CW00665169

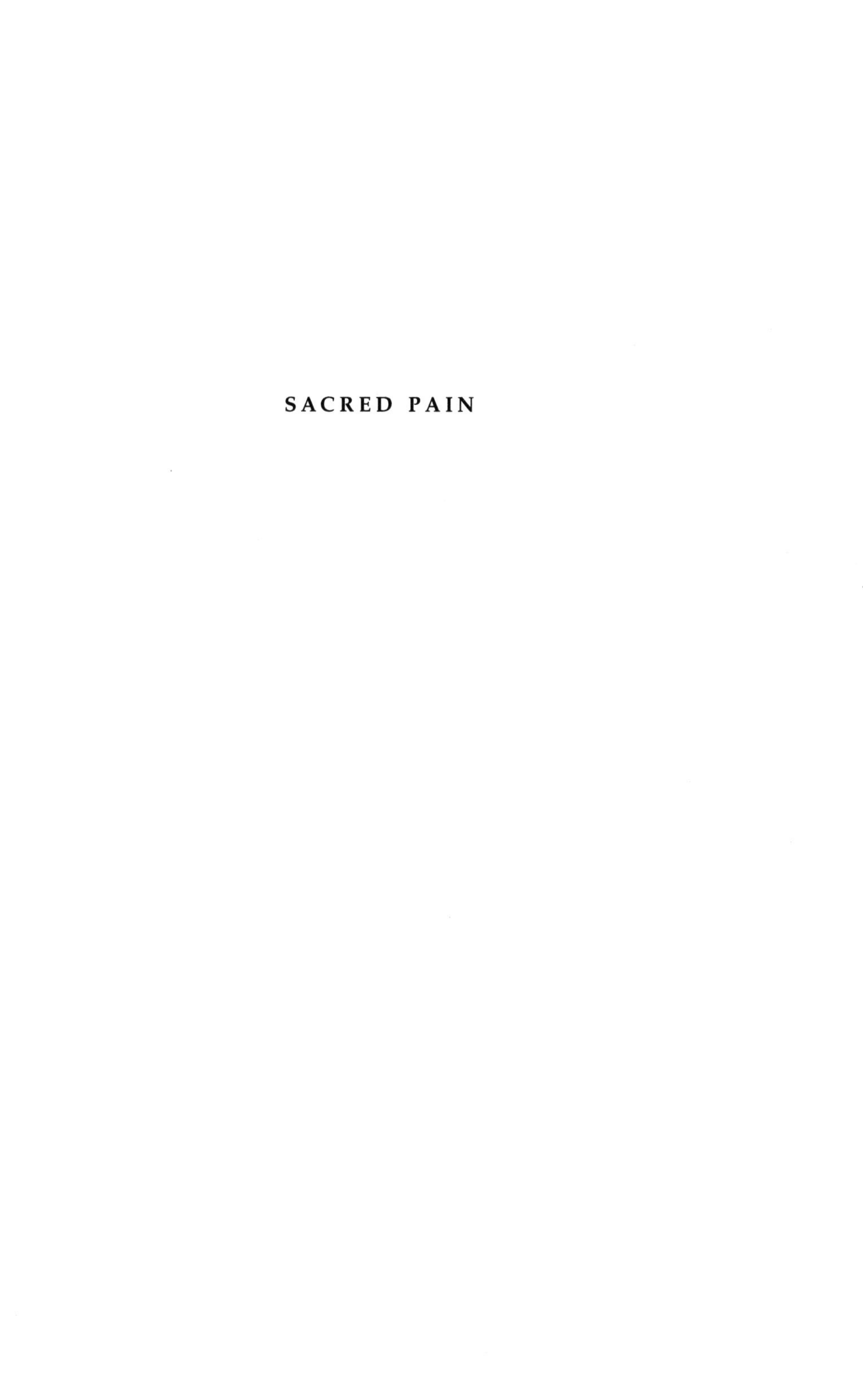

SACRED PAIN

Sacred Pain

Hurting the Body for the Sake of the Soul

ARIEL GLUCKLICH

OXFORD
UNIVERSITY PRESS
2001

OXFORD
UNIVERSITY PRESS

Oxford New York
Athens Auckland Bangkok Bogotá Buenos Aires Cape Town
Chennai Dar es Salaam Delhi Florence Hong Kong Istanbul Karachi
Kolkata Kuala Lumpur Madrid Melbourne Mexico City Mumbai Nairobi
Paris São Paulo Shanghai Singapore Taipei Tokyo Toronto Warsaw

and associated companies in
Berlin Ibadan

Published by Oxford University Press, Inc.
198 Madison Avenue, New York, New York 10016

Library of Congress Cataloging-in-Publication Data
Glucklich, Ariel.
Sacred pain : hurting the body for the sake of the soul / Ariel Glucklich.
p. cm.
Includes bibliographical references and index.
ISBN 0-19-513254-8 (alk. paper)
1. Pain—Religious aspects. 2. Ritual—Psychology. I. Title.
BL627.5 .G58 2001
291.3—dc21 2001018528

Chapter 2 previously appeared as "Sacred Pain and the Phenomenal Self." *Harvard Theological Review*, 91:4, 1998; and Chapter 4 appeared as "Self Sacrifice and Sacred Pain." *Harvard Theological Review*, 92:4, 1999.

2 4 6 8 9 7 5 3 1

Printed in the United States of America
on acid-free paper

For my parents
Rachel and Joseph Glucklich

Contents

Acknowledgments

I owe a profound debt of gratitude to many people who have helped me over the years. At St. Lawrence University, Mark McWilliams, Michael Greenwald, and Randi Kristensen have been supportive and helpful. At Georgetown University, I have benefited from the material support of the Theology Department (Landegger Fund), and from the comments of many colleagues, including Diane Yeager, Theresa Sanders, Tony Tambasco, Elizabeth McKeown, Joel Sweek, Julia Lamm, and others. I have also benefited from the input of Oliver Sacks, Ronald Melzack, Wendy Doniger, Emma Sweeny, Avner Glucklich, Joseph Glucklich, Aviva Gali, and Rony Oren. Jennifer Hansen was especially helpful throughout the final phases of the book and with the index. I owe her a special debt. Cynthia Read of Oxford University Press did her very best, as usual, to save my reputation.

SACRED PAIN

Introduction

A few years ago I visited Israel during the Passover holiday. I was watching television one night with a friend and the state-run network ran a show on several Easter practices. One practice that caught our attention was a ritual crucifixion in a small Philippine town. We were shocked to see volunteers being nailed to crosses, then lifted high up above a crowd of devoted onlookers. My friend, Jacob Goren, who is a retired professor of engineering, a socialist and atheist, immediately launched into a tirade against the superstitions of religion. He ridiculed not only the Catholics of the Philippines, but all the other similar practices he could think of—the Shi'i, self-beating for the martyrdom of Husayn at Karbala; Native Americans who suspend themselves from hooks inserted in their chests; and medieval penitential practices he had seen in movies. "Why," he asked with a mixture of curiosity and derision, "would anyone in his right mind do this? I would say they're crazy, but they can't all be!"

And true, among the oddest forms of the religious life around the world are rituals of self-hurting and even a theological glorification of suffering that seems entirely inconsistent with common sense. Goren knew only three or four examples, but I could have offered many more. Several types of traditional practices such as pilgrimages, funerals, initiations, mystical disciplines, annual celebrations of various sorts, along with sermons, religious biographies, authoritative pronouncements, poetry, and a multitude of other religious discourses manifest a positive attitude toward physical pain. No religious figure is more eloquent or prolific on this topic than the great Sufi mystic Rumi, who once wrote:

> Pain renews old medicines and lops off the branch of every indifference. Pain is the alchemy that renovates—where is indifference when pain intervenes?[1]

The sentiment is still heard today. In 1984 Pope John Paul II delivered a pronouncement "in liturgical remembrance of the Blessed Mary, Virgin of Lourdes." The Pope quoted one of the epistles of St. Paul: "I am now happy in the suffering that I endure for you":

> The joy comes from the discovery of the meaning of suffering. . . . What we express with the word "suffering" seems to be particularly *essential to the nature of Man*. . . . Suffering seems to belong to Man's transcendence. . . . Christianity . . . is not a system into which we have to fit the awkward fact of pain. . . . In a sense, it creates, rather than solves, the problem of pain.[2]

This is sacred pain, precisely what the modern patient cannot understand. Simone Weil called it "affliction," by which she meant the state of participating in the suffering of Christ on the cross.[3] But it is far broader and more complex when viewed across cultures and time periods.

Just as mystifying as this counterintuitive religious attitude toward pain is the general indifference to it in scholarly literature. To be sure, in the large corpus of publications that appears every year, violent rituals such as sacrifices and theological discourses on suffering and theodicy feature prominently. But specific studies on religion and physical pain are rare, and the few recent ones have been mostly inspired by the work of a literary critic, Elaine Scarry.[4]

Jacob Goren had not read C. S. Lewis's *The Problem of Pain,* which excoriated the Christian glorification of the heroic resignation to pain, but he became immediately curious as well as repulsed. He was a retired captain in the British army who had served in World War II and lost a limb in battle. For decades he has suffered extreme phantom-limb pain, and his attitude was dominated by a strong desire to eliminate physical suffering, to wipe out pain with medication—anything from sleeping pills to morphine. For Goren, pain is a medical problem and its persistence signals only the failure of current pharmaceutical technology. The idea that throughout human history and around the world people would actually seek pain, or if struck by disease or accident find some positive meaning in it, could testify to only two possibilities: either they were sick as individuals or they belonged to cultures where superstition held sway. Goren's genuine bewilderment over religious pain, especially in light of his own medical situation, is my motive for writing this book. *Sacred Pain* seeks to find the causes of religious self-hurting and uncover the hidden rationality behind the representation of pain as a good thing.

This book, then, is an answer to Jacob Goren's question, but it is more. It is also a response to the chronic-pain patient, the scientist, and the secular socialist. The book lays aside any scholarly pretension to "cover the topic" of religious pain and instead it answers a specific question posed by a specific person. This implies several limitations on the scope and trajectory of the ideas I shall discuss.

To begin, the answer has to be scientific in a reductive way—a true explanation for an observed problem. I cannot argue that pain is important because people who use it, such as Muslim mourners, say it is. Nor can I merely say that they hurt themselves to mourn the death of Husayn, however true that may be. At the very least, the pervasiveness of such behavior, with no corresponding beliefs, on a cross-cultural scale, suggests a more basic explanation. Mourners in Australia and elsewhere also hurt themselves, as Emile Durkheim noted decades ago, so the question of how to relate mourning with pain persists. Meanwhile, initiates into societies and religious groups allow themselves to be hurt for altogether different reasons. Is there one scientific explanation for all instances of religious pain? Goren himself made the (false) assumption that self-hurting indicates a masochistic or pathological attitude.[5] Some researchers have argued that religious self-hurters are surfing a wave of euphoria induced by beta-endorphins (natural opioids) triggered by the trauma they inflict on themselves. Both masochism and biochemistry are truly general theories, meeting some formal requirements for explaining the observed self-injurious behaviors. Although I shall reject both later on, my own approach has to share some of their formal properties.

Another limitation imposed by the nature of the man who asked the question is the scope of the answer. I could easily have written a book of three or five thousand pages, a sort of *Golden Bough* of religious pain. I hardly mentioned the Romans, or the Celts, South and Central American rituals, religious wars, priestly contests, hundreds of monastic biographies and hagiographies from Europe, and too many other instances. Instead I opted to develop one theory of sacred pain, which is neurodynamic and psychological at its foundation, and then test it in a limited number of cultural and historical situations that mean something in Jacob Goren's particular circumstances. The choice of topics for discussion in this book, as the table of contents reveals, is not a comprehensive survey of a field but the specific trajectory of my answer to one man's question. If this answer leads through Christianity and Europe more than Taoism or Islam, the reader should not misconstrue this as representing the actual distribution of sacred pain.

Here then is the short answer to Goren's question. Pain is not a simple matter: There is an enormous difference between the unwanted pain of a cancer patient or victim of a car crash, and the voluntary and modulated self-hurting of a religious practitioner. Religious pain produces states of consciousness, and cognitive-emotional changes, that affect the identity of the individual subject and her sense of belonging to a larger community or to a more fundamental state of being. More succinctly, pain strengthens the religious person's bond with God and with other persons. Of course, since not all pain is voluntary or self-inflicted, one mystery of the religious life is how unwanted suffering can become transformed into sacred pain.

The first chapter of the book shows that pain is a prolific topic within religious literature and practices around the world. It is articulated according to several conceptual models including juridical, medical, military, and athletic. Some modes of representing pain, such as pain-as-punishment, indicate an aversive attitude; others indicate that pain can be perceived in a positive light. Ultimately, the dozen or so models of pain boil down to two fundamental types, according to their effect on the individual self. The task of sacred pain is to transform destructive or disintegrative suffering into a positive religious-psychological mechanism for reintegration within a more deeply valued level of reality than individual existence. Chapter 2 proposes a psychological-neurological theory that accounts for the transforming benefits of pain. The following chapter builds on this naturalistic approach and shows how pain is communicated and perceived in a natural and spontaneous manner. I will show that pain depiction and perception is not just a matter of artistic or cultural convention, but is intrinsic to the way humans are biologically adapted to communicate pain to others. The socially integrative effects of pain depend on these natural facts. Chapter 4 looks at the psychological effects of pain on the self in its relation to significant objects and the emerging social self. The positive transformations brought about by pain must be understood without recourse either to pathological concepts such as masochism or to a metaphysical Self, and with the use, instead, of developmental concepts such as object relations and systemic ego psychology.

By now the basic question of the book is no longer, Why do religious persons hurt themselves? Rather, it is, What is the effect of self-induced pain on the religious person? Once the psychodynamic benefits of pain are understood, it becomes possible to isolate the effects of pain within diverse contexts in order to move forward toward an answer for Jacob Goren. The next few chapters build on neurological and psychological dynamics but situate the hurting subject in a number of ritual and cultural contexts. Chapter 5 discusses possession and exorcism. The material is cross-cultural and general, but the point of the chapter is to isolate the role of pain (trauma) in the personality changes that are brought about in cases of possession and exorcism. The prevalence of pain in the inducement of possession, its perpetuation, and its termination illustrates the mixture of biological principle and cultural idiom in the shifting contours of personality and identity. The same holds true for rites of passage and initiation. Chapter 6 shows that these traditional rituals seek to bring about changes in identity and status by utilizing similar neurological and psychodynamic mechanisms. A child becomes an adult, or an outsider becomes an insider when ritually controlled pain weakens the subject's sense of empirical identity and strengthens his or her sense of attachment to a highly valued new center of identification. Chapter 7 argues that even the medieval and Spanish Inquisitions were in the business of transforming identity, but adds another level of analysis. It shows how a sense of guilt, or moral subjugation to an internalized authority, is inculcated by means of the inquisitorial use of torture, which was a carefully modulated use of pain in a roughly psychoanalytical manner.

The biggest obstacle to understanding the value of sacred pain is not its feel but our insistence that pain can signify a medical problem only. This is not an intellectual failure or a poverty of the imagination, but the amnesia that descends with the emergence of a radically new worldview. Chapter 8 looks at the invention of medical anesthetics in the 1840s as one central factor in the birth of that medical outlook. The modern self is now the legal owner of a biomedical body that gives off signals of illness in the form of painful symptoms. As a consumer of medical services, the patient enters a contractual relationship with those who read his pain, reinforcing his own inalienable rights to painlessness by purchasing the best services possible. That person thus shares an adversarial alienation from his own body with the physician to whom he entrusts the elimination of pain. One hundred fifty years of this bourgeois medical psychology have all but erased the memory of pain as an experience that signifies something other than personal disintegration.

But perhaps not altogether? Closer examination reveals that "sacred pain," or pain in the service of higher ends, has not entirely vanished from the modern world, even outside the Vatican. Contests and sporting events are still often about the endurance of pain, either in performance or in training. Initiations still often hurt, whether they lead to the Marines or a fraternity. On a deeper level yet, some pain patients still accept their pain with more than stoic resignation. According to pain clinicians, too many patients feel that they "deserve to hurt," or that they are somehow being tested by God.[6] The Conclusion to *Sacred*

Pain will reflect briefly on the pain patient who no longer seeks consolation but relief of symptoms, and on our irrevocable loss of pain as a source of religious meaning.

In a sense, *Sacred Pain* is a simple book. The question of religious pain is answered through the effects of ritualized pain on human consciousness and identity. The book seems to cover a wide range of topics but it is, in fact, singularly focused on that one theme only—the effect of ritual pain on consciousness and identity. I cannot possibly hope to contribute to the scholarship of the Inquisition, possession, passage, and all the rest. I can only isolate the role of pain in these contexts in order to highlight the psychological transformations that take place as a result of regulated pain. The sequence of chapters is not a matter of surveying the history of pain, but an analytical deepening of the psychological transformations, leading finally to the consciousness and identity of the poser of the question himself. The entire process begins with the particular, moves to the general, and closes the expositional circle by returning to the particular.

This trajectory has required that I make implicit choices in a number of basic methodological areas. These may have a broader interest outside the scope of religious pain, bearing on general issues of cross-cultural and religious scholarship. The first issue is how to construct an explanatory theory in the study of religion. The history of religions is notorious for its pursuit of methodological autonomy while scholars of religion in fact borrow methods from every other field in the humanities and social sciences. A religious phenomenon—pilgrimage, for instance—lends itself to a variety of explanations based on the social-scientific or symbolic understanding of culture. These approaches may be too "reductive" for religious scholars when they fail to take into account the religious consciousness of the pilgrim. On the other hand, if religious actions require a truly sui generis explanation or interpretation, such a theory is in danger of becoming indistinguishable from theology or some confessional narrative, which is not really explanatory. Is it possible in principle to explain a religious ritual or belief in a nonderivative but properly reductive manner?

The second issue is closely related. Assuming that psychology holds the key to the first issue, how does one apply it to a cross-cultural question—the practice of self-hurt in religious contexts—without going to two opposite reductive extremes? On the one side is biological materialism, which takes cross-cultural similarities as indications that human nature is the cause of the observed phenomenon. Two examples are Freud's drive theory and neurochemical production of natural opioids in the brain of self-hurters. On the other side is cultural psychology, such as Richard Shweder's, which takes the position that psychological explanation can only be culture-specific because the appearance of cross-cultural similarity is indeed just appearance.[7]

Sacred Pain does not set out to solve these methodological issues but to answer the question of pain. It so happens that the particular topic at hand forces a decisive stance in relation to both sets of options. Pain is neither a simple biological event—say, tissue damage—nor an idea. It occupies a space "in between," a middle-of-the-road phenomenal position between the material organism and the mind. Pain is a conscious signal (it does not exist if you are not aware of it) and participates in those qualities of consciousness that are essential for a broad-based wellness of some biological systems, including human beings. To a large extent, then, the study of pain is the study of consciousness, or phenomenology. So my position "in the middle" is not just a matter of compromise or convenience; it follows the path of its subject matter. But it is not precisely in the middle, either.

Truly explaining religious phenomena requires a position that is strategically placed between religious data and intellectual theory, in an appropriately reductive stance. The participants, who explain their self-hurting ritual as an imitation of God or give some other religious reason are offering a folk theory. In fact, the ritual itself can be regarded as a performed folk theory. Academic theologies are simply more elaborate versions of such conceptualizations. A scientific explanation of religious self-hurt must reduce these prevailing theories to another level, but it cannot go too far. Reduction is a relation between two theories, one reducing or encompassing the other.[8] Several logical and formal properties must remain between the two theories for the reduction to be effective. If the reduced theory is not recognizable at all in the new one, then it is displaced. For example, the demonic possession theory of certain behaviors has been completely replaced by nervous disorder theory. It has been so thoroughly junked that demons have no ontological existence at all within the new theory. This is not a reduction, properly speaking, but a complete displacement. In contrast, the reduction of optics to electromagnetics at the turn of the last century is an example of effective reduction. Light is still light but its theoretical explanation moves from one theory to another.

The progress of scientific understanding hinges on reduction rather than displacement. Unfortunately, effective reduction is quite rare and difficult to achieve. Even within psychology the reduction of some theories remains in the future. In the starkest example, representational theory (such as propositions about emotions and cognitions) is still not reducible to nonrepresentational theory (propositions about sensory and nervous stimuli). In other words, for the time being, material theories of human behavior must compete with mental or cognitive theories, but they run parallel. Consequently, the notion that we could, at present, reduce religious folk theory to neurobiology (for instance, the production of beta-endorphins) is silly. Even in principle there ought to be a number of intermediate-level theories between neuropsychology and religious beliefs. When we do discover a likely candidate for a reducing theory, it will *not* displace or eliminate the beliefs and values of religious folk theory, but will incorporate them into the logic and form of the reducing theory. It will have to avoid the justified derision that scholars of religion feel toward existing reductive theories, such as Freudian drive theory, or "God in the brain" theory. *Sacred Pain* stakes its claim in this tricky no-man's land by proposing an experiential category that underlies both the beliefs of religious self-hurters and the psychological events that take place at one remove. This category is the systemic and cybernetic nature of consciousness, which encompasses both ego and body. However, the book does not aim for a methodological revolution in the study of religion, only a reasonable answer to a difficult question.

ONE

Religious Ways of Hurting

The following are self-evident: Spilling a few drops of hot tea on your wrist will make you cringe; when your dentist's probe finds the cavity in your tooth your whole body contracts. You may rest assured that an ancient Egyptian would have felt the same way, as would a Siberian Russian today. Pain is the most familiar and universal aspect of all human experiences, and it binds us with many animals as well. The American Medical Association (and the International Association for the Study of Pain) defines pain somewhat redundantly as an unpleasant sensation related to tissue damage. However, nearly everyone recognizes it for a wholly undesirable sensation that seems to be localized in a definite part of the body.

Despite being so obvious, so intimately bound in our bodies as a noxious feeling, pain remains conceptually elusive. To begin with, pain must be distinguished from suffering; it is a type of sensation usually—though not necessarily—associated with tissue damage.[1] Though unpleasant—to say the least—by definition, pain is a sensation that is tangled with mental and even cultural experiences. As such it has been pursued and glorified throughout history, and not only by clinical masochists. Suffering, in contrast, is not a sensation but an emotional and evaluative reaction to any number of causes, some entirely painless. The loss of a child, for instance, is a cause of deep suffering and sorrow, but not pain. We regard such suffering as painful in a derivative, even metaphorical sense. On that distinction Montaigne wrote, "The types of sufferings which simply afflict us by tormenting our soul are much less distressful to me than they are to most other men: . . . but truly basic, corporeal suffering, I experience fully."[2] In fact, one may go so far as to say that pain can be the solution to suffering, a psychological analgesic that removes anxiety, guilt, and even depression.

Discourses on pain, around the world and throughout history, have been pervasive and oblique at the same time. It is difficult to imagine ancient medicine, in Greece, India, or anywhere else, without the need to overcome pain. And yet most premodern systems of medicine touch the subject of pain in a roundabout manner. Similarly, it is hard to imagine ancient jurisprudence without pain: the pain of the crime-victim and the pain inflicted by the law to put things right. And yet, here too, even the most vivid descriptions of gruesome mutilations and executions seem to treat the body of the prisoner as an insentient object. Pain, of course, also figures in military affairs. The side that wins is usually the one that can sustain the highest level or the most extensive amount of pain and continue to fight. One needs to read between the lines of medical, juridical, and military documents to discover the pain that permeates these domains of human activity. And yet, surprisingly, all three areas have left a profound mark on the way pain is conceptualized, perhaps even experienced, within the literature that eventually comes to describe pain explicitly.

This is the literature that may cautiously be called "religious": scriptures, sermons and teachings, biographies and writings of mystics and saints, monastic guides, theologies, myths, and even rituals. These writings frequently discuss pain in detail, but often in a paradoxical and counterintuitive fashion. The modern reader expects, as a matter of common sense, that religious literature would insist that pain is a cause of suffering, the "problem of pain" in the words of C. S. Lewis's famous book. In the Christian and Jewish traditions of the West, the book of Job seems to epitomize how religion treats, how in fact it ought to treat, the problem of pain. The book is an unfulfilled theodicy, a problem of evil. But its inconclusive lesson is acceptable to us because we have come to believe that the only true solution to pain is medical. Religion may explore the mental terrain of pained anguish (as Job certainly does) but the solution proper is just around the corner.

But the book of Job is hardly representative of religious literature on the subject of pain. Casting a very wide net and looking at dozens of references to pain, I have found that, in fact, religious literature around the world is far richer and more ambiguous in its evaluation and even description of pain. Pain is frequently not a problem at all, but rather a solution! The contexts in which pain is discussed are impressive. There are ascetic disciplines, martyrdoms, initiatory ordeals and rites of passage, training of shamans, traditional forms of healing such as exorcism; there are contests, installations of kings, rites of mourning, pilgrimages, vows, and even celebrations. For some reason or reasons—these will be the heart of this book—the most highly revered religious documents (taken in the broad sense) around the world have often treated pain not as an "unwanted guest" but as a useful and important sensation worthy of understanding and cultivating.

In this chapter I shall look at major ways of describing and evaluating pain in religious literature around the world. The survey will reveal a remarkable depth and subtlety in the manner of using pain, and in the way pain has been situated in the religious imagination of humankind. The richness of the data resolves itself into a definite number of patterns—I call them "models." There seems to be a limited repertoire of imaginative resources for describing pain and for evaluating its role in life. This may not surprise biologists who insist that pain is an organic feature of the species, but it would surprise psychologists and cultural theorists who feel that descriptions of pain are always cultural constructions subject to the vicissitudes of historical circumstances. At any rate, the models of pain I will discuss are juridical (punitive, business law, law of evidence—including tests and gnostic models), medical (curative, preventive), military, athletic, magical (alchemical, purifying), educational, shared (communal, vicarious, sacrificial, imitation of a god and social bonding), and psychotropic. These are not areas of life in which one finds instances of pain. Rather, these are the ways in which a pain is characterized and perhaps even experienced. For instance, one may suffer intense chronic backaches and come to feel that the pain is punitive, that it is due to some evil one has committed. That would be a juridical way of conceptualizing and experiencing the hurting body. The McGill Pain Questionnaire, which will be discussed in a number of places in this book, contains evaluative terms from which pain patients select to describe their pain as perhaps punitive, vengeful, or some other judgment.[3] Its assumption is that pain is frequently accompanied by an emotional or intellectual judgment. In the literature that I will survey, such judgments seem to be essential to the way pain is perceived. For example:

> One day Gabriel appeared and said, "O Prophet of God, leave the mosque (and go) to Batha' in Mecca, that you may see one of your companions who is honored by the seven heavens and the earth." The Prophet went out and saw a man, naked, rolling in the dust and rebuking his soul. In that heat of Mecca, which melts lead, he rolled among the stones, saying, "O soul taste this punishment, and wait for the punishment of Hell! O soul, at night you are a fallen carcass, and by day you go about idly; like the beasts of burden, you do nothing but eat and drink." The Prophet summoned him and asked, "What is this?" He replied, "My soul had prevailed over me." The Prophet said, "Receive then the good tidings that Heaven's doors have been opened, and the angels of the

> seven heavens glory in you." Then he told the Companions, "Let whoever desires God's mercy touch this man and ask for his prayers." They all went and entreated him to pray for them.[4]

In this instance taken from medieval Islam, the pain of rolling on an extremely hot surface is characterized as a form of punishment, "earned" by a sense of moral outrage at one's spiritual failings. Of course, the models I have listed are only heuristic devices. Many expressions of pain communicate in a polyvalent or ambiguous way, the boundaries between models may be fuzzy, or a pain may be articulated in one way but function in another. For instance, penitential pain tends to be conceived in a juridical manner, but it may be imagined positively within initiatory ordeals for specialized societies.[5]

Cultural theorists will be quick to argue that a broadly comparative collection of material based on "models" makes no sense. After all, the material is not the spontaneous grunting, moaning, or crying of specific individuals in pain. Rather, it is a collection of discourses *about* pain, literary representations authored within specific cultural contexts. Pain discourse represents embodied experience—sensation as well as its emotional/evaluative aspects—and is consequently a social and cultural construction, regardless of the biology of the pain. We may be even more specific on this point and follow the theorists who have set the agenda for the cultural construction of embodiment over the last couple of decades, namely Michel Foucault, Julia Kristeva, Luce Irigaray, Gilles Deleuze, and Felix Guattari. Their theories require that pain discourse reflect the way cultures "construct" the individual as a self and as a member of a community. It is not possible for individuals or cultures to talk about pain without simultaneously expressing social relations of power and the ideologies that contain them. This situates pain in a specific time and place. The notion of transcultural models eviscerates the very heart of what is essential in pain discourse—namely, its participation in the unique dialectic between culture and individual experience.

Cultural constructionists, as such theorists are sometimes called, are correct of course, up to a point. Embodied experience, including pain and its representation, are a mix of biological facts and cultural consciousness (metaphors, emotions, attitudes). The problem, and they are sharply aware of it, is precisely how this mix works, and how scholarship may combine objective description with subjective experience. As we shall see in a later chapter, this is the struggle behind the sociology of Pierre Bourdieu, and perhaps an inevitable consequence of a lingering struggle with positivism, which has dominated Anglo-American material sciences. Be that as it may, the cultural construction of pain experience, and the rejection of transcultural models, is based on a top-down view of the culture-body dialectic. There is much to say on behalf of the other perspective—the bottom up. As Roselyne Rey puts it:

> All the same, despite its many individual, social, and cultural characteristics, pain is not an historical subject in the same sense as fear, or hell, or purgatory. Pain is based on an anatomical and physiological foundation, and if there is one experience where the human condition's universality and the species' biological unity is manifest, pain is certainly it.[6]

The point is not to substitute biological description and analysis for cultural interpretation. Instead, the agenda for this book is to explore with some precision that fuzzy area where culture meets biology. This is the place where sensation becomes representation, and conversely consciousness is experienced somatically—in the body. I thus agree with Rey's own agenda, which is to find "how do these sensations convert into perceptions and how do they reach our awareness" (the bottom-up agenda), but I shall also keep an eye on the reverse point of view.

This bifocal perspective is more consistent with the richness and ambiguities of the models than either the biological or the cultural reductions. For instance, some cultural theorists insist that subjectivity is an internalization of power relations, and the models of pain should reflect that one-directional flow. Pain narratives record the development of moral agency, for instance, when they uncover the guilty conscience of the victim, who has now internalized society's aggression and turned it on himself. Foucault's work on the confession and on punishment—the "technology of self"—is a famous example of such theorizing. But in fact, the survey of pain discourses reveals a wide range of images and values, many of which project the very opposite evaluation of pain. An obvious example is pain as medicine.

The transcultural models are not designed to produce cultural-comparative knowledge about diverse traditions in search of universal symbolic ideas. This is not an exercise in the comparative religion of pain. Instead I am looking at the very possibility of representation, at the simple fact that pain can actually be articulated as an experience despite being a "body feeling." This requires that I move beneath the models to the origins in experience and in language of how the body feels when "it" feels pain. That mechanism—the phenomenological construction of pain—is universal, though it operates in culturally constrained spaces.[7] Discovering it requires that we suspend the culturally specific, for the time being, and operate in a comparative fashion. It will be possible to see, after the discussion of the models, that the phenomenological construction is binary, and as such it is a suitable way of discussing the dialectic of culture and biology, or mind and body.

Models of Pain

The discussion of models will be simply descriptive. Although the collection of material is already a selective and therefore interpretive act, I will postpone the temptation to reduce the data to psychology or theology. Nietzsche famously refused to do this; his descriptions were already literary in their interpretive passion. On the self-hurting of ascetics, for instance, he wrote that they "inflict as much pain on themselves as they possibly can out of pleasure in inflicting pain—which is probably their only pleasure."[8] This reads very well, and the pseudoparadox, hardly masking the writer's contempt, has inspired a vast amount of writing, especially in France, on transgression. But of course, the pronouncement is both too quick and off the mark.

Juridical Models

Narratives and discourses about pain that describe it in terms taken from the world of jurisprudence are included in this model. The clearest is pain as punishment, an obvious feature considering the very etymology of the word. But pain may also be described as a debt or damages owed, and it may also be related to laws of evidence when it is linked to methods of eliciting truth. This model accounts for a large percentage of the cases found in religious literature, and many pain patients still use it today.

Within this model, pain is described as a punishment by some personal agency (God, Satan, demons) or by some impersonal mechanism such as karma. The punishment may be perceived as just, as we saw in the case of the man who rolled in the heat of Mecca, or it may be entirely unwarranted and tragic. Such of course is the case of Job who flails at God in pained rage at what he knows to be injustice, or the cry of Prometheus, who rightly calls Zeus a tyrant: "This is a tyrant's deed; this is unlovely, a thing done by a tyrant's private laws."[9] Among the three Western monotheistic religions, due to the legacy of Adam and Eve, punitive pain is endemic: "To the woman He said: 'I will greatly increase your pangs in childbearing; in pain you shall bring forth children, yet your desire shall be for your husband, and he shall rule over you.'"[10] This constitutional sentiment, if taken seriously, situates the pain of parturition in a moral universe in which pain is not meaningless, or even merely biological. It is the automatic moral consequence in an iron logic of action and reward.

But the suffering blamed on Adam's misconduct is far more general:

"In Adam's fall sinn'd we all: human life became penal and the world hostile."[11] Punishment, fortunately, is not the same as vengeance; it has the advantage of removing guilt.[12] Or else, it covers the shame and regret of having done wrong, and more importantly, pacifies the anxiety over an indefinite mechanism of justice waiting to pounce. Thus, to be punished, or to punish oneself, may be a good idea. Ascetics and monks have often conceptualized their pain as a punitive but preemptive measure: How much better is it, writes Thomas à Kempis, to suffer in this world than to save the accumulated "matter" of sin for the fire of purgatory.[13] Henry Suso amplifies this sentiment to explain the extravagance of his own self-punishment: "Brother, it is necessary for thee to be punished in this life or in purgatory: but incomparably more severe will be the penalty of purgatory than any in this life. Behold, thy soul is in thy hands. Choose therefore for thyself whether to be sufficiently punished in this life according to canonical or authentic penances, or to await purgatory."[14] The pains of monastic discipline are "enjoyed," in Nietzsche's scornful term, because they remove something more hurtful—the fear of the afterlife. Such a pain may, in fact, hurt hardly at all, if such a thing is possible. Some martyrs may have experienced their last pains in a surprisingly analgesic manner due to the way they evaluated their pain. St. Peter Balsam had the presence of mind to debate his own torture with the emperor Severus, who was attempting to cajole the Christian into sacrificing to the state gods.

> Severus, on hearing these words, ordered him to be stretched upon the rack, and whilst he was suspended said to him scoffingly, "What say you now, Peter; do you begin to know what the rack is? Are you willing to sacrifice?" Peter answered, "Tear me with hooks, and talk not of my sacrificing to your devils; I have already told you, that I will sacrifice only to that God for whom I suffer." . . . The spectators, seeing the martyr's blood running down in streams, cried out to him, "Obey the emperor! Sacrifice, and rescue yourself from these torments!" Peter replied: "Do you call these torments? I feel no pain: but this I know that if I be not faithful to my God I must expect real pain, such as cannot be conceived."[15]

There is no "transgressive masochism" here, though perhaps the bravado of a man who is confident that his body's sensations belong in a larger and more powerful context. So the paradox Nietzsche had discovered, the counterpleasure, is actually a different paradox, a more puzzling one. On the one hand, the martyr and the ascetic regard pain as the phenomenal face of a divine mechanism—retributive and just, while on the other hand, their certainty produces a strange insensitivity to pain. This is true not just for martyrs (with their anesthetizing adrenal rush) but for patients as well. An ascetic named Stephanus was suffering from cancer under the care of a physician. "'While his members were being cut away like locks of hair, he showed no sign whatsoever of pain, thanks to the superiority of his spiritual preparation.' Stephanus explained to his visitors that 'it may well be that my members deserve punishment and it would be better to pay the penalty here than after I have left the arena.'"[16]

Juridical pain straddles the boundary between *lex talionis* and law of debts in a variety of cultures, from Judaism and Greece to Hindu versions of karma. The difference between pain as punishment and an exchange of debts involves the legal distinction, which became important in ancient Greece, between owing to a private party and being accountable to society as a whole. The strongest Jewish instance of this distinction may be found in the Yom Kippur (Day of Atonement) liturgy with its notion of redemption as exchange (*pidyon*) or a debt.[17] Pope John Paul II, in that same 1984 address quoted in the Introduction, states that those who wish to enter the kingdom of Christ must suffer: "Through their suffering they, in a sense, pay back the boundless price of our redemption."[18] Here pain does not act by removing a certainty of culpability—in phenomenal terms, the sense of moral guilt. Instead it restores a balance, either in terms of psychic processes or in the cosmos. For Plato suffering pain can be punitive in such a beneficial way. Pain (as punishment) restores order in the soul, which is not about a subjective sense of guilt but more of a medical conception of balance. Still, it also prevents eternal torments in Tartarus.[19] The juridical model conceived as repayment of damages or debts plays out with either a magical or a sacrificial mechanism that guarantees the efficacy of the exchange. This principle also seems at work in the acts of self-torture performed as *vrat* (vow) in the Hindu and Buddhist worlds. The accused man's pain will keep him out of prison or healthy.[20] Perhaps behind this is a sociological force, which anthropologists have called "prestation" but whose mechanism is most interesting when considered psychologically. The certainty of automatic or built-in reciprocity seems to be very pervasive, sometimes burdensome as well. In the subtle wryness of Hobbes: "To have received from one, to whom we think our selves equall, greater benefits than there is hope to requite, disposeth to counterfeit love; but really secret hatred; and puts a man into the estate of a desperate debtor, than in declining the sight of his creditor, tacitely wishes him there, where he might never see him more. For benefits oblige; and obligation is thraldome; and unrequitable obligation, perpetual thraldome, which is to one equall, hatefull." To turn away from such obligations leads to the depth of shame, to have oneself irrevocably shown up.[21]

Finally, the juridical model of pain also branches off into the law of evidence, where pain acts as an instrument for obtaining truth from reluctant witnesses or from the accused. This principle operates not just in cases of ordeals or religious inquisitions, as one might expect, but also in the cases of asceticism and initiatory ordeals. However, the dominant sphere of influence, as we can see in the case of ordeal by fire in India, is the revelation of hidden truth wrested by means of pain. In ancient India, for instance (as in England and most of Europe), ordeals were regarded as uncanny methods for establishing legal facts in the absence of reliable witnesses. Ordeals acted as a method of invoking divine insight in order to discover a hidden truth, and pain somehow pointed at this truth. The following is a brief summary of the fire ordeal in medieval India:

> Having made red marks on all sores of the hands of the *sodhya* [accused] on which grains of rice have been rubbed, he (the judge) should place seven leaves of the *aśvattha* tree on them and also grains of rice and curds and should fasten round them threads. Then the judge should carry the red-hot piece by means of a pair of tongs and place it in the hands of the *sodhya* (that are covered with leaves). Then the *sodhya* holding in both his hands the red-hot piece should walk from the first to the eighth circle not hurriedly but slowly and at ease. Having reached the 8th circle he should place the red-hot iron piece on the 9th circle. Then the judge should rub on the hands of the *sodhya* rice grains and when the latter shows no hesitation at the rubbing and no injury on his hand at the end of the day he is declared to be innocent.[22]

The ordeal was a common method for introducing divine perception into uncertain legal cases. Pain acted as one feature; the other equally important sign was the scarification of the hands. The innocent were not only expected to overcome the fear and discomfort of pain, but its tissue damage as well! Unlike in India, European ordeals (ancient Jewish too) were most commonly reserved for women. However, the same "truth mechanics" dominated the European conception of juridical ordeal.[23] The following poem from the Edda describes a hot cauldron ordeal meant to settle a common accusation of adultery:

> She put her hand into the water
> and gathered up the glittering gems:
> "My lords, you have seen the sacred trial
> prove me guiltless—and still the water boils."
>
> Atli's heart laughed in his breast
> because Gudrun's hand had not been harmed:
> "Now let Herkja go to the kettle,
> she who hoped to hurt my wife."
>
> No man has seen a pitiful sight
> who has not looked at Herkja's scalded hands;

then they forced her into a foul swamp—
Gudrun's grievance was well avenged.[24]

The correlation between pain and truth in these cases is not punitive but "gnostic" (truth-eliciting). The power of pain, or the miracle of insensitivity to pain, is attributed to a divine oversight of the proceedings. But pain also acts in subtle ways without the divine. It is geared to what Foucault has called a domain of introspective thought: "What is in play [in legal torture] is an entire technique for analyzing and diagnosing thought, its origins, its qualities, its dangers, its powers of seduction, and all the obscure forces which may be hidden under the aspect which it presents."[25] This is why the replacement of ordeals by legal torture has been regarded as a moment of progress in the history of European rationality. But more basic evidence suggests that pain is always and mysteriously related to truth as the essence of things—whether psychic, social, or cosmic. This goes beyond the effectiveness of pain to elicit confession—a highly distortive and unreliable quality as far as justice goes. Instead, pain simply points to the way the world presents itself to consciousness, like its complement—pleasure. In Buddhist and Hindu traditions this often implies that pain is not to be resisted (nor desired), but closely observed. In the 1930s a Thai Buddhist teacher, Sao Man, was accompanied by two disciples. One contracted a very severe case of malaria, which caused him deep pain. "Man believed that instead of trying to relieve physical symptoms, monks should go to the root of distress and cure their minds. He instructed ill disciples to observe the pain without reacting, for thereby they would realize the truth of suffering."[26] The most familiar example in the West is the fairy tale of the princess and the pea. The girl's true identity is vouchsafed by her extreme sensitivity to pain. The most familiar example in India is the episode in the *Mahabharata* in which Karna, a Kshatriya, tries to conceal his identity from his guru in order to pass as a Brahmin. His stoic tolerance of a vicious bug-sting, as his teacher rests against his lap, reveals his scheme and his true social nature. In such instances pain uncovers the truth to those who do not know it, namely outsiders. It is pain observed. However, similar pain can also be experienced subjectively as a test, an indicator of one's true resolve, virtue, love of God, or even identity. In such a way Rabbi Akiva, reciting the Shema, regarded his extreme pain while the Romans were combing the flesh off his bones in the most striking instance of Jewish martyrology.[27] This is a separate, though related, model (pain as test), and it can be found in the New Testament. There the agony Jesus experienced in Gethsemane is characterized as a test, a type of ordeal or trial. Elsewhere the text is explicit: "Because he himself was tested by what he suffered, he is able to help those who are being tested."[28] Later, St. Anthony became the exemplar of suffering as a test, a struggle with "the phantoms of lions, bears, leopards, bulls, and of serpents, asps, and scorpions."[29] Though obscured by hagiography, such narratives seem to be describing pains, phantom or illusionary pains, which are experienced as a test of one's spiritual state.

Related to the juridical-punitive model is the punitive-educational way of speaking about pain. The most famous biblical reference is Proverbs 13:24, "He who spares his rod hates his son."[30] The theme recurs with some frequency in a number of related senses: "I will be a father to him and he will be a son to Me; when he commits iniquity, I will correct him with the rod of men and the strokes of sons of men, but My lovingkindness shall not depart from him."[31] Pain may be taken as punishment, but the loving punishment inflicted by a metaphorical father, by God, in order to educate those whom He loves. It educates them for patience and perseverance, which are necessary for salvation. Clement mixed this theme with medical terms when he wrote: "Though disease, and accident, and what is most terrible of all, death, come upon [the true Christian], he remains inflexible in soul—knowing that all such things are a necessity of creation, and that, also by the power of God, they become the medicine of salvation, benefiting by discipline those who are difficult to reform."[32]

Medical Models

Even though medical authorities today characterize pain as an aversive sensation, religious sources often describe it as medical, and in so doing, evaluate it as a beneficial experience. A dramatic example comes from Prudentius, a fourth-century Christian poet who attributes to Saint Romanus (the martyr) the following words: "You will shudder at the handiwork of the executioners, but are doctors' hands gentler, when Hippocrates' cruel butchery is going on? The living flesh is cut and fresh-drawn blood stains the lancers when festering matter is being scraped away." Consequently, to those who grieve his imminent death he adds: "That by which health is restored is not vexatious. These men appear to be rending my wasting limbs, but they give healing to the living substance within."[33] The claim is not that pain is pleasant, but that it benefits the soul. One need not seek it like a martyr, but if afflicted naturally, the pain ought to be taken as a spiritual sign—not just a reason for running to a doctor. In fact, it may be left untreated for healing by Christ himself.[34]

Medicine, of course, is both preventive and curative. It either cures diseases that have already been contracted (sin), or prevents ills to follow (punishment). In either case, a familiar feature of classical medicine—and the attendant aspects of the model—is that the remedy is as bitter as the disease. In its Christian version this model may owe a great deal to the classical dictum that "medicine is the philosophy of the body, and philosophy the medicine of the soul."[35] The ancient physicians, including Hippocrates, recognized the powerful effect that the mind exerts over the body's health, and they refused to separate the mechanics of healing the body from the more subtle work of the mind. By logical analogy, if healing the body often requires painful medicine, so did the healing of the soul.

Epictetus, comparing the philosopher's teaching room to that of the surgeon, claimed, "You ought not to walk out of it in pleasure, but in pain."[36] The work of the surgeon, in fact, as Saint Romanus insisted, often resembles that of the executioner who cuts at living flesh. But while the surgeon may look like a butcher, his bloody tortures head off greater pains. Saint Basil explained: "It is shameful, indeed, that they who are sick in body place so much confidence in physicians that, even if these cut or burn or cause distress by their bitter medicines, they look upon them as benefactors, while we do not share this attitude toward the physicians of our souls when they secure our salvation for us by laborious discipline."[37] The classical medical notion that the medicine can be as painful as the disease may be one of the most persistent ideological axioms in Western cultural history. It unfolded in the conviction of any ascetic, monk, or martyr who, like Henry Suso or Marguirite Marie, tormented his or her own flesh in order to avoid the greater torments to the soul in the present or future life.

The classical medical doctrine that medicine is often bitter and in its mental aspects requires abstention from the free reign of desire also survived in Islamic metaphors of religious pain. *The Sea of Precious Virtues* warns the man who seeks worldly gains:

> Woe to you! You suffer such pains and abasement seeking gold, and in seeking health you abandon all your desires on the advice of an ignorant physician, and know not even this, that Hell is harsher than the illness of poverty, and the duration of the Hereafter is longer than the life of this world![38]

Those who do not take pains, the author warns, will not escape pain. Similarly, Shah Abdul Latif, an eighteenth-century Indian sufi, explored the theme of religious pain and medicine with great insight and ironic subtlety. On the true lover (of God) he wrote:

> Whilst the physicians were seated, the friend entering came to my
>   door
> The pain went far off with the coming of my wonderful (friend).
> [And the lover cries out]:

O physician! Do not give pulverized medicaments!
May I not become better!
My beloved may arrive, and help me one day![39]

The pain metaphor takes a life of its own in this mystical poetry, and medication no longer seems appealing. Instead, the illness—the pain—becomes an invitation for the divine healer. The reason for avoiding the medication for pain is made even more explicit in the words Ghalib sang in Delhi a century later: "When pain transgresses the limits, it becomes medicine."[40] Only in a state of absolute and helpless suffering does the lover stand any chance of beholding his Beloved, so intolerable pain is no longer a metaphor for spiritual illness, and it becomes true medicine for the soul. The medical model does not deny or suppress the bitterness of pain, but it affirms (either reluctantly or aggressively) its spiritual usefulness. A far less ambiguous and more assertive stance is articulated in the equally pervasive military metaphors.

The Military Model

Most people who suffer pain today, especially chronic pain, regard it as an enemy, or at the very least—in the name of a recent book—an unwelcome guest. This is certainly the attitude of Job to his pain; the arrows flung at him by mortal enemies.[41] A similar metaphor runs through a magical charm against severe cholic pain in an ancient Indian text, the *Atharvaveda,* but there the arrow belongs to the god Rudra.[42] The psalmist at Psalm 22 (Jeremiah's vision of the pain suffered both by Israel and the messenger of God), shares a modernist aversion to pain with Job.[43] These examples define the military model as a way of conceptualizing pain as an enemy or invader of the patient's body. However, Christian and Muslim writers have turned this over on its head. Often the enemy is not pain but the body, or the embodied soul.[44] Pain is the weapon by means of which the body is subdued, demons exorcised, temptation averted, in a battle for salvation. Calvin famously conceived of the spiritual life as a battle against the flesh, or "the old man." One must slay the flesh with the sword of the Spirit in order to achieve the mortification that is required for salvation. This warfare manifests in a continuous struggle in which following the example of Christ—bearing his cross—is crucial. The cross brings humiliation, discipline, and chastisement, which means that illness and pain are not merely to be suffered but welcomed as tools for this battle.[45] Much earlier Augustine had described his own spiritual crisis as a battle between the Spirit and the flesh, his mind and the members of his body.[46]

Ascetics and mystics who take this psychology seriously relish the

pain they inflict on themselves, or the natural pains that strike them involuntarily. Simeon the Stylite engaged in a painful battle with his body, bound on top of the column, the bones and sinews visible on his feet due to the pain. Simeon loved his pain so much that he tortured himself to death.[47] Macarius once responded to an ego-boosting job offer by throwing himself down on the floor of his cell. He commenced a prolonged and violent battle with his "fiends," entrenched, of course, in his own body. A friend who saw him and wanted to relieve his pain was turned away with the following: "I am tormenting my tormentors."[48] Catherine of Siena wrote to the Abbess of the Monastery of Santa Marta in Siena: "'Our perverse will!' What does the loving Paul say? 'Discipline the members of your body.' He doesn't say the same of the will; no, he wants the will put to death and not merely disciplined. Oh sweetest treasured love! I can see no other answer for us but the sword that you, dearest love, had in your own heart and soul."[49]

Muslim ascetics have been prolific in their conceptualization of *jihad* as, first and foremost, combat against internal enemies, specifically the "soul" (in its Aristotelian sense). *The Sea of Precious Virtues* quotes Abu Bakr Wasiti as saying: "Within each man's body is enthroned a soul, which rules, commanding and forbidding. Were it not for fear of the sword, it would become aware and claim divinity, just as accursed Pharaoh said, 'I am your supreme Lord.'"[50] The "sword" is used metaphorically, of course, in reference to self-discipline and mortification of the flesh. The same chapter, on the conduct of holy war, contains the following episode:

> One day the Prophet asked his Companions, "What would you say of a friend who, if you honor him and exalt him, betrays you and acts with perfidy toward you, but if you despise him and treat him basely will exalt you?" They replied, "What an evil friend is he!"—"He is your own souls that lie between your ribs; they will lead him to Hellfire who exalts and honors them, gives them food and drink, and follows their desires . . . (And whoso) shall have chosen this present life verily hell shall be his abode."[51]

The chosen pain of asceticism is thus the instrument of combat, the weapon used against one's own soul.[52]

The Athletic Model

The word *ascesis* in Plato and Aristotle means training. It is closely related to virtue because athletic training requires the manly virtues of discipline, physical control, and endurance. In *Epictetus,* Plato uses the athletic ethic for religious purposes, quoting Diogenes: "Now God says to you, come to the contest, show us what you have learned, how you

have trained yourself. How long will you exercise alone? Now the time has come for you to discover whether you are one of the athletes who deserves victory."[53] Philo applied the athletic virtue to ascetic discipline in his admiration both for gymnastics and the Essenes, whom he called "athletes of virtue." The wide use of the athletic model in the ascetic world of early Christianity reflects a somewhat softer attitude toward the body and its pains than the military model. But its imaginative range goes beyond asceticism as preparatory training for a future life. Hebrews 10:32 uses athletic language (*athlesin pathematon*) to characterize the appropriate attitude of those who suffer pains inflicted on them by others. Similarly Hebrews 12 describes pain as God's training for his faithful, designed not merely to be endured but actively sought.[54] In fact, martyrdom could be imagined as an athletic contest, played out in the arenas of Rome, against paganism, or against one's own weaknesses. Colin Eisler argues that the New Testament events of the passion, agony in the garden, the stripping, the flagellation, and the crowning with thorns represent an inversion of the athletic ideal and the triumphant athlete.[55] The preparation, discipline, and crowning of the contestant is here the torturous path of Christ's sacrifice. This identification between martyrdom and the athletic contest would extend to other figures in early Christianity, such as Tertullian and Prudentius.[56]

Magical Models

Numerous instances of religiously induced pain appear to be connected, usually in an implicit manner, with magical thinking. Pain is an alchemical force, like the forger's fire, which magically transforms its victim from one state of existence to a higher, purer state. Or the pain inflicted by striking or biting acts like an agricultural instrument that magically produces growth. Finally, pain can be the mysterious source of superhuman powers.

Gregory of Nyssa explained that pain comes naturally to those who are being "drawn up" to God because of the transformation that the adherent must undergo: "Just as those who by means of fire, purify gold mixed with matter, not only melt the impure matter, but also melt the pure gold along with the counterfeit . . . so, also, when evil is being consumed by purifying fire."[57] Shah Abdul Latif, whose remarkable inventiveness in the trope-making of pain we have already seen, explored the theme of the blacksmith's fire as a metaphor of ascetic pain. The theme is an old one, present in Rumi's mystical exclamation, "I am the fire!" and further before that in the Christian mystical writings of Origenes. For Shah Abdul Latif, just as the blacksmith transforms ore into steel, so the mystical guide prepares his disciple by putting him through the fires of pain and suffering in order to transform an ordinary individual into a brilliant receptor of God's unity.[58]

Agricultural metaphors seem to dominate in rites of passage and initiation. The Rajasuya, or ritual of installing a new king, in ancient India is one example. It is an enormously complex ritual, but one of its central acts features the striking of the new king with canes. After the king casts the dice that had been placed in his hand, the Adhavaryu priest and his assistants silently strike him on the back with Udumbara sticks. "By beating him with sticks they guide him safely over judicial punishment, whence the king is exempt from punishment" for inflicting pain on others.[59] The explicit rationalization of the ritual is jurisprudential, and it rests on a pun involving the noun *danda* (staff). Jan Heesterman, who describes this ritual in great detail, correctly interprets the beating as a fertility theme associated with rejuvenation and growth.[60] Heinrich Kisch has similarly noted that in ancient Greece infertile women would visit the Temple of Juno in Athens where they would receive flagellation from the priests.[61] The striking may also be a symbolic sacrificial act, as are other elements of the ritual. From a phenomenological perspective it is also related to the imitative character of agricultural rites of seasonal regeneration and vegetation.[62] Implicit again is the magico-agricultural motif in the initiation rituals cited by Durkheim: He claims that the Australian ritual act of severely biting the scalp of the initiate is meant to make hair grow. In other instances the hair is pulled out, as are teeth in often-cited instances of initiatory ordeals. The ritual torture of genitalia—that is circumcision, clitoridectomy, and subincision—are related to the theme of regeneration as well.[63] The "magic" behind these applications of pain seems to rest in the connection made between the burning, beating, cutting, or mutilation and the anticipated results of the ritual.

Whipping has been a widely pervasive magical remedy for a large number of conditions and situations, as a brief perusal in Frazer would immediately reveal. In the New Testament, flagellation was a means of driving out ghosts (see Chapter 5 of this book). In the *Satyricon* of Petronius the mariners Encolpus and Giton were whipped in order to assure calm seas.[64] This appears to involve a sacrificial motif, in which the victim is a willing participant in the magical compulsion laid at the feet of a god.

Related to this theme, in its fiery aspect, is the Indian doctrine of *tapas*.[65] The word *tapas* was used in the Rig Veda to designate a certain type of pain: "My ribs pain (or burn) me all about as co-wives plague (their husbands)."[66] The combined meaning is a painful heat, which generations of Vedic and post-Vedic ascetics cultivated in order to gain extraordinary powers and great fame. Of course, the feats of pain tolerance had to be proportional to the goals: legendary powers in exchange for years of standing on one leg or with one arm raised; standing still on top of a swarming anthill; suffering extreme cold, heat, or hunger; and ritual penances such as suspension of the body by hooks, insertion of iron rods, and so forth. The ascetic who breaks his ascetic vows (of *tapas*) must undergo a specific expiation: "By means of fire they enveloped (the body) with a skin. Now fire, being *tapas*, and the Diksa being *tapas*, they thereby underwent an intermediate consecration; and because they underwent that intermediate consecration, therefore this intermediate consecration (is performed [by man]) . . . and [therefore] so does he thereby make atonement for what heretofore he has done injurious to the vow [of asceticism, i.e., *tapas*].[67] In Taoist texts extremely painful methods of suicide are described as methods for assuring immortality. The *Zhengao* states, "If an adept ingests a spoonful of the 'White Powder of the Perfected of the Great Ultimate for Abandoning the Waisband,' he will feel a sharp, stabbing pain in the heart. After three days he will become thirsty and drink a *hu* (about 20 liters) of water, after which he dies—or so it seems. The corpse later disappears, leaving only the clothes. At this point, the adept becomes an 'immortal released in broad daylight.' "[68]

Closely related to the magical model, though conceptually distinct, is the notion that pain purifies. When the body is either imagined or experienced as a filthy and putrifying encasement of the pure soul, pain is felt as cleansing. Such a view was consistent with the extreme dualistic views that flourished in the first few centuries of the common era, in the writings of the Manicheans, Gnostics, and Marcionites. According to Celsus, who was quoting Heraclitus, the body is worse than dung. This sentiment was never far from the mouths of mainstream Christians throughout the centuries.[69] The Christian apologist Arnobius declared that the body is " 'a disgusting vessel of urine' and 'bag of shit' "[70] St. Bernard of Clairvaux was eloquent in his revulsion, stating, "The flesh . . . is no better than filthy Rags. . . . Consider a little those constant evacuations, the discharges of thy mouth, and nose, and other passages, without which the body cannot subsist."[71] The only way to purify this disgusting flesh is to discipline it harshly and mercilessly by means of asceticism—extreme mortification. "The flesh of God's revered servant, hardened and virtually mineralized by tough vigils and pared to the bones by pitiless dieting, would smell after death as 'sweet as a perfumed apple.' "[72] Gregory of Nyssa, who described pain in terms of the alchemical (purifying) fire also compared the body to a rope smeared with mud which is pulled through a narrow hole. The mud comes off through the "violent tugging," like the soul purified of the polluted body through ascetic pain. The reason I place these sentiments under the heading of the magical model is that it may belong with the extremely common practice of passing people (sick, sinners) through holes in trees, rocks, walls, and scraping off ghosts, diseases, or pollution.[73]

Both eastern (nondualist) and European ideas about pollution—the removal of sin as though it were dirt—often require submersion in cold water. According to classical Hindu legal sources, the colder the water, the more effectively it purifies. The Jatila ascetics of ancient India would bathe in the freezing Neranjara river in cold winter nights, removing their sins (*papa*) in the cold wet pain of submersion. As noted earlier, medieval European penitents, Christians and Jews alike, often performed penance while sitting in freezing cold streams.[74]

Also related to the magical model is the conception of pain as an instrument of passage. This theme is most frequently performed in rites of passage, but it has also been articulated theoretically. Pain is an essential aspect of passage from one state of life to another, from limited states of consciousness and identity to other, broader identifications. The Baha'u'llah is reported to have said: "The steed of this valley is pain; and if there be no pain this journey will never end."[75] A striking recent example of pain-as-passage is the statement by the Midwives Alliance of North America that natural childbirth is "hugely empowering." Shelly Girard explains: "Labor is challenging, a powerful process marking the miracle of bringing forth a new life and a new being onto this planet. It is a rite of passage, a psychospiritual training ground for both mother and child. The laboring woman must put aside her own comfort and learn to surrender to a process so intense that it threatens to consume her. . . . When a woman is able to release into her own intuitive consciousness, she gives birth to the spirit of the 'Divine Mother.'"[76] Similar terms have been used recently in debates over Oregon's assisted suicide law. Marjorie Williams framed her argument, in opposition to the law, in terms of dying as passage, and the pain of dying as that feature which makes the transition both meaningful and empowering.[77]

Models of Shared Pain

Contemporary patients think of their pain as profoundly isolating and as entirely their own. *The Death of Ivan Ilych* may be the quintessentially modern way of expressing this feeling, although the ending of the story hints at a premodern sensibility. Ivan Ilych finds his only relief and consolation through the tender care of a simple country boy—Gerasim. On his deathbed he can finally feel for his surviving family, and his suffering gives way to peace. Indeed, numerous religious sources from around the world portray pain as a transitive experience. The victim of pain may suffer it on behalf of others, while the others are deeply affected by this pain. This vicarious property of physical suffering stands at the center of Christian life, beginning with the sacrifice of Christ and running through the capacity to imitate the suffering Christ.[78] Vicarious pain culminates in Christianity, perhaps, with stigmata, showing the co-suffering on one's own body of Christ's wounds from the crucifixion. But the shared-pain model transcends Christology and mysticism. The public execution of heretics and witches, the judicial spectacle, is a ritual of communal identification, a sacrifice of sorts, in which the victim touches the mob, either by moving it to a frenzy of derisive joy or to a riot of anger and protest. The very existence of hell is a testimony to the power of vicarious experience. Rites of passage in which groups of boys and girls are hurt achieve their social ends through the bonding effects of shared suffering. Rites of mourning in which self-mutilation is extreme also play out the bonds that exist among the survivors or reinforce the lasting bond with those who have died.

The concept of shared pain is archaic, and in its Greek versions it overlaps with pollution. *Miasma* is the term for the polluting afflictions caused by a single agent, which becomes the scapegoat sacrifice who removes the suffering of the entire community. Oedipus gets this right—but in reverse—when he declares: "I suffer the misfortune of all these men even more than if it were my own."[79] The intimacy between the instigator and the communal suffering underwrites the bond between the sacrificers and the sacrifice, the dwellers of heaven and hell, the city and its criminals, and at times in European history, Christians and Jews (or witches, heretics, Muslims). This bond will be discussed in subsequent chapters of the book.

Colossians 1:24 states: "Now I rejoice in my sufferings for your sake, and in my flesh I do my share on behalf of His body (which is the church) in filling up that which is lacking in Christ's afflictions." The assertion that a sacrifice can be effective as an instrument of communal bonding through divine mercy depends on the transitivity of the sacrificial victim's pain above any other ritual mechanism. This is explicit in Hebrews 13:11–12: "For the bodies of those animals whose blood is brought into the holy place by the high priest as an offering for sin, are burned outside the camp. Therefore Jesus also, that He might sanctify the people though His own blood, suffered outside the gate." The early church is identified as a community through this shared pain, at the center of which stands the sacrifice of Jesus.[80] Later on this model figured in the way mystics came to feel their intimacy with Christ, and more rarely with the community around them. Catherine of Siena wrote that just as Christ went the way of suffering, "it is by such suffering that we become conformed with Christ crucified."[81] And Julian of Norwich claimed that she had "desired a bodily sight, in which I might have more knowledge of our saviour's bodily pains, and of the compassion of our Lady and of all his true lovers who were living at that time and saw his pains, for I would have been one of them and have suffered with them."[82] All of this is extremely familiar to Christians, and it may be tempting to think that vicarious pain is merely a secondary aspect of the theology of sacrifice at the heart of the New Testament and subsequent *imitatio dei* mysticism. In fact, the phenomenon of shared pain is extremely pervasive.

The *Zohar* adds to the Yom Kippur liturgy a discussion on the death of the righteous ones, who atone in their death for the sins of the entire generation. To feel a sympathetic sorrow for the suffering of the righteous is thus to have one's sins atoned.[83] The Taoist text *Mingzhen ke* contains ritual liturgies that require participants in the ritual to inflict pain and humiliation on themselves to expiate the sins of others and to free souls of dead sinners from the tortures of hell. The ritual consists of reciting petitions while the participants kowtow and slap their own cheeks repeatedly, sometimes over six hundred times. The text states:

> It is so that by prostrating yourself in worship, kowtowing and hitting yourself, you administer words of humble confession. Thereby with your earnest heart and devoted mind, your sincerity is thorough and your suffering is sufficient; naturally [your petitions] will move [divine beings] pervasively.[84]

Psychotropic and Ecstatic Models of Pain

Anesthesiologists and neurologists know that certain levels of pain possess analgesic qualities and can even induce euphoric states. A low level of nerve irritation or stimulation can mask deeper pain, as anyone knows who has been given a Novocain shot by a compassionate dentist who shakes the patient's lip as he inserts the needle. Similarly, a sharp and brief pain can produce an effect called "hyperstimulation analgesia," which is based on the production of endogenous opioids resulting in temporary states of euphoria that may also be related to the reduction of psychological drives and the experience of dissociation or trance. The voluntary ordeals undergone by shamanic initiates and perhaps a very wide range of practices among ascetics may be related to such a model.[85] A particularly revealing contemporary manifestation of this model—chosen because it is contemporary—can be seen in the rituals and discourse of a man who calls himself Fakir Mufasar and publishes the journal *Body Play*. Fakir is a leading player in a subculture that centers on body modifications: piercings, tattooing, and a variety of so-called modern primitive rituals. He has subjected himself to an eclectic assortment of mutilations, modifications, and tortures gathered from several sources, including Indian Sadhus, American Plains Indians, Christian ascetics, Sufi mystics, and others. On hanging himself by hooks inserted into his chest, like the O-KEE-PA Ritual, Fakir writes:

> As a change-of-Bodystate progresses, be it BRIEF/INTENSE or LONG-TERM/GRADUAL, I finally reach a point where a shift occurs in my internal workings. Mental self-objectification becomes an emotional (feeling) going on in my body. Spirit and body co-exist now. Aware of each other but separate. It's an ecstasy state where no matter what happens in the body, no matter how much more intense the physical sensations become, I feel no more. Sensations just "are."[86]

Traditional mystics and religious practitioners do not use biochemistry to describe their experiences, of course. The language of psychotropic brain states, or even "altered states of consciousness" is modern and scientific, originating in the nineteenth century. Although mystics, shamans, and others have always used biochemical agents, such as the ancient Indian Soma plant or native American mushrooms, they spoke about their experiences in spiritual terms, in line with their beliefs about the ultimate nature of reality. Consequently, the psychotropic model is a modern phenomenon.

Why Hurt?

I have cited or quoted well over one hundred instances of pain, conceptualized in any of ten or so manners. The range of hurting styles is immense, and even the ways of imagining pain impress the modern reader, whose aversion to pain is clear and monolithic. It is thus hardly surprising that theories that have sought to explain the use of pain in religious history have tended to rely on single and reductive explanations. Some of these theories will be discussed in later chapters, but an overview should reveal the limitations of current explanations for the wide-ranging religious attitude toward pain.

Theories of pain fall into four broad categories: normative, critical, descriptive, and reductive. A normative "theory" is a theological argument for the value of pain articulated within a distinct tradition. When Calvin or Pope John Paul II writes about pain or mortification in theoretical terms meant both to situate pain within Christian psychology and to justify it on theological grounds, he embodies the tradition's own theoretical stance toward its practices.[87] The critical approach carries on a conversation with the first stance, in which the theorist has not altogether disengaged his discourse and reduced it to a separate level. In the case of pain, Friedrich Nietzsche and William James provide familiar examples as they critique Christian practices. Descriptive theories are those arguing that the reasons for using pain are the ones stated (explicitly or symbolically) by the practitioners themselves. The work of Mircea Eliade provides a rich example and is ultimately not altogether distinct from the first category (normative), despite its claims to the contrary. Such theories or more recent cultural-constructive variations do not really explain the pain. Instead they restate it in somewhat theoretical terms that merely paraphrase the reasons given by the practitioners. Reductive theories are the only true explanations of religious pain. They explain hurtful behavior by reducing it to a more abstract "fundamental" level of description such as biology, sociology, or psychology. The most familiar example is the work of Freud, who reduces self-hurt to the biology of drives and to psychopathology. But there are several other reductive theories, including the ethologically based work of Walter Burkhert and René Girard, the historical psychology of Michel Foucault, the literary criticism of Elaine Scarry, and others. Clearly I am overstating the boundaries between types of theory, but that is perhaps inevitable. The reason is that, with the exception of Scarry, none of the theorists I have seen has been interested specifically in pain. Freud's discussions on masochism and inward-turned aggression are not truly about pain. Neither are Girard's or Burkhert's interpretation of sacrificial violence, Durkheim's sociological reduction of violent rituals, or Foucault's descriptions of executions and his ideas about inscription. One must interpret their theories before applying them to actual pain, and this third-level reduction is bound to produce overlap and fuzzy boundaries.

It is most rewarding to critique theories of pain on specific points, as I shall do in context. Fundamentally, though, they all (with the exception of Eliade's history of religions) share this fault: They reduce all forms of religious pain to a single principle, and yet none of them gives any indication of the wealth of pain types being reduced. It may be appealing to explain the self-mutilation of a teenage nun in terms of erotic-aggressive drives, but how does this account for the Zen monk who focuses his undivided attention on the pain in his knees as he sits in Zazen? Some mystics may be riding the rush of beta-endorphins as they scourge their bodies, but what about the martyrs who allow their bodies to be hacked by Roman executioners or consumed by beasts? Clearly, no single reductive theory can answer the question, Why is pain used—even welcomed—in the history of religions?[88]

I will change the question and set a slightly different agenda: What is the effect of pain on the consciousness of those who hurt, and how does the consciousness of pain contribute to the religious life? Or put somewhat differently, What is the effect of pain on the self and on the sense of identity of those who engage in painful practices, and what is the role of the pained self in religious and social life? This book then is a psychological theory, a reduction of religious pain to self-psychology. I am fully aware that this psychological reduction cannot explain all cases of pain, but I am also confident that the theme I have selected is central enough to warrant the trouble. And, just as important, it is the only approach that can answer Jacob Goren's question, which calls for a scientific reduction but also has to make sense to him in his own unique cultural and historical circumstances, and this requires a culturally sensitive and nonreductive awareness.

Pain and Self

Based strictly on pain's effects on the self, it may be possible to reduce all conceptions of pain to two fundamental "types."[89] The two are disintegrative and integrative pain, or what David Bakan calls "telic decentralizing" and "telic centralizing." The pain Job experienced was disintegrative: It entirely disrupted his life, isolated him from the world, devastated his sense of well-being, his very desire to live. Disintegrative pain is extremely likely to be described as punitive, or as an enemy. In contrast, the pain that a woman undergoes during labor—as intense as anything Job felt—is more ambiguous. Despite being characterized in Genesis as punitive, it is also described by the American Association of Midwives as integrating. It strengthens, so they assert, the woman's sense of identity, her ability to situate herself within nature and within her social and spiritual world. Such a pain is more likely to be described as healing, or transforming than punitive. These two examples should make it clear that the difference between the two types of pain is not intensity—healing pain can be as intense as punitive pain.

It should also be clear that the description of pain is extremely context-sensitive. The same pain can be either punitive or transforming. Indeed, disintegrative and integrative pains are not two logical (and mutually exclusive) categories for classifying pains. Nor are they two physiological effects of pain on their victims. Both of these options are too objective and suffer from what postmodernists call "closure." Labor pain shows that one and the same pain can be either integrative or disintegrative or both at the same time or at different times. The types, instead, are two ways of talking about pain from the (shifting) perspective of the ego in pain. I use the word *ego* in a broad sense that points to Freud but only to differ. Ego will be discussed in detail in Chapters 2 and 4, but it should be understood here as the conscious "steering mechanism" of the human organism. Or, ego can be understood for the time being as the end or goal (telos) of the system that constitutes the person. By system I mean more than the individual organism: It includes the family, friends, church, and even inanimate objects that surround the individual and define his or her identity in a broad context ("lived world" in phenomenological terms).

The first fundamental type of pain—disintegrative, or telic decentralizing—emerges from descriptions of pain that weaken or destroy the ego and that disrupt the relationship of ego to its lived world. The second type emerges from narratives that describe the strengthening of the system's telos. This may not be the individual ego; it may be the sense of identity with the interests of the community or with a god, but the empirical individual feels empowered by the sensations of the hurt.

The two fundamental perspectives of ego on pain represent an extremely subtle mix of cultural, psychological, and biological principles. It would be absurdly simplistic to say that pain is evaluated as healing when an authoritative theology or worldview superimposes its norms on the pain patient, compelling him to disregard his natural aversion to pain. But it would be equally simplistic to argue that pain is evaluated as punitive simply because it hurts the individual. This book will focus on the margins of biology and culture and explore the dialectic that operates between the injured organism and the mental world of the person in pain. I will not only show how culture and pain come together but also that the aversive disintegrative type of pain can be transformed into integrative pain. Only religious language can describe how "bad" pain becomes "good" pain, though it is not only religion that brings about this transformation.[90] In exploring the transition from one type of pain to the other, I will show that pain can act as a socially and spiritually integrative force that defines and broadens the individual's sense of identity within the traditional community.

Pain in Ritual

I have noted earlier that pain is actively produced in a number of religious rituals around the world. Three chapters in the book will discuss ritualized pain in some detail within the context of rituals of possession and exorcism, rites of passage and initiation, and the ritualized tortures of the Inquisition's investigations and executions. These three contexts represent a small minority among the numerous rituals that use pain. The reasons for discussing only those three, aside from a sheer lack of space, are embedded in the aims of this book: I am discussing the effects of religiously conceived pain on the development of the self, or the moral agent within his or her community. Because this discussion must lead to a specific answer for a particular questioner (Jacob Goren), the direction of the book is limited to those contexts that are most persuasive for Goren and similar readers. Still, pain figures just as prominently in other ritual contexts, such as mourning rituals, pilgrimages, rites of atonement, vows and intercessionary rites, and celebratory performances of annual holidays. In San Fernando, the Philippines, for instance, Good Friday has been celebrated by the performance of self-flagellation and voluntary nailing to the cross in identification with the crucified Christ, but such rituals will be excluded from this book.[91]

Ritualized pain—self-flagellation, crucifixions, barefoot pilgrimages, piercing of the body, walking on hot coals, rolling naked on a hard terrain, and so forth—raises distinct issues of conceptualization. To be sure, ritual pain is related to the primary models in a variety of ways. The example just cited is an imitation of Christ and thus shows vicarious pain in action. But ritualized forms of hurt are more difficult to understand. The meaning of the pain is rarely explicitly discussed, and it usually unfolds within a complex symbolic performance, which hides its meanings. I shall briefly discuss mourning rites and pilgrimage to highlight the presence of pain and also to indicate the unique problems in understanding the meaning of ritualized pain.

Mourning

Self-mutilation is extremely pervasive in rites of mourning around the world. A recent survey of seventy-eight societies has documented thirty-one in which self-injury prevails and thirty-two in which it is attempted in varying degrees of success.[92] Acts of self-hurting vary from mild hair-pulling and chest-beating to extremely violent forms of self-abuse. Some of the most vivid descriptions, and possibly the most influential in the anthropological literature, were cited by Emile Durkheim out of Spencer and Gillen's observations of the Warramunga in Australia:

> Some of the women, who had come from every direction, were lying prostrate on the body, while others were standing or kneeling around, digging the sharp ends of yam-sticks into the crown of their heads, from which the blood streamed down over their faces, while all the time they kept up a loud, continuous wail. . . . To the side, three men of the Thapungarti class, who still wore their ceremonial decorations, sat down wailing loudly, with their backs towards the dying man, and in a minute or two another man of the same class rushed on to the ground yelling and brandishing a stone knife. Reaching the camp, he suddenly gashed both thighs deeply, cutting right across the muscles, and unable to stand, fell down into the middle of the group. . . . As soon as [the dying man] had given up his last breath, the same scene was re-enacted, only this time the wailing was still louder, and men and women, seized by a

> veritable frenzy, were rushing about cutting themselves with knives and sharp-pointed sticks, the women battering one another's heads with fighting clubs, no one attempting to ward off either cuts or blows.[93]

Durkheim makes it clear in the next passage that this is not a random and spontaneous mayhem of grief, but that the acts of wailing and hurting are carefully scripted, which is why they are described here as a ritual. He regards the rites as "piacular"—that is, rites of penance. Obviously, grief can result in spontaneous acts of self-injury, but the French sociologist insists that emotions and their outlets are carefully channeled by social factors. The precise relation of emotion and this cultural form of action (in the case of mourning) is not entirely clear and has been debated forcefully over the last few years. On the "left" side, if I may borrow a political term for extreme social construction, are scholars who feel that the ritual prescriptions generate the emotions. The acts of violence are scripted in order to evoke grief, sorrow, regret, anger, and all the other feelings that are evidently present.[94] At the other end of the spectrum, and more recent, is the argument that the emotions of grief are natural and spontaneous and that the acts that follow, including self-hurt, must be understood first and foremost as expressions of these feelings.[95] In the middle is an intermediary position that claims a closer allegiance to Durkheim, arguing that the relationship between emotion and ritually prescribed action is "cybernetic."[96] This means that although the emotions are natural, they are scripted and magnified according to a repertoire of culturally meaningful norms.

The relationship between emotions (and pain) and ritual script is extremely important and will be discussed in some detail in the chapters that deal with possession-exorcism and rites of passage. For the time being, what is at stake is how we interpret the meaning and function of the pain that accompanies self-mutilation. The ritual practitioners do not often explain their pain. If the hurt is understood as a spontaneous display of grief it could be conceived in terms of psychological explanations that are consistent with a number of the models above. For instance, extreme grief may consist of an uneasy balance of guilt and anger, and if this is so, self-hurt may be imagined in terms of the punitive aspects of the juridical model.[97] But if the self-mutilation is rigorously scripted in order to provoke strong emotions or even beliefs, its meaning would have to be conceptualized in a different manner. For instance, such pain might belong in the communal-vicarious model, as a sacrificial act that is aimed at furthering the journey of the departed spirit, or easing the emotional burden of the surviving relatives.[98] In either case, the researcher has to supply the pain model, and do so on the basis of unclear evidence. Similar problems pervade other rituals, such as the ritual of pilgrimage.

Pilgrimage

The study of pilgrimage has become increasingly sophisticated over the last two decades since the work of Victor Turner reduced the phenomenon to liminality and communitas (the egalitarian community of initiates), which are extensions of Arnold Van Gennep's seminal observations on the structure of passage. Scholars no longer seem to agree on what precisely constitutes a pilgrimage, let alone what pilgrimage means.[99] However, a strong agreement persists that pilgrimages are often accompanied by discourse about pain and conceptualized as sacrifice, imitation of God, penance, tests, and so forth. Ethnographic descriptions of pilgrims in pain abound, ranging anywhere from voluntary self-flagellation and whippings in the Andes and barefoot walking in Sabari Malai, South India, to the unwanted travails of pilgrims at Lourdes. The same ambiguities I have noted in reference to mourning apply here as well, and the correspondence between painful conduct and the representation of pain is highly problematic. The best description of pilgrims in pain, or for that matter of ritualized pain of any kind, that I have seen is the Ayyappan pilgrimage description of E. Valentine Daniel.[100] Although the pain descriptions there are multilayered and include imitation of God, penance, and purifying and gnostic pain, the author's analysis of the psychological effects of pain are precise and clear. I will therefore quote him at some length. The pilgrimage to Sabari Malai is seasonal and takes place between mid-December to mid-January. It marks the path of the god Lord Ayyappan, son of Shiva, in his encounter with, and deflection of, a beautiful demoness. The pilgrims who undertake the journey commit themselves to vows of austerities, including celibacy, moderate eating, bare feet for the duration of the journey, sleeping on the hard ground. The hardest aspect of the forty-plus-mile journey is the pain induced by walking barefoot:

> The path was either covered by sharp-edged stones and gravel or by the softest and finest earth. . . . As it was, this soil merely absorbed and retained the heat of the sun and blistered the soles of the pilgrims' feet, which had already been lacerated and made tender by the stone-strewn pathway.[101]

Daniel very carefully observes the modulation of the pains produced by barefoot walking over the course of several miles in the heat, uphill one time, downhill at another. His pain is not monolithic or inarticulate:

> One tells oneself, "I shall walk on this side or that" or "Look! There's a patch of grass. Let me go and walk on that. It will make my feet feel good, even though the patch is only three feet long." During this phase, one is able to differentiate between the pain caused by the blisters under one's toenails and those on one's heels. Then again, one is able to distinguish between the pain caused by blisters, wherever they happen to be, and the pain arising from strained calf muscles and tendons. . . . The headaches caused by the heat of the noon sun and the load of the *iru muti* can be distinguished from the pain resulting from the straps of the knapsack biting into one's shoulders.[102]

All of this hurting is essential to the devotion (*bhakti*) of the pilgrimage, and according to Daniel it is a critical mediator between personal experience (the psychotropic effect of pain toward mystical consciousness) and the elaborate theological psychology of Samkhya-Yoga. In other words (for Valentine these words are out of Peirce), the spiritual ends of the pilgrimage—loving union with Ayyappan—spring from pain. This is how it happens:

> Sooner or later, however, all the different kinds of pain begin to merge. . . . The experience of pain makes one acutely aware of oneself (ego) as the victim, and the outside (undifferentiated as roots, stones, and hot sand) as the pain-causing agent. . . . With time, pain stops having a causative agent, and ego is obscured or snuffed out because it has nothing to contrast itself with or stand against. . . . There is a "feeling" of pain, of course, but it is a sensation that has no agent, no tense, and no comparative. . . . Pain is the only sensation belonging to the eternal present.[103]

With regard to his fellow pilgrims the author notes: "Several pilgrims seemed to believe, however, that after a while, pain, having become so intense, began to disappear. In the words of one pilgrim from my village, 'At one moment everything is pain. But at the next moment everything is love (*anpu*). Everything is love for the Lord.'"[104] This is the goal of the pilgrimage, to attain a devotional love for Ayyappan in such an intense manner that all other thoughts and feelings are blotted out. In the case of this pilgrimage the method is a transforming pain.

It is hard to say how much of this vivid description is colored by the author's use of an elaborate epistemology derived from the great American semiotician Charles Peirce. His ritual description could easily serve as the masthead for this book because it illustrates the transition from aversive pain to transformative, even love-inducing pain. In a word, it is a splendid instance of sacred pain. But due to the essential ambiguities and self-contradictions of ritualized pain, such rituals must be used with great care. I will avoid interpreting or analyzing the meaning of the ritualized torments, and focus instead only on those instances of ritual pain where the function of the hurt, regardless of its cognitive meaning, is clearly related to transformations in the status of the hurting self. Many rituals that use pain are aimed at such transformations, as Valentine Daniel so clearly shows. My work will thus involve isolating certain features of the rite, sometimes ignoring its manifest purpose in favor of its implicit effects.

TWO

Pain and Transcendence: The Neurological Grounds

If You want to saw my limbs,
I will not flinch.
Even if You kill my body,
I will not stop loving You.[1]

Kabir is not unique and his claim is no boast. Pain not only fails to alienate the true lovers from God, it seals their love. Why do Sufis, Hindus, Christians, and many others think so? What does one make of a pain described as ecstatic or as healing to the soul? It sounds like a weak theodicy: religious dogma rationalizing the unavoidable suffering of a complicated existence. This is too simple. Recall, first, that around the world, in rituals and private devotions, people have actually scourged themselves, branded their bodies, sat in frozen rivers or next to hot fires. Self-inflicted pain is no theodicy. Next, consider that even the language of punitive pain is not closed-ended, that any religiously conceived pain can potentially be transformed into good pain: educational, healing, bonding with God. In its relation to pain, the goal of religious life is not to bring anesthesia, but to transform the pain that causes suffering into a pain that leads to insight, meaning, and even salvation. This is the essential paradox of sacred pain: that the hurting body does not suffer silently. It offers a potential voice, if one has the tools to make the soul listen.

Pain was muted in the nineteenth century when suffering became a medical problem and when the polyvalence of pain language was boiled down to illness—whether somatic or psychological. Modern pain now requires not only anesthesia, but a "theory," a unified answer to the question that opened this book: Why would religious discourse ever glorify pain and encourage painful behavior? In fact, several theories explain sacred pain, falling into two basic categories: reductive and nonreductive. A nonreductive theory does not explain; at best it interprets. For instance, it may read initiatory ordeals as symbolic ritual forms of death and rebirth. The nonreductive theory, most famously Mircea Eliade's, may further be expanded to Sufis and other mystics who are, after all, seeking initiation into a direct experience of the sacred.[2] The witch is executed in an exceptionally painful manner because her death is conceived, obscenely to be sure, as spiritual passage, initiatory rite, or saving violence, not merely a removal from society.[3] Unfortunately, a nonreductive theory never explains exactly how pain "symbolizes" death, or why a symbol based on sensory experience should acquire such an immense authority.

Reductive theories have been more thorough. Freudian psychoanalytical theory regards religious self-hurt—"holy" masochism—as the ego's response to guilt induced by factors embedded in the superego.[4] Voluntary pain is a form of self-punishment that subdues such voices by suppressing the effects of instinctual drives, especially sex, that conflict with higher social interests. The Christian mystic who wears a nail corset is fighting the battle of social repression against a seductive body. Or the torture of novices in rites of passage inflicts the repressive force of society on the no longer infantile subjects and harshly initiates young people to an authoritative order of being. Psychoanalysis is far more persuasive than Eliade's symbolism, but it fails to account for the phenomenological voice of participants who undergo pain. The guilt that perhaps induces self-flagellation among penitents seems entirely absent from the actions of ritual mourners, pilgrims, or yogis and shamans who train their bodies in rigorous ways. Victor Turner cautions that inserting subconscious forces into religious or cultural history is bound to distort the meaning of conduct that is determined by cultural motivations. And, of course, Freud's own explanation of clinical masochism no longer holds paramount position in psychological literature on self-hurt.[5] Still, psychoanalysis is important enough to discuss in detail, as I shall do in Chapter 4.

Other reductive theories come from a variety of disciplines such as sociology, neuropsychology, and even ethology.[6] Most focus on the function of pain rather than the way it feels. They explain violence or aggression as factors that determine religious behavior and belief, but this does not go far enough. A successful explanation of sacred pain needs to account for the subjective phenomenon, that is, the experiential contours of pain. A good theory also needs to explain how hurting contributes to a sense of the sacred in a way that is not reducible either to pathology or social determinism.

A dozen years ago Elaine Scarry published a book, *The Body in Pain,* which has been extremely influential among scholars of religion as they interpret sacred pain.[7] Scarry seeks to demonstrate the power of pain in the unmaking of worlds, and conversely, in the struggle to make worlds as acts of overcoming pain. Her point of departure is the unique and overwhelming muteness of pain as an experience that eludes language. Prolonged and unremitting pain has the effect of destroying its victim's ability to communicate and finally shatters his or her entire world, including even the self. These are profoundly political observations, at least potentially, because Scarry argues that pain can never be articulated, or even imagined, without the instruments that inflict it—instruments of torture. Still, the tools of pain are only imagined. Pain is unique among human experiences in being entirely objectless; the instruments in pain language are metaphorical inventions, an effort to conceptualize a subjective experience that has no external objective features. This is why pain requires imagination as its counterpart. Scarry emphasizes that "any state that was permanently objectless would no doubt begin the process of invention."[8] Directly opposed to pain, the imagination is a state that consists wholly of objects, so the process of world-building, of moving away from the corporeality of pain, calls on the imagination as its first means. It is the imagination that first transforms weapons into tools, that substitutes symbols for actual victims of violent acts, a process that makes the building of a world possible from the first moments of civilization.

One easily sees how Scarry's ideas might influence scholars of asceticism and martyrology. Maureen Flynn has recently written: "For the mystic seeking to chain the human mind in order to acquire a higher, more perfect form of understanding, pain provided the necessary psychic shackle. This is why we see the mystics conscientiously intensifying pain on the surface of their bodies through vigorous scourging and within their bodies through concentration on the Crucifixion, until finally the contents of the world were canceled out in their minds."[9] Pain unmakes their profane world with its corporeal attachments and leads the mystics away from the body to self-transcendence.

Scarry's is a dense and complex argument, and no brief summary can do it justice. However, her fundamental axiom, that pain eludes language and is therefore completely subjective and objectless, is incorrect. Scarry bases her observations on the devastating effects of pain in the context of political torture, and she adds to this the methods of clinicians who seek to improve the ability of patients to communicate their pain. I will shortly return to the language and epistemology of pain, but first a few comments on torture and pain. Torture does indeed have the power to destroy the world of its victims, to unmake their identity, their language, their memory. However, it is not clear that pain is more effective in this process than other means. The torturer has other, perhaps more decisive, instruments: isolation, sleeplessness, starvation, darkness, light, terror (mock executions, screams from other cells, threats against the prisoner's family), suffocation and drowning, which are not painful. Examples, unfortunately are easy to find. Consider the testimony of Eric Lomax, who was tortured by the Japanese during World War II:

> A bench had been placed out in the open. I was told by the interpreter to lie down on it, and I lay on my front to protect bandaged arms by wrapping them under the seat. But the NCO quickly hauled me upright again and made me lie on my back while he tied me to the bench with a rope. . . . The NCO suddenly stopped hitting me. He went off to the side and I saw him coming back holding a hosepipe dribbling with water. . . . He directed the full flow of the now gushing pipe on to my nostrils and mouth at a distance of only a few inches. Water poured down my windpipe and throat and filled my lungs and stomach. The torrent was unimaginably choking. This is the sensation of drowning, on dry land, on a hot dry afternoon. Your humanity bursts from within you as you gag and choke. I tried very hard to will unconsciousness, but no relief came.[10]

Ascetics and mystics know that they possess effective techniques, short of raw pain, for unmaking their own profane selves: First is a rigid diet, then isolation, sleepless nights (vigils), ongoing prayer or chanting, hard physical work, and other psychotropic techniques. Pain is one example in a range of methods, but it must neither be elevated above the others nor reduced to them. Similarly, specific mystical and ritual methods are not mutually reducible: The effects of isolation and a restricted diet are distinct, and dancing to the beat of drums is different from both.

Pain and Communication

Scarry builds on the axiomatic assertions that pain is uniquely private, an objectless experience beyond (or beneath) language that, in fact, undermines every effort to communicate. This is a familiar observation. Virginia Woolf once remarked about the English language that it "has no words for the shiver and headache. . . . The merest school girl, when she falls in love, has Shakespeare and Keats to speak for her; but let a sufferer try to describe a pain in his head to a doctor and language at once runs dry."[11]

This entire book takes the opposite perspective, following the first chapter, which amply demonstrated the language of pain. *Sacred Pain* argues that religious individuals have hurt themselves because the pain they produced was meaningful and is not only subject to verbal communication but also figures in our ability to empathize and share. In other words, the symbolic and experiential efficacy of pain derives from the way it bridges "raw" sensation with our highest qualities as human beings in a community of other humans.[12]

The clinical specialists in the area of pain working in North America and in the English language have long recognized the difficulties of verbally expressing the subjective sensations of pain. Ronald Melzack, a psychologist at McGill University, devised a questionnaire that could be given to patients in order to pinpoint the quality of their pain and diagnose the nature of their problem more effectively.[13] The terms listed in the questionnaire, from which the patients choose the most accurate, are divided into distinct experiential categories, such as sensory, affective, and evaluative. Listed below are twenty-five terms out of the seventy-seven in Melzack's original version, which has been revised and updated several times. The words represent answers to the question posed to the patient: What does your pain feel like? Flickering, throbbing, shooting, pricking, drilling, sharp, pinching, gnawing, tugging, burning, stinging, heavy, splitting, tiring, suffocating, terrifying, punishing, blinding, intense, radiating, piercing, squeezing, freezing, nagging, torturing. Clearly, some of the terms apply to the "physical" sensation (throbbing, shooting), others to emotional response (terrifying), and yet others to an evaluation (punishing, torturing).

There are clinical-neurological reasons for evoking the patient's description on all three levels. For our purposes it is sufficient to note, as Scarry does, that the terms make metaphorical references to fictitious agencies, usually tools or weapons, and the type of bodily damage these produce: cutting, shooting, drilling, and others. Scarry adds: "Physical pain is not identical with (and often exists without) either agency or damage, but these things are referential; consequently we often call on them to convey the experience of the pain itself."[14] The spine may feel as though a hammer had come down on it, and though nothing of the kind happened, speaking in such terms somehow feels right. In sum, it is difficult for us to communicate, perhaps even imagine, the nature of pain—even our own—without resorting to metaphors of agency or instrumentality: the weapon that penetrates, the vice that pinches and pulls, the ice the freezes, the scorpion that stings. Melzack may have put together the McGill questionnaire with his graduate students, but the terms are not his arbitrary inventions. They are meaningful because we speak about our experiences of pain by using these very words.

I will shortly show that pain is not the only experience we verbalize metaphorically. It may first be useful to note that English does not stand alone in using such metaphorical devices due to some intrinsic paucity in its ability to describe subjective states. Sanskrit and biblical Hebrew act in a similar way. A brief collection of pain terms in Sanskrit may include the following: *pīḍa, vedanā, rūjā, vyathā, ārti, śūla, vega, toda,* and of course, *duḥkha.* The first term, *pīḍa,* comes from the root *pīḍ,* which means to squeeze or press, as one does to obtain the Soma juice. The second, *vedanā,* is related to the causative form of the verb to know, and refers to making something known through torture.[15] The third term, *rūjā,* originates in the root *rūj,* which means to shatter to pieces or break open. The next term, *vyathā* originates in *vyath,* to tremble, waiver, be agitated or restless. Next is *arti,* from *ār* = *a* + *ri,* which means to insert, fall into (misfortune), and in a causative sense, inflict. In the Indian medical literature it describes a sawing pain. *Śūla* is Śiva's weapon, a fork, spear, lance, or dart, and is used to describe a lancinating and sharp pain, often translated in the medical literature as colic. Prisoners condemned to death by impailment die on the *śūla.* The term *vega* comes from *vij,* violent agitation, and describes the effect of poison or the painful expulsion of feces. The *Bhagavata Purana* (3.18.6) describes *toda* as a pricking pain; the term is derived from the instrument used to drive cattle or elephants. Finally, *duḥkha,* which means pain, grief, or suffering, derives from the root *duḥkh*—to pain, which in turn may originate from *dū*—to burn or consume with fire.[16] Clearly, those who used Sanskrit for describing their experiences also had to resort to a metaphorical extension of language into the realm of agency. A pain is described in terms of the tool or weapon that causes it, or in terms of the effect such a tool may have—squeezing, ripping, and so forth.

Biblical Hebrew is extremely rich in the way it describes pain, and its use of pain language tends to be poetic and very visual. The best single source is, of course, the book of Job, but several Psalms are equally descriptive, as are Jeremiah and a smattering of descriptions from other books. As in the case of Sanskrit, the list of terms will be intentionally brief. Job 6:3 describes his physical suffering in terms of divine arrows that have penetrated his person (*ḥiṣei šadai'imādi*), a crushing by means of a storm, breathlessness (*lo yitneni hāśēb rūḥi;* Job 9), fatigue, shriveling, being torn apart, being gnashed with teeth, being broken in two, being seized by the neck and dashed to pieces (*weāḥaz be'orpi wayepaṣpeṣēni*), having his kidneys slashed open (*yepalaḥ kilyotai*), having his gall poured on the ground (*yiśpoḥ lāāreṣ merērāti*), being burst open (*yipreṣeni pereṣ;* Job 16), having his bow-string loosened, being tossed about on a storm, having his skin turn black and fall off (*'ori śāḥar mē'ālai*), his intestines boiled (*mē'ai rūtḥu;* Job 30).

Unfortunately, the translation of pain terms in the New Revised Standard Version is not always clear. For instance, Job 9:17, "he crushes me with a tempest," is the English rendering of "*bisše'arah yeśūpēni.*" The verb derives from the root *shuf*, which does not mean "crush" but "blow" (to blow sparks; the wind blows), "poison" (a snakebite), and in other forms, to lose consciousness and even to smooth or rub. The most likely meaning in the quotation is to be blown away in a storm. Still, the overall meaning of the visual description of Job's pain is clear even in translation. It is inflicted on him by external agencies (arrows, a storm) and feels like his body is being ripped open, his innards spilling out, his bones burning, and so forth. Readers may safely conclude that the reliance on metaphors of agency and instrumentality to describe the subjective experience of pain is not limited to modern speakers, or to the English language. Pain, which is a universal biological and psychological fact, must be intrinsically elusive, putting human language to work in a surprisingly similar fashion across a variety of cultures and time periods.[17] This observation seems to support the thesis that an experience—or sensation—that takes place in our subverbal awareness can serve as an instrument of annihilation, both in the negative (political) sense and in the positive (mystical) sense. But does pain, by virtue of being an "objectless" experience, occupy an exclusive place in the nonverbal awareness of humans? I think not. Consider pleasure, for instance.

Kenneth Mah, a doctoral candidate at McGill University's Clinical Psychology program, has recently applied the basic principles of Melzack's questionnaire in a study, under the supervision of Dr. Irv Binik, of adjectives used to describe the orgasm. Subjects were asked to rate their experiences according to numerous adjectives, which were organized along sensory, emotional, and cognitive categories (like Melzack's pain adjectives). Again, the number of adjectives was substantial, but here are only a few examples: shuddering, quivering, building, shooting, exploding, hot, throbbing, spreading, flooding, immersing, loving, ecstatic, euphoric. Obviously the list is not identical with the list of pain terms in its use of metaphors of weapons or tools. The level of refinement also pales in comparison with the pain questionnaire because no diagnostic purpose is served by completing a pleasure questionnaire. However, as with pain, all the terms are metaphorical. The description of the temporal structure of orgasm as shooting or exploding is an obvious example. The point here is basic: The mere fact that a sensation or experience can only be described by means of metaphors does not render such an experience uniquely a-linguistic. The metaphorical function of language as a semantic instrument is familiar to every beginning student of linguistics. Consider the following examples taken from a linguistics textbook:

a. Let me chew on these ideas for a while.
b. They just wouldn't swallow that idea.
c. She'll give us time to digest that idea.[18]

In these instances, "words from a physical realm are being extended into a mental realm, perhaps because the physical vocabulary provides a familiar and public frame of reference for discussing our private mental life."[19] Of course, this is a very general observation. One needs to state far more precisely in what way the metaphor is an appropriate extension of the experience for which it stands, whether the relation is arbitrary or grounded in other principles. The similar situation in English, Sanskrit, and Hebrew may suggest that the relation of the pain metaphor and the sensation it describes is more than an arbitrary device, a sign that signifies by convention in Peirce's semiotic terms.

The Origin of Pain Metaphors

Speaking of pain in terms of tools and weapons extends a private sensation or experience into the public domain.[20] Everyone knows what a knife does, and many can imagine a scorpion sting. That is the public face of the metaphor. But perhaps we are moving too quickly. How many of us have been shot, crushed, gnawed (by rats?), seared, or pierced? In what way is it safe to assume that we are communicating meaningfully when we tell someone that our stomach feels as though it were being sawed, or that our tooth feels a shooting pain? As a matter of fact, the sensation of being shot is not "shooting" at all, it is more of a blow followed by heat. The selection of metaphors to describe pain is based on an entirely different principle from an extension of the effects of a tool or weapon on our body. What is at work, instead, is an analogy based on the formal properties of different senses. The metaphors are overwhelmingly visual (sometimes tactile) and based on a common form perceived to exist in the visual, tactile, and nociceptive realms. The awareness of pain (nociception) is not sensory, properly speaking. But it shares certain structural forms (*gestalten*) with the forms of sensory perceptions. The metaphors are based on these "similarities," or what Gestalt theorists call isomorphism.[21] If a painful experience has the temporal form of starting suddenly, moving to an adjacent or deeper space, and ending abruptly, while being limited to a narrow region, we call it a shooting pain. It resembles the visual form of a shot, not the nociceptive properties of its consequence. By the same token, an orgasmic experience with similar spatiotemporal properties is also described as "shooting." A "sawing" pain projects the temporal structure of sawing (rhythmic, repetitive, possessing frequent peaks and lulls) to the visual characteristics of a saw. This type of perceptual correspondence is quite common, and according to the psychologists in the phenomenological-Gestalt school, it is fundamental to the way we organize our experience. It allows subjects in experiments to match roundish and jagged figures with corresponding names, which are vocal (temporal), not spatial.[22]

Douglas Hofstadter has discussed an extreme, and beautiful, example of the ability to perceive isomorphic (corresponding) forms in a multisensory fashion. As an amateur musician he found himself fascinated by Frederic Chopin's Etude no. 1 in C major from Opus 10. The music was printed by Donald Byrd's SMUT program at Indiana University and reproduced in *Metamagical Themas*.[23] The visual form of the score is stunning and immediately suggestive in an emotional way. James Huneker writes about it: "The regular black ascending and descending staircases of notes strike the neophyte with terror. Like Piranesi's marvelous aerial architectural dreams, these dizzy acclivities and descents of Chopin exercise a charm, hypnotic, if you will, for the eye as well as the ear, here is the new technique in all its nakedness, new in the sense of figure, design, pattern, web, new in a harmonic way."[24] Chopin was conscious of what he was doing, setting the visual pattern of his musical score to correspond with some of the auditory and emotional properties of the music. In fact, he consciously worked on two levels, or with two types of pattern that he sought to unify: the emotional and intellectual (perceptual). The latter is a syntactical and nonrepresentational property of the music, which corresponds to the alliteration, rhyme, meter, repetition of sounds and other techniques of poetry.[25] The first, semantic, pattern in music is far more elusive than poetry but is nonetheless present, because the etude does not fail to move its listeners, and often in predictable emotional ways. Of course, Chopin's score provides a strikingly unusual example of the correspondence between spatial pattern and emotional response. The match between the pattern of notes seen on the page and the pattern of sounds that the ear perceives is based first and foremost on convention (musical notation), but the subject's ability to perceive the correspondence, as Hofstadter and Huneker indicate, is natural. It is an intrinsic property of music that it moves us, that it communicates to us semantically, based on pure form, with very little representation. Music can be sad, happy, sentimental, patriotic, devotional, serious, humorous, without recourse to any words. These emotions are conveyed, as Gestalt theorists and art critics have observed, by formal structures such as *crescendo* and *diminuendo, accelerando* and *ritardando*, to mention only a few.[26] Musical structure can move us because it creates patterns that correspond to the patterns of our mental and emotional life. Susanne Langer observed "that there are certain aspects of the so-called 'inner-life'—physical or mental—which have formal properties similar to those of music—patterns of motion and rest, of tension and release, of agreement and disagreement, preparation, fulfillment, excitation, sudden change, etc."[27]

We communicate the concept of pain based on the spatiotemporal patterns of the sensation. The choice of instrument in the metaphor we use has nothing to do with the actual pain it inflicts. The "form" of the pain is due to neurological principles, not the agent or tool, a significant fact for pain researchers and diagnosticians. That is why the language of pain gets across, even if it lacks the richness of Shakespeare's eloquence on love. We understand another person's pain in the same way that we perceive the mood of a nocturne, due to the same neurological principles at the root of verbal communication. Of course, what I have presented up to now is a very schematic picture of how pain may be communicated. Gestalt epistemology and cognitive psychology are far more comprehensive. There are several ways of considering how the correspondence between pain perception and neurological dynamics might work in detail, most of them hypothetical. Oliver Sacks discusses a number of theories that account for the duration and expansion of neurological information experienced as migraine.[28] The experience itself is an aura that spreads in waves of a certain temporal and spatial form. The aura is perceived through visual, tactile, and other hallucinations that take on characteristic patterns called "migraine scotoma." When asked to draw the patterns, victims of migraine depict jagged arches consisting of sharp zigzags that split the scene into two halves. These illustrations resemble one of the conventions used in art and cartoons to convey sharp pain. According to Oliver Sacks's summary of Ralph Siegle's work, the illustrations of the hallucinations correspond to the migraine sensations, which can be explained in terms of the patterns of the firing of neurons across a wide range of synaptic maps. In other words, the experiential forms (hallucinations) are prefigured in the function of the neuroanatomy. This supports the case for isomorphism.

Interestingly, from the neuropsychological point of view, the depth structures of Noam Chomsky's syntactical linguistics resemble Gestalt perceptual principles. Both schools of thought take the position that there are built-in brain functions that influence—in a top-down fashion—the contents of our perceptions, cognitions, and language. This is a very vague way of putting the matter, but it achieves a basic task: disposing of the notion that pain is a uniquely raw and private sensation in futile search for a voice in language.

But pain requires more than communication; it calls for empathy and healing. Here matters become more complicated. The observer of the person who hurts may indeed vicariously experience the pain, but his own suffering (if he is empathetic) or thrill (if he is sadistic) is due to deeper psychological reasons than either the patient's words or the perception of his pain behavior. For a deliciously wry analysis of the tormentor's psyche one turns to Dostoevsky:

> I don't know how it is today, but in the not-too-distant past there were distinguished people to whom beating some victim afforded feelings similar to those of the Marquise de Sade and Marquise de Brinvilliers. I think that there is something in these sensations that, in these people, makes the heart stop in agonizing delight. There are people like tigers who long for a taste of blood. Anyone who has once experienced this power, this unlimited control over the body, blood, and spirit of a man like himself, a fellow creature, his brother in Christ—anyone who has experienced the power to inflict supreme humiliation upon another being, created like himself in the image of God, is bound to be ruled by his emotions.[29]

The key here is "brother in Christ." It is the shared humanity that makes the thrill of the sadist possible—the vicarious identification with the victim. Freud, who was a careful Dostoevsky reader, recognized this aggressive-erotic bond between the victim and the sadist: "Sadomasochistic object relations are a way of loving (and hating) others and oneself and are especially concerned with intense ways of engaging another so as to mitigate dangers of separateness, loss, loneliness, hurt, destruction, and guilt. Aggression and sexuality are adapted to this end of intense connectedness with another person."[30] The painful event assigns a distinct role to the victim and to the perpetrator, but the roles resonate and the torturer needs his victim in order to fully play out his own fantasy. Dostoevsky continues: "Once when the victim refused to cry out, the flogger, a man whom I knew and who, in other respects could even be considered kindly, took it as a personal offense. At first he had intended to make the punishment a light one. But when the usual cries for mercy were not forthcoming, he grew furious and ordered fifty extra lashes, seeking both cries and begging—and he had his way."[31] But notice that even the bystander—say, the reader of torture accounts—normally identifies with the victim and his pain rather than the tormentor. Psychoanalysts call this reaction "libidinal sympathetic excitation," and since Freud clearly linked sadistic aggression with sexuality, there is something pornographic about our human fascination with victimization, even if it does also manifest an ability to empathize.[32]

I intend to show that both Dostoevsky and Freud were on to something important, but their modern sensibilities distorted it. This is the fact that shared pain (empathy) requires a community—a "brotherhood"—and that pain has been instrumental in constructing such a community. But precision is important here. "Community" is not a catch-phrase for people who like each other, or who believe in the same god. I use the term in a far more specific way: It is a group of people who share the same language. One member of a community must understand the other very well when she reports a gnawing pain in her foot. This requires that the metaphor be entirely transparent. As we have seen, what makes pain metaphors work is their use of gestalt principles, based on the similarity of different senses, and these in turn correspond to the way the nervous system functions. The experiential basis of communities that share pain terms, ultimately, is neurological, and the broadest community of all, as Dostoevsky put it, is humanity. Every pain term ever used ultimately belongs in a limited repertoire of ways of thinking about pain because as human beings we are constrained by the dynamics of the nervous system and its effects on communication.

Pain and the Nervous System

Contrary to common perception, the body and pain are not as clearly connected as cause and effect. It is possible to hurt without trauma to the body, and it is also possible to experience painless injury to the body. This observation is critical to understanding the neurological pain mechanism as a system of controlled input and output.

Before proceeding any further it is important to recall a distinction that was made in the previous chapter. Two major types of pain are implicated in life and in religious discourse: acute and chronic. The suffering inflicted on prisoners under torture, like the sudden stab of gallstones, must be termed acute pain. In contrast, the lower backache of a construction worker who suffered a fall ten years earlier is chronic pain. The pain sought voluntarily by religious specialists is more closely akin to chronic pain, while the trauma inflicted on teenage boys at their circumcision ritual is acute. The difference is not one of intensity, as both types can be ferocious, but of duration. Chronic pain exceeds the relatively short-lived trauma of a gun wound, or even the days or weeks of political torture. Both types of pain involve complex psychological factors, but the difference is profound. Chronic pain sufferers deal with a range of issues that never occur to patients of acute pain, and in fact, their very identity becomes linked with their pain. In either case the relationship between the sensation of hurting and actual damage to the organism is tenuous. As Harold Mersky explains:

> Activity induced in the nociceptor and nociceptive pathways by a noxious stimulus is not pain, which is always a psychological state, even though we may well appreciate that pain most often has a proximate physical cause.[33]

In other words, the confluence of psychological, social, and cultural factors cannot be separated from the physical event in the overall experience of the pain, although this applies far more prominently in the case of chronic pain. Thus, the lifelong voluntary suffering of a mystic must be analyzed and interpreted on a variety of levels, but the distinction between acute and chronic pain must always be kept in mind.[34] A nun may become accustomed to the stings of back scourging and the freezing of her toes on the bare winter ground. But if she suddenly becomes severely ill, her newfound (acute) pain may be experienced as a problem that she needs to solve, perhaps by incorporating it into chronic behavior.[35]

Even the type of acute pain that is associated with clear physical causes and tissue damage is, to a very large extent, a mental event. For example, under certain circumstances a bad injury may be minimized, or not perceived at all. Soldiers may suffer bullet wounds in battle but continue to function with no awareness of their injuries. Patrick D. Wall reports the case of a young Israeli woman officer who had her leg blown off in an explosion with no immediate pain. Her first reaction, in the moment following the explosion was to ask: "Who is going to marry me now?"[36] On a lesser scale this may happen to athletes in the midst of their games. The pain is not ignored in such cases, nor is it always "sedated" by natural opiates. Instead, pain is masked or blotted out in the preoccupation with, or awareness of, more urgent or interesting matters. Hours after the injury, the soldier or athlete may suddenly become aware of the injury, or rather aware of a pain that can be so intense as to require powerful sedation. Most people know these facts, and classical medical systems in Europe, as well as Asia, discussed them extensively. However, as a medical-neurological phenomenon, this so-called paradox of pain was not fully explained until the 1960s and the "gate-control theory," authored by Ronald Melzack and Patrick Wall.

The theory, subsequently supported by numerous clinical studies, posits a mechanism in the spinal cord that controls the flow of neuronal stimuli from the body's peripheries to the brain, where pain registers. The gate-control mechanism operates by means of inhibiting signals that "descend" from the brain to the gate and block the incoming signals.[37] The search for the exact inhibitory neuronal cells has led to the discovery of two types of endogenous opiates: enkephalins and dynorphins. These are secreted in response to certain traumatic events, though it would be a mistake to believe that every traumatic injury triggers the production of natural sedatives in the brain. In general terms, the success of the gate-control theory has led to the recognition that the intensity, duration, and nature of pain depend on decisions of the central brain, not just on peripheral stimulation. The underlying psychological and even philosophical implications are far-reaching, because they seem to imply that our experiences—British empiricism notwithstanding—are shaped in significant ways by "central," and perhaps genetically built-in, structures (dare one call these a priori categories?). In other words, experience is more than periphery-to-center input; it also relies on center biasing in the form of synthesis, interpretation, and inhibition. We shall see in a later chapter that this means that cultural and linguistic factors can actually shape (top to bottom) the way people experience pain.

Clearly, we should not be surprised then, that René Descartes was deeply interested in the mechanism and implications of pain, particularly as it weighed on the debate of "peripheralists" versus "centralists." In order to highlight the sharp contours of the issues, to the advantage of a centralist position where he stood, Descartes had to find a case of pain that did not depend on external nerve stimulation. He found his example in the case of a girl with an amputated arm:

> A girl suffering from a bad ulcer in the hand, had her eyes bandaged whenever the surgeon came to visit her, not being able to bear the sight of the dressing of the sore; and, the gangrene having spread, after the expiry of a few days the arm was amputated from the elbow [without the girl's knowledge]; linen clothes tied one above the other were substituted in place of the part amputated, so that she remained for some time without knowing that the operation had been performed, and meanwhile she complained of feeling various pains, sometimes in one finger of the hand that was cut off, and sometimes in another.[38]

Descartes did not understand the precise function of the nervous system and imagined it in mechanical terms, the dominant neurological metaphor of his time. Still, the philosophical upshot of the girl's phantom pain was similar for Descartes as it is today for leading neuropsychologists such as Ronald Melzack and Patrick Wall. Descartes concluded: "And this clearly shows that the pain of the hand is not felt by the mind in so far as it is in the hand, but in so far as it is in the brain."[39] Anyone who has been to the dentist for a root canal knows the phantom sensation. Novocain locally anaesthetizes the area where work is being done, but it also deadens sensation in a part of the lip. As a result the lip feels larger than it really is, and it often tingles as well. This is phantom lip. Individuals who have undergone amputation of a limb, due to a variety of causes from war injury to diabetes, experience similar and additional sensations (heat, cramps, stabs) "in" the missing limb, though far more painfully. This is true for 72 percent of amputees a week after amputation, 60 percent six months later. Only 10 to 12 percent of amputees find relief even years after the amputation.[40] Phantom-limb pain is a profoundly intractable and devastating affliction, which has up to now completely eluded efforts to cure. Many who are unfortunate enough to suffer this form of chronic pain have given their lives over to various drugs that work only by recourse to unconscious states of medicated sleep. Any attempt to block nerve impulses from the region, say by electronic or chemical blockage at the base of the spine, fails to cure the pain. As Descartes remarked, the pain is located in the brain, not in the periphery.

Peripheralists—those who believe that the brain processes only stimuli obtained through the peripheral nervous system—have claimed that the phantom experience can result from such sources as nerve pathology at the stump (neuroma), or alternatively as a form of "memory," or patterning in the brain. The failed blocks in the spine discredit the neuroma argument, while studies have shown that children born with missing limbs often also experience phantom-limb pain.[41] Melzack, who has studied this phenomenon more thoroughly than anyone else, is convinced that the sensation and the pain are due to a built-in central structure, which he has described in a relatively new theory as the "neuromatrix."[42] Though technical and relatively inaccessible to scholars of religion, such a theory is worthy of a hearing due to the fact that every religious self-hurter finds meaning in pain by virtue of the function of the neuromatrix.

Melzack begins by observing that the areas of the brain that process the pain experience are widespread and extensive. The experience of the phantom limb, which subjectively feels as real as any other part of the body, is subserved by the same brain regions that process pain, including the limbic system and somatosensory projections. The anatomical network that consists of neural loops between the thalamus and the cortex as well as the cortex and limbic system is termed the neuromatrix. This is a system that is hard-wired inasmuch as it is anatomically genetic, but it is also soft-wired in possessing plasticity, that is, a flexibility for changing synaptic connections according to learning. As a function of its (flexible) systemic structure, the neuromatrix processes incoming nerve impulses according to a characteristic pattern, which Melzack calls "neurosignature." All the inputs from the peripheries of the body flow through the synaptic connections of the neuromatrix, where they are molded into the patterns, which eventually become converted into the structures of awareness. In Melzack's words: "The neurosignature, which is a continuous outflow from the body-self neuromatrix, is projected to areas in the brain, known as the *sentient neural hub* (SNH), in which the stream of nerve impulses (the neurosignature modulated by ongoing inputs) is converted into a continually changing stream of awareness."[43] Meanwhile, a similar pattern proceeds through a neuromatrix circuit ("action-neuromatrix") that eventually activates neurons in the spinal cord for muscle activity and complex actions.

Melzack could be wrong as far as the precise anatomical features of his theory are concerned. The theory itself, at least in its philosophical-epistemological foundations, is far from new. It goes back through H. von Helmholtz to Immanuel Kant and the notion that phenomenal experience is formed by a combination of empirical inputs from the outer world and some built-in active template that organizes experience. A critical aspect of the neuromatrix, according to Melzack, is its body-self function, a nonanatomical neurological pattern that coordinates input and output in such a way that we can have the experience of "owning" our own body. This allows us to function as a unity within an enormously complex anatomical system and sensory environments.

The neuromatrix theory provides a coherent link between anatomy and experience. It also has significant phenomenological implications. The psychologists of perception in the Gestalt school have recognized that our experience is shaped by characteristic patterns (*gestalten*) and posited an isomorphism with underlying neuronal patterns.[44] We have seen that the temporal structure of music was correlated to the patterns of emotion that we experience: agitated or joyful, sad or upbeat. What makes this correspondence possible, according to Gestalt, is the structure and function of the nervous system. This is the principle they have termed "isomorphism." Unfortunately for Gestalt theorists, they were not able to find any such corresponding anatomical structures, but here, with the neurosignature, or even with the plastic neuromatrix, the Gestalt school may find an extremely rewarding program for future studies on isomorphism.

So what is the origin of phantom-limb pain? It is important to keep in mind that the neuromatrix is a system with input and output circuits channeling information and feedback. Melzack notes that in the absence of modulating inputs from the limbs or body, the active body neuromatrix "produces a signature pattern that is transduced in the sentient neural hub into a hot or burning quality. The cramping pain experienced in the phantom limbs may be due to messages from the action-neuromatrix to move muscles. In the absence of limbs, the messages to move the muscles become more frequent and stronger in the attempt to move the limb."[45] The same principle, he adds, applies to the shooting pains. The three types of pain are familiar to those who suffer phantom-limb pain: extreme heat, severe cramping, and shooting pains. The heat is a type of neuronal "noise" or false alarm, while the cramping and shooting are equivalent to the ringing of a doorbell when no one answers: louder and more frequent.

Because the neuromatrix is a fundamental anatomical structure, and because it acts as a system that underlies perception and action, it provides a coherent explanation for what the Gestalt theorists called the "similarity of the senses." Our auditory perception of musical pattern can be matched by visual structures, as the case of Chopin's score sheet demonstrates. The perception of forms and patterns across different sense modalities may be due to this underlying neurological mechanism. If this observation seems excessively speculative it can be tested empirically; it has already produced clinical tests for the practical goal of treating phantom-limb pain. V. S. Ramachandran and his colleagues from the Brain and Perception Laboratory at the University of California in San Diego have recently published a report of an experimental treatment in *Nature*.[46] The authors note:

> When motor commands are sent from the premotor and motor cortex to clench the hand, they are normally damped by error feedback from proprioception. In a phantom, such damping is not possible, so the motor output is amplified further and this outflow itself may be experienced as a painful spasm.[47]

In order to fool the system into perceiving some type of feedback, the scientists placed a mirror in such a way that the patient would see the normal hand superimposed on the phantom or amputated hand. They hypothesized that "visual feedback from the mirror may act by interrupting this loop" and eliminate the spasms. The visual feedback consisted of viewing the good hand unclench, or in other cases, touching that hand. The results were successful, though the entire program is too preliminary for any certain therapeutic benefits at this time. It is not clear how many times one can fool the brain, and more importantly, how long the synesthesia would last. However, the tests indicate that visual and tactile inputs can modulate the output of a motor neurosystem; and further, that our bodily sensations (proprioception), our sense-based embodiment, is structured by a variety of senses acting in standard patterns as Gestalt theory predicts.

Sacred Pain

Phantom-limb pain may be regarded as a type of hallucinatory experience. The pain is absolutely real, of course, but the certainty of its localization in the missing limb is an "illusion" that results from the absence of input from that limb. Visual hallucinations are common among ascetics and mystics who retreat to environments where sensory input is reduced to minimal levels. Geoffery Schultz, a student of Melzack, has recently conducted a study showing that visual hallucinations need not be caused by psychopathology or impaired cognitive functioning, but may result from the disruption of sensory input among patients suffering eye damage.[48] The neuromatrix, in Melzack's theory, overfires its output messages in the absence of stimulation from external sources (or temping feedback), and creates images—often fantastic or exaggerated—that may be experienced as real.

The fact of visual and other types of hallucination can be explained by the systemic properties of the nervous system, as outlined by Melzack.[49] However, the contents of the hallucinations, their phenomenal features, are conditioned by different facts. Christian mystics will not experience a vision of Kali or a bodhisattva, but will draw on material that has been incorporated through learning and memorization within their own cultural context.[50] In the absence of incoming stimulation—of any sense modality—such stored neuronal information is amplified by the neuromatrix and triggers vivid phenomenal apparitions, which may be visual, auditory, or other phantoms.[51]

It is even possible that hallucinations—tactile ones, for instance—result in somatic effects ranging from raised blood pressure or pulse rate to loss of hair, incontinence, false pregnancies, paralysis, rashes, blistering, and others. The phenomenon of stigmata, most famously associated with St. Francis but documented in far less exemplary figures such as Jane Hunt or Ethel Chapman, may indeed be a psychogenic event with somatic manifestations.[52] The phenomenal contours of the stigmata "hallucination" (the location and feel of the wounds) correspond to learning and beliefs about the location of the injuries to Jesus, although the etiology is neurological and systemic.

To summarize up to this point: Phantom pain and hallucinations are generated by the absence of incoming neuronal signals from the peripheries of the body.[53] The neurosignature gradually overfires due to the absence of modulating or damping feedback from the extremities, thus producing physiopsychological experiences characterized by nervous excitation but shaped by other factors as well. If input were blocked from the entire peripheral body, the body-self template as a whole would be affected, resulting in a profoundly distorted sense of the phenomenal self.

The system, however, acts in the other direction as well. When the organism is bombarded with incoming signals moving afferently (from periphery to center), the neurosignature begins to underfire its characteristic output signals, which results in the minimization of *all* mental phenomena, including hallucinations.[54] The contrast between the two aspects of the system can be illustrated by means of the following example. Inside a sensory deprivation flotation tank (dark, silent, water warmed to body temperature and salted to enhance flotation), a bather quickly begins to experience extremely vivid mental images and visions. In contrast, submerged in a cold stream of water—say, the Ganges on a January morning—when the skin surface is assaulted with unpleasant sensory stimulation, the phenomenal field becomes radically simplified and free of mental images; in fact, it becomes reduced to simple embodiment.[55] Ramachandran's therapeutic work in the San Diego lab is based on this well-known feature of the nervous system in which—as in all information systems—incoming signals temper output. His innovation was based on the synesthetic assumption that visual feedback could be substituted for proprioception, but the principle is the same. An extreme bombardment of incoming signals, in whatever sensory modality, can produce a virtual shutdown of outgoing signals, resulting in dissociative states, either trance or psychotic breakdowns.

Melzack's contribution to these insights goes beyond the postulation of an anatomical structure (neuromatrix) with functional properties (neurosignature). The neurosignature, among its more important tasks, functions as the basis for the body-self template—the neuropsychological foundation of the phenomenal self. The body-self template is one functional aspect of the neuromatrix. At the basic information level it is a spatiotemporal organization of inputs and outputs relating to the bases of unified perception and proprioception. It provides the structure of the phenomenal self, a schema or schemata rather than a symbolic or metaphysical construct. Consequently, it is susceptible to ongoing modulation by perception and perceptual distortions. A familiar example can illustrate these dynamics. Everyone has experienced the manner in which a suitcase appears to become increasingly heavy as we hold it for a length of time. In fact, the suitcase stays exactly the same weight, and its pressure on our muscles does not change either.

What changes is our level of muscular fatigue, which is perceived through proprioception, followed by the center's (neurosignature) instruction to increase effort.[56] The basic (schema) perception of self in relation to world (the suitcase's increasing weight) is determined by the organization of input and output of an information system. The neurological structure (neuromatrix) is still hypothetical but its correspondence with Gestalt theorists' understanding of the phenomenal self, and their experimental ingenuity, suggest that a program for verifying these hypotheses can indeed be devised.[57]

One could predict, by implication, that an overload of incoming sensory signals—say, in the form of ongoing self-inflicted pain—would progressively weaken the body-self template, resulting in the diffusion of the self or its complete disappearance.[58] This would be a "reverse phantom"—the disappearance not of sensory or mental images (though these are simplified), but of the subject who experiences them. In other words, if you scourge your body repeatedly, the sensory overstimulation would not eradicate your thoughts, sense perceptions, and so forth. But your experience of being a self, an agent who undergoes these perceptions and thoughts, would gradually disappear, until it seemed that these belonged to someone or something else. You would enter a dissociative state, which could be modulated through pain.[59] For the sake of convenience, the two aspects of the neurosystem may be outlined in the following way:

I. Sensory deprivation→hallucination (expansion of mental experience)
II. Sensory overload→"reverse"-hallucination (shrinkage of mental experience, weakening of body-self)

I have noted earlier that the phenomenal properties of the hallucination are due to a variety of factors (learning, expectations, beliefs, emotion). For the sake of convenience I shall call these properties "cognitions" and note that they are affected by the plasticity of the neurosystem and the control action of the neurosignature. The neurosignature itself changes with learning and life experiences roughly in the same way that a disc (if you can imagine an organic one) changes with the program stored in it. A middle-aged Iowa farmer experiences ten inches of snow differently from the way a twenty-year-old Harvard student does. The impact of "cognitions" on pain perception is also considerable. A soldier and a car passenger who suffer the very same injury, one in battle and the other in an accident, will experience their injury very differently. The soldier may be relieved to be removed from harm's way, the passenger devastated at his loss. The first will feel far less pain and interpret his pain differently (for instance, as a lifesaver). The way the trauma is interpreted ("cognition") influences the action of the neurosignature in processing the damage signals from the periphery and the way the pain is felt.

The subjective sense of agency or self is deeply bound by these factors. At its most basic level the self is the phenomenal upshot, a schema that emerges from the function of characteristic neurosignature patterns. However, it is important to keep in mind that this self is not the ego. The ego, as Chapter 4 will show, is more complex and it straddles the boundary between the body-self and what I have called "cognitions." Mystics, shamans, and other religious technicians, who manipulate their bodies either through sensory deprivation or stimulus overload (pain)—or both—are playing with several factors: phenomenal experiences (hallucinations and their opposite), the body-self template (neurosignature function), ego, and cognitions (emotions, beliefs). And because many combine several spiritual techniques (pain, sensory deprivation, sleeplessness, starvation) the psychodynamics of religious practice become enormously complex. For instance, while sensory deprivation—say, isolation in a dark cell—produces sharper "visions," pain weakens the subject that perceives the visions, which thus take on an unusual autonomy in relation to ego.

But hurting is unique; it produces a singular effect. Pain does not eradicate experience, it makes the experiencer transparent. It weakens the most basic level of the body-self as the agent who "owns" every experience from pain itself to beliefs about God. As we have seen in the previous chapter, this can be either terrifying or exhilarating. For the hospital patient it is a momentous loss, a premonition of death. For a monk or nun it may be the gateway to transcendence. The link between pain and self, and the evaluation of the loss of self, yields the dualism of pain, which becomes manifest in the models I have listed in the previous chapter: punitive or healing, bad or good. Recall a few examples from the models of the previous chapter:

1. Medieval European monastic guides were explicit about the value attached to pain that monks were expected to inflict on themselves: "Brother, it is necessary for thee to be punished in this life or in purgatory: but incomparably more severe will be the penalty of purgatory than any in this life. Behold, thy soul is in thy hands. Choose therefore for thyself whether to be sufficiently punished in this life according to canonical or authentic penance, or to await purgatory."[60]
2. An equivalent evaluation, expressed in a different metaphor, is the following quote of Abu Bakr Wasiti in *The Sea of Precious Virtues*: "Within each man's body is enthroned a soul, which rules, com-

manding and forbidding. Were it not for fear of the sword, it would become aware and claim divinity, just as accursed Pharaoh said, 'I am your supreme Lord.' "[61]

3. Mirza Asadullah Ghalib is quoted as saying: "When pain transgresses the limits, it becomes medicine."[62]

The three examples (punishment, warfare, medicine) present a gradation in attitude toward pain in relationship to the self. Annihilative pain is horrific but its power to annul the self is compensated for by what it does after all earthly existence passes: It preempts future punishment. The same pain, though negative, can be harnessed for the task of subduing the self, which in the second example is the "enthroned soul." Finally, inasmuch as the unmaking of the self is a good thing, the pain that brings this about can be conceptualized, perhaps even experienced, as medicine.

In an important book that links the physiological aspects of pain to its psychology, David Bakan distinguishes pain in relation to two primary aspects of the individual: telic-decentralization and telic-centralization (the breaking up and the reinforcement, respectively, of a system in relation to its goal—in our case, the self.)[63] Bakan identifies several hierarchical centers of telos (goal or end) in the individual organism, ranging from mechanistic-biological (the nervous system, the immune system) to the ego and superego, which contain goals based on intentionality and purpose. Bakan observes that the experience of pain "is the psychic manifestation of telic decentralization."[64] This decentralization involves a threat to the system either from external sources (pathogens, injury) or a breakup from a larger system yet. However, because there are several hierarchical centers of telos, pain need not be equated with tissue damage, which explains Melzack's "paradox of pain." The soldier who is injured in battle may identify with his ego as a higher end that sacrifices the telos of a subsystem—say, a lost leg—and thus experiences less pain compared with the car passenger. In fact, the ego is saved (telic-centralization) by the loss of the limb. In religious literature, pain that is conceptualized as a problem (punishment) is experienced as a decentralizing threat to the telic center (ego). In contrast, pain that is conceptualized as a solution (medicine) assumes a higher telos than ego and is centralized or reinforced by the sacrifice of the ego.

The task of religious practitioners is often to convert accidental pain or illness (conceived perhaps as punishment) into a positive force acting on behalf of passage, healing, or some other spiritual advantage. In Bakan's Freudian scheme, the hierarchy of telic centers extends to the superego. This higher level of telic organization is reinforced or centralized by the type of stimulation (pain) that diminishes or decentralizes the lesser telos of the ego. Thus, if a pain can be transformed into a sacrifice, higher ends benefit at the expense of lower ends, and oddly, suffering is reduced. The modern individual, in contrast, who locates his highest purpose in the well-being of the individual ends of the body and ego, experiences the same stimulation as something to be avoided, or a problem of theodicy. For this "victim" the solution lies in medical treatment rather than in a reconfiguration of experience.

Clearly, these observations require further discussion in light of both Freudian and post-Freudian psychology. Since telos is a systemic principle, in what sense, for instance, do the ego and superego constitute broader systems that encompass the somatic systems? What is the relation between biological-mechanistic goals and the telos of ego, which involves intentionality? Such questions will be addressed in Chapter 4. Here we see that the two basic ways of conceptualizing pain in religious history are consistent with a systemic view of the neurological system. Our ability to communicate pain is a synesthetic feature of this system. The loss of the sense of self through self-hurting is based on the system's homeostatic properties (control toward balance), and the twofold evaluation of the phenomenon of pain is related to the psychological perception of the system's purpose.

THREE

The Psychology and Communication of Pain

We have seen in the previous chapter that the insurmountable privacy of the body in pain has been decisive in the way cultural theorists and scholars of religion evaluate religious pain. But we have also seen that several pain models, richly textured and widely distributed, situate pain at the heart of religious discourse around the world. It is inconceivable that the suffering of Christ on the cross, or that the astounding martyrdom of the saints, or for that matter Rabbi Akiva or Al-Hallaj, would mean anything to anyone unless pain was intrinsically shareable. There is a link, I have shown, between the language of pain, the tropes used to communicate the very sensation, and the function of the system that processes the neuronal information. Pain communication, then, is not just a matter of convention; it is also a matter of biology and cybernetics. I will discuss this idea in terms of the concept of *empathy*, a nineteenth-century theory used to analyze our natural capacity to perceive the emotions and pain of others. In this chapter I will develop this theme in a bit more detail, providing both a brief historical sketch and a systematic overview of the Gestalt theories that laid the ground for a psychology of pain communication.[1]

Empathy and the Perception of Emotion

The publication in 1873 of Robert Vischer's *Uber das optische Formgefuhl* (On the Optical Sense of Form) is generally acknowledged as the beginning of the theory of empathy. The work concerned the expressive qualities of form itself: lines and surfaces, vertical and horizontal properties, straight and uneven lines, and so forth.[2] Vischer looked for some universal law by which the form holds an emotional content that is visible to the human eye. The principle that he finally advocated was similarity to the human body. An abstract form that resembles the structure of the human body, its symmetry and proportions, is pleasing. Nonsymmetrical forms that lack balance and are irregular are displeasing to the eye and convey negative emotional qualities. For Vischer, such forms are impersonal and are often aspects of inanimate nature. But definite emotional qualities are imputed onto such abstract realities and not only onto humanly crafted forms (art), or indeed, the human face. This imputation involves a projection of one's own sense of form, and one's own emotions, onto the object of vision. Vischer called this act *Einfuhlung* (feeling-in) and the American psychologist E. B. Titchener translated it as "empathy." Vischer's work, much like that of Gustav Fechner, was not lacking in metaphysical assumptions. Specifically, he noted that the projection of emotion onto the world in the form of empathy was essentially due to some pantheistic urge toward union with the world.[3] Nonetheless, he had proposed an empirically verifiable principle, something like "the law of the human body," that explains the nature of the projection.

The theory of empathy was further developed by, and is today largely associated with, Theodor Lipps. Lipps was no longer an applied psychologist, but was interested in aesthetics.[4] His *Grundlegung der Aesthetik* explains the intrinsic expressiveness of body movements based on principles that allow the observer to understand the emotions expressed. Lipps, like Darwin, did not feel that the movement was intrinsically expressive, but he felt that there were universal principles of perception that make communication possible. These inter-linked principles were "participation" (*Mitmachen*) and "inner imitation." The observer of the expressive gesture "participates" in the gesture by making it his own. This entails repeating the gesture internally, in a mental fashion, and experiencing the emotions attendant on such a behavior. The perceived object need not be human, of course. A thin column supporting a massive portal expresses vulnerability and imminent destruction in a very articulate fashion by means of this "inner mimesis." The observer internally imitates the gesture of holding something that is too heavy.[5] The notion of inner mimicry was taken to extreme lengths by some writers: "We see and think with our physiological equipment, particularly with our muscular, skeletal . . . systems." So when we see a weeping willow our body subconsciously mimics its bent-over stance, which instantly evokes sadness and sorrow.[6] What makes this imitation effective in reproducing the same emotion in the observer and the observed object is no longer a metaphysical entity like "world soul," but a structural correspondence between the forces that operate in the two separate forms:

> And to (the knowledge of these mechanical forces) is furthermore attached the representation of possible internal ways of behavior of my own, which do not lead to the same result but are of the same character. In other words, there is attached the representation of possible kinds of my own activity, which in analogous fashion, involves forces, impulses, or tendencies, freely at work or inhibited, a yielding to external effect, overcoming of resistance, the arising and resolving of tensions among impulses, etc. Those forces and effects of forces appear in the light of my own ways of behavior, my own kinds of activity, impulses, and tendencies and their own ways of realization.[7]

One need only recall Susan Langer's comments on music and emotion to see how influential Lipps was. "There are certain aspects of the so-called 'inner-life'—physical or mental—which have formal properties similar to those of music—patterns of motion and rest, of tension and release, of agreement and disagreement, preparation, fulfillment, excitation, sudden change, etc."[8] The more abstract the work of art, or the form that one observes, the more expressive does it become as a correlate of our own inner experience. This principle became a guiding force in the work of abstract expressionism, as we shall shortly see in reference to Kandinsky, and as a fundamental aspect of Gestalt psychology. The principle—correlation of abstract nonrepresentational forms in separate objects (or levels of reality)—became known in Gestalt as isomorphism. It was discussed in some detail earlier in this book. Where emotions are concerned, the Gestalt principle of isomorphism reveals directly the meaning of expressive behavior. From a structural point of view, the forces that shape bodily and mental behavior are isomorphic, as are forces operating in different media or sense modalities. The structural similarity does not reduce either mental or physical processes to the other, but remains ontologically "neutral." At the same time, the existence of such structural correspondences is an empirical matter, subject to falsification.

Gestalt Theory

Lipps's structural similarity represents a dramatic opposition to the predominantly British forms of empiricism (called associationism). This structuralism was a more synthetic-Kantian approach to reality, which in experimental form became Gestalt psychology. Gestalt, in its earliest expression in the works of Max Wertheimer, Kurt Goldstein, Kurt

Koffka, and Wolfgang Kohler, exhibited a near-Romantic fascination for humanity's place in the natural world. However, it tackled this relationship experimentally, by focusing on perception. The basic premise of Gestalt theories of perception was the notion of top-down organization. For instance, an assortment of dots or visual objects will be perceived as patterns when certain conditions (size, distance, background, color, and so forth) are present. These patterns do not result from the assembly of individuals but from the perception of the overall form as a totality before the individual parts are distinguished. The parts do not precede the whole but vice versa. The underlying physical assumptions of this theory—and many Gestalt theorists started out as physicists—was that the organizational principles that become manifest in pattern inhere in the objective world, including the human perceptual system. Another way of putting this is that the human nervous system is structured in a manner that allows it to perceive a nonrandom and structured world. Again, this correspondence has been called isomorphism. This approach is consistent with field theory or system theory in physics, which seeks to identify the broadest systemic parameters that encompass units within the field, be they optics, energy distribution, biochemical transmission, and so forth. The physics of systems, worked down to biology and psychological dynamics, allow a perceiver to know the emotional state of a person (or inanimate object!) due to a series of correspondences along the path of communication. The state of mind of an observed person is isomorphic with neurological processes, which in turn correspond (isomorphically) with muscular forces and these with kinesthetic dynamics that become manifest in the shape and movement of the body (face). Hence, psychology, electrochemical impulses, mechanics, psychology (again), and geometry "interact" by being isomorphic. From the observer's point of view the retinal projection of the movements of the emoting person (geometry) are isomorphic with cortical projections (electrochemical impulse), which in turn correlate with perceptions (psychology).[9]

Historically, the advantage of Gestalt over other schools in the understanding of expression is chiefly the avoidance of the two extremes of metaphysical mentalism and crude behaviorism (or associationism). Gestalt was also an experimental approach to the psychology of perception, its conclusions always subject to verification or falsification. Contemporary theories of the perception of pain—nociception—still utilize various aspects of Gestalt theory such as figure-ground phenomena, perceptual wholes, perceptual stability, closure, and others.[10] These will be retained in the exposition of a theory of the perception of pain.

The Expressive Line

The series of isomorphic correspondences along the path of emotional expression and perception does not end where I stopped. The last step was a psychological perception of sensory images. The beholder views a face contorted in some emotion, or a work of art that expresses one thing or the other. The main question remains, In what way does the specific form of the line or shape convey its own isomorphic relation to the emotion that gives it life? Why does a crooked line express one thing and not the other? For example, most viewers under conditions of testing report that a circular curve looks "harder" than a parabola, which is gentler.[11] We have seen this in Chapter 2 in connection with the two shapes ("takete" and "maluma") that "correspond" to the sound of their names. The old associationist approach to perception would argue that the connection is the result of some learned—but ultimately arbitrary—linking of circularity with rigidity or some similar value. The early form of empathy, which was based on projection, would argue that the quality that supposedly inheres in the circle and parabola is a mere extension of some inner state of the beholder, and would vary widely from one to the other.

Gestalt is far more ambitious than both of these positions. If expression and perception are subject to the same organizational principles, the line ought to appear intrinsically expressive. In fact, the line itself, or the shape it carves in its background, is subject to the same forces that govern the perceptual system, the emotions, and any of the other factors in the chain of communication. The line of the parabola marks in space a trajectory that represents a compromise between competing forces such as acceleration, vector of motion, and gravitational force. This is true in ballistics, and it is also true in the case of the hand that draws a parabola on paper.[12] The circle represents no such compromise; it is executed by a decisive force that overwhelms all other competing forces. It would be more accurate to say, in every case, that it is not exclusively the line that expresses some force or affect. Instead, it is the line in its context, that is, as part of a field of competing forces, of relations in a pattern.

One need not be a Gestalt theorist to recognize that line and abstract shapes express affects in their relationships. Wassily Kandinsky remarked: "The more abstract is form, the more clear and direct is its appeal."[13] *In Point and Line to Plane* he analyzed the affect of lines in their relationship to other figures in the two-dimensional space. He analyzed the concepts of tension, the expression of lyrical and dramatic affects, and even spiritual properties of graphic art. And he based his observations on the qualities of lines such as angles, curvature, proportion and length, and so forth. For example, sharp angles represented for him the conflict between two competing ("alternative") forces, while curved lines represented the action of two cooperating ("simultaneous") forces.[14] Although I find no evidence that Kandinsky read early Gestalt papers, he shares an important insight with Gestalt theory. For both, the forces acting on the angular line are not metaphorical or representational. It's not that the ninety-degree angle symbolizes the side of a house, or some numerical property "out in the world." The forces expressed by the "tense" angular figure are there on the page as they are in the world of ballistics, in optics, in the dynamics of the central nervous system and the cortical centers.

For that matter this is also the field of forces in which a dancer moves and expresses emotions—even when not intended—through the distribution of weight: moving in a hemisphere that consists of center, forward, right side, backward, forward, left side, backward, center; or moving downward or upward, smoothly or rigidly. Accelerating or slowing down, every movement in the space that surrounds the dancer is intrinsically expressive, not due to convention but naturally.[15] The agitation or serenity expressed by the dancer could equally emerge from the motion of a flame, a falling leaf, a willow tree, a steep rock, the cracks in a wall, a glazed teapot, lightning and thunder, and every other object or event around us.[16] These objects do not require a mind or consciousness to express emotion; the affect is communicated by the pattern of lines, motions, and sounds. But just as important, the emotion is not a projection of the human observer's inner states arbitrarily imposed on mute objects. Certain trees express sadness while others are agitated not because they possess these emotions, nor because the viewer simply decides that they are a fitting mirror for his own feelings. The expression is a patterned action of forces in a field of perception.

There are compelling evolutionary reasons for the expression of emotions by means of optical information. Both animals and humans, at an earlier stage of development, had to read their immediate physical environment in a glance and determine that it was either safe or hostile. Sudden noise or movement in a bush must be perceived as threatening, the sudden screech of a bird in a tree signifies agitation or fear, the unbalanced movement of a prey indicates vulnerability. The piping plover *Charadrius melodus* (Wilson plover as well), which nests in the sands of the eastern United States, is known to feign injury when it sees a predator approaching its vulnerable nest.[17] It is not clear whether the bird mentally calculates the benefits of a charade ("better pull out the old act, I see a predator coming").[18] What is clear is that the bird starts walking and hopping away from the nest while dragging one of its wings as though it were broken. This behavior is known among cognitive ethologists as "Broken Wing Display." The predator immediately picks up on this show of vulnerability and follows the jerky motions of the bird, drawn by its vulnerable hurt expression. Fishermen rely on a similar principle when they use a broken lure and jerk it in the water to simulate the uneven motion of an injured fish. They know that this increases the chances of a predator strike. The bird, the lure, or, for that matter, the weeping willow, do not truly project emotion, of course. The point is that the lines and trajectories of their motions act in a fundamental biological manner to produce in the observer the impression of emotion. Human perception of the emotion of others begins at this rudimentary level of reality; it is grounded in biological principles.

The most heavily discussed area of natural display of emotion since the time of Duchenne and later Darwin, has been facial expression.[19] While it is clear that various contortions of the face do in fact communicate affective information, neither Darwin nor modern researchers seem able to settle the natural-learned debate. The correlation between a specific facial gesture and a specific emotion may either be universal and therefore natural, or limited to a culture and therefore learned. The issue is currently complicated by other experimental considerations—for instance, response or manipulation of an audience as opposed to the audience's spontaneous displays. If facial gestures are important in controlling an audience and are not merely the expression of inner emotional states, then the question of cross-cultural variation is mediated by the context-specific function of facial contortion, which strengthens the naturalistic interpretation.[20] One thing is clear. Facial expression in general is a universal aspect of human communication and it operates in a powerful visceral manner. But either way, the face expresses by means of visual cues that constitute patterns in space: lines, shapes, and colors. Even if the expression is conventional, the capacity for registering it immediately, reliably (for social communication), and empathetically is based on neurological principles and universal dynamics. In other words, the ability to encode and decode emotion in muscular tension is itself a natural capacity shared by humans with other animals.

The relationship between expression and pattern is not exclusively visual, of course. The vocal communication of animals, birds, and even humans contains nonrepresentational elements that clearly convey affective information. The European blackbird (*Turdus merula*) territorial male communicates frequently with intruders. Researchers have measured the relationship between the qualities of the sound and motivational states and found that the bird utilizes "high-intensity" songs when displaying aggression, competition, or threat, and produces low-intensity songs at other times.[21] Humans too communicate aspects of language on a level that is known as prosodic, paralinguistic, or melodic. A strong correlation between emotion and such features of language as pitch level, pitch range, pitch variability, loudness, and tempo have been measured.[22] Even common observation reveals that certain vocal characteristics such as softness, halting pattern (stop and start), tight aspiration, and so forth express emotional states.

The Psychology of Pain

The case of pain communication raises some of the same problems encountered in the case of the emotions, and a few unique challenges. Darwin situated human pain behavior within the overall context of animal response. His work on the expression of emotions was published before precise pathways for ascending pain signals were known, or for that matter the two major types of pain signals distinguished. Consequently he was only able to describe one major type of pain behavior: "Thus a habit of exerting with the utmost force all the muscles will have been established, whenever great suffering is experienced."[23] Severe pain causes the muscles to contract violently, Darwin claims, because the organism is acting to escape the source of pain. At the same time the vocal organs are also put into violent action, producing a loud cry. The function of the sound is not evasion but summoning assistance, especially in the case of the young. Darwin was correct to situate human pain response in a biological-evolutionary context. His observations have been superseded, of course, but not the principle that the perception of pain is grounded in a biologically adaptive context.

At its most fundamental level, pain constitutes a number of distinct anatomical and functional events. Pain involves the activation of nociceptors that register mechanical, chemical, thermal, or electrical stimulation. The pain signals travel in a number of ascending pathways up the nervous system. The systems that are relatively constant among species include the spinoreticular system (SRS), the paleospinothalamic tract (PSTT), and the propriospinal system (PSS).[24] Each system conducts by means of distinct cellular structures or fibers. For instance, the cells for spinothalamic transmission consist of low threshold neurons, wide-dynamic-range neurons, high threshold neurons, and deep neurons that respond to deep tissue receptors.[25] Although the specificity theory has now been rejected, it seems that distinct *types* of nerve fibers specialize in transmitting different types of pain (see Chapter 8). For instance, high threshold stimuli (mechanical injury, chemical irritation) that damaged tissue produce 10 to 25 percent of the A-beta fibers. These generate a fast, bright pain sensation that is well localized. In contrast, 50 to 80 percent of unmyelinated C fibers respond to noxious stimulation, which is experienced as poorly localized nagging ache. There are specialized nociceptors for mechanical stimulation (crush), thermal stimulation (burn), and combinations. There are distinct cutaneous nerve endings, where C fibers dominate, and different ones for deep tissue nociception.

If one can generalize about a complex process, two basic functions stand out with the perception of pain. The first function, which is localized in the A-beta fibers, "is a warning system that provides immediate information about the presence of injury, the extent of injury and its location." The second function, which is localized in the C fibers, is a reminding system: "By generating slow, diffuse, particularly unpleasant and persistent pain, the second system repeatedly reminds the brain that injury has occurred and hence that normal activity should be restricted."[26] The first system is based on exteroception and the second on interoception. The sharp and bright pain of the first function generates an immediate muscular escape response, the hand that quickly withdraws from the hot stove, for instance. The dull ache of the second function produces inactivity and avoidance of unnecessary motion. These responses are natural and characteristic of animals as well as humans.[27]

In fact, "response to pain" is not a behavioral category that requires a mind or calculating intentionality in order to understand. Even when both types of pain generate reactions with social consequences—nursing the wound or immobilizing the area, for instance—these must first be understood as the organism's response to extreme novelty. Walter Cannon was the first to recognize the systemic nature of organismic response to extreme situations.[28] It was Cannon who began using the concept of homeostasis to describe the controlled features of the organic system that seeks to restore equilibrium of forces after some disrupting threat or damage. He assembled research results from the beginning of the twentieth century that measured the physiological response to pain (as well as emotions such as fear and rage). These studies indicated that pain results in a dramatic rise in the secretion of adrenin, which helps produce carbohydrates in the liver, thus flooding the blood system with sugar. It also results in the effective distribution of blood in the heart, lungs, central nervous system, and limbs while removing blood from the organs of the abdomen. All this eliminates the results of muscular fatigue and enables the organism to respond quickly and vigorously to the threat.[29] Cannon cites Darwin as well as other biologists on the specific behavioral manifestations of response to pain—the bristling hair, the cries, the contortion of the muscles. He explains them in terms of a fight-or-flight response to the threat, but in either case the organism requires the immediate physiological arousal brought about by andrenal and sugar secretions.

It is easy to discern a fair number of levels at which pain events operate or cause responses. At the most basic are the physical forces acting in nature that "collide" with the organism. Then there are the neurological registering of these, accompanied by biochemical cellular processes. The central nervous system responds on a number of levels, including motor responses and sympathetic nervous responses that trigger hormonal and chemical events throughout the body. At a higher level yet these become manifest behavioristically in the movement of the muscles, the arousal of the skin, drying of the mouth, extreme palpitation of the heart, and so forth. At a more conscious level, the organism experiences pain, or perhaps fear or rage, and seeks to avoid the stimulus at all cost, or perhaps strike back at it. The basic system theory of Cannon is based on the first type of pain, the exteroceptive pain, discussed earlier. He did not discuss the physiological responses to the aching sensations of healing and recovery. But in either case the organism ought to be taken as a cybernetic system that regulates itself toward balance or homeostasis.

Cannon was correct to note that pain is an extreme form of novelty, which is a great stressor. The responses triggered by pain can be taken as the organism's attempts to remove novelty by means of avoidance, elimination, nursing, and so forth. The victim of a toothache who repeatedly feels the sore spot with the tongue or finger is seeking to minimize novelty by reducing the sharpness of the pain into a dull ache. Anticipation of and preparation for painful events reduce the element of novelty and lessen the sensation of pain. Natural childbirth classes illustrate this principle, as do the instructions given to Chinese patients before receiving acupuncture analgesia.[30] Many of the actions that help reduce the sensation of pain are conscious and involve intentional attitudes toward pain. But nociception, like the perception of other stimuli, involves systemic processes at the numerous levels of the events involved. Consequently, psychologists of pain have utilized Gestalt theory to account for many of the features of pain perception.

Pain and Gestalt

Pain is not experienced as an isolated stimulus that is divorced from its context. It takes place in a very complex process that consists of at least three fields—the immediate external physical and social environment, the immediate internal somatic environment, and cognitive processes that involve memory, expectation, attention, moods, and so forth.[31] The relation of pain stimulus to these contexts is a figure-ground phenomenon that defines the nature of the experience of being in pain. An awareness of a sudden ache in the stomach generates no anxiety when it happens at noon time, about the time one usually has lunch. A splinter in the finger generates no sensation at all in the midst of a heated basketball game. A sudden contraction in the chest is felt sharply and arouses some concern after a visit with an uncle at the hospital. All pain perception takes place in a fluid and constantly changing field of foreground and background phenomena. At this perceptual level, as at the organismic, novelty is recognized only in context, and successful function requires adaptation—which is a reduction of novelty. Extreme pain emerges dramatically into the foreground and pushes everything else into the background. It comes to dominate the attentional field.

Pain perception also involves configurational units (*gestalten*), rather than discrete and separate phenomena. People do not perceive their pain as minute particles of sensation traveling up their nervous systems. Just as a face is perceived as a total unit before the elements that "constitute" it, so pain is perceived as a drilling or shooting sensation that has a complete perceptual structure. The figure or "shape" of the sensation does not assemble itself out of separate nociceptive units, but feels like a whole, even when it is experienced as motion, as is shooting pain, or the spread of migraine aura.

It is very important to emphasize that the forms of pain perception are not exclusively spatial but take place in time as well. The next chapter will show that pain is essentially a conscious signal, and as a fact of consciousness it must take place in time or possess duration. Pain's configurational pattern involves form in space and time, which generates the perception of ongoing events such as drilling or shooting. In the McGill Pain Questionnaire the sensory terms are all present-continuative.[32] This temporal structure of time (time and space units acting isomorphically) has presented unique problems for the graphic rendering of pain in frozen spatial media such as drawing and painting.

Other elements of pain perception that involve Gestalt principles, according to psychologists of pain, include perceptual stability, closure, and isomorphism between the levels of pain perception. Closure and stability are particularly relevant to the phantom-pain phenomenon, which is a sensation generated by the *absence* of input, to which the control system responds by over-firing output. In other words, it generates the perception of a whole body (closure) but overdoes it in the absence of tempering feedback (see Chapter 2).

Communicating Pain

According to neurophysiologists there are only three fundamental sensations of pain: burning, piercing, and throbbing. Each corresponds to a distinct type of neurological event and must be diagnosed as such for proper treatment. However, this objective observation seems inadequate in the light of introspection. The actual feel of pain, as everyone knows, is infinitely richer and more complex than these three qualities, even when the sensations do not translate well into words. Anyone who has visualized his or her pain—as we all do—knows this well. Noreen Meinhart reports the following descriptions of pain by some of her patients: One man visualized his pain as a large rat eating a hole through his stomach (he was dying of cancer). Another patient described his pain as exactly 132 squares covering his body, and no matter what was done, at least two squares could never be relieved. He was a real estate developer. Yet another patient described the aching muscles of his lower back as raw bleeding hamburger meat.[33] Although it is difficult to describe pain precisely, the sensation itself often evokes extremely vivid images, which are multilayered. That means that the image is not just an allegory for sensation (the rat that gnaws) but that the image has powerful cognitive-evaluative, emotional, and social aspects.

According to Karoly's guide to diagnosis of pain ("The Pain Context Model"), the complex and multilayered quality of pain must be taken into account by the health practitioner, along with the systemic properties defined by Gestalt.[34] The health worker is encouraged to treat the pain patient as a distinct and integrated individual. This requires creating a model of the pain that takes the following into account: the pain description must be nonreductionistic; it should be contextualized within the emotional and cognitive life of the patient. The model should regard pain as a systemic event and not just one result of a single cause. In other words, pain is context dependent. The context is not just biomedical but social as well, and the approach to healing should be regarded as an integrated process.

The most comprehensive effort to date to sort out the various levels of pain perception has been the McGill Pain Questionnaire (MPQ). It is a diagnostic tool used for incoming pain patients that takes into account the multidimensional quality of pain. It gauges the sensory, affective, and evaluative properties of the reported pain based on the selection of terms, which are divided into twenty categories. Some of the categories are sensory (flickering, quivering, pulsing, throbbing, beating), some are affective (fearful, frightful, terrifying), and others are evaluative (annoying, troublesome, miserable, intense, unbearable).[35]

A man who experiences his cancer as the gnawing of a rat would be expressing an emotional attitude such as fear or revulsion, along with a judgment that the pain is vicious. The questionnaire forces patients who have not experienced their pain in vivid images to express its various layers. Despite the respect that the MPQ commands, several researchers have pointed out serious limitations. Marion V. Smith has indicated that the Canadian English used in the questionnaire imposes parameters tied to the associative and connotative properties of the words used. Some of the terms may be either ambiguous or multilayered themselves. Some groups contain terms that do not seem to belong together; other groups are missing words that ought to be there. Smith claims that stabbing ought to appear with shooting or piercing, though it does not, and that boring could go either with drilling or blunt and unremitting.[36] There are additional criticisms that could be made: The quesionnaire fails to focus on social consequences (isolating, ignored) and cognitive factors (confusing, mystifying). The general point is that the rigid structuring of pain adjectives can be distorting, which common sense accepts readily. On the other hand, long and impressionistic descriptions of one's pain, which are probably the most accurate methods of communicating its complicated nature, are far too time-consuming for health care professionals. Reading such a narrative requires a type of literary interpretation that would probably delve into these "levels" of the patient (these are subjective-phenomenal levels, pertinent to the way the patient lives in the world; they are not objective ontological categories): the patient's lived body, self (including emotions and thoughts), social relationships, and cosmos.[37] M. C. Rawlingson has divided these levels slightly differently into the body, relationships with others, the will, and sphere of universal alteration.[38] Sorting out the layers and reading the effects of pain in each entails a near anthropological depth that has recently been attempted in an admirable fashion by Mary-Jo DelVecchio Good and her colleagues.[39]

The multilevel and narrative approach to the evaluation of patients in pain is a response to the medical harm done, paradoxically, during the nineteenth-century progress in neurophysiology and pain management. The medicalization of pain at that time resulted in the separation of the pain symptom from the person, and its fragmentization into discrete phenomena. The vast majority of nursing and pain clinic guides today focus on this depersonalization of the pain patient:

> The elevation of sensation over emotion in traditional medical and psychological approaches results in the lack of attention to subjectivity, which in turn leads to a limited approach towards suffering and a neglect of broader cultural and sociological components of pain. In other words,

> a far more sophisticated model of pain is needed; one which locates individuals within their social and cultural contexts and which allows for the inclusion of feelings and emotions.[40]

For the embodiment of the sensation of pain—its localization in our lived body—the reader can refer to anything as common as a toothache or a bad headache, a bone fracture, and so forth. But extreme pain summons extreme images:

> The first sharp pain of metal thrust
> fiery tip bores pinioned flesh
> no resistance to its force
> no protection from its lust.[41]

The author is describing a bone marrow biopsy, which involves a needle, hence the "metal thrust" in these pained words. As the description progresses one comes across words such as pressure, explosion, burn, and bite to go with the bore and thrust of this quote. All of these words suffer from the ambiguities and imprecision attributed to the McGill Pain Questionnaire. But in the narrative context they clearly convey the sense of a body invaded, a weak and soft unity violated by a lustful and powerful intentionality. Thus, although the pain is "in the body" its sensations are far more than purely somatic; they also devastate the self. The decentering effect of pain on the self has been described in the following way: "I was too enveloped by pain even to acknowledge anything else. The pain was the centre of a boiling solar system, and I was spinning around it in a trajectory that I could do nothing about."[42] Notice that the description begins with a metaphor of envelopment and moves effortlessly to its opposite, the pain now at the center. This suggests a complete sense of the spatiality (not to mention centrality) of one's self, and the consequent loss of control. In order to feel that we possess a will, we must be able to experience agency in some space relative to the body and the world, on which we can exert our will.

This is the conclusion that emerges from this and other pain narratives: Pain acts in a similar fashion at the levels in which the victims experience themselves in the world. It acts as a force of disruption, disintegration, invasion, decentering, alienation. At the body level, patients feel that the pain is invasive and destructive. At the level of self, pain causes disintegration and decentering (recall Bakan's telic decentralization); at the level of social relationships, the pain is disruptive and consequently isolating; and at the level of the lived-in cosmos, the pain is a problem of evil—a theodicy—and therefore a disruption of meaning and good order. At every level pain breaks the order of things, becomes a foreground phenomenon, and shatters the rest. This is indicated in the choice of words to describe the action of pain at the various levels—the tools or weapons first (metal), the wielders of these tools or the creature who can inflict such harm (rats), the fragmenting psychic consequences, the terms of social disruption and isolation.

But the homology between the levels, the structural correspondence, makes comprehension and empathy by outsiders possible, as long as they move beyond the single symptom and the isolated trope to the broader context of the sufferer in his world. It is the tragedy of the modern patient (not to mention the political prisoner) that the invention of modern biomedical models in the nineteenth century (see final chapter of this book) has cut off the person and reduced him to patient—a tangle of symptoms and the legal right to demand their removal. I will show in the next chapter, and those that follow, that in traditional religious contexts pain has been voluntarily pursued because its devastating effects in one cultural context are highly meaningful and desirable in others.

FOUR

Self and Sacrifice: A Psychology of Sacred Pain

We have seen that the actions of the peripheral and central nervous systems shape the way humans experience and communicate pain. Neural function, particularly Ronald Melzack's "neurosignature," also accounts for the body-self, which supports our sense of agency. Pain and self are thus intimately related through neurodynamics. We have seen how intentionally painful manipulations of the body could lead to states of self-transcendence or effacement. Of course, the mystics and monks who flagellated themselves in their cold cells in order to feel more Christlike did not know any of this. The processes that transform pain into meaningful religious experiences take place beneath the level of consciousness. They constitute neuropsychological events, not intentional mental states. So what happens at the conscious level, in the awareness of the self-mutilator? How do the neurological dynamics become decisions to hurt oneself, and what is the experiential face of such voluntary pain? To answer these questions we must move on to the psychological level of description, building carefully on the theories of the previous chapters which were grounded in the cybernetic view of the nervous system. There will be no deus ex machina, or even "ghost in the machine" Self who becomes magically "reborn" or "purified" through the ordeals of pain. "Self-transcendence" also does not mean that a metaphysical self, encased within the empirical person, becomes actualized through pain. Instead, the subject who undergoes pain will be discussed here merely as an expansion of the biological processes, specifically those that accounted in Chapter 2 for the emergence of the embodied self (body-self).

Pathological Self-Mutilation

Andre Vauchez's *Sainthood in the Later Middle Ages* says that Blessed Clare of Rimini had herself bound to a pillar and whipped on Good Friday. Hedwig of Silesia scourged herself, and Blessed Charles of Blois wrapped knotted cords around his chest.[1] Caroline Bynum's *Holy Feast, Holy Fast* states that Christina of Spoleto perforated her own foot with a nail.[2] Above all, Heinrich Suso may have tortured himself in more ways than many of the other saints and mystics combined.[3] The lives of Christian saints and mystics abound with descriptions of self-tortures and even self-mutilation. I shall look at one instance in some detail shortly. But in order to de-theologize these phenomena it may first be useful to put such religious individuals in a far broader context of modern self-destructive behavior. Consider, for example, the self-mutilations that prevail in a wide range of populations in contemporary America.

The feature article of the *New York Times Magazine* of July 27, 1997, focused on a teenage girl, Jill, who was a self-mutilator.[4] Jill was an attractive and charismatic cheerleader in a South Chicago Irish neighborhood, a member of a close-knit and caring family. Her social success appeared to be accompanied by extremely high levels of stress and a complete preoccupation with efforts to please others, especially boys. At age fourteen Jill discovered that by cutting herself with a razor and watching the blood come out, her psychic pain would vanish, at least temporarily. Jill began to cut herself in the bathroom and other places with razor blades, or, when these were not available, broken glass, compass needles, and other items. She usually cut the upper thigh area where she claimed the cuts could not be detected. She thus became part of a current epidemic that runs especially among young women. The epidemic has been called "bodies under siege" by Armando Favazza.[5] What is the explanation for the widespread phenomenon in which young women, who appear well adjusted, secretly hurt themselves, sometimes with extreme violence? Is the comparison with the sacred self-hurt of saints and mystics fair, or entirely baseless?

Favazza, who is a professor of psychiatry at the University of Missouri, Columbia, defines self-mutilation as "the direct, deliberate destruction or alteration of one's own body tissue without conscious suicidal intent."[6] He is referring to moderate self-mutilation, which differs from the coarse psychotic infliction of major traumas and amputations, or involuntary acts, like head banging of autistic or some retarded individuals. Acts of violence perpetrated on their own bodies by young women like Jill usually include cutting, burning, plucking of hairs from the head or body, bone breaking, head banging, needle poking, skin scratching, and others.

The "PsychLit" abstracts of professional journals from 1991 through 1997 list well over two hundred articles dealing with the topic of self-mutilation. The scientific journals describe and analyze the phenomena of self-injury from the full range of disciplinary approaches—from the neurophysiology of pain and brain states, to family dynamics, social context, and the religious orientation of victims. Psychoanalytical theory is still pervasive and will be discussed shortly. The population of self-mutilators in the literature also ranges from teenage girls to male prisoners and even animals in captivity. Self-mutilation was recorded among black slaves in the nineteenth century and has been seen among soldiers who seek to avoid combat or extreme exertion.

Given the enormous diversity of approaches and the variety of self-mutilators (though the single largest group seems to consist of young women in their teens and twenties), it would clearly be foolish to reduce self-injury to one or two causes. On the neurophysiological level, the injury seems to produce natural endogenous opiates known as beta-endorphins that can lead to temporary states of euphoria after the infliction of the injury.[7] At an entirely different level of analysis, self-mutilation has been linked with post-traumatic stress syndrome, particularly following sexual abuse or rape, imprisonment, and war experiences.[8] Naturally, none of these explanations has been universally recognized as a definitive and exclusive factor. Jill suffered neither rape nor war, but she was a victim nonetheless of extremely high stress levels.

It is clearly futile to decide here which theory is right for which population of cutters, or what is the "true" cause of self-mutilation. Far more interesting, I believe, is the phenomenological question: What is it like—from the subjective point of view—to injure oneself with cuts, burns, and bruises? Surely those who commit such acts experience them differently from the way even the most empathetic "healthy" observer imagines. Self-mutilators seem to experience the injuries they cause in a positive way, and the subjective feel of their experience is never identical with the causes attributed to the actions by others. In other words, the voice of the agents, their personal narrative, reveals surprising and important facts about self-injury, and despite the variety of causes and diversity of the practitioners, their accounts ring in a strikingly consistent manner. Often they sound like religious self-mutilators without the theology.

Jill, for instance, reported little pain when she was interviewed by Jennifer Egan, and described a feeling of somehow taking charge of her life with the help of the razor. Another patient at the program Egan surveyed, whose name was given as Jane, had made a list of reasons for cutting herself in which she included more than thirty items. However, the word that recurred most frequently in that list was *power*: "I cut right in the fold of a finger. . . . It was so sharp and so smooth and so well hidden, and yet there was some sense of empowerment. If somebody else is hurting me or making me bleed, then I take the instrument away and I make me bleed. It says: 'You can't hurt me anymore. I'm in charge of that.'"[9] Although Jane had suffered sexual abuse at a young age while Jill did not, both were the victims of powerlessness, having been dominated by the wills of others.

Few self-mutilators report intolerably high levels of pain. An anonymous writer who describes self-mutilation in great detail and with a professional level of sophistication (via the Internet) claims rather typically: "The slicing through flesh never hurt, although it never even occurred to me that it should."[10] Indeed, this absence of pain refers back to the distinction between injury and pain, which was discussed in the Chapter 2, and which is important for understanding religious self-injury. At any rate, the self-mutilation of some patients, regarded from the subjective point of view, may not be entirely different from the self-injury of mystics or saints. The heuristic concept of pathology, which differentiates the patient from the saint, might actually distort an important insight. Both types of violence appear to revolve around a sense of empowerment and a positive affirmation of some sort.[11] After looking at a case of religious self-hurt I shall consider a psychological theory that could explain both "pathological" and "sacred" pain.

Sacred Self-Mutilation: The Torments of Maria Maddalena de' Pazzi

The mental life of individuals who injure themselves rarely matches either the traumatic shock that observers attach to injury or the reductive processes of neurological and psychological sciences. If anything, in its complexity and ambiguity, the inner world of self-hurters more closely resembles that of mystics and other technicians of the sacred who acquire, or claim to acquire, "spiritual" power by austerities and discipline.

The following is a description taken out of Vincentio Puccini's biography of Maria Maddalena de' Pazzi:

> On the eight of September in the same year of 1587 . . . going into a room where the wood was kept, and there having first bolted the door, she gathered together rugged sticks, and thornes, etc., she tumbled therein. . . . Sometimes she would afflict her [self] with disciplines of

> iron, and gird herself about with a most terrible girdle, which in coursest canvas, she had imbordered with piercing nails, in such sort, that in truth the only sight thereof maketh them shrink and even tremble who look upon it.[12]

These were just a few, and far from the most horrific, tortures that Saint Maria Maddalena inflicted on her body. The information we have on that woman, whether hagiographic or biographic, lends itself to easy psychologizing on various forms of masochism.[13] She was born in Florence to a very distinguished family and baptized Caterina, after her maternal grandmother. She received religious instruction in a Jesuit-sponsored institution, and though precociously sensitive, she did not exhibit any unusual psychological traits before her entry to the Carmelite monastary of Santa Maria degli Angeli in 1582. She took the habit as Sister Maria Maddalena de' Pazzi in 1583.

Maria Maddalena's self-tortures are not only vivid illustrations of sanctioned "masochism." They provide an unusually detailed map of the subjective experiences of the religious self-hurter. The details put to easy rest any notion that pain is a monolithic experience lacking subtlety, ambiguities, or inner contradictions. It is possible, based on information obtained from Maria's confessors, superiors, and sisters, to distinguish at least three major types of pain in her monastic life: voluntary self-inflicted pain, pain she felt inflicted on her by devils and which may have been nonconscious forms of self-mutilation, and natural pain (disease).

Voluntary, Self-inflicted Pain

A vivid illustration of the first type is available from very early in her monastic career. Puccini tells that Maria took long stalks of orange trees, which are covered with thorns, and tied them tightly around her head in the manner of the crucifix. She kept this crown of thorns on her head for a full night.[14] Indeed, Maria's identification with the crucifix was such that she sometimes would remove it from the cross at the monastary's Quire, and wipe off the sweat and blood she saw on the face of her beloved.[15] But the conscious forms of self-inflicted pain went beyond the imitation of Christ. Maria on various occasions had herself tied to a post, hands bound behind her back. At other times she lay on the ground and members of the congregation stepped on her body. She slept on rough straw, walked barefoot in the winter, dripped hot candle wax on her own body, dressed in a coarse and irritating garment. When not imitating Christ, she described these and other forms of torment as ways of testing and fighting bodily temptation (like Daniel in the lions' den), fighting the urge to eat too much, or battling the pleasures of comfort and sexual desire. Pain for her was also a way of driving away possessing devils and evil spirits, or it was an alchemical agent for transforming her body and mind into instruments of Providence.[16]

Pain Inflicted by Devils

Every now and then Maria was subject to pains and injuries which she experienced as though inflicted by devils: "Sometimes the envious spirits would throw her down the stairs, and sometimes she was cruelly bitten by them, as by so many venomous vipers, whereby she suffered extreme pain."[17] On another occasion "she was then cast down to the ground with great fury, and beaten with incredible rage. For sometimes the Devil struck her over the head, sometimes he cast her down precipitously, so that her face was swollen in such a way that for the space of many days it was necessary for her to be under cure."[18] It is hard to know what to make of these and similar descriptions. The agent causing the pain is experienced as though it were someone other than Maria, the devil no less. Maria's biographer clearly shares this point of view and in fact he describes her throwing stones at the devil.[19] But these events seem strikingly delusional, which is not only a clinical observation, but an ontological judgment about the nature of hallucination. At this point it is safe to say that from the phenomenal perspective the injury is not caused by ego, but by some other agency.

Natural Pain

The third form of pain that Maria Maddalena experienced was natural. Shortly after joining the monastery she became extremely ill and was not expected to recover. She was hit with sharp burning fever and a "vehement" cough that was accompanied by extreme pain. Puccini describes the young woman suffering gravely from her illness until she seems to have discovered a valuable secret that transformed her pain into something else. The biographer quotes Maria as she points at the crucifix: "I contemplate the great sufferings which that cordial and incomprehensible love endured for my salvation; he sees my weakness, and with that sight of his I am comforted, since all the pains and grief which all the chosen children of God have endured, did pass through that most holy Humanity of Christ, where they grew to be sweet, and to be desired by his members."[20] The pain of her illness, she discovered, could be transformed into a desirable sweetness, like the sweet pain of Teresa of Avila, by means of Christ. In a stunning transformation, pain became a meaningful experience rather than a problem she had to resist and reject. It remains to be seen what this profoundly important religious discovery means in psychological terms. But undoubtedly, the wealth of Maria's pain experiences cautions that a theory of sacred pain must take its subject as a complex and ambiguous phenomenon.

Psychologizing Religious Pain

Maria Maddalena's self-tortures were not always gladly tolerated by her superiors, but they were ultimately accepted as part of her extraordinary rigor in visiting penance and discipline on herself. This reluctant abidance by the singularity of a precocious nun would gradually erode in Church history, or, at least, the conceptualization of its meaning would change drastically with the rise of psychological sciences. During the late nineteenth and early twentieth centuries there was a strong tendency to link some phenomena of mystical ecstasies with psychological pathology, particularly hysteria. The church itself had struggled for centuries to distinguish between mystical experience and various forms of "insanity," such as epilepsy, possession, humoral imbalance, and others.[21] Previously, women who had possibly been suffering from a variety of traumas and other forms of mental disorders sought outlet in behavior that, if not sanctioned, may at least have been recognized in religious terms. Maria Maddalena's superiors certainly gave up fighting against her self-torments, and after her death even left the nail-studded corset on display. But with the rise of the psychological sciences the religious hysteric was "stripped of her borrowed halo, she has lost her rights to the stake or to canonization. She has the honor today of being a sick person, and depends directly on the doctor."[22]

After Jean-Martin Charcot and Sigmund Freud, the emergence of Jungian depth psychology produced less reductive and more influential explanations of religious self-tortures. Carl Jung himself differentiated between "pathological" self-hurt and religious forms of self-sacrifice. On the first type he was not particularly insightful and regarded self-destructive behavior as a method of manipulating others. In contrast, he considered self-sacrifice a sacramental act, a surrender of the ego, which also amounted to a mastery of the ego. In the denial of ego that self-sacrifice entails, one brings to consciousness the forces of profound metaphysical (unconscious) realities. Here Jung went beyond Freud's understanding of ego and its role in the conflict between drives and social constraints. On Jung's understanding of religious sacrifice, a potential self is actualized and transformed into a fully conscious Self. In Christian terms, the model of Self is Christ as the Original Man, and the goal of discipline is imitation of Christ, which corresponds to the individuation process.[23]

Jung's basic metaphysical assumptions were incorporated into a more recent and somewhat more rigorous school of religious psychology. Transpersonal psychology is "the study of human nature and development, which proceeds on the assumption that humans possess potentialities that surpass the limits of the maturely developed ego. It is an inquiry that presupposes that the ego, as ordinarily constituted, can be transcended and that a higher transegoic plane or stage of life is possible."[24] This reality is called "dynamic ground," something like Brahman or Tao, which can be reached through discipline, including austerities. Jungian and "transpersonal" reductions are both metaphysical and cultural. They define religious experience either in terms of the mystic's own symbols, or using such language as "transpersonal reality," which reads like paraphrasing jargon. Although few students of religion take this approach seriously, the influential theories of Mircea Eliade are not that different in principle.

Freudian theory, in contrast, is more comprehensive and rigorous in its reduction. It promises to explain both the mystic and the neurotic teenager by means of biological as well as social causes. Psychoanalysis is the most promising and incisive tool we can bring to the discussion of self-hurt, but it must be applied with caution and without recourse to such clinical concepts as hysteria and masochism.

The Faults of Masochism

The nineteenth-century science of psychology went beyond distinguishing true spirituality from mental illness. For Freud and his immediate followers, all forms of religious activity—from simple rituals to self-mutilation—were expressions of deep underlying psychic causes, ranging from neurosis to clinical masochism. Freudian psychoanalytical theory would regard Maria Maddalena's self-flagellation as her response to guilt induced by factors embedded in the superego's relation to the ego.[25] Voluntary pain is a form of self-punishment that subdues guilty inner voices by suppressing the effects of instinctual drives, especially sex, which conflict with broader social constraints.

For Freud there could be no valid distinction between a Maria Maddalena and a clinical masochist like Lise in Dostoevsky's *The Brothers Karamazov*, which Freud had read avidly:

> And Lise, as soon as Alyosha had gone, unlocked the door, opened it a little, put her finger in the crack, and slammed the door as hard as she could. Ten seconds later she released her hand, went slowly to her chair, sat down, and looked intently at her blackened, swollen finger and the blood that was oozing out from the nail. Her lips quivered, "I am a vile, vile, vile, despicable creature," she whimpered.[26]

The subjective emotional life of the self-hurter, in the psychoanalytical view, is shaped by conflict and is experienced as punitive. Pain—the means of punishment—serves as a negative force, a repulsive sensation that one feels she has earned by the moral logic of a deep neurosis. In other words, the function of the pain—the removal of mental anguish associated with guilt (even unconscious guilt)—limits it exclusively to contexts in which self-loathing prevails. Pain resembles here an analgesic device: If you have a headache but you get kicked in the shin, the headache vanishes.[27] For Freud such self-loathing is linked to the entrapment of the ego in the conflict between biological drives and superego, and it is erotic. It results from a repression of the ego's hidden desires and culminates in aggressive impulses toward the ego. Freud's followers—Anna Freud, Theodore Reik, and even Bruno Bettelheim—also paradoxically associate the sense of guilt with erotic, as well as aggressive, drives.[28] According to Anna Freud, and Melanie Klein, as we shall see later, the self-inflicted hurt is an ego defense mechanism that operates by means of a symbolic reversal.[29]

The literature on masochism is both large and riddled with inconsistencies, especially on the relation of pain and sexuality. A general working definition of masochism follows Krafft-Ebing in emphasizing the sexual component and associating it with one or more of these three features: receiving pain, giving up control through bondage, and undertaking humiliation or embarrassment.[30] Although studies of masochism have undergone significant changes over the last few decades, newer psychoanalytical theories have retained key Freudian ideas, primarily the axiom that masochism is a form of sexual perversion. According to Rudolph Loewenstein, all the mechanisms that have been discovered for masochism "center around the crucial problems with which human sexuality has to deal during its development: namely fear of loss of the object and fear of loss of its love, castration fear, and superego anxiety."[31] By punishing themselves, masochists alleviate the fear of being tortured or abandoned by others, thus controlling fear and guilt by means of pain—eroticized pain.

The specific problems with psychoanalytical drive or conflict theory on the clinical level are beyond the pale of this chapter. The broadest problem in the application of psychotherapy theory to saints such as Maria Maddalena is the monumental methodological reduction it entails. The assumption that a single culture-bound clinical theory can explain vast amounts of cases across cultures and centuries is tenuous.[32] A culturally mediated action that *looks* like the masochist's "perversion" cannot be equated with material that is dominated by the puritanical work of a Victorian superego.

More decisive and substantive critiques are empirical. Freud's biological/sexual reduction fails to acknowledge the importance of conscious experience in dysfunction and in therapy. His theory, for instance, would have to equate all self-abusers roughly with Jill and her difficulties in dealing with authority and the love of her parents. The prisoners and the slaves who inflict injuries on themselves have to fall somewhere in the same group, according to such a distortive flattening of experiential nuances. The theory, bred to treat specific types of patients, overreaches when it tries to embrace every case of self-injury. In this reduction, the language of various self-hurters, including mystics, is dissolved into clinical concepts, and intentional cognitive states are marginalized. Still, in some cases Freudian theory can sound persuasive. The three types of pain Maria Maddalena experienced could represent three permutations of the ego's relation to the superego. The first is ego acting on behalf of the Father (God), the second is the repressed Id (sexuality, aggression) acting in rage against the Father in the person of the Devil, and the third is Fate as the distant embodiment of paternal oversight.

As noted, Freud's biological drive theory requires that conscious experiences be demoted to a secondary role. There is, however, no compelling reason to discount conscious experience in favor of such concepts as Id and repression, or reduce all relations to sexuality. Heintz Kohut's self psychology, by contrast, analyzes sadism and masochism not in terms of subconscious drives and their conflict, but in terms of the subject's frustrated relation to a primary "self-object," a non-nurturing parent for example, and her need to strengthen a depleted self. The fulfillment of the nuclear self's ambitions and needs makes even "martyrdom" appealing if it substitutes the love of a parent in strengthening the self. It is the phenomenal self, the self that develops in conscious relation to caregivers, not the biological organism and its drives, that determines the meaning of hurt.[33]

Finally, the Freudian assumption that pain is monolithic and intrinsically aversive or punitive also needs to be reexamined. If pain is a single sensation, always "bad," then anyone who desires it must be perverse. But in fact, there is no such single and simple pain. Nociception is largely a mental event, a conscious experience that cannot be separated from emotional and evaluative contexts. In the words of the neurologist V. S. Ramachandran, "Pain is an *opinion* on the organism's state of health rather than a mere reflexive response to an injury."[34] The possiblity of "good pain" can be illustrated with common examples. When you go to a massage therapist with a sore back and he runs his thumbs powerfully down the sides of the aching muscles, the hurt is experienced as satisfying. Similarly, some recovering patients of chemotherapy describe the discomforts and pain of the treatment in positive terms, because it is experienced as the destroyer of the invading tumor.

But common sense rebels against the idea that pain can actually be experienced as something good. If it is pain, we say, it is by definition felt to be bad. Pain can never be anything else; it can only be interpreted as good, usually after it has passed. Perhaps the pressure on the muscle is really not powerful enough, and we confuse heavy touch, a pleasurable sensation, with pain that one perversely enjoys. An example from Chapter 2 takes the discussion further: A soldier emerges on command from a foxhole, where he has been under constant gunfire, and charges up a well-fortified hill. Bullets whistle all around him and his comrades are getting hit. Suddenly a bullet hits him, taking away half of his hand on the spot. He drops back and is evacuated. In contrast, another man drives in a convertible to a restaurant with his wife to celebrate their wedding anniversary. Without warning a pickup truck pulls out of a side street, colliding with the smaller vehicle. The convertible flips over and the man, whose arm is outside the vehicle, loses part of his hand. The two injuries—to the soldier and the driver—may be regarded as identical, for the sake of argument. Research has shown that the soldier is likely to experience less pain than the civilian in the car.[35] The injury is not just evaluated in different terms; it is *experienced* differently.[36]

A more mundane example of different pain perceptions would be two football players going up for a ball that is sailing toward the end zone. The attacking player catches it and the two athletes collide violently and land in a pile on the turf. The attacker, who has just scored a touchdown, is more likely to leap back to his feet while the defender limps off the field. Both players register some pain, but for the victor pain becomes an emblem of his achievement. It almost feels good. Any theory of self-mutilation that takes pain as a monolithic sensation, directly linked to tissue damage, is bound to fail. It fails first and foremost by distorting the fact that pain is a mental event, and an extremely nuanced one. The range of mental factors that influence the perception of pain is impressive. They include belief, immediate context, cultural and ethnic background, fear or stress, fatigue, perception of danger, and even more subtle factors such as cognitive tendencies to overestimate or underestimate distances and sizes.[37]

Neuropsychology can explain that the soldier experiences less pain than the car accident victim because of the massive stress that precedes his injury. In experiential terms, the soldier feels relieved because the loss of his hand will remove him from the battle and the threat of far greater harm. In fact, the injury to the hand may actually have saved his life. In other words, the soldier may feel as though he sacrificed a "part of himself" for a more urgent goal—his personal survival. What is unclear is why emotional relief should result in a lesser experience of pain, or even a pain that is experienced in relatively positive terms.[38] After all, the organic hand undergoes the same trauma and the nerves process the same "information" to the brain. Surely judgment plays no role in these physiological processes. But such commonsensical doubts are contradicted by clinical observation, which in the early 1960s led to the "gate-control" theory of pain.[39] Mental facts at the central brain do in fact block or modify the quality and intensity of signals arriving from the periphery and modulate the sensation of pain.

The perceptual ambiguity of pain undoes psychological theories of masochistic pain—such as Freud's—which interpret it as the bringing on oneself of something hurtful and vindictive. The behavior of girls like Jill and mystics like Maria Maddalena cannot be reduced to the perversion of enjoying something hurtful that they inflict on their bodies. In order to understand the nature of self-inflicted injury and its positive function, we must look at the nature of the person as ego and organism, and at pain as a special signal within this complex organization.

The Phenomenal Self: From Biological Organization to Experience

In Chapter 2 we considered the body-self as a neurological template, a function of neurological dynamics such as the "neurosignature."[40] It is necessary, in fact, to separate the body-self into two closely related concepts. The first is the "body schema" that accounts, from a neurological perspective, for the organism's ability to operate consistently and effectively within complex and shifting physical environments.[41] The second—"body image"—is the phenomenal or experiential aspect of the body schema: It is the sense that the agent has of "owning" a cohesive and coordinated body-self. Counting both of these, the self at its most basic level is the body-self, a phenomenal upshot of organized neural functions.[42]

For the French phenomenologist Merleau-Ponty, who was deeply influenced by Gestalt psychology, the self emerges from an intuitive sense of being embodied, of being first and foremost a self in a body.[43] William James too wrote half a century earlier: "The world experienced (otherwise called the 'field of consciousness') comes at all times with our body as its centre, centre of vision, centre of action, centre of interest. . . . The body is the storm centre, the origin of coordinates, the constant place of stress in all the experience-train. Everything circles around it, and is felt from its point of view."[44] The body-self develops for the child in tandem with the body's own changes, before there is any knowledge of the body as separate from a "self." The body image—the perception of owning one's body—develops as the body becomes the "mirror-body," the stage in human development posited by Lacan at six to eighteen months when the child recognizes its own image in the mirror.[45] Basic identity comes in the visual and cognitive recognition of one's self as other—the self projected as body in the mirror. And very much like the body in the mirror, the body-image is itself an abstraction: In reality it is never a thing—not even a constant phenomenon—let alone an entity. It shifts endlessly with the changes and movements of the body and with the changing vantage point of the subject. Some researchers (Van der Velde) even suggest that we possess innumerable body-images, phantoms without ontology—a view that tallies with theories ranging from early Buddhist psychology to William James and postmodern thought.[46] This view is also consistent with contemporary philosophical analysis of the self (Tom Nagel, Daniel Dennett, Marvin Minsky), and perhaps most impressive of all, neurological science. Some neurologists (V. S. Ramachandran, W. Hirstein) have identified at least six or seven distinct "selves," each a function of separate brain structures.[47]

Although the body-image is a phantom, we do in fact experience ourselves *as though* possessing an integrated and concrete body-self. The essence of phenomenology is that "as though" experiences—phantoms—can acquire a reality that seems more vivid and concrete than what is "truly so." Folk-psychology, as Jerome Bruner calls psychological common sense, strongly reinforces the notion of a constant and clearly defined self. This fictive unity implies that the changes of brain states at the root of the body-image must be coordinated or regulated (notice that these are noncausal terms) in some fashion. For Bruner the regulating principles are cultural and linguistic. Identity, personality, and the self are thus situated somewhere between mental-cultural factors and neurodynamics. It is not surprising that a cultural psychologist like Bruner recognizes the mutual influence of brain states and mental-cultural factors, or that this coevolutionary view should influence a cultural anthropologist like Clifford Geertz.[48] More surprising, many neuropsychologists, following the work of the neurologist A. R. Luria, attribute the coordination of dispersed and flexible neural functions, those that underlie the body schema and image, to higher mental principles based on culture.[49] According to Luria, numerous separate brain operations are structured in an anatomical and functional way by means of devices such as language, arithmetical systems, and other symbolic constructs called "codes." A child acquires these cultural codes along with language, which in turn aids the development of functional systems in the child's growing brain. For example, as the child learns to speak, verbal instructions given by parents on appropriate behaviors and similar matters are gradually replaced with inner speech that regulates the child's behavior. This inner speech creates networks of cerebral connections for organizing behavior and inhibiting irrelevant actions. The process results in a virtual rewiring of the frontal lobe in a way that actually controls motor actions. Lesions in this region of the brain result in a failure to regulate motor behavior based on verbal commands.[50] Synaptic connections—much like Melzack's neuromatrix—are formed and produce functional patterns that translate into behavioral and cognitive templates. This happens not through the specialized and separate role of distinct brain centers but through the relationship among centers, established by means of the connections of higher functions. In the words of Luria: "The chief distinguishing feature of the regulation of human conscious activity is that this regulation takes place with close participation of speech . . . higher mental processes are formed and take place on the basis of speech activity."[51] In other words, culture has as much of an effect on brain function as brain function has on culture. According to another eminent Russian neurologist, Lev Vygotsky, culture fashions psychological tools, which are internalized by the developing individual in the form of higher brain functions that ultimately integrate the body-schema.[52] The consciousness of a unitary self, in sum, owes itself to a combination of cultural and biological processes.

In fact, the "self" is grounded in a complex hierarchy of organizations that can be described from different perspectives as either organic or psychic. From the biological point of view, the human organism consists of numerous systems and subsystems of cellular organization. At the most basic level are single cells, then individual organs, and moving up the scale there are complex functional systems such as the circulatory system, the reproductive system, the immune system, the nervous system, and so forth. In calling a unit a "system" we are making several assumptions. For instance, the separation into systems is functional rather than anatomical. The same organs can be "shared" by more than one system. This organizational principle implies at least three critical features: communication within the system, the notion of telos or systemic goal, and isomorphism between different levels of subsystems.

Communication and Telos

Communication between elements in the system is critical for its survival and success, which is its ultimate goal (telos). David Bakan gives a clear example of the biological development of form in the case of the cellular slime mold.[53] The process begins with a single cell that multiplies into numerous identical cells. These move around without a fixed location until some join to become a disk while others develop into a stalk, others form a body at the top, and so forth. The special form each cell takes is not predetermined but emerges from its location, and this is communicated to other cells, which then become specialized in other ways. But "location" in what? The biochemical signals of specific cells assume an end toward which the entire ensemble—the finished organism—progresses. This is the telos of the overall system, an overarching purpose that requires some form of communication, even if no intentionality is present.

Consider in contrast the following system. A kindergarten teacher instructs her group to run up a hill, and she specifies one condition: The children must maintain a straight line at all times. As the children run up the slope, their behavior can be simple or complex, depending on circumstances. Any time one stumbles, the rest must stop or slow down; as the steepness and contour of the terrain change, parts of the line must accelerate while others slow down. The telos of this group is defined by the simple order to keep a straight line. This goal organizes the children's behavior intentionally but mechanically, and it results in specialized though predictable behavior. The behavior is then adjusted through visual inspection and auditory instructions, both conscious forms of communication. Individual units within this system act rather mindlessly, but the whole ensemble displays a certain kind of intelligence toward its task. In elementary biological systems, such as cellular slime mold, the goal (telos) is mechanistic or chemical; there is no consciousness or sense of purpose, only a systemic pursuit of homeostasis or balance. A major exception is the open or chaotic system such as regional climate, which acts according to indeterminate ends.

Isomorphism

Subsystems within a larger organization can also possess the characteristic of isomorphism: Each subsystem structurally or formally resembles the others in important ways. At its most basic level isomorphism means, for Gestalt theorists, that the organization of perception in space corresponds to the organization in time.[54] For instance, sequential knocks on a door will be heard as patterns—they will be organized into temporal groups. This organization corresponds to the way random dots on the ceiling will be organized visually into some pattern. In turn, the spatiotemporal organization of perception corresponds isomorphically to the way the nervous system receives and transmits data. The world we experience consists of patterns that are established by such perceptual correspondences. I gave examples of isomorphism in the second chapter—for instance, in the similarity between the form of notes on a musical score and the music's emotional effects. But this is only similarity, a weak type of isomorphic relationship.[55] Since I am going to show that pain is a signal among biological subsystems within the human organism, it is important to keep in mind that the isomorphic relationship that holds between them is stronger than similarity.

At a more radical level the variety of subsystems within a larger organism are isomorphic in being subject to mathematical rules by which the physics of the entire system can be described. For example, a measurement of the rhythm of leg movements among the animals cruising the Serengeti in Kenya will reveal that their timing obeys subtle but discernible biomechanical laws in relationship to the weight of the animal, its bone structure, length of limbs—all subject to gravitational forces.[56] Measure the pace and bounce of an urban stroller and the same laws still apply. Such measurements seek to describe systems and subsystems, including ecological conditions, weather, and down to limb size and joint plasticity, and assume that isomorphic equivalencies apply. In both cases the physics and mathematics of broad, open-ended systems account for the observed behavior of apparently unrelated systems such as strolling New Yorkers and African elephants. This is the thesis of synergetics, which is the scientific theory that supplanted cybernetics or closed-systems theory.[57]

These theories are important in the way they allow us to understand the structure of self, or agency, as a systemic principle of biopsychological characteristics, without recourse to a Cartesian mind that is engaged in Freudian perversities such as masochism. Such an understanding must be consistent with the neurological basis of the body-image, as well as its phenomenal aspect as described by Heinz Kohut, Jacques Lacan, R. D. Laing, and others.[58] There are a number of alternative models linking the phenomenal self with its biological underpinning, but James J. Gibson's ecological psychology is among the most persuasive. Gibson argues that the conscious self can sometimes be described as part of a biomechanical system. Patterned intelligent behavior does not necessarily require symbolic cognition, let alone an a priori agent. For instance, how does a driver know exactly when to start braking the car when approaching an obstacle, and exactly how much pressure to apply to the pedal? Cognitive psychology, and perhaps common sense, suggest that this decision is based on learning complex computations of an increasingly abstract nature, performed by the mind of a rational (and sober) adult agent. But Gibson and his followers note that birds slow down just as efficiently when they swoop on their prey, and for that matter, so does the common house fly as it reaches the wall. Gibson argues that the "optical flow field"—the subject's moving field of vision—expands or shrinks at the rate of the object's movement forward or back. He posits a simple parameter that has evolved biologically and indicates time to contact. There are no complex mental calculations, only structured energy distribution within a dynamic system, a system that applies to a fighter pilot as well as to a falcon.[59]

Of course, all mental operations are not as simple as stopping a car or slowing down motion. Certainly language use is far more complex. But the fact that intelligent behavior does not require a Cartesian mind indicates that computation and other mental processes are subject in principle to a scientific analysis that discards the "little man in the head" theory. The isomorphism that Gestalt psychology identifies between levels of organization is based on the fact that subsystems obey fundamental principles of physics. Antimetaphysical theories may seem overly behavioristic or materialistic to some readers, but they have been very successful at describing and predicting patterns in perceptions and even behavior. Patricia Churchland regards such theories as the proper goal of all psychological reduction. I believe that material and cybernetic theory is appropriate for understanding voluntary pain. The work that pain accomplishes begins at such basic levels of embodied experience. The "higher" cultural-symbolic aspects must await discussion until the more basic principles become clear.

Ego and System Control

The telos (goal) of a system is defined by its survival needs, but is not identical with the existence or well-being of individual subsidiary elements. Telos is a function of higher systemic principles and entails that the lesser systems subserve themselves to the higher end. David Bakan calls this function "telic centralization" and it registers at the human level as health.[60] The breakdown of the overall system's goal, which is not necessarily an attack from the outside but can be an internal reaction to perceived external threat, is "telic decentralization," or disease.

For humans, the overarching body-mind telos is the ego. Of course, the folk-psychological conception of the self is psychic—it insists that the self is separate from, but located "within," the body. But neuropsychologists, Gestalt theorists, and philosophers of mind argue that the self is an emergent property of several organic systems and is not in fact separate from the body. And although Freud focused predominantly on depth structures and processes, his view of the ego was not that far off, at least from a structural point of view, from the phenomenological-embodied view. Here he sounds much like William James: "The ego is first and foremost a body-ego; it is not merely a surface entity, but is itself the projection of a surface."[61] In 1923 Freud hinted at a systemic understanding of ego: "We have formed the idea that in each individual there is a coherent organization of mental process; and we call this his ego."[62] Decades later, after Walter Cannon's theory of homeostasis and control systems became better known, followers of Freud such as Hartmann characterized ego in more elaborate systemic terms. This is an ego that derives from bodily sensation and perception, and acts as an organization of basic perceptions.[63] Such a neo-Freudian ego transcends the metaphysical agent—as the self did for Jung, for instance. In fact, the ego can be imagined as more of a steering mechanism than the proverbial "little man in the head." It is the ego's coordination of several complex functions that allows the human organism to survive in ambiguous natural and social contexts. These functions of the ego include motility, perception, intentionality, reality testing, anticipation, judgment, and synthesis.[64]

It is possible to conceive of the ego as an overarching organization, a broad system that subsumes or encompasses the other (organic) systems by experiencing them phenomenally as one's own. Here the concepts of isomorphism and communication become very important because the ego is phenomenologically different from the other subsidiary systems in being conscious and intentional, and yet it must subsume them in effective functional ways. Of course, once an organic system is subsumed to ego it becomes a phenomenal subsystem. The digestive system, an organic functional structure, becomes "my stomach, guts, regularity, tummy ache" and so forth. These refer to the body-image, a body in the mind, which is distorted according to the principles discussed in neuropsychology textbooks under the heading of "homunculus"—the little man in the head (Penfield's neurological map).

But by incorporating the functions of the organic body into its phenomenal-systemic organization the ego does not take absolute command. It is important to note that ego does not *control* motility, perception, synthesis, and the rest. Ego is only the systemic organization of these functions following biological principles; there is no proper causality in this relationship of ego and basic function. For example, ego's systemic tendency to simplify tasks in daily functions does not necessarily involve a conscious "executive" decision to do so. Try an experiment on a friend: Place two objects in front of your friend and have him or her reach for the two objects with both hands, one object farther from the right than the other is from the left. Despite the fact that one is closer, the two objects will be picked up simultaneously (as long as the subject is unaware of the purpose of the experiment). Voluntary action, such as moving your hand to turn on a radio, is constrained by physics; not just the mechanics of the arm and hand, which are closed systems with predictable features, but even the physics and mathematics of open-ended ("chaotic") systems that regulate the timing and rhythms of the act, the transition from one phase to the next, and other elements of the action. What we commonly take to be mind (intention to act in a specific way) and body (governed by Newtonian mechanics) turns out to be a far more complex and subtle naturalistic picture. Most of the operations we perform throughout the day take place without the regulation of intentionality.[65]

Because the systems that ego incorporates are biological, communication (feedback) to the ego is critical for the existence of a unitary telos—the person. But while cellular communication is a nonconscious biochemical reaction, the ego requires signals that register in a conscious though immediately effective way. This is precisely what pain does. It signals the ego in an intrinsically conscious manner of a threat to one of the subsystems or to the telos of the organism as a whole. Pain is a signal to the ego in its capacity as a conscious steering mechanism of the overall system. That is why pain is conscious by definition: If you are not aware of pain then you have no pain. This too is why pain hurts rather than registering as a sound or a flashing light. The hurt causes the ego to register the signal as an urgent messsage from one's own body to act in a specific way—flee or rest. According to evolutionary biology this quality of pain is due to the organism's capacity for representing scenes and generating sensory images that would allow it to make correct choices. Plants—both those that are eaten and those that "eat" (Venus's-flytrap)—do not register pain because they lack mobility and hence the need to make decisions involving their environment.

Pain and the Purpose of System

Experience suggests that what pain signals is tissue damage or some similar organic harm. However, this may only be a necessary condition—itself a debatable point. It is definitely not sufficient.[66] Recall the two football players in the end zone. Assuming they suffered a similar bruise, why should one register pain while the other does not? Clearly there is more here than just tissue damage. The same applies to the soldier versus the car accident victim, phantom-limb pain sufferers, or for that matter even self-mutilators as opposed to victims of torture. Pain is not a simple signal of tissue damage; it is rather a signal to the ego of the breakdown of a system's goal or telos. In Bakan's words: "Pain is the psychic manifestation of telic decentralization."[67] Again, pain signals to the conscious steering mechanism (ego) of the whole organism that the functional purpose of a subsystem is jeopardized. Or perhaps it indicates that the overall function of the entire system is threatened, perhaps by death. Pain relates to system function (telos), not directly to tissue. Pain, in other words, is the message, not the medium.

There are compelling evolutionary reasons for this ambiguity of pain. The capacity for perceiving pain (and pleasure) relates to evolutionary choices involving reproduction, response to danger, predation, and so forth. Overregistering either pleasure or pain would result in the failure to function on any level. For example, temporary painlessness can be essential for surviving predatory attacks. A buffalo attacked by wolves and bitten at her flanks can go for hours before the pain sets in, as long as mobility and calculation are necessary to get her out of danger. An immediate and overwhelming sensation of pain, like its total absence, would render the entire species vulnerable to quick extinction.[68] The overregistering of one's own body tissue as alien entity by the autoimmune system produces the pain of rheumatoid arthritis due to a biological-adaptive failure. In contrast, the loss of feathers, shedding of skin, hardening of tissues, the loss of excess brain cells, the loss of the tadpole's tail as the larva becomes an adult frog, and other cyclical phenomena serve purposes that represent necessary and painless "loss." Pain, then, is a signal of systemic breakdown rather than the loss or damage of organic parts.

The same principle applies to systems that include both organic and "mental" elements. It is well known that Freud reduces the human psyche to biological causes such as instincts and drives, with even ego regarded as a biological steering mechanism. Such a biological reduction makes it possible to extend the neurobiological facts of pain-free loss to psychological processes such as differentiation and integration (evolutionary adaptive concepts), object formation, narcissism, and repression. According to the Freudian analyst Margaret Mahler, the increasing organization of the child's ego, the process of separation and individuation, requires a relinquishment of symbiotic identification with the parent. This entails acts of psychic renunciation and the overcoming of necessary frustration and even pain—most characteristically hunger.[69] The point is not that psychological processes should or should not entail physical pain (although they do), but that the function of pain in psychological integration or disintegration corresponds (isomorphically) to its function in organic processes. We have also seen that from a phenomenal point of view there is no absolute distinction between organic-mechanistic systems and the psychic-intentional system of the ego. The isomorphism discussed by Gestalt assumes that there are structural correspondences between organic and psychic systems. This means that the "body's" organic systems under specific conditions can be supervised by the ego's control function. Or, in other words, ego as an organization principle can be made to extend from the intentional to the organic and back. That pain, a conscious fact, is an essential signal to ego demonstrates that the overarching system—the one that encompasses "body and mind"—is in fact a phenomenal system. Systemic information is a phenomenal signal—pain. To ego, the body is part of the phenomenal "I" feeling. Consequently, what I have noted in regard to organic systems applies to the psychic as well: A subsystem or individual organ can be "sacrificed" for the telos of the overall system (the person or ego) and relatively less pain will register, or pain will be experienced as beneficial.

Self and Sacrifice

The soldier in battle suffers extreme states of stress and a constant awareness of his imminent death. (The first is a neurological condition, the second cognitive-emotional.) The loss of a hand represents the sacrifice of one organ for the sake of the entire organism—removing the soldier from the battlefield. For a while, his injury will be almost welcomed, his pain far less than that of the car accident victim. But the sacrifice is not an intellectual process, a matter of deciding that the hand can be given up and that the horror of amputation will surely be a lesser evil than death.[70] A hunted animal undergoes the same state of painlessness, despite being bitten deeply, as long as the entire organism is in grave danger. In fact, there are recognized biochemical causes for insensitivity to pain at such times, including inhibiting output signals and the production of natural opioids. In the case of the soldier—we know too little about animal minds—the systemic information has two interrelated aspects: conscious, intentional relief accompanied by a surprising body-state of relative painlessness.

The girls who slice their thighs with razor blades experience a similar process due to the intentional nature of their self-hurt. Anyone who is cut accidentally, even a nick on the chin while shaving with a razor, winces in pain. That is the usual reaction in which pain temporarily dominates consciousness. In contrast, the girls are carrying out a sacrifice of sorts. The cutting of skin and the spilling of blood are performed intentionally for the sake of a higher telos or goal. Self-directed violence asserts the dominion of their ego over lesser bodily subsystems. It does so by manipulating conscious signals—hurt—through the information circuits of the body-self. Consequently, these become acts of autonomy and even empowerment—in the very words of many self-mutilators. And surprisingly, while ego inflicts pain on the body-image, the hurt registers in a different manner from the pain of an accidental nick with a razor blade, not to mention being cut by a torturer.

Sacrifice is not simply the destruction of a body part or system, just as pain is not simply a signal of tissue damage. Phenomenally speaking, something more significant becomes incorporated at the very same time that the loss takes place. Sacrifice is the act of subserving a lower telos in favor of a higher one, a way of establishing a hierarchy of phenomenal embodiment. It is a principle of organizational supercession and encompassment. The removal of one's diseased tonsil or a cancerous organ is a way of eliminating disease, of altering one's body, in favor of a more highly valued body—the healthy body. The soreness inflicted on the muscles at the beginning of a training regimen does this as well. Or, to give a more unusual example: Amputees who use prosthetic limbs often report that they have to hit their stumps in the morning before putting on the prosthesis. They do this in order to "wake up"—or bring under the control of the conscious mind—the silent or missing organ, so that it may "slip into" and "operate" the prosthesis.

A lesser system within the body-image is subdued or brought under control by an assertive act of ego, while a higher system becomes claimed by ego. Sacrifice does not always imply intention, certainly not at the lower levels, such as an individual cell sacrificed for the entire immune system. Moreover, sacrifice is not necessarily painful. It is performed for the integration of the overall system, that is, toward telic-centralization. As a result, the level or quality of pain remains relatively low. Or it may be perceived as "good" pain. But why is it necessary to sacrifice parts of the body, or more precisely the body-image, in order to assert a higher purpose, and why must it be a violent act? Clearly, simple body-modification is not enough, and one does not perform these operations surgically under anesthesia.

I have argued that stress in the form of sensory overload or pain has a powerful effect on the phenomenal body-self. Under extreme conditions the sense of self can actually disappear or become transparent. In other, less traumatic situations, the sense of body-self is merely weakened or changed. It is important to emphasize that pain does not modify beliefs, memories, and cognitive functions in a direct way. What it affects dramatically and immediately is the subject of these experiences: the phenomenal self, which includes perception of basic orientation within one's body, even the sense of agency that controls the body. Changing the perception of this agency will obviously affect beliefs, attitudes, emotions, and the rest—but this is an indirect result and is not the topic under discussion here. The saint and the girls who cut their own skin have discovered something more basic and visceral than new beliefs about their identity and their power. The changes they undergo depend on the twofold process I have described:

1. Pain changes the perception of one's body-self.
2. The sacrifice of a lesser system-goal reinforces the goal of a higher system; this higher goal may range from identity with an abusive father-image to identity with a god or savior for religious self-tormentors.

Both of these dynamics result in a new ego organization, which is experienced as either empowerment or identification with a higher Being.

The careful reader may assent to the first of these two propositions, but wonder about the second. True, pain weakens the old body-self, and sacrifice makes pain tolerable—even good. But how does a new telos, a higher purpose or "Self," emerge out of this? Clearly the argument is still missing an important step, and it may be the most elusive in the chain of exposition. Up to now the argument has been grounded in neuropsychological principles, which rest on relatively firm ground. This is how we discovered that stress makes the body-self transparent. The argument has also been rigorously phenomenological: The body-self has been defined as a perceptual schema, an organization. Its relation to the organism with its many subsystems has also been phenomenological, based on system theory. But the basic questions of sacred pain remain. Toward what goal do saints change their ego by means of austerities? What is the systemic connection between a theological goal and a psychological mechanism?

The metaphysically inclined interpreter will argue that such activities unmake the human self in order to connect with a higher level of Being, a transcendental Reality.[71] This is the fallacy Carl Jung committed decades ago and the reason I have tried to keep the discussion at a phenomenological level. The importance of this limitation cannot be overstated; it reverses the fundamental tautology of Mircea Eliade and the history of religions in general, which was discussed in Chapter 2. If my purpose is to stay clear of metaphysics and explain, rather than paraphrase, how pain and sacrifice help create a higher telos (conceived in theological terms but achieved psychologically), I must look at the role of pain in the formation of identity. "Higher ends," to a great extent, are symbolic entities. How do they integrate into the emerging sense of empowered Self? The task is to show how the symbolism of the new telos emerges out of the instruments and sensations of pain that bring it about.

Pain Symbols and the New Self

The problem is not as difficult as it seems once we abandon Cartesian dualism and keep an eye out for Freud's occasional lapse into it. Self-torture is not a dualistic theater in which self or ego hurts the "other"—that is, the body. Moreover, the act of hurting is not the extension of the ego's domain over the body, properly speaking. Instead, the self as a phenomenal organization of perceptions, motivations, commands, and actions emerges out of the violence and out of the hurtful feedback it generates. In Kohut's terms, the pain nurtures the girl or the mystic because it enriches an impoverished self. Still, both the tools and the goals of the violent act are loaded with symbolic meanings, and it is not obvious how these are integrated as phenomenal information into the emerging self. This is especially true when self-destructive behavior seems so inconsistent with the goal of the self's empowerment. This final section will consider some of the psychological difficulties in appraising the phenomenal significance of symbolic actions and tools.

Objects with symbolic value are critical elements in the formation of identity. All developmental theories agree on this in principle, though profound functional and ontological differences separate, for instance, Sigmund Freud, Melanie Klein, Jacques Lacan, Heinz Kohut, or Donald Winnicott. The classical psychoanalyst would explain the symbols of the tools and the body in terms of various psychic-adaptive transformations such as defense mechanisms. A theorist who follows Lacan's version of psychoanalysis would refuse to limit the symbols to fixed biological or psychic values, and might also look for more flexible semiotic meanings based on linguistic principles. The nail corset and the razor would not just be objects associated with sexual feelings toward a parent, but would also take their meaning from a broader range of cultural values (economic, political). In other words, while drive theory tips its hat to a biological a priori, various forms of self psychology give a stronger role to culture. It is important to emphasize that phenomenology makes no judgment about the origin of the symbols and tools themselves, whether a cross, a razor blade, or a Porsche a person buys to affirm his sense of worth. Instead, the focus remains on the integrative mechanisms by means of which any symbol and symbolic object becomes experienced as an aspect of one's own identity. Here depth psychology is not as useful as the study of surface structures. And phenomenology, which consists of information and feedback loops, is far more consistent with neurological research than either depth psychology or cultural construction theory.

A mystic such as Maria Maddalena or a girl like Jill transforms her sense of self in a variety of ways that include hurting the body with meaningful objects. The objects used tend to be carefully chosen by the subject. They may include a nail corset and razor blades as pain tools; but also parts of the body are selected for hurting—the torso perhaps, or the upper thigh. The language contained in these objects—the symbolism—will be read by the analyst according to his own theoretical orientation. Leon Wurmser outlines and defines several defense mechanisms (operating against anxiety to ego) that include repression, denial, reversal, projection, and externalization.[72] He states: "When a drive arises that could present dangers—either in one's relationship to the outer world, or to one's conscience, or to one's need for integration and meaningful cohesion—this drive needs to be stopped, searched, and released only when its dangerous aspects have been removed."[73] A variety of mechanisms, including those listed above, are brought into play, usually nonconsciously, to displace or even reverse the drive. Melanie Klein regarded masochism as a defense mechanism that employs reversal and identification. The instruments of aggression against the subject become tools of desire, and ego identifies with the master of these tools—say, an abusive father. The symbolism of the razor blade and the nail corset is unlocked in such depth structures—the drives and the ego defense mechanisms. The grammar (reversal, projection, and the rest) is indirect and hidden rather than phenomenal.

A more phenomenological reading of the symbols of self-hurt would have to take into account the conscious awareness of the subject and her relationship to the objects of her desire and fear. Object Relations theories argue that the issues of the self-hurter must be examined in light of the failure of her parents (idealized self-objects) to properly respond to and nurture her infantile self. As a result of this failure, the parental image breaks up into fragments, which are sexualized. (Kohut does not deny the primacy of the drives). Meanwhile, the nuclear self is depleted, so the breakup of the parental image is followed by a "sexualized merger with the rejecting (punishing, demeaning, belittling) features of the omnipotent parental imago."[74] The razor and the nail corset are directly related to an aspect of the fractured parental image, as extension of the parental self-object, though in a highly distorted manner. The father who performs his masculine but domestic ritual of shaving or the mother who puts on her feminine underwear are no longer persons but are condensed into the fetishlike objects with which they are associated. The application of the emblematic object to one's body—however painful—is gratifying because it substitutes the feedback lacking from the parent. The application is then experienced as merging with that aspect of the parent (the father's masculine love, the mother's femininity) who witheld appropriate (ego nurturing) feedback. This meaning of the symbol would thus be consistent with its experiential quality of being empowering and gratifying, despite causing some pain.[75] The relation to the hurting object is based on the illusion that it substitutes for the primary object (parent-nurturer), but the certainty of the illusion is not delusional or pathological. It is based on the same principles that Donald Winnicott identified for transitional objects in the normal process of separation and individuation in child development.[76] What is unusual about mystics and self-abusers is the age at which such illusions are generated and the violent means.

The key element here is feedback—the information that is processed between the self and the self-objects. Feedback, in fact, is the major phenomenological feature shared by all schools of Object Relations, starting with Melanie Klein, through Donald Winnicott and more current theorists.[77] The essential fact of human psychology is not the a priori primacy of drives, but relationships. The individual subject is a nexus of relationships, of internalized others and projected I, of a body experienced as self and one's self experienced as an object. The field is clearly too rich to discuss here, but it seems that Object Relations psychology is both clinically and conceptually consistent with modern sociological thought (Emile Durkheim, Peter Berger, Pierre Bourdieu), philosophy (Thomas Nagel, Daniel Dennett), and ancient Hindu and Buddhist psychologies. The clinical assumptions imply that the patient is altered through the information exchange, the discourse that takes place, with the analyst.[78]

The feedback "circuits" by means of which the infant's sense of self evolves are sensory and include input as well as output. Sensory feedback continues throughout life to generate the shifting images of the self in a variety of ways. Even well-adjusted adults experience themselves as altered by a new purchase—say, a car or a home. The object becomes a self-object, an extension of one's identity. Depth and self psychologists may agree that such object-dependence can be due to unhealthy compensation for a lack of primary nurturing by parents. But the phenomenologist and the Object Relations theorist would look at the nature of the relationship for a different type of symbolic grammar, which is not related necessarily to drives (sex and aggression), conflict, or other depth structures and mechanisms. The grammar of the object's relation with the self would be closer to its surface meaning, at the level of awareness. The narrative of the subject is profoundly valuable because the meaning of the event takes place at the level of the altered identity, not at the level of a deep and disguised metaphysical (or biological, which is the same thing) entity.

Saying that we identify with objects may seem either metaphorical or trivial. But V. S. Ramachandran demonstrates the manner in which sensory feedback (vision, touch) can generate profound alterations of body-image relative to other objects. In one experiment the subject places his right hand under a table and a plastic hand is located above, just next to the subject's left hand. An assistant taps the plastic hand, while also tapping in synchronization on the real hand under the table. Within minutes a phenomenal sense emerges in the subject that the plastic hand on the table belongs to his own body. A hammer blow on the plastic hand produces psychic pain, measured electrochemically. The hand, Ramachandran concludes, "had now become coupled to the student's limbic system."[79]

The symbols of self-hurt owe their meaning to the relational objects from which they come. The razor blade is associated with the father; it is an aspect of the father-object. The corset may be connected with a mother. The cross Henry Suso pounded into his own back was, of course, a Christian object. None of this is the primary phenomenological fact. Instead, the symbols become self-objects proper, real experiential "illusions" that belong to the phenomenal self through their application to the body and by means of the sensations they generate. The same holds true for the body itself. The upper thigh is first an organic location, as is the torso. Second, it is a social body, that is, a place loaded with values acknowledged by the subject. The upper thigh is almost sexual; it is hidden, it is a place vulnerable to weight gain. Finally, the body is the experiential body, the body-image. This is a neurological and perceptual system, as outlined earlier in the chapter.

The information that travels in the phenomenal circuits of the self-hurter crosses the thresholds between these levels. It is cognitive, emotional, and nociceptive, all at different times and in different manners. This is as true for the man who puts on a prosthetic leg as it is for Jill or Maria. The self-hurter, however, generates self-objects and object relations by means of pain, a unique sensation. This means that the objects that are used for hurting oneself, resonate not only because their symbolism (e.g., association with the abusive father) is powerful. Their resonance increases because the sensation of pain weakens the preexisting self-image due to the neurological principles that have been explained in Chapter 2. The newly emergent self thus lacks the "as if" quality of less effective integrating feedback information, such as the visual effect of a new car, or even the pleasures of a new relationship. The phenomenological power of pain signals (weakening the old self) makes the transformation of the self-hurter far more effective than any defense or other depth mechanism ever could. The power is at the surface.

FIVE

Ghost Trauma: Changing Identity through Pain

An extraordinary thing happened to Maria Maddalena de Pazzi when she scourged her body in order to bring God into her life and into her very person. She became intimately acquainted—possessed in fact—with a demon, who threw her down the steps, slammed her against the floor, and caused more bruises and pain than she herself could inflict in pursuit of God. Maddalena remained unaware of bringing these pains on herself, and she felt that some other agency was brutalizing her. It was her confessor and biographer who described these events as possession by demons: "For sometimes the Devil struck her over the head, sometimes he cast her down precipitously, so that her face was swollen."[1] One cannot be sure whether Maddalena's prolific self-mortification brought about the episodes her biographer describes as possession. Painful trauma is undoubtedly linked to phenomena like possession, but the relation needs to be clarified. This chapter will build on the previous discussion of Object Relations theory and body-self changes to examine the way in which painful trauma contributes to changes in identity, and how such changes figure in religious life.

In her convulsive and involuntary tortures at the hands of an alien presence acting from within her body, Maddalena resembles a large number of men and women around the world, even today, who succumb to invading psychic forces. These are depicted by the cultures in which they take place in a variety of ways, as demons, ghosts, spirits of deceased relatives, or spirits that inhabit trees, ponds, and other locations, as psychic derailment by the evil-eye, spells, curses, and so forth. Possession is so common that even the *DSM-III-R* (*Diagnostic and Statistical Manual of Mental Disorders*, 3rd ed. rev.)—the primary psychological diagnostic tool until recently—recognizes it as a traditional idiom for some types of mental affliction.[2] In India, where I witnessed several cases of possession and exorcism, ghosts are implicated in numerous psychosomatic conditions. The following description from Sudhir Kakar is not unusual.

Asha and Her Spirits

Asha was a twenty-six-year-old woman from a lower-middle-class family in Delhi who had come to Balaji accompanied by her mother and her uncle. A thin, attractive woman with sharply chiseled features and a dusky complexion, Asha had a slight, girlish figure that made her look younger than her age. She had suffered from periodic headaches ever since she could remember, though her acute distress began two and a half years ago when a number of baffling symptoms made their first appearance. Among these were violent stomach-aches that would convulse her with pain and leave her weak and drained of energy. Periodically, she had the sensation of ants crawling over her body, a sensation that would gradually concentrate on her head and produce such discomfort that she could not bear even to touch her head. There were bouts of gluttony and fits of rage in which she would break objects and physically lash out at anyone who happened to be near her. "Once I even slapped my father during such a rage," Asha told us. "Can you imagine a daughter hitting her father, especially a father who I have loved more than anyone else in this world?"

Treatment with drugs (her uncle was a medical doctor) and consultations with an exorcist did not make any appreciable difference to her condition, but what really moved Asha to come to Balaji was her discovery, six months after her father's death, that her skin had suddenly turned dark. This caused intense mental anguish, since she had always prided herself on her fair complexion. Asha now felt that she had become very unattractive and toyed with the idea of suicide.

After coming to Balaji, Asha's peshi [the hearing of the ghost] was immediate. She had barely finished eating the two laddoos in Balaji's "court" when she fell down on the floor and revealed that she was possessed by two spirits. The first spirit, who caused the stomach aches, stated that it was sent by Asha's brother's wife. Its name was Masan, it said, a ghost that inhabits cemeteries and cremation grounds and whose "specialty" is the eating of unborn babies in the womb. The second spirit admitted its responsibility for the sensation of crawling ants and for Asha's rages, and further revealed that it had been sent by the elder brother of Asha's fiancée.[3]

Asha did not seek out the violent stomachaches and headaches that plagued her and hinted at her psychological condition. In contrast, Maria Maddalena was a connoisseur of pain and her problem with the invading demons was not the pain they caused as much as the spiritual indecency of their presence. By inhabiting her body they left no space for the spirit of God, whom the mystic was attempting to inject into the center of her being. If the *DSM-III* describes possession as a culturally defined belief connected with certain dissociative conditions, such as Multiple Personality Disorder (Dissociative Identity Disorder in the *DSM-IV*), is it possible that the mystic-saint who seeks unity with God in fact causes trauma to herself in order to induce dissociative states (trance, out-of-body experiences, fugues, ecstatic faints)? In turn, is the infusion with divine spirit just another case of possession? After all, shamans around the world, oracles in traditional cultures including ancient Greece, the Zars in Ethiopia, Vodun practitioners in Haiti, *bhaktas* (ecstatic devotees) in India, and many others literally possess themselves with divine energy by the application of hypnotic and dissociating procedures.[4] And if so, why not argue that the self-torture of religious specialists is a mechanism for producing dissociative states—like self-hypnosis—in order to bring about psychodynamic benefits, or even complete change of identity? Clearly, in order to avoid the reduction of religion to pathology it is necessary to develop a descriptive language that can capture the phenomenology of hosting an "alien" self in one's own body. Only such a language may effectively distinguish between "pathological" possession and union with a god, and separate spiritual growth from severe personality disorders.

Maddalena's possession and the other cases described in ethnographic and historic literature are too complex and ambiguous to reduce either to the clinical concept of "personality disorder" or to purely religious experience. Questions of overlap between religion and psychology persist and ought to be sorted out. A strong relationship undoubtedly holds between culturally defined conditions like "spiritual union" with the divine, or spirit possession, and psychological events related to ego defense mechanisms such as Multiple Personality Disorder or Dissociative Identity Disorder. But in either case, trauma and pain can bring about profound changes in personality, sense of identity, and the integrity of the self. This chapter will confirm William James' observation that the self is an "attitude" that can change dramatically under the appropriate conditions, either in the direction of disintegration (Bakan's telic decentrialization) or integration (telic centralization). In the religious literature this may manifest as spirit possession at one extreme, conversion and spiritual rebirth at the other.

Problems of Method

The previous chapter explored several key features in the psychology of religiously sanctioned pain. It defined the ego as an organizational principle, a systemic regulator of several psychological functions. Self-sacrificing pain—hurting subsidiary subsystems—was a way of strengthening ego, or fortifying the central goals of the system (person in context) as a whole. The chapter concluded by showing that the objects used to inflict such pain on oneself—a knife, razor blade, or a corset studded with nails—are not incidental tools. They are symbolically pregnant and become objects with which the self-hurter enters into an emotionally powerful and intimate relationship. This object-relationship is made possible, to a very large extent, by the feedback operation of the pain that the knife and other objects generate. The searing, but always desired, pain weakens the subject's body-self. Self-hurt wipes out the agent's sense of engaging in role playing when she feels herself one with the wielder of the knife, an abusive father perhaps, or even with Jesus on the cross. The "as if" quality of these roles disappears along with the vanishing body-self, thanks to the pain of symbolic objects.

But not only physical objects (knife, corset, cross) can act as the fulcrums of psychological and cultural signification. Emotions do as well, along with personality, beliefs, and cultural values. Or, to be more precise, no mystic-saint, and no teenage self-mutilator, enters a violent relationship with any object in the absence of powerful emotions and ideas. To the neurodynamics and the ego-dynamics of the earlier chapters we must now add an increasingly social and cultural analysis. The use of pain to produce specific states of consciousness and to give birth to a new self now points to culturally defined psychological and religious phenomena where individual and culture meet. At the most basic level these phenomena include spirit possession, exorcism, and dissociative psychological events.

Possession

> And they sailed to the country of the Gerasens, which is over against Galilee. And when he was come forth to the land, there met him a certain man who had a devil now a very long time, and he wore no clothes, neither did he abide in a house, but in the sepulchres. And when he saw Jesus, he fell down before him; and crying out with a loud voice, he said: What have I to do with thee, Jesus, Son of the most high God? I beseech thee, do not torment me. For he commanded the unclean spirit to go out of the man, For many times it seized him, and he was bound with chains, and kept in fetters; and breaking the bonds, he was driven by the devil into the deserts. And Jesus asked him, saying: What is thy name? But he said: Legion: because many devils were entered into him. And they besought him that he would not command them to go into the abyss. And there was there a herd of many swine feeding on the

> mountains; and they besought him that he would suffer them to enter into them, And he suffered them. The devils therefore went out of the man, and entered into the swine; and the herd ran violently down a steep place into the lake, and were stifled.[5]

The phenomenon of possession ranks among the most pervasive in the religions of the world, ranging from the battles waged by Jesus, to the oracular ecstasies in Delphi and the Dionyisian bacchanalia of ancient Greece, and all the way to the Okiyome rituals of contemporary Japan and the charismatic healing of Pentecostals in Central America and in New England. No culture is without some form of possession; one easily thinks of Muslim jinns, of Jewish dybbuks. The biggest story in the Israeli press one week before the election of Ehud Barak in 1999 was the possession of a woman by the spirit of her deceased husband.

Similarly, the secondary literature on possession and exorcism is vast, diverse at its very core, and spills over into ethnographic studies of cultures at its boundaries. The term *possession* usually refers to the cohabitation in one organism of plural agencies (be they spirits, egos, selves), easily blurring the distinction between religion and psychology. Religious literature tends to describe possession as an invasion of an ordinary person's body by a spiritual entity, perhaps a demon. But some scholars, such as Sheila Walker, ignore the experience of dual agency in favor of altered states of consciousness, which are consistent with hypnosis and hypnotically induced behavior.[6] The most comprehensive study of the subject, T. K. Oesterreich's monumental *Possession Demoniacal and Other*, skirts the need to reduce the phenomenon to psychology by stating that the "new" theory posits a duplicity of egos in the organism while the "old" theory called such agencies spirits.[7] The experience itself of an alien agency in one's own body is the same.

It may be relatively easy to agree on basic criteria for defining possession, but a thorough reading of descriptive and analytical literature on possession quickly confuses the reader. Reports are so diverse, one becomes uncertain whether possession is a single phenomenon. The possessing entity could include a deceased relative; a spirit that normally resides in a tree, a pond, or other objects; the spirit of a living teacher currently in a distant location; an animal; a god. The possessor may be one or, as the case from the New Testament shows, legion. More important, the act of possession sometimes occurs involuntarily, and even accidentally, or it may be intentional and produced through complex ritual manipulations. Possession can take place in an instant, or it may take years to achieve. Some possessions are unique, others seasonal. The possessing force can be hostile and painful, or benign, and even highly desirable. On some occasions possession is a problem—

an illness—and at other times possession is the healing procedure. In many instances the possessed individual loses sense of her own identity and becomes entirely consumed by the invading presence, but at other times both agents govern simultaneously. Possession may either be a complete transformation, a temporary loss of identity, or mere play-acting. The strong cases can result in unusual and visible distortions of the physical person; the weak rarely do. While some possessions are associated with violence and pain, others are not.[8] Similarly, some possessed individuals exhibit analgesic trance while others are highly susceptible to pain. There are recorded cases of mass possessions, but most are individual.

Two sets of features will be distinguished in the maze of facts: strong and weak identification of ego with possessing spirit, and voluntary and involuntary possessions. The strong-weak distinction extends from a complete failure to separate one's consciousness from that of the invading entity (whether it is single or multiple, good or bad, divine or demonic) to a relatively casual playing of the role of the possessed—common among healers and shamans. The strong case usually involves a victim who is unaware of even being possessed. Below are two cases: a strong one followed by a weak.

Strong Identification

> Suddenly, one morning, after two days of apparent death, Achille [Pierre Janet's pseudonymous patient] arose, sat up with both eyes wide open, and broke into a frightful laugh. It was a convulsive laugh which shook his whole body, a laugh of unnatural violence which twisted his mouth, a lugubrious laugh which lasted for more than two hours and was truly satanic.
>
> From that moment everything was changed. Achille leapt out of bed and refused all attention. To every question he replied: "Do nothing, it is useless, let us drink champagne, it is the end of the world." Then he uttered horrible cries, "They are burning me, they are cutting me to pieces." These cries and wild movements lasted until the evening, then the unhappy man fell into a troubled sleep. . . . The devil was within him and forced him to utter horrible blasphemies. In fact Achille's mouth, for he declared that he had nothing to do with it, abused God and the saints and repeated a confused mass of the most filthy insults to religion. Yet graver and more cruel was the fact that the demon twisted his legs and arms and caused him the most hideous sufferings which wrung horrible cries from the poor wretch.[9]

Weak Identification

In his ethnopsychiatric work in Morocco, Vincent Crapanzano witnessed several cases of possession and exorcism. The most notorious spirit among the Hamadsa, which he studied, is that of Aisha Qandisha, a *jinniya* (demonness) associated with erotic impulses and evil consequences:

> A man is walking along a road, and suddenly his vision blurs. He thinks there is something wrong with his eyes, but in fact it is Lalla Aisha Hasnawiyya [one of Aisha Qandisha's manifestations]. He sees only her in front of him, and he looks on and sees only her. When he comes to an isolated crossing or path, she takes him by the hand. She asks him why he is following her and where he knows her from. The man tries to excuse himself and says that he thought she was a woman he knew. She says, "Fine, Welcome. Come with me."[10]

If a person is "struck" by a spirit he may manifest a variety of bodily symptoms, such as deafness, blindness, mutism, paralysis. If he is possessed he may fall unconscious, or display convulsions or tremors; he may speak in tongues, act like a stranger, or have flight of thoughts.[11] In other words, being struck is a phenomenologically weak case of possession because the sense of self is relatively unchanged. In fact such a "possession" may be a case of theodicy, a way of explaining a sudden onslaught of physical troubles lacking in obvious organic causes. Many other weak cases of possession involve technicians such as shamans and exorcists who voluntarily become possessed by a spirit of a god (or goddess) in order to combat the presence of a strong possession spirit in the shaman's patient.[12]

In the first (strong) case, Achille is unaware of being possessed; the spirit that takes over his body completely dominates his consciousness. Like Linda Blair's character in *The Exorcist* he may lapse back into his own ego, but would then have no recollection of having been someone else. While dominated by the possessing spirit Achille is entirely other. I will shortly discuss the reasons and mechanism for such complete transformations, but it is important to note that these are not always exclusively psychic. Physiological changes may also take place, sometimes including a change of facial features, skin complexion, muscle tone, an increase in strength or flexibility, and extreme cases of analgesia to pain. There are cases on record that include asthmatics and diabetics who are well when possessed and vice versa, whose allergies and other medical conditions change dramatically during episodes of possession.

In contrast, the agent of a "weak" possession, or the healer or shaman who becomes ritually possessed, may sometimes be merely playing the role of the god, goddess, or spirit. The healer can lapse in and out of multiple roles and there is little evidence of deep change in states of consciousness. For instance, the Indian exorcists (*ojhas*) move into such roles at will, though sometimes they work up more intense states of identification with the deity they possess. Similarly, the process of exorcism that Crapanzano describes in Morocco builds up, at the Hadra, to a frenzy of dance and self-mutilation (head slashing) in which the technicians submerge their identity completely within a state of trance.

The distinction among weak and strong cases, based on level of psychic identification with the possessing spirit, is not identical with the distinction between voluntary and involuntary possession. The following two cases demonstrate, the first in India the second in France, that it is possible for ritual specialists to become voluntarily possessed and attain temporary states of complete phenomenological unity with the spirit they embody.

Voluntary Possession

> In the morning a large number of people congregated in the courtyard of the house. Several men were seated in one corner singing javara songs to the accompaniment of cymbals and two large drums. . . . Some of the men then began a kind of dance. They trembled and jerked as they moved around the courtyard. Each dancer held a long slender rod which was shaped into a *trishul* (trident) at one end and was sharpened to a keen point at the other. A lemon was impaled on the sharpened end of each of these rods. The dancing continued to gather fervor. Finally one of the dancers went into a seizure. He froze in one spot and began howling and barking. This was evidence of possession by the goddess.
>
> A goat was then led into the courtyard and over to a man who stood in a corner holding a large knife . . . and the goat was quickly decapitated. . . . One of the dancers then threw himself prone and began licking at the blood slick on the floor. Another produced a whip resembling a cat-o'-nine-tails, which he brandished at the spectators in a threatening fashion. Another dancer appeared with a chain festooned with barbs. This he kneaded in his right hand until blood appeared. These phenomena, again, are indications of possession.[13]

Such ritual performances are common around the world; in South and Southeast Asia alone there are several festivals, holidays, pilgrimages, and other occasions where devotees bring themselves to possess a god or goddess such as Skanda, Murugan, Shitala, Durga, and others.[14] To the ethnographical observer the possession manifests itself in extraordinary displays of bodily gesticulations, indifference to pain, changes in vocal intonations and unusual verbal demonstrations, frothing of the mouth, fainting spells and other symptoms. Witnesses can usually observe the transition from role playing to strong identification by means of such external signals. In contrast, the following case of possession is an insider's view, the view of the Jesuit Jean-Joseph Surin who became involuntarily possessed as a result of dealing with the infamous mass possessions that took place in Loudun in 1633.

Involuntary Possession

Things have gone so far that God has permitted, I think for my sins, what has perhaps never been seen in the Church, that in the exercise of my ministry the devil passes out of the body of the possessed woman and entering into mine assaults and confounds me, agitates and troubles me visibly, possessing me for several hours like a demoniac. I cannot explain to you what happens within me during that time and how this spirit unites with mine without depriving me either of the consciousness or liberty of soul, nevertheless making himself like another me and as if I had two souls, one of which is dispossessed of its body and the use of its organs and stands aside watching the actions of the other which has entered into them. The two spirits fight in one and the same field which is the body, and the soul is as if divided. According to one of its parts it is subject to diabolic impressions and according to the other to those motions which are proper to it or granted by God. At the same time I feel a great peace under God's good pleasure and, without knowing how it arises, an extreme rage and aversion for him, giving rise to violent impulses to cut myself off from him which astonish the beholders.[15]

One readily sees that voluntary possession may be extremely intense while involuntary possession may be relatively mild, gauged at least from the perspective of the participant's ability to recall and describe the episode, which suggests that a sense of his own ego persisted.

The two distinctions I have made obviously do not exhaust the field. Strong and weak, voluntary and involuntary are only distinctions that serve the task of this chapter, which is to analyze the malleability of identity and self, and the ritual means—using pain—to manipulate these. This takes me back to the topic of pain.

Possession and Pain

There is a strong, but poorly understood relationship between cases of possession and painful trauma. Certainly not all cases in the literature on spirit-possession describe pain, whether self-inflicted or as the trauma that triggers the possession. However, this may be due to the lack of interest in pain among the ethnographers of possession—even those who focus on the violence.[16] When an oracle, diviner, healer, or devotee enters ecstatic states by going through "violent gestures and bodily manipulations" does this include pain? Can a mere dance be painful? According to Vincent Crapanzano, the Hamadsa, who dance into a possessed trance, move vigorously on the soles of their feet, jarring the entire spinal column. Similarly, the barefoot dancing of the Sundancers in the hot July desert can be very traumatic. Still, it is not always clear how pain relates to trauma and stress. Are extreme temperatures (heat or cold) examples of pain? There are cases of severe stimulation and stress that are not commonly described as painful but are sufficiently irritating to the organism to produce the neurological effects described in Chapter 2. Loud noise is one example, but so perhaps is overcrowding or, in some contexts, itching, tickling, swaying, shaking, spinning. To make things simple, pain will be taken as an aversive sensation that is sufficiently intense to place a stress on the neurological system.[17]

Pain is implicated in the initiation and progress of possession episodes according to four general theoretical possibilities, each exhibited in some cases, none in all:

1. Pain acts as a distant cause of the possession (anywhere from a past traumatic experience to ideological factors such as the wish to imitate a suffering God).
2. Pain acts as the immediate trigger that brings about the radical shift in consciousness we call possession.
3. Pain, caused by violent behavior, is made manifest in a variety of ways during the possession itself.
4. Pain is used by an exorcist to drive out the possessing spirit.

Any discussion on the importance of pain for the phenomenon of possession must specify which of these four is meant. Weak cases of possession, whether voluntary or involuntary, rarely exhibit any of these four types of pain. Strong cases of pain are far more likely to display painful factors, depending on whether the possession is voluntary or involuntary. Strong voluntary possessions are commonly triggered by painful stimuli such as scourging, cutting, banging or slashing of the head, or violently shaking it from side to side (a form of torture according to Amnesty International). But pain also acts as a more distant cause in these cases if the ritualists are imitating a god or some religious model, or are following a model that defines pain as a desirable end. Many of these strong voluntary possessions maintain a high level of violent or painful behavior during the course of the ritual—for example, the piercing of tongues and insertion of hooks in the back during Javara or Kavadi in Hinduism. However, given the nature of the descriptions at hand it is difficult to say whether these self-mutilative acts are triggers of the possession, whether they are necessary for the maintenance of the possessive trance already attained, or whether they merely accompany the possession.

Strong and involuntary instances of possession share many of these uncertainties. Such cases often exhibit violent or self-abusive behavior, like Anna Maddalena throwing herself on the ground in a similar way to the possessed in Bharatpur, Uttar Pradesh, or Babba Bahadur Sayyid in Banaras. Victims of a spirit or demon who has taken over their consciousness seem to be engaging in battle with that entity, or more precisely, they behave as though they were under an attack against their body.[18] The pain following these assaults is the third type, a pain that accompanies the change of consciousness and perhaps makes possible the continuation of the trance. The causing pain, whether distant or triggering, is often unknown either because the researcher is not present (researchers usually spend most of their time with the exorcists, not the patients), or because the cause(s) have been forgotten or repressed.

The presence of pain in cases of possession varies with other factors. Invasion by a demon or evil ghost implies greater pain than possession by a relative or god and determines, in turn, the nature of the emotions implicated in the entire affair. The emotional and evaluative levels of experience also carry important sociological implications, because it is the social and cultural context that largely shapes which emotions are inappropriate and must be displaced into the form of a ghost.

Exorcism pain is particularly facinating. While the triggering pain, as we shall see in the next section on dissociation, separates the ego (executive self) from subsidiary mental functions causing dissociation, exorcism pain can actually produce reintegration.[19] It does so by bringing the sensorial body under the control of the body-self, creating a pain-body, which is phenomenally integrated. The slapping or whipping of the possessed by the healer, said to "drive out" the ghost, acts in a psychodynamic manner. The pain serves as the phenomenal signal that brings the body into the realm of the perceiving self and reestablishes a hierarchy of self-control. From a psychological point of view the effects of such exorcizing behavior—for instance, the self-mutilation of abused girls—are temporary and should not be equated with full mental health.

Dissociation

The second chapter of this book discussed the systemic function of some neurological events such as phantom-limb pain. The discussion highlighted the conditions under which neural output is shut down due to pain or stress on the system as a whole. The psychological term for such a shutdown is *dissociation,* though it may be safer to say that the neurological event is connected with a whole range of dissociative disorders. In a very general sense, dissociation (Pierre Janet's *desagrega-*

tion) "means that two or more mental processes or contents are not associated or integrated."[20] Clinicians and therapists usually assume that as a matter of mental health these dissociated elements should be integrated in conscious awareness, memory, or identity.[21] Ethnographers and historians of religion with an interest in possession have followed suit. Beginning with William James and Pierre Janet himself, they have noted the correspondence between cases of dissociation and possession. The clinical fascination with dissociation at the turn of the century owes its origins to a number of infamous possessions, or possessionlike incidents. The case of Ansel Bourne in New England was the one that drew the attention of William James.[22] Among the clearest recent statements is Winston Davis's in *Dojo*: "The formation of semi-autonomous ego organizations [connected with the defense mechanisms of dissociation] within the structure of ego itself is obviously of prime importance for explaining the behavior of people who believe themselves possessed by or filled with spirits, good or evil."[23] The conduct and verbal narrative of individuals who suffer from possessions so closely match the clinical accounts of patients diagnosed with personality disorders that the reduction seems unavoidable. Possession may often be a form of Dissociative Identity Disorder.

The *DSM-III-R* is explicit about this connection: "The belief that one is possessed by another person, spirit, or entity may occur as a symptom of Multiple Personality Disorder. In such cases the complaint of being 'possessed' is actually the experience of the alternate personality's influence on the person's behavior and mood."[24] Multiple Personality Disorder (MPD; but Dissociative Identity Disorder [DID] in the latest manual—*DSM-IV*) is the primary dissociative disorder in the manual. It is described as "the existence within the person of two or more distinct personalities or personality states" where personality is understood as a relatively enduring pattern of perception, thinking, and social experience.[25] Multiple personality disorder is often accompanied by phenomenological and physiological features that match those of possession. The accompanying personality may be a diametrical opposite of the hosting one, aggressive to its passive, or promiscuous to its conservative. The personalities may have differing IQs and respond differently to medication. One—but not the other—may be allergic, and one may have an extremely high pain threshold or display complete analgesia. The manuals also indicate that episodes of MPD or DID may be accompanied by self-mutilation or self-hurt, violent behavior, or suicide attempts.

Dissociative disorder is a broad umbrella for several conditions. These include psychogenic fugue and psychogenic amnesia, depersonalization disorder, and various other episodes related to specific contexts such as dissociated states resulting from brainwashing and indoctrination, captivity by terrorists, trance states that immediately follow physical abuse or trauma among children, and others.[26]

From the early studies of Jean-Martin Charcot, Morton Smith, and Pierre Janet, a strong correlation has been identified between dissociation and trauma.[27] The causes ("predisposing factors," that is, possible distant causes, not triggers) listed by the *DSM* for this dissociative disorder include abuse and severe emotional trauma in childhood. The disorder is far more prevalent than has commonly been thought, and the gender ratio is three to nine times more frequent among females than males. A variety of taxonomies differentiate levels of dissociative phenomena including Khilstrom's and Cardena's.[28] Cardena conveniently distinguishes the severe (pathological) from the "normal" intensity of dissociation (as one encounters in hypnosis, or even daydreams, or just "blanking out"), and just as important, he lists the neurological along with the psychological symptoms.[29]

Researchers fail to agree on precisely what dissociation is and what function it serves, or how to sort out its biological, historical, intrapsychic, and psychosocial factors.[30] There is considerable—if not unanimous—agreement, however, that dissociation serves some defensive purpose, both preserving the adaptability of the organism under conditions of trauma by reducing stress and by maintaining minimal ego viability. This functional-adaptive aspect is most necessary when the cause of the dissociative event is extremely traumatic, endangering either the organism as a whole or its integrative health (systemic goals). Because such a trauma is frequently involved in possession, this is also the topic at hand, following the lead of Ernest Hilgard, whose neodissociation theory revived the psychological field of dissociation after a half-century eclipse by psychoanalysis.[31]

Hilgard's Neodissociation

Ernest Hilgard claims that the aspects of neodissociation theory that place it beyond traditional (Janet's) dissociation theory include the following three:

1. The notion that we consist of totally unified consciousness is attractive but false. Instead, there are subordinate cognitive systems, each with some degree of unity, persistence, and autonomy of function.[32]

Hilgard concedes that the science of psychology is not yet at the point of identifying the basic units of meaningful function or information, but he has decided that for the purpose of recognizing autonomous functions "the identifiable activities that a person can be engaged in are referred to as subsystems to distinguish them from the larger control and monitoring functions that regulate them. These subsystems are the visible or reportable behaviors that occur when a person is engaged in any definable activity—reading a book, operating a machine, scratching his or her head, solving a problem."[33] Like digestion and circulation, these subsystems are functional and not ontological (for instance, anatomical). They share a variety of flexible neurological, perceptual, and cognitive aspects according to task. Although these systems can interact, many functions take place independently, and often without the awareness of the "central" consciousness. Long-distance car driving can exemplify the relative autonomy of motor-control operations, as do typing, playing the piano, or signing a check.[34]

2. The second assumption is that "some sort of hierarchical control exists that manages the interaction or competition between and among these structures"—that is, functional systems.[35]
3. There must be some executive, an "overarching monitoring and controlling structure." In the absence of such organization the semiautonomous systems would compete for attention and the most powerful or "noisy" would overshadow the others.

Hilgard leaves himself vulnerable to charges of promoting a homunculus when he says that the central control structure "plans, monitors, and manages functions involving the whole person, so that he or she thinks and acts appropriately.[36] But in fact, this executive must be regarded as one more system, a "master loop" of information input and output that regulates the other systems, and which has evolved due to adaptive—biological—factors. Such a view of ego as systemic control function was discussed in the previous chapter. The implications in relation to the role of pain in causing dissociation, and conversely, the role of hypnosis (an induced dissociative state) in analgesia and anesthesia, are significant.

In the second chapter we have looked at the model of the gate control mechanism, by means of which higher level output can moderate incoming pain signals. Hilgard was aware of the model's limitations but regarded it as generally consistent with hypnosis. He added a similar model, which complements the gate control in showing more precisely how dissociation modifies the information exchange at the levels he has called "central control process." Taken together, both conceptions show, hypothetically and without explaining, where pain acts in dissociative events and why people in dissociative states often display analgesic abilities.[37]

The notion of semiautonomous subsidiary systems is unexceptional.

Hilgard cites numerous researchers, including K. Lewin, E. C. Tolman, and F. C. Bartlett, who have discussed these systems and their functions. Hilgard also cites Noam Chomsky's ideas about the existence of independent cognitive structures that allow children to learn language. And I have indicated in a previous chapter that neurologists identify at least nine "selves" as constituting what is commonly regarded as an individual.

According to neodissociation, based primarily on experimentation under conditions of hypnosis, severe constraints on ego from some external source (either the hypnotist, or some traumatizing event) may influence the executive functions of the ego and change the hierarchical relationships of the subsidiary systems. This can result in changes to motor control, distortion of perception and memory, and mistaking hallucinations for external reality. Hilgard discovered the existence of a "hidden observer" during periods of hypnosis, an agent who can respond to the hypnotist's questions but has no awareness of any of the actions performed by the subsidiary system under hypnotic command. That hidden observer may receive sensory feedback from the outside world, but none from the activated subsystem, nor does it issue motor commands to the subsystem performing the task. The neurologist V. S. Ramachandran gives a poignant example of this potential separation of performance from awareness. He tells of woman who lost her sight while taking a hot shower in contaminated water and fell into a coma. When she returned to consciousness she was blind. Surprisingly, in the laboratory the woman was able to reach out and grasp an object such as an envelope with precise and sure hand movement. She was not aware of the location or position of the envelope—she could not "see" it—but her hand performed the task perfectly.[38] According to Hilgard the hidden observer behind autonomous actions is the executive system. It is not a self, or ego, commonly speaking, but somehow corresponds to the supervisory aspect of the network of semiautonomous systems. The monitor "as part of the central control-system, is a member of the family of controls that includes the conscience and the superego."[39] To a large extent this monitor merely rides piggyback on the subsidiary systems that regulate themselves once a function is mastered. But it is at the level of monitor that the sense of agency emerges. With these observations Hilgard seems to be equating the monitor with what other scientists have described as the body-self, which I have discussed in previous chapters.

Hilgard has been one of the most influential researchers in the field of dissociation. His neodissociation theory is particularly attractive to phenomenologists because it is based on a systemic understanding of the person and the ego. It is consistent with the systems view of ego, and at the same time it accounts for the strange behavior that often becomes evident as a result of dissociation. More important, it accounts for the type of cognitive processes that take place during dissociation, such as implicit learning and changes in personality and identity, while it also explains psychosomatic events such as analgesia, increased strength, hearing voices, changes in facial features, bodily convulsions, and violent or lewd behavior.

Hilgard would have a great deal to say about Maria Maddalena's demons, as he would about other extreme cases of possession. The *DSM-III-R*, as noted, implicates trauma and abuse—often sexual abuse—in the onset of dissociative disorders and certainly MPD. While there is no evidence that Maddalena suffered such abuse, certain cultural-ideological factors coupled with her own self-torture could have produced the organic and psychological retreat into dissociation. Ongoing scourging and cutting could sustain the shutdown of feedback between the executive and subsidiary systems, which results in fragmentization and a weakened sense of identity and the embodiment of an alien presence—a demon. The subject experiences the "other" as different, but somehow a part of one's self too.[40] Electrocution or shock therapy can create this perception, as Robert Pirsig's chillingly vivid narrative shows:

> And yet strange wisps of his memory suddenly match and fit this road and desert bluffs and white-hot sand all around us and there is a bizarre concurrence and then I know he has seen all of this. He was here, otherwise I would not know it. He had to be. And in seeing these sudden coalescences of vision and recall of some strange fragment of thought whose origin I have no idea of, I'm like a clairvoyant, a spirit medium receiving messages from another world. That is how it is. I see things with my own eyes, and I see things with his eyes too. He once owned them.[41]

But this raises difficult questions: When is the alien presence a demon and when is it a god, or even Jesus? Or to put it more colorfully, "How are we to distinguish between the leadings of the not-I who is the Holy Spirit and of that other not-I who is sometimes an imbecile, sometimes a lunatic and sometimes a malevolent criminal?"[42] Where does the "other" take its personality and why is it either "evil" or sublime, but rarely indifferent? In more technical terms, one must identify the emotional and evaluative aspects of the subsidiary systems that take a life of their own during dissociation and discover their origin in biographical fact and psychological process. Up to now I have discussed mainly the psychodynamic or systemic aspects of dissociation and/or possession. It is necessary to turn to a richer phenomenological domain that hangs on systemic function but takes into account the perceptions, emotions, beliefs, and sociocultural evaluations of both self and its environment.

Naming Your Ghost: Emotions and the Symbolism of Defense Mechanisms

The ghosts or demons that possess people within a given culture make interesting characters: They are passionate, extreme, and usually unpredictable. But they are not arbitrary. An intimate bond links ghosts and spirits to the people they invade. The repertoire of personalities ghosts assume comes both from a cultural cosmology and the "behavioral environment" into which they emerge.[43] In a modern American setting—group therapy—the appearance of a "ghost" or hidden aggressive personality takes on a familiar form of aggression:

> [The patient] has said, "I can kill anyone here with the strike of my hand." He was a black belt in karate. So I told B [another team member], "Hey one of the evil spirits has to be a death wish on other people, murder and so forth . . . karate, which is not just a defensive technique at that point. She told P [the team leader], "Hey, ask about that spirit." And sure enough, it came out.[44]

But the dynamic mechanisms that make possession possible transcend either culture or individual psychology. Hilgard, following Janet, pinpointed biological and systemic reasons for the defensive response to dissociative trauma. One is the mechanism of adaptation. Adaptation usually involves differentiation and change, and acts as the very antithesis of identity, which is integrative and strives for stability. But this is too general and biological. For the semiotics (symbolic quality) of the changes that take place in defensive mechanisms one is best advised to turn to psychoanalysis. Anna Freud, building to some extent on her father's work, identified ten ego-defense mechanisms that assist the ego "in its struggle with its instinctual life."[45] These methods of defense are regression, repression, reaction-formation, isolation, undoing, projection, introjection, turning against the self, reversal, and sublimation. Several of these defenses may work in tandem or sequentially, as illustrated in the case Anna Freud gives of a patient who suffered from the repeated failure of successive defenses—splitting, projection, introjection, and others—caused by her ambivalent feelings toward her mother. According to Freud, her ambivalence was due to instinctual issues—penis-envy toward her brothers and jealousy of her mother's pregnancies. The symbolic meaning of ego defense mechanisms is familiar in this case and needs no detailed repetition.

The ambivalent feelings toward the mother are transformed through splitting and projection. The girl finds another female figure that she can hate without a sense of guilt, and that woman now becomes evil.[46] On Freudian psychoanalytical theory, the ego defense mechanisms are driven by three types of anxiety: instinctual, objective (relating to the object of instinctual gratification), and relating to conscience. In other words, the ego needs its defense mechanisms in order to mediate between the id (instinct) and the superego (conscience). Melanie Klein, W.R.D. Fairbairn, and other Object Relations theorists identify the source of conflict outside of the individual psyche in a troubled relationship with a primary caregiver—a parent.[47] But either way, the defensive mechanisms tend to generate very distinct "personalities" among those dynamics that come to the aid of the faltering ego. When these personalities gain secondary autonomy, sometimes to the point of vivid delusions, their character may become that of either idealized friends or kind relatives, or aggressive, vicious, or licentious figures who act on forbidden impulses.[48]

In sum, "fictitious" creations of the psyche, molded within given cultural parameters, can become a vivid "person" who takes up residence in one's body. This happens usually, though not necessarily, as a result of trauma, which triggers the process. Freudian psychology identified the root of the trauma (and the character of the invading self) in erotic or aggressive pathology and the ego's attempt to preserve viability. Later psychoanalytical research modified the function of ego defense mechanisms (along with ego psychology as a whole) to refine both its biological aspects as an adaptive function (Heinz Hartmann) and to expand the role of extrapsychic factors (R. Spitz). Hartmann's view of ego psychology went beyond conflict (of drives) to ego functioning as a domain of autonomy, and defensive operations as responses to external stimuli that are not connected with instinctual conflict.[49] Spitz emphasized the unique object relationship that characterizes the life of the infant fused with the mother. Both of these post-Freudian innovations prefigure the emerging prominence of Object Relations theory, which is based on nurturing feedback in the infant's relationship with the primary caregiver. The type of trauma that might call for extreme defensive methods—and chief among them, dissociation—are no longer the inner conflicts between drives. Such a trauma is more likely to originate in the relationship with the primary caregiver and deprive the emerging ego of its capacity to self-organize. Several theorists regard dissociation as the failure of integration of subsystems ("self-organizations") caused by relational trauma.[50] Such a dissociation is a "rent by vertical splits between different self-states that have not been integrated with one another."

In cases of involuntary possessions, which are equivalent or identical to DID, the possessing ghost takes its personality from the material supplied by several sources:

1. Unintegrated self-organizations (systems), such as the moral self, the aggressive self, the self-sufficient self, the musical self.
2. Problematic areas in the relationship with primary objects, such as parents. These may include neglect or overprotection, competition, verbal or physical abuse.
3. Social issues such as gender and class bias, suppression of social autonomy, unchecked conflict, and irregular power hierarchies.
4. Radical separation (Janet's *desaggregation*) of the self-organizations, and the absence of direct feedback to the executive system responsible for feeling the "mine"-ness of these organizations.
5. Transformations brought about by splitting, denying, reversing, projecting, and other ego defense mechanisms coupled with the conscious work of imagination and fantasy, and material taken from a multitude of possible cultural sources.[51]

Pain may be part of the trauma that sets the dissociative proccesses into motion. A parent, husband, or employer may be physically and unpredictably abusive. But the deprivation to the ego is most severe when it is psychological, not directly painful to the body. This certainly holds true for the distal causes of dissociation. In fact, the dissociation often takes place years after psychological trauma has done its damage, and may then be triggered more directly by physical stress. The abused former child may be married to a man who strikes her and triggers an episode of dissociation. Or she may begin to suffer from severe migraines that trigger the event. At other times, the teenage girl may suddenly develop a strong urge to cut herself, and dissociation follows the cutting. Pain is thus implicated in the direct triggering event as a strong contributing cause, but it is rarely sufficient. The integration of the girl's personality must be sufficiently weak that the pain would trigger dissociation by cutting off the executive ego control. Of course, when the pain is severe enough or prolonged enough and ego has few escape options, such as in cases of prisoners of war, the dissociation might take place despite the relative strength of ego integration.

Scholars of possession have emphasized the sociological implications of these psychological facts. They have noted that possession is the escape of the weak and disadvantaged. The *DMS-III-R* claims, as noted, that dissociative phenomena are three to nine times more likely to happen to females than males. It is not just that female infants are less likely to be nurtured psychologically, though this is true in some cultures, but that they are more vulnerable to the social censorship that accompanies the free expression of certain emotions. A girl is less likely to express rage, anger, or desire in a culture that defines females in terms that exclude such expressions. Consequently, these and other emotional features are less likely to be integrated into her ego organization, and they become vulnerable to the distortive workings of ego defenses. At the same time, women are more likely to be victims of abuse and physical trauma of varying kinds. Such triggering events will thus produce dissociation that may take the shape of multiple personality, or in some cultures women become possessed by ghosts who bear the name of the repressed, split, or otherwise displaced emotion.

Studies of possession in India and South Asia have focused on class (caste) and gender as the primary factors. Kathleen Gough, for instance, analyzed ghosts among the Nayars as expressions of theodicy and the need for justice, and as an outlet for aggression in the relationship between the castes.[52] Similarly, Bruce Kapferer has shown that ghosts are implicated in illness that involves transformations in identity and social views of self in Sinhalese Sri Lanka.[53] The ritual contexts in which illness is identified and treated as the result of possessing demons allow for the negation and reconstitution of a self in a manner that traditional society would otherwise disallow. Richard Lannoy has reviewed these ethnographic descriptions and concluded: "The fact that someone violently possessed can express his most secret aggressive thoughts with impunity, but, as it were, 'in character' with the deity who has seized him, and articulate repressed social grudges of the collective while convulsed by histrionic exhibitionism, is indication enough of disordered unconsciousness subjected to relatively well coordinated cultural control."[54] The split implied here between psychological events and cultural scripts should not be taken too strictly. The imagination of the patient, in every instance of dissociation, feeds on a variety of cultural sources in order to generate the phenomenal sense of the possessing entity. As Melanie Klein noted, the imagination accompanies the internalization of relationships in Object Relations and feeds consciousness with vivid and complex images of self.

The separated and objectified system or organization comes to be experienced as a person (however ghostly) in extreme cases of dissociation such as MPD or strong possession. But the phenomenology of this "personalization" is not different in principle from the process by means of which one normally comes to experience oneself (or others) as persons. Unfortunately, this is one of the most difficult areas in psychology and in philosophy, in the exasperated words of Wittgenstein: "The I, the I, is what is deeply mysterious."[55] The process by means of which subjectivity comes about, the consciousness of being a self in a world, is profoundly elusive. As the dissociative event overtakes a patient, the usual personality recedes and a new one surfaces. How does the individual come to experience this personality as relatively integrated and as one's own?

Philosophers have been split on such basic questions as whether the self is a metaphysical entity or whether it is the phenomenological face of sensations, perceptions, movement, and attention. The second point of view, phenomenology, owes its contemporary agenda to Merleau-Ponty and, more recently, James Gibson. Among the best recent expressions of this perspective in the context of an anthropological study of healing rituals is the work of Thomas Csordas, who defines the self as "neither substance nor entity, but an indeterminate capacity to engage or become oriented in the world, characterized by effort and reflexivity. In this sense self occurs as a conjunction of prereflective bodily experience, culturally constituted world or milieu, and situational specificity or habitus."[56] The last term is taken via Pierre Bourdieu from Marcel Mauss who understands it as the culturally patterned uses of the body. It is designed to bypass the mind-body dualism that confounds ritual scholars, but of course, it only defers the problem to a deeper psychological level.

The case of either (strong) possession or Dissociative Identity Disorder is unusual in that the objective body remains roughly the same but it is appropriated by a new self. Pain is a contributing factor in both systemic and phenomenal ways. Pain interrupts the feedback between the features or aggregates of the empirical individual (the subsystems) and the executive self which is about to disappear. This unmakes the proprietary relationship between the subject and the body. Recall the phantom-limb sensation discussed in the second chapter of the book. The sensation of having a limb that is no longer there, or occasionally the sensation of missing a limb that is still there, may be due to a central brain feature called "neuromatrix" which generates a neurosignature. Body image and the sense of possessing a distinct body is due to this neural function, the neurological ground of the embodied self. Pain interrupts the input and output features of the neuromatrix resulting in the sense of alienation from one's body. This is the systemic contribution of pain to possession. It results in the phenomenal certainty that the possessed person has of his or her guest self. The "as if" quality of weak possession is removed. From the phenomenal point of view, pain contributes programmatically. It could be a way of battling the old self, a way of torturing a hated body, it could be the implementation of a cultural or ritual agenda, such as healing (pain as medicine) or penance, or it could be a way of appropriating the characteristics of a god one is about to become.

William James on Dissociation and Conversion

The topics of possession, even voluntary possession, and conversion do not appear related. By conversion I mean the inner transformation that individuals undergo from secular to religious life. It is true that in some of the notorious cases of conversion some trauma, physical or psychological, has instigated the process that led to a new life. The transformation of Saul into the great Christian missionary Paul is probably best known ("The Road to Damascus" syndrome). But even where pain or trauma can be demonstrated, is it fair to say that the convert assumes a new self, or even that conversion and possession belong in the same broad religious category? William James thought so, and his reasons are worth restating, however briefly.

According to William James, both Christianity and Buddhism exhibit the most methodical cures for the sick soul, the soul steeped in evil—defined as alienation from the Real.[57] Paradoxically, it is the sick soul, the incompletely unified or discordant one, that has the greatest potential for religious experience. The dualism or multiplicity of such a soul can be conceptualized as a type of possession—even the lives of the saints give evidence to invading foreign agencies such as demons or Satan. Conversion, on this understanding of the psychological basis of religious experience, is the unification of the soul: "To be converted, to be regenerated, to receive grace . . . are so many phrases which denote the process, gradual or sudden, by which a self hitherto divided . . . becomes unified."[58]

William James carefully defines the soul as a process, "successive fields of consciousness" rather than as a metaphysical entity that is an ontological monad.[59] It is a habitual center of personal energy, a concept that owes much to Buddhist psychology in its refusal to posit a permanent and irreducible core of the self. James continues that the conversion of an individual means, on these terms, that "religious ideas, previously peripheral in his consciousness, now take a central place, and religious aims form the habitual center of his energy." In other words, conversion is a reorganization of psychological states—the subsystems of contemporary psychological jargon—rather than a theological event. Such a dramatic event is more likely to happen due to some shock, whether physical or emotional, that jars the individual and makes his or her habitual center of gravity collapse.[60] These shocks may sometimes be emotional occasions, especially violent ones, which precipitate the "mental rearrangements." However, the same can take place as a result of hypnotic suggestion, which can send powerful subliminal messages that change the control of the habitual self.

James develops his argument claiming that the same psychological processes underlie the more ordinary conversion that adolescents undergo in passage from childhood to adulthood. This may account for the ordeals that adolescents suffer in numerous cultures in the form of puberty rites or rites of passage. That will be the topic of the next chapter, but according to James, the effectiveness of such rituals is due to the "exhaustion" of the habitual self and the consciousness-altering rearrangement of shock and suggestion. Such a transformation takes a few unique individuals beyond mere membership in a religious community. Saints are such people who have subdued the lower appetites of their habitual self, who have applied the psychological tools for controlling the self to their fullest extent. Using ascetic techniques of self-mortification they not only displace the soul from its habitual center of consciousness but torture it to the point of annihilation. The boundary between saintliness and pathology is thus fuzzy, and James cites both Henry Suso and Marguirite Marie (founder of the Sacred Heart order) as illustrations of such ambiguity.

In conclusion, William James was aware, both as a historian of religion and as an experimental psychologist, that there is a strong connection between violent or painful behavior and religious experience. His theory is capable of accounting for rites of passage and initiation, along with mystical union, in the same breath as clinical cases. The neurological and psychodynamic details are no longer consistent with current theories but the reduction is splendid—the near equal of Freud's. Its greatest appeal, as far as I am concerned, is the supreme role assigned to experience and consciousness above and beyond "theology."

SIX

The Emotions of Passage

Cases of spirit possession show that traumatic stress can lead to the emergence of a new identity, the splitting up of one's habitual identity, or even the cohabitation of several selves within one body. But possession is usually unwelcome, an illness. Even god-possession, often highly desirable, frightens most people with its violently energetic displays. Is there any evidence that some cultures use trauma to bring about similar changes in identity in a more ordinary way? Does pain ever figure in rituals that are not the earmarks of unique individuals—ecstatic specialists—but are the domain of ordinary members of the community?

Among the most frequently performed type of life-cycle ritual around the world, and possibly the most intensely scrutinized, is the rite of passage, including both initiation and puberty rites.[1] And like possession, voluntary or involuntary, puberty rites display an astounding inventiveness in the use of pain. In one New Guinea community alone one finds bleeding the penile urethra, the nose, the tongue or gums, and the back. The methods vary: The penis bleeding is caused by twirling twigs in the urethra, scraping with nettles, or stabbing with an awl. The back bleeding is inflicted by cutting and scarifying.[2] Around the world, children have been subjected to pain, from whipping to circumcision (boys and girls), subincision, or superincision; piercing noses, ears, or cheeks; scarification; knocking out teeth; kneeling in hot coals; getting beaten by sticks; hanging from hooks; and so forth.[3] This violence ranges from the Americas to Africa, Asia, and Europe, and at all known times in human history.[4] These facts are so familiar that they do not merit a sordid repetition of detail. And, of course, the rituals are not limited to puberty rites but include initiation rites, and then not only to religious societies and fraternities, but also to military, academic, athletic, and other so-called secular organizations, which require some form of ordeal for acceptance.

Although traumatizing pain figures prominently in the change of status and identity, the extension of the psychodynamics of possession to passage is neither simple nor straightforward. It raises a variety of new issues that transcend the physical and emotional upheaval of possession: Why do ordinary and common rituals use pain, and how does the ritualized form of the physical ordeal contribute to the specific psychological ends of passage? This chapter seeks to find out why so many cultures insist that identity be changed through pain and by means of ritualized pain, rather than simple brutality.[5]

Ritual Violence: The Extreme Reductions

Consider the following case of initiation. In 1954, at the gathering to discuss "Man and Transfiguration," Mircea Eliade, who would become the leading figure in the history of religions, gave a paper called "Mystery and Spiritual Regeneration in Extra-European Religions." It contained a richly textured and imaginative interpretation of rites of initiation, beginning with the Australian Karadjeri. He interpreted the structure of initiatory rituals in which physical tortures of the initiates appear to be a pervasive and perhaps essential aspect. Eliade cited instances of mutilations, scarifications, tattooing, and other forms of ritual pain, and particularly marveled at the initiation torture of the "Maudan of Dakota": "The torture exceeds anything that can be imagined: Two men pierced the muscles of the chest and back with knives, plunged their fingers into the wound, passed a strap under the muscles, attached ropes to it, and hoisted the neophyte in the air. But before he was hoisted, pins were affixed to muscles of his legs and arms, and heavy stones and buffalo heads were attached to the pins."[6] Still in the shadow of the great war in civilized Europe, Eliade was perhaps moved to defend the "natives" against charges of viciousness by interpreting their action as symbolic of deep metaphysical beliefs:

> And it is primarily these ordeals that constitute the religious experience of initiation—the encounter with the sacred. . . . The central moment of every initiation is represented by the ceremony symbolizing the death of the novice and his return to the fellowship of the living. But he returns to life a new man, assuming another mode of being. Initiatory death signifies the end at once of childhood, of ignorance, and of the profane condition.[7]

This symbolic and metaphysical explanation of ritual passage absorbs the meaning of the painful manipulations that take place: "For all traditional societies, suffering has a ritual value, the torture is held to be administered by superhuman beings, its aims being the spiritual transformation of the victims."[8] Eliade's interpretation thus represents an example of an extreme symbolical reduction in which ritual behavior is interpreted according to comprehensive metaphysical presuppositions.

But Switzerland was also home to opposite ways of understanding violent rituals. The Eranos conference in which Eliade gave this paper was sponsored by a wealthy Swiss philanthropist Olga Groebe-Kaptyn, who was in turn inspired by Carl Gustav Jung and his work. Throughout the Second World War she hosted the annual conference at her Laggo Maggiore estate, completely disregarding the viciousness that took place all around this island of tranquility. While the serene conferences were proceeding in defiance of the savagery beyond the estate walls, another Swiss—a scientist—developed an altogether more realistic theory of human cruelty. The underlying assumption of Konrad Lorenz was simple: Humans are biological beings—animals—who share with other animals aggressive instincts related to mating, territory, feeding, and so forth. The undeniable evidence of pervasive violence in human history is ultimately reduceable to our genetic heritage. In fact, even religiously orchestrated ritual violence—for instance, initiatory ordeals—are ultimately expressions of biological drives, such as the natural aggression of adults against young sexual competitors. Rituals owe their origins to phylogenetic principles; their careful staging can no more conceal the biological origin than can the complex actions of the Common Shelduck.[9]

Despite their obvious differences, the metaphysical and biological reducers share two major points. First, both appeal to common sense because they are sweeping and simple. Second, for different reasons both have come to define the two extremes of anthropological understanding of passage. Some psychologists and historians of religion subscribe to one or the other of these reductions, but most of the work is being conducted in the vast middle ground between the two.

Hurting Teenagers

Unfortunately, researchers cannot even agree what rites of passage are and who they include, let alone what they mean or what function they serve. Is the ritual a social phenomenon, a psychological mechanism, or a spiritual test? The differences can be decisive in how ritualized pain functions and who it serves. Here are three distinct approaches, illustrated by Victor Turner, Vincent Crapanzano, and Sam Gill.[10] They discuss Ndembu initiation, Morrocan circumcision, and Hopi whippings, respectively.

According to Turner, the main purpose of the Mukanda (male initiation) is to turn a boy into a man. "The extended circumcision rites, therefore, act to purify him, break his connection to the world of women, and induct him into the male hierarchical power system."[11] Successfully changing from boy to man depends on the manner by which the ritual depicts and resolves basic social tensions—for instance, between the matrilineal principle of descent and patrilocal habitation and government. The boy gets his early sense of identity from his mother, but needs to enter the broader village social relations, which are dominated by men. The ritual must symbolically incorporate such tensions and potential conflicts and resolve them, or at least play them out. Therefore, just as the women wail when the boys are led away to be circumcised, the boys may cry at the cutting, but they are only to cry for their father. Crying out a mother's name will peg the initiate as a coward and failure. In short, the ritual dramatizes the tensions that dominate Ndembu social life and subjects the initiate to them as a process of giving him an adult identity.

Vincent Crapanzano denies that rites of circumcision always serve as passage from childhood to adulthood. On his evidence from Arab villages in Morocco, the seven-year-old boy is taken for circumcision long before he is ready for an adult identity. The boy is cut, then returned to his mother, and he must only be old enough to remember the trauma of both temporary separation from mother and the pain of the circumcision. The ritual does not focus on identity—a complex social construct—let alone try to resolve social tensions. Crapanzano understands the ritual, instead, in a Freudian-functional way as a traumatic conclusion to the oedipal fantasy. The ritual reinforces an already existing anxiety in relation to the father and separation from the mother, and traumatizes the boy permanently in order to repress his desires, allowing him to develop compensatory psychological mechanisms, which are essential for healthy adult relationships.[12]

According to Sam Gill, the whippings that accompany Hopi initiation rituals are either a type of payment for the new teachings that the youth will acquire or a warning not to reveal the secrets of these teachings to the uninitiated. However, at the heart of the passage ritual is a shocking revelation. The masked Katchinas whom the boy has always seen dancing as gods are, in fact, none other than his own male relatives. Passage thus includes a revelation of betrayal, a lie exposed. Gill calls this a rite of "disenchantment" and claims it is designed to replace juvenile fantasy with a reality marked by complexity and discord.

Despite such divergence of opinion on the nature of passage, a number of features are universally acknowledged. The first is that rites of initiation and passage involve notable acts of violence, which are neither spontaneous nor merely brutal. The second is that the subjects of these rituals, usually young men and women—sometimes children—undergo profound changes in their social identity. It is important to add one more to these two fundamental features, namely, that the pain caused by the acts of violence is the link between the symbolism of the ritual and the psychology of identity change.

Violence and Pain

The communication of pain discussed in Chapter 3 shows that violence and pain are distinct phenomena. Ritual contexts, and the rich ethnographic literature that describes them, reinforce this observation by emphasizing violence while virtually ignoring pain. There is a simple reason for this: Violence is a semiotic event while pain is a subjective sensation that is not easily observed or represented. Because cultural anthropology favors symbolic analysis above psychological reductions, the meaning of passage rituals is usually localized in the violent actions and in the way such violence is situated in a broader cultural context. For example, we have seen that the Gnau of New Guinea manipulate the boys' penises in a variety of ways. They cause penile bleeding among boys at puberty, without actually removing the foreskin.[13] The bleeding penis thus *resembles* menarche and the ritual seems to produce in an artificial way a first menstruation for boys. Unfortunately there is no evidence, Gilbert Lewis claims, that in the minds of the Gnau penile bleeding stands for menstruation. The Wogeo, in contrast, use the same word to describe ritual penile bleeding and the menstruation of women, both of which remove sexual impurity.[14] Here then, the identity between the symbol and the reality it represents is far more convincing. This divergence, even on one island (New Guinea), illustrates the essential aspect of symbolic interpretation: A symbol always signifies something to someone.[15] In order to avoid extreme regionalism, cultural anthropologists acknowledge that more must be said about the symbols of violence. According to Corinne Kratz, the vital aspect of the violence is broader than the physical manipulation of the body and its visual symbolism: "Initiation is a culturally created danger point, with both personal, physical danger from the operation and the wider danger of public shame and cowardice. In braving these dangers initiates move away from parental control, display their personal control, and emerge with the power of adult capacities."[16]

Symbolical interpretation, the tool for analyzing culturally scripted violence, hangs in a precarious balance between the empirical fact and its objective meaning. The fact is the blow and the cut and the meaning is passage—but how are these connected? Roy Rappaport shows the intractability of these problems, better perhaps than he has himself intended. He argues that the dubbing of a knight confers a new status on him not by the power of the blow of the sword on his shoulder, but by *informing* him of his knighthood. Change of status, Rappaport claims, is the awareness of the meaning of the gesture with the sword.[17] Similarly, passage is conferred on the young man, not simply by the physical damage to his body—the scar, the cut penis—nor even by the pain of the operation: "The significant transformations produced by such operations are obviously not physical, nor are they outcomes of the physical changes per se wrought by such operations but of the meanings those changes carry."[18] The actions bundle meanings on several levels and in a variety of media; they are markers of rich units of information.

But if the ritual is about the symbolic understanding of gesture, why must the initiates hurt? Here is Rappaport's answer. "When that sign is carved on the body the abstract is not only made substantial but immediate: Nothing can be experienced more immediately than the sensations of one's own body—and if the mark is indelible, as in the cases of the subincision, the excised canine, the lopped finger, the scarified face, chest or back, it is ever-present. As the abstract is made alive and concrete by the living substance of men and women, so are men and women predicated by the abstractions which they themselves realize."[19] In other words, the participant's body is a text on which adults inscribe the message that society considers authoritative. The reading of the message creates the reader, who is the new adult. Ritualized hurt simply makes the message immediate and permanent.

It is too easy to stumble over the dichotomy between the body with its sensations and perceptions, and the culturally determined mind (the reader of the sign). Victor Turner ranks among the first to draw the attention of anthropologists to the need to incorporate both "poles" of the symbol into a resonant dualism in which the two—signifier and signified, body and mind—get equal play. Turner's method, developed in the sixties, has now been undercut by a variety of approaches that tilt the description toward mental constructions (the reader of the sign) by rejecting the autonomy of the body's "raw" sensations. The social and linguistic construction of experience has simply removed the body from the equation, even as talk of "embodiment" has proliferated. Feminist theory with its investigation of the political nature of the body, the social construction of gender experience, and its Foucault-inspired textual reading of the body have produced a corpus of influential psuedo-monistic (social-constructive) lines of thought.[20] Mauss's concept of the habitus, adopted by Bourdieu in his theory of practice, has essentially eliminated the primordial nature of body and sensation from objective description.[21] And, of course, in the context of pain Elaine Scarry wrote her *Body in Pain* with the premise that embodied experience is constituted by social and linguistic invention.[22] Eliminate the word through inarticulate pain and experience itself becomes mute.

Two problems persist in the face of such theories: First, the children's hurt remains completely irrelevant to analysis. Pain is merely something that draws the attention of the victim, but other than that it is mute and meaningless (unlike everything else in the hypersymbolic ritual!). Second, the dualism is not really eliminated, only pushed underground when sensation is reduced to perception and ultimately to social consciousness.[23] The surviving dualism is inconsistent with the goals of performative semiotics, which include the need to avoid separating the message from the medium. I see no reason that the sign on the body should be separated from the reader of the sign, and the only way to mediate the two is to look at the intrinsic expressivity of pain, which is unavoidable when the knife cuts.

A strong effort to resolve the dualism of semiotics in connection with the violence and pain of the subject in rites of passage has come from T. O. Beidelman who has written *The Cool Knife*. Beidelman is aware that pain serves as the mediator between the cultural goals of the ritual and its subjective effects. It is therefore not surprising that for his analysis of the use of pain in the ritual he turns to Elaine Scarry (as quoted by Morinis). Beidelman writes:

> Pain is central to such ritual transformations. As Scarry observes, the infliction of pain is a powerful means of verifying an invisible reality, in the Kaguru case, the moral order of society and the elder generation who convey it. "To have pain is to have certainty"; "the physical pain is so incontestably real that it seems to confer its quality of 'incontestable reality' on that power that has brought it into being." . . . Pain is related to imagination. The instructing elders wield pain and the easing of it as tools to cultivate social (moral) imagination in their young charges. "Pain and imagination are the 'framing events'; within whose boundaries all other perceptual, somatic, and emotional events occur; thus, between the two extremes can be mapped the whole terrain of the human psyche." At initiation, an objectless pain shatters words but is followed by a succession of recovery states associated with ever-diminishing discomfort and a corresponding construction through words and songs of an imagined world of objects, along with ideas as how to control them.[24]

Beidelman's observations represent substantial progress in our efforts to understand how the violence of the ritual actually achieves psychological goals (changes in identity and social status). But too much vagueness remains. The claims that pain confers a quality of "incontestable reality" on the power that wields it, and that it "shatters words" while building up an imagination are problematic in light of the critique of Scarry's work in Chapter 2 of *Sacred Pain*. The neurodynamics of that chapter and the psychology of Chapter 4 could be applied to Beidelman's agenda in order to gain a more detailed understanding of what pain achieves in rites of passage. However, that level of analysis would not fully resolve the problem of dualism at hand. In order to see how pain—the subjective response to the violent act—mediates between cultural and social ends and subjective psychological processes, it is necessary to move beyond neuro- and psychodynamics. Consequently I shall focus on the emotions triggered by the painful stimulus and analyze the way these emotions mediate objective and subjective realities.

Emotions and the Body

The pain of the cutting is intimately connected with very strong emotions. The various social conflicts and tensions ritually acted out on the body of the initiates generate a profoundly articulate pain on three levels at least: First, the painful manipulations of the body trigger a variety of nociceptive sensations. Second, these manipulations trigger neuromuscular responses that release powerful feelings and emotions that are locked up in the body. And third, the emotions mediate body sensations with social perceptions and cognitions, that is, with the fundamental social issues that play out in the ritual. The pain of initiation, whether adulthood is achieved or only implied, is not incidental to other descriptions of the event and is not mute.

William James was not the last researcher to think that emotions are identical with physiological states, or behaviors. Obviously the behaviorists (J. B. Watson, B. F. Skinner) reduced mental phenomena such as emotions to stimulus-response learned behavior, with no inner states to speak of. But Gilbert Ryle (*The Concept of Mind*) and Ludwig Wittgenstein (*Philosophical Investigations*) also reduced emotion to its behavioral expression, taken as a sequence of actions. These positions ring jarringly against our commonsensical notion that emotions are feelings about inner states, about qualia, which are only *accompanied* by bodily sensations and behavior. We feel angry *at* someone, and our anger has to have that focus, with its true or assumed cause (he slighted us) before we can feel flushed and before our fists clench and jaw tightens.[25] In contrast with the position of the materialists, the mental perspective on emotions also has its reductive champions. Social constructionists, for instance, claim that emotion is identical with the mental or cognitive conceptions that define its orientation. A culture that has no ideological conception of righteous indignation has no righteous indignation.[26]

This latter position—call it "the propositional attitude theory"—has been thoroughly and forcefully debunked by Paul E. Griffiths and other researchers. It is certainly inconsistent with the approach of *Sacred Pain*.[27] Many psychologists maintain that emotions consist of several simultaneous aspects: sensory, physiological, behavioral, cognitive, and social.[28] Empirical research reveals structural and functional "correspondences" among such aspects, or between the activity of the central nervous system and emotional states. Similarly, biological and systemic thinking have rejected the essentialist reduction of emotion to one feature, whether mental (culture) or physiological. It may thus be relatively prudent to view emotions as the bellwether for total organic wellness. If the individual is analyzed as a complex open system that constitutes physical, mental, and environmental dynamics and information flow, emotions provide indications—these are the subjective feelings—of how well such a system is functioning in relation to its adaptive goals. This is how Lazarus puts it: "Emotions are complex, patterned organismic reactions to how we think we are doing in our lifelong efforts to survive and flourish and to achieve what we wish for ourselves. Emotions are like no other construct of psychology, sociology, and biology in that they express the intimate personal meaning of what is happening in our social lives and combine motivational, cognitive, adaptive, and physiological processes into a single complex state that involves several levels of analysis."[29] The cybernetic approach implies that the information that passes through the circuits of this system move in a variety of different directions and that consequently emotion is never the product of just one sequence of events. Again, the standard folk-psychology must be rejected. It tells us that something happens "out in the world" and that we react to it based on cognition, social norms, and psychological upbringing, and that the reaction becomes manifest in a variety of actions, which are mediated by physiological responses. In contrast, systems theory argues that emotion can originate at the body, with no corresponding external triggering event. Or the same triggering event can produce two diametrically opposing somatic reactions and emotions. A razor cut across the thigh can produce fear or elation, a manipulated shoulder (by a somatic psychotherapist, not an inquisitor) may flood awareness with either joy or sadness. And yet the feelings are there, triggered by a pressed muscle or irritated nerve before any mental image or conceptual attitude intervenes. The same could be said for breathing exercises, rapid eye movements, and yoga postures and rituals.

The function of body-mind systems determines that information (the experiential aspect of neurotransmission) can flow in a number of directions; it is stored in numerous loops—not all of them limited to the brain but extending to neurotransmitters or hormones, to muscles, joints and tendons; and that the information is not discrete but consists of elementary units—*gestalten*—that pervade both neurological pattern and perception. I have discussed Gestalt theory in the second and third chapters, in connection with pain language and perceptual isomorphism. Those observations could be extended to body work and emotional reactions to somatic manipulation. The force, direction, rhythm, temperature, and other aspects of touch, for example, correspond to and trigger emotional states, in the same way that the structure of music corresponds with emotions, as noted by Susan Langer. Still, one must go beyond the language of correspondence or isomorphism.

A growing body of literature, some of it following the work of Wilhelm Reich, has been exploring the interaction of body states with emotional and psychological phenomena and its effect on therapy.[30] This corpus represents one distinct, and clinically successful, way of thinking about the articulateness of the body and its role in our mental life. Wilhelm Reich was a student, then colleague of Freud, who gradually developed an interest in the body as a focus of psychotherapy. He came to feel that without attention to the body the changes brought about by psychotherapy would not last. The reason was that the mind, emotions, and intellect were inseparable from muscle and bone, that all belonged to a unified whole that must function in an integrated manner in order to achieve either physical or psychological health. Reich began to describe muscular holding patterns in relation to personality traits, and discovered correspondences between characteristic bodily attitude and psychological issues. He termed the bodily attitudes muscular "armoring." This is how Myron Sharaf describes Reich's work: "Then gradually in the late 1930s, he began more intensive use of touch to attack the body's armor directly and elicit emotions bound up in muscular spasms. He would press hard with his thumb or the palm of his hand on a particular segment of the body armor; the jaw, neck, chest, back, or thigh. Such pressure often stimulated an outburst of crying or rage."[31] Reich recognized the systemic nature of the human organism and postulated an organic energy flow that follows scientifically describable dynamics. The energy becomes manifest as a pattern of tension, charge, discharge and relaxation. In the absence of proper energy flow and the appropriate release of psychological tension, blocks in the organism form at specific locations. In many animals, according to Darwin, the expression of anger becomes manifest at just below the seventh cervical vertebra, in the junction of the neck, shoulders, and trunk—in the form of bristling hair and arched spine, for instance, among cats, baboons, and other animals.[32] Such locations (among humans), Reich posits, retain emotional energy, which can be released, at least in principle, by manipulation, and would then be experienced in the form of released anger. Reich called this energy "orgonomy"—a concept that has been rejected, if not ridiculed, by most mainstream therapists. Still, hundreds of Reichian and other somatic psychotherapists practice throughout the United States using somatic techniques to enhance psychological change. Reich noticed fairly early that such an armoring of the body is functionally identical with the defensive posture of the ego intent on protecting the individual.[33] In other words, he was able to argue that Freud's defense mechanisms become manifest in characteristic bodily gestures and postures—such as a limp or incorrect way of carrying the head—which in turn ossify in fixed bodily patterns.[34] Perhaps there is a more general way of putting this. Just as ego defenses lead to characteristic personality traits—mental phenomena—they also lead to patterned bodily postures. For example, repressed sexual issues become manifest not just in splitting, projection, and other mental attitudes, but in pelvic tightness, chronic pain, or physiological-sexual dysfunction.

The followers of Reich, including Elsworth Baker, Alexander Lowen, Stanley Keleman, and Robert Hall, continued both to treat psychoanalytical patients by means of somatic work along with analysis, and to chart the anatomy of what Lowen called "bioenergy." They agree on several correspondences between body characteristics and emotional states, such as tight jaw and anger, tight chin and sadness.[35] More specialized work has followed in the wake of Wilhelm Reich. Lowen cites Sandor Rado, who claims that at the root of all language is the proprioceptive sensation of one's body.[36] Lowen insists that what we call body language is deeply grounded in body sensation and awareness, and that it transcends the cultural or social values attached to the body as trope or as conventional sign. This is not to say that cultural attributions expressed idiomatically in America by such expressions as "he has both feet on the ground"; "he has a soft heart"; "she is tight fisted" do not shape attitudes toward the body, but that these have the body at their root and not vice versa. Culture (language) translates embodied experience into meaningful communication by means of experiential metaphors.[37] Bioenergetics, as this field is often called, states that as energy flows through the organism (human or animal), certain regions process that energy into different affects, and that consequently we experience our emotions as localized in different parts of the body (because on the bioenergetic level they are). In that sense the heart is an organ of feeling, primarily love, joy, anxiety, deep sorrow.[38] The fact that expressions such as "you broke my heart" are accompanied by a proprioceptive sensation in the chest indicates that the "energetic flow" is stopped or accelerated in that region of the chest. The area can literally expand with joy at the right occasion. Part of the upper rib area—the thoracic cage, the sternum, the chest muscles—are all conduits of emotional energy and may be the blocks to the free flowing of that energy. This may become manifest in typical body posture (a sternum protuberance designed to keep people away, tight breathing, overly developed—sometimes intentionally at the gym—chest muscles). It is currently hard to accept bioenergetics, especially when it tries to bridge emotional tropes with proprioceptive sensations, although the research program defined along these lines is extremely lively.[39]

However, Lowen's argument is ultimately biological, and although it tries to bridge biology and experience, it ought to be challenged or even discarded on biological rather than cultural grounds. A more conservative biological approach identifies emotions with the dynamics of the nervous system and with the activity of hormones that serve as neurotransmitters and as regulators of metabolic and motor activities.[40] Due to the adaptational success of these neurophysiological mechanisms certain "affect programs" have developed in response to key environmental situations. Emotions reflect adaptational success both on the level of social communication and in mobilizing psychological and physiological responses to goal-threatening environmental hazards. The localization of sensation in regions of the body corresponds to the defensive or aggressive motor response necessary for dealing with a given situation. The sensation is generated by the impact of hormonal secretion on muscular and other gross motor senses (proprioception). There is no "energy" in any empirically meaningful sense, except as an abstraction of neuromuscular activities.[41]

The release of energy in a certain region of the body—say, the chest—represents catharsis. Individuals who have developed characteristic blocks (armoring) associated with certain regions of the body have difficulties releasing the emotional energy stored there. In some cultures mourning rites are accompanied by violent behavior; scholars claim this either imitates sorrow or induces it. Renato Rosaldo protested against the notion that sorrow needs to be ritually induced, but there is no doubt that in some cultures this happens. Manipulations of the body at such times may indeed produce the desired emotion by a cathartic effect, that is, by freeing "pent up" emotional energy. This may be done by self-hurt (tearing out one's hair, beating the chest, whipping one's back).[42]

There is no compelling evidence that we can precisely chart the body manipulations in rites of passage, relate them to precise emotional release, and link these emotions to the social values implicit in the process. The somatic psychological work cited is not focused enough, and its application to cross-cultural and symbolic material needs to be worked out in considerable detail. We may be sure, however, that the symbolic actions of the wielders of the knife are met by equally loaded somatic and emotional responses on the part of the initiate. Every rite of passage involves the body of the initiate, not just passively as the paper of a text, but actively as the fulcrum of psychophysiological events. The same imagination with which the ritual language has been interpreted must extend to the body of the boy or girl, in which emotions are brought to the surface, moved around, reburied, and so forth. In order to do this properly the ethnographer has to consult physiology, neuropsychology, biocybernetics, and psychoanalysis.

A Case of Passage

Despite the four decades that have passed since its writing, Victor Turner's description of Ndembu passage still remains one of the best. Turner claims that the passage and circumcision of boys is designed to unify in the person of the boy many of the social tensions that run through Ndembu society. The ritual is a complex and multilayered symbolic enactment of such a process: "The corporate unity represented by *muyombu* results from the overcoming of cleavages. An individual is incorporated into a series of groups as a long-term member—matrilineal segment, village, vicinage, perhaps chiefdom. . . . To produce the category *'anyadi'*, 'novices', corporate groups such as villages—each organized around a matrilineal core—have to be robbed of their male children and aggregated together in a new way."[43] The ritual of circumsicion is meant to produce a unity on the level of moral order instead of the particularistic order based on birth and motherhood. On the symbolic level the ritual depicts such a transition, and its incorporation into the person of the boy, in diverse ways. Among other elements, Turner discusses the color symbolism of the ritual—the transition from whiteness to redness (and from milk to blood; from feminine to masculine, from simplicity to ambiguity). He also interprets the use of three trees (*mudyi, muyombu, mukula*), which act as vital stations in the ritual passage and embody the values of the social and psychological states through which the boy passes. Turner describes the movement toward the circumcision site, the setting up of a gate (*mukoleku*), and the very suggestive passing through the legs of the male elders who hold up their genitals. The description is ethnographically rich and symbolically meaningful, and it conforms extremely well with Turner's sociological thesis.

Among the more striking features of the description, from my point of view, is Turner's psychic distance from the initiate. There are clear references to pain: the drum-beating to cover the screams, the paternal concern for the bleeding son, the care for isolating the penis after the operation. There is much about the cutting, the need for speed and precision, healing time, and so forth. But in the virtual "forest of symbols," this aspect stands out for its relative poverty. The ethnographer is simply too far removed from the consciousness of the initiates, which figures little in the semiotic structuralism of the narrative. Consequently anything I could say in line with the agenda drawn above would be speculative.

One could speculate, for instance, that the pain of the cutting produces a traumatic dissociation, anywhere from mild to extreme. Since the boys are at or around puberty, their genitals have started to become erotic zones, a source of pleasure, the focus of strong, though increasingly ambivalent, object relations with the mother. The extreme pain at the genitals thus triggers rage, sexually charged anger that accompanies the psychodynamic dissociation. The rage can be directed neither toward the mother nor the father (the objects of desire and fear, respectively), although the first allowed this to happen and the second acted with the party of the perpetrators. The ambivalent pain could result in splitting, and the rage, with its negative evaluation of the situation, is projected at the circumcisers.[44] These individuals, and the knife with which they inflict the pain, become, in D. Winnicot's term, "transitional objects" endowed with the projected anger, which had been split from pleasure and love.[45] The split is evidenced in the hostility and fear generated by the circumcisers, who are red-stained, the "killers" of the boys. They are reviled by the mothers and threatened by the fathers. After the bleeding stops, when they try to feed the boys a sweet mush placed on the cutting knife, the fathers grab handfuls and feed the boys by hand, in a very maternal manner.[46] The knife and its wielder are not allowed to become part of the healing process but must remain the objects of negative feelings. From the start of the operation the fathers begin to act in a very solicitous and encouraging way, unlike their customary behavior before the ceremony. The love and attachment that had been the exclusive domain of relations toward the mother are now transferred to the father, who helps with the feeding and healing, and who benefits by the role of the cutter who takes away all of the rage. The pain-based attachment is also directed at the other boys in the group, who undergo the same pain. The boy's psychological upheaval, the transference and objectification of his feelings, is enhanced by dissociation, which strengthens the liminal quality of the entire process surrounding the circumcision and its aftermath. As a result the boy now conceives of his world in dualistic terms and becomes prepared to embody some of the ambiguous values that dominate the Ndembu worldview. These include, according to Turner, masculinity and femininity, courage and fear, killing and healing, life and death, good and evil, fertility and barrenness, pleasure and pain, and so forth.

To summarize the role of pain for now: The sharp pain of the cut leads to a fairly strong psychological dissociation and triggers extremely powerful emotions. These emotions are objectified and projected onto temporary objects, which take on some of the ambiguities that dominate the boy's emotional life. The emotions are split into good and bad, and the objects onto which projection takes place become part of a bifurcated reality.[47] Due to the dynamics of dissociation the boy is able to identify in a very strong phenomenal way with the "good" male elders, his father and shepherd. As the burning hot original pain gives way to a throbbing ache of recovery, and as the boy heals while spending time in the community of men, he is able to integrate his anger with his love. He experiences two sides of Ndembu dualism, without rejecting and permanently displacing one side or the other. Being an adult means embodying conflict in a functional way within a community, and this is what the pain allows. There is also a strong cognitive learning process, which is enhanced by pain, but I will discuss it later.

This psychological speculation may be accurate, but it is very impoverished without subjective pain and trauma narratives. The initiate's point of view must be voiced before a detailed analysis of the function of pain can be discussed. Since I know of no such narrative in the context of puberty rites I shall discuss an initiation ritual, which is closely related—the one that so impressed Eliade in 1954—and for which a wealth of subjective information is available. This rite is the Sun Dance.

Initiation: The Sun Dance

The Sun Dance is a generic name given to a number of ritual types performed by the Arapahos, Cheyennes, Crows, Blackfeet, Sarsis, Teton, Dakota, Kowas, Plain Crees, Plains Ojibwas, Wind River Shosohonis, Utes, and several additional plains and Rocky Mountain reservation communities. It ranks among the most prolifically described and analyzed Native American ceremonies, and has also produced a wealth of personal narratives.[48] Although it is not a puberty rite, it shares many of the transitional elements of rites of passage and may be used to fill out subjective detail lacking in classical anthropology for rites of passage.

The Sun Dance has been characterized in a number of ways. According to Joseph Jorgensen, the Sun Dance is a ritual aspect of a "redemptive movement" that has for its goal "the total change in the individual by supernatural means and human efforts, provides a loose code of conduct (obligations and responsibilities) for each adherent, rejects and castigates the evils of white society, and helps to resolve the conflict between Protestant ethic individualism preached by whites, and the collective ethic preached by Indians."[49] The dance is a sacrificial performance, for the good of others, for the purification of one's own community, and for the improvement of the world.

But the ritual has also been described as a calendrical rite of renewal, with cosmological symbolism of a world center and the solar god moving around the tree axis.[50] In yet other analyses it is a ritual of defiance against the white man—a reservation phenomenon, a rite of mourning for dead warriors or hunters, a mobilization of power for war, a ceremonial enactment of capture, torture, and release.[51] The meaning of the rite changes from one community to the next, one scholar to another. The same issues of symbolism discussed earlier in connection with the spilling of blood in New Guinea surface here. What is the range of appropriate symbolical reading, who reads the symbols, and is there meaning with no awareness of symbolic meaning?

The Sun Dance, which usually takes place in late June or early July, varies from one tribal group to another, and even one performance to another. Based on Robert Lowie's detailed description, Fred Voget divided the event into five subsidiary stages: 1. The initiation of the Sun Dance cycle. 2. Public announcement and consecration by means of buffalo hunts. 3. Selection of Sun Dance bundle owner to supervise the ceremony. 4. Construction and consecration of the lodge (including erection of central pole). 5. The dance for power around the pole in front of the sacred effigy.[52] The dance lasts for three or four days and is performed by participants who have taken a vow to sacrifice for their families and the community. Dancers are barefoot and bareheaded, and they dance with their heads raised to the sun, while blowing on eagle-bone whistles and dancing to the rhythm of ongoing drumming and singing from nondancing participants. The rules for the dance vary. However, everywhere the Sun Dance is undertaken the dance is an enormous physical and psychological trial. The dance usually lasts from early morning till midnight every day, and the dancers fast and avoid water, either for the entire period, or while dancing. Many performances, though by no means all, are accompanied by the piercing of some dancers' chests with sticks or eagle claws that are fastened with rope to the central post. The dancers must break free by tearing their own flesh. The Sun Dance may also be accompanied with other forms of torture, as we shall see.[53]

Various narrative accounts of individual experience support all the meanings attributed to the Sun Dance in one case or another. Here are two examples for the way personal experience correlates with the stated meaning of the ritual.

Reconciling Cosmological Opposites

Jorgensen argues that the religious significance of the Sun Dance is its capacity for synthesizing "opposing yet compatible forms in which power is evidenced."[54] This cosmological power is evident at the most abstract level in the opposition of "dry" and "wet" and "hot" and "cool." Ritualized attainment of power takes place through the interaction with the sun and the sunrays, sources of both heat and coolness, both dryness and moisture. The first three days of the dance are characterized by a buildup of heat and dryness, by meditation on the increasing difficulty of the sacrifice, which the dancers have undertaken. The dancers are painted, and this dries them; even the singers and drummers, whose throats get parched, increase their heat and dryness. Meanwhile, the central pole, identified with man, who needs water for survival, is also painted; it too dries out and makes the sacrifice. As the sacrifice is rewarded, the participants become cooled down and wetted, their thirst miraculously quenched and their hot bodies cooled. Dancers who attain vision are literally knocked off their feet and lie flat, unconscious for several hours.[55] They are carried off to remain in their vision, their bodies surprisingly cool and moist. Lesser dancers also experience a similar transformation:

> I ran to the tree. The heat was terrific. The top of my head was so hot, and the bottom of my feet was just burning. I danced two or three times, and on the last attempt I was running to the tree, when a drop of water struck me in the middle of my back. That drop of water—where it came from I did not know—for there were no clouds in sight, only the heat. I thanked the Maker for that drop of water on my back, feeling relief. I started again, and again a drop of water hit me right in the same place, and I danced . . . [until] the end of the song. . . . I felt relieved as if I had had a cup of cold water.[56]

The localization of power by reconciling cosmological opposites generates new shamans, individuals who are endowed with wisdom and the capacity to heal. However, the opposing forces synthesized are not merely natural, but are social as well. The principles of individuality, often inculcated by white values, must be reconciled with collective identification, which is a more traditional Indian value. And even these values contain subsidiary distinctions, such as individuality that is group-sanctioned and serves the ends of the group, as opposed to individuality aimed at the benefit of one's own self alone. Similarly collectivism is not a monolithic value. Jorgensen argues that illness is the disharmony between such oppositions and health is their reconciliation, something that can be achieved through the synthesizing power of shamanism. The argument resonates very well with Turner's observation that rites of passage for Ndembu boys enact a variety of social and psychological conflicts, which are resolved in the new status of the boy. Readers who are quick to congratulate the authors on the discovery of a universal principle should recall that both authors were writing at the heyday of structuralism, a time when everyone was discovering oppositions mediated by rituals.

As noted earlier, one of the interpretations of the Sun Dance describes it as a mock captivity, torture, and release. The dancers are pierced in the skin above the pectoral muscles or scapulae where wooden skewers are inserted. These are attached to thongs leading to the Sun Dance pole. Other skewers may be attached at the back or upper arms and tied to buffalo skulls. The dancers move toward the pole, then run backward with great force, tearing themselves free. At times the piercer, who is the "captor," makes the cut too deep and the tearing free becomes hard: "If he was unable to tear the flesh in that time by means of the motion of the dancing, he might give horses for his release, or his relatives might give them in his behalf. In that event the man who had done the cutting was allowed to cut the flesh either partially or entirely."[57] If his relatives have no horses or valuable with which to buy his release, the man is jerked downward until the flesh tears. These performances, particularly the purchasing of freedon, are indeed consistent with captivity and release. Some participants would at times make a vow to be entirely suspended between four poles above the ground by means of thongs inserted both in the front and the back of the torso. In such a case there is no question of dancing free, and gifts always have to be given for release.

The symbolism of captivity and release and the symbolism of reconciled cosmic oppositions may seem incompatible. Or perhaps they are easy to reconcile due to the voluntary nature of the captivity and its community-enhancing self-sacrifice. At any rate, my concern, and the reason I am citing these descriptions in the context of a chapter on rites of passage is to show how pain serves the overall purpose of the ritual, whatever its symbolic meaning. Ritual pain is both prevalent and instrumental regardless of how the scholar or even the participants interpret the ritual. Pain is psychologically effective in mediating the cultural meanings of the ritual with individual experience, regardless of conceptual interpretation.

The Pain of Sun Dance

Dancers who choose to do so hurt themselves very deeply at the Sun Dance. Eagle Feather writes that in a 1974 dance he began to use eagle claws instead of a wooden pin. The eagle was the first messenger of God, so the symbolism is powerful, but the eagle claw does not break easily and the flesh must rip open for release. He adds: "I repeat that we do not use antiseptic or anesthetic to cleanse to wound or to dull the pain. And it is very painful, believe me, it is very painful! I have gone through twenty-five piercings, and I know."[58] Eagle Feather also describes the groaning, begging, praying, and the way those who are pierced grab the man who pierces them. Some plead for a small cut, others cry.

A detailed subjective description of the ritual and the piercing can be found in Manny Twofeathers's autobiographical *The Road to the Sundance*. The book is a candid portrayal of a middle-aged man, a Native American, whose life gradually disintegrates around him. His marriage collapses, he becomes distant from his children, and he is alienated from any sense of community. The reasons, Twofeathers confesses, are his own failures, his self-indulgence. The book moves through the Sun Dance to a new life, and the readers are not promised an integrated and healthy life. The author still comes across as troubled, as my students have all insisted. But for the duration of the Sun Dance itself, as Manny Twofeathers undergoes the tortures described above, a noticeable transformation takes place. This is an outward movement from personal to community identification. The following passages are taken directly from his account:

> "Okay, where do you want to be pierced?"
>
> I pointed to the places on my chest.
>
> He asked, "Once or twice?"
>
> "Let's go for both sides. I came from too far away to get pierced on only one side."
>
> He took the time to explain to me, "Manny, this is your first time, are you sure you want both sides? Most new guys and first-timers will only pierce once to make sure they can endure the pain."
>
> "I'm sure. I want both sides done. I can do it. The Spirits came to me this morning and told me that I was ready."
>
> . . .

I lay there on the ground, looking up into the sky. Then I handed Lessert my piercing bones. He got down on his knees next to me, and his father knelt by my left side.

I felt both of them grab my chest and rub it with some dirt, because I was sweaty and slippery. This way their thumbs and fingers wouldn't slip.

They pinched my skin, and I felt as the knife went into my flesh.

I felt a sharp, intense pain in my chest, as if somebody had put a red-hot iron on my flesh.

I lost all sense of time.

I couldn't hear any sounds.

I didn't feel the heat of the sun.

I tried to grit my teeth, but I couldn't—my crown was in my mouth.

I prayed to the Creator to give me strength, to give me courage. I was doing it for my children.

. . .

When I stood up, I did feel pain. I felt pain, but I also felt that closeness with the Creator. I felt like crying for all the people who needed my prayers. I prayed that they could get enough to eat. I prayed for all the people who are sick in the world. It brought tears to my eyes. . . . The pain did not compare to what I was receiving from this sacred experience. . . . I was tied to the tree with that rope as securely as a child is tied to its mother by the umbilical cord. The only way off that cord was by ripping myself off.

. . .

Every time I leaned back on my rope, I felt intense pain in my chest. It became a raw ache that reached all the way down to my toes. Every time I looked at my piercing bones, I saw the faces of my children. . . .

It felt glorious and explosive. The energy was high and brilliant.

The narrative proceeds to describe Twofeathers's affection for the pole, his intimacy as he hugs it, while being tied to it. He states again that breaking free would be like breaking the umbilical cord connecting him to his mother. But he knows he must do so, like a warrior:

I went back, back. I looked at the tree and said silently, "Grandfather, please give me strength."

I ran faster and faster and faster.

I hit the end of the line.

I heard my flesh tear, rip, and pop.

I saw the rope bouncing way up into the tree.

It dangled there for a second, then dropped.

While this was going on, I fell backwards.

I had broken loose.

. . .

I was so happy, I let out a big yell.[59]

Manny Twofeathers is not a scholar of Native American spirituality or ethnography. He supports himself by making artifacts and selling them at fairs or wholesale to merchants. His experiences play out some of the themes found in the ethnographic literature, but are also unique and even eccentric. However, his pain narrative is very illuminating and contains all three levels identified in the McGill Pain Questionnaire. These are the sensory (sharp, like red-hot iron on the flesh), affective (explosive), and evaluative (glorious).

The pain clearly triggers a flood of emotional responses that are both intense and pervasive. The dominant emotions are sorrow (aimed at the poor and sick), love (his children, mother), compassion, dependence (I embraced the tree), fear (give me courage to finish this), shame (it shamed me to have tears appear), courage, happiness, exultation (I brought that Sun Power down on myself and all the people). There is no question that without the pain of the pierced chest he would not have had these emotions surface and would not have experienced them so profoundly. It is the piercing that triggers massive emotional responses related both to courage and love. Twofeathers reports the buildup of his courage, though his first emotional response to the actual pain is love—a sense of deep compassion for his children, to whom he had been a failing father. Contrast these feelings to what the Ndembu initiates must be feeling (how can we truly know from reading Turner?). The cutting of the penis is connected with social conflicts relating to gender roles, to the distribution of power in the village, and to the role of the village in its broader context. The pubescent boys begin to arrive at sexual maturity, and their identity as young men now includes the genitals, where sexual energy would be flowing in a relatively free way if not for the trauma induced. While the Lakota torture frees up emotional energy (among fairly mature individuals), the Ndembu trauma seems designed to stop the energy, control the emotions related to sexuality. However, in both cases, the Sun Dance and the circumcision ritual, the ritual involves conflicting emotions that become reconciled experientially: courage and love in one case, desire and rage in the other. Both sets of emotions are experienced consciously in the ritual, as both opposites must be integrated in the emerging self.

For the Native American the piercing is made tolerable by the greater social end that motivates the initiate (in the person of the spectators and other participants). A pain-induced subservience to a greater telos turns the torture into a ritual of self-sacrifice. That greater cause is then "internalized" in the sense of uniting conscious emotions with somatic feelings. The magicalism that Catherine Bell identified in the work of Turner, Mary Douglas, and Steven Lukes on the question of how social values are ritually internalized is here eliminated.[60]

Pain and Learning

Strong feelings induced by pain affect our capacity to perceive and know reality.[61] In fact, the conceptual separation between emotion and cognition, due so much to Piaget, is highly misleading. The goals of rites of passage, or initiation for that matter, include emotional synthesis along with the acquisition of new knowledge, both embodied in one's developing sense of identity.[62]

In normal growth, the infant's sense of reality emerges in tandem with the loss of the complete symbiosis with the mother. The existence of such an "external" objective reality is deeply bound with pain (hunger), discomfort (wetness), and frustration (waiting for the mother). If the child's needs were met instantaneously it would not be able to separate the primary object from its own body-self. The painful fact of having to wait for the gratification of basic needs is the origin of the possibility of reality knowledge. Or, to be a bit more precise, it is the sequence of frustration and gratification that aids cognitive development, the differentiation between one's biological self and the sense of other objects that possess continuity and permanence. Without the gratification that follows frustration the external world would lack coherence and predictability.[63] In terms of Object Relations theory, which I have been using throughout this work, "separation and individuation from external objects and the formation of internal psychic organization and structures develop in a reciprocal way, and a lack of differentiation of the external world may be paralleled by a lack of internal differentiation."[64]

Discriminating between fantasy and reality is thus both a perceptual matter and a function of emotional development. The sense of reality cannot be separated from the ability to have certain emotions in relation to one's primary objects, beginning with the nurturing mother. In other words, love and knowledge go together, as do knowledge and misery.[65] Successive developments in life—"stages," as Melanie Klein calls them—involve several "decentrations," the painful giving up of safe certainties that are bound to our emotional security.[66] After infancy and childhood come the upheavals of adolescence, young adulthood, and so forth. The key difference between the infantile learning and adult learning, on this model, is the trauma required for giving up certainties. Infants and young children whose sense of reality is relatively weak require "transitional objects" (in Winnicott's terms) such as Linus's blanket to move beyond primary process fantasy to secondary process reality testing.

The only transition that matches that one in its radical depth, is the one in which ordinary reality gives way to spiritual reality. Rites of passage, in addition to their psychological and social agendas, introduce boys and girls into the world of spiritual beings, moral values, mythologies, and sacred lore. The legitimacy of such knowledge is acquired at the expense of both ordinary reality and childhood fantasy. A child needs to give up the illusion of Santa Claus and replace it not with free market commercialism but with the reality of charity, love, or whatever Santa Claus is meant to symbolize. As Sam Gill noted in his example, this may involve the traumatic discovery that what the child took for true spirits were in fact his relatives in disguise. That disappointment must give way not to bitterness and cynicism, but to a recognition of the symbolic reality behind the mask. This is an invented reality that consists of abstractions, which are animated by emotions and the objects of emotions. This is an enormously difficult leap, and on a cognitive level is the goal of rites of passage.

That rites of passage emulate the process of death and rebirth is a truism. However, the similarity is not a mere trope, a device for conceptualizing transition as such. The similarity is paradigmatic in that both indicate a loss and then recovery of consciousness. The initiates are severely traumatized, which leads to dissociation of various levels and qualities. The dissociation is accompanied by powerful—often forbidden—feelings, which are then split, projected, or otherwise deflected from the taboo objects (mother, father). The emotions are localized in transitional objects, the cutter or other functionaries in the ritual, who are thus perceived as evil, defiled, horrific, monstrous. The child's peers who undergo the same torture are endowed with the good qualities that are no longer the domain of the absent mother.[67] They are the other pole of the split and the other transitional objects. As the child begins to heal and listen to the teachings of his elders, the transitional objects become less one-sided and more ambiguous, and endowed with the complex qualities the child must come to possess in order to be an adult. Cultural lore too is recognized as intrinsically ambiguous (or perhaps polyvalent), bad and evil in tandem, rather than absolutely good in opposition to the absolutely evil—a childish fantasy.

Pain thus acts as the mediating force that makes the acquisition of third-level (spiritual) reality possible and compatible with the emotional maturation that takes place at the same time. This is an enormously fecund pain that produces a wealth of benefits. The trauma reduces the initiate's sense of body-self and allows the identification with the sociocultural goals embodied in the spiritual role models of the child. When the painful dissociation is effective it removes the psychic distance from the assumed role. Failure to go beyond the "as if" distance could mean the failure of initiation.[68]

Why Ritual?

Hurting initiates in rites of passage and initiations is a form of applying force on them. Force, or power, is brought to bear by those who already belong to the adult world, or to the society of the initiated. But initiates are not simply brutalized, and highly ritualized force becomes sacrificial pain. Rites of passage are rites of supercession. In order to become adults, the initiates sacrifice or give up their lesser identity as boys or girls. Instead of being victims—however symbolic—the children must hurt in a voluntary manner. Only then can the psychological mechanism of self-sacrifice become effective. The fourth chapter of this book discussed the psychodynamics of voluntarily inflicted pain as a means of identifying with higher and more abstract goals than ego. Rites of passage attempt to institutionalize this identification with higher ends, and the means of doing this is the ritual. If adults were to hurt their children in a brutal manner and with no ritual, the pain would not be transformative. The reductive theories of ethologists like Konrad Lorenz would then make sense. But what is it about the ritual that allows a victim to become a self-sacrificer?

Rites of passage mediate the flow of power that takes place between those who have it and those who do not. The symbolic language in which they are couched, and, more important, the performative structures with roles precisely assigned to the participants, create a universe with relative autonomy in which even the young initiate has a degree of power. Catherine Bell calls this "resistance" (to the flow of power) and defines it as the assent given by ritual participants to the ritual itself, and through the ritual, their stake in the control society tries to exert over them. The ritual first creates ritual agents, individuals who appropriate knowledge and values by their mastery of the ritual schemes embedded in their bodies—by mastering, in short, the ritual itself. Ritual becomes a performed cultural sieve. The internalization of social control in ritual contexts is experienced "as relatively empowered, not conditioned or molded."[69] If all social relations are about power—in Foucault's sense of power/knowledge—then all ritual is about the sharing of power, whether the ritual is the flogging of a prisoner, the initiation of boys and girls, or weddings.

Ritual participation is assent, and assent is the fount of self-sacrifice. Turner insists that the voluntary submission to the tortures of passage is, to a large extent, a pious fiction enshrined in the terminology of the rite.[70] This may be so, but Catherine Bell would counter that the very ritualization of the torture (after all, families could send their boys to be circumcised in the mission hospital) creates "resistance," a mock-autonomous realm that defines ritualized action. This is required if the pain is to be effective as a form of self-sacrifice, a principle of social growth.

SEVEN

The Tortures of the Inquisition and the Invention of Modern Guilt

Conscience is like an ulcer in the flesh
—Plutarch, *De Tranquilitate Animi*

Humiliation is worse than physical pain
—Talmud, Sota

On April 6, 1568, Elvira del Campo was brought before the inquisitors of the Spanish Inquisition in Toledo to explain why she refused to eat pork and why she put clean linen on the table for Saturdays. She was suspected of secretly practicing Judaism, though this charge was never made explicit.[1]

> She was carried to the torture-chamber and told to tell the truth, when she said that she had nothing to say. She was ordered to be stripped and again admonished, but was silent. When stripped, she said, "senores, I have done all that is said of me and I bear false-witness against myself, for I do not want to see myself in such trouble; please God, I have done nothing." She was told not to bring false testimony against herself but to tell the truth. The tying of the arms was commenced; she said "I have told the truth; What have I to tell?" She was told to tell the truth and replied "I have told the truth and have nothing to tell." One cord was applied to the arms and twisted and she was admonished to tell the truth but she said she had nothing to tell. Then she screamed and said "I have done all they [the witnesses] say."

The historiography of the Inquisition has been greatly enriched by the exquisite detail and detachment with which officials of the Church witnessed and recorded such interrogations and tortures. Numerous instances, some of which will be quoted later on, began with a pathetically uneven sparring over truth, followed by a vigorous application of torture, and the willing confession of the accused to the charges—any charges. In fact, the Inquisition has entered the popular imagination as an institution of crushing power, the brutalizer of individuals into conformity and correct belief. An analysis of its repressive power would seem to call for the type of methodology with which Michel Foucault claimed that the state exerts power over its subjects. Although this insight is wrong—in fact, because it is so wrong—the present chapter must begin with Foucault's analysis.

Pain and Power

Michel Foucault launched his study of the rise of the prison—*Discipline and Punish*—with a vivid description of the appalling execution in France on March 2, 1757, of a man convicted of attempted regicide. The sentence against Damiens read that he was to be

> taken and converted in a cart, wearing nothing but a shirt, holding a torch of burning wax weighing two pounds; then, in the said cart, to the Place de Greve, where, on a scaffold that will be erected there, the flesh will be torn from his breasts, arms, thighs and calves with red-hot pincers, his right hand, holding the knife with which he committed the said parricide, burn with sulphur, and, on those places where the flesh will be torn away, poured molten lead, boiling oil, burning resin, wax and sulphur melted together and then his body drawn and quartered by four horses and his limbs and body consumed by fire, reduced to ashes and his ashes thrown to the winds.[2]

Foucault's account follows the detailed eyewitness version of Bouton, an officer of the watch. The readers can follow with their mind's eye, if they wish, as the executioner—"a sturdy fellow"—struggled to tear off pieces of flesh from the screaming prisoner with those red hot pincers. Or the readers can marvel at the structural integrity of a man's body, as four then six powerful horses failed to quarter it, while the man lay conscious. Many readers may flinch or turn the pages quickly, but Foucault's gaze is unwavering; the description is even and textured, with no detail elevated above another, and none spared to the readers.

And what is the purpose of Foucault's demonstration? It is a retelling of a public execution by torture, designed to chronicle—surprisingly—the disappearance of the judicial spectacle and the rise of the penitentiary in eighteenth-century Europe. But perhaps the gruesome beginning to Foucault's study is not surprising, let alone perverse. After all, the story is about the disappearance of the body as the target of penal repression, and its replacement with the soul: its confinement, surveillance, and discipline. In other words, "physical pain, the pain of the body itself, is no longer the constituent element of the penalty. From being an art of unbearable sensations punishment has become an economy of suspended right."[3]

These observations are very surprising for a scholar writing a book that advances a resoundingly monistic psychology. Foucault's book has been criticized on many grounds, empirical as well as conceptual.[4] Its psychology, however, is important, at least in principle. Foucault rejects the distinction between metaphysical subjectivity and objective realities such as social and political contexts in which a subject presumably exists. He understands the subject as the fulcrum of social forces—"power"—in a type of Marxist effacement of a priori consciousness. Reduced to its bottom line, Foucault's method states that "power and knowledge directly imply one another."[5] Or, in more contemporary terms, information is both the substance and the structure of social and psychological reality, and it flows from those who control power to those who do not. Foucault's point was set in historical terms, of course: Penal law (infliction of power through pain) and human sciences developed out of a common matrix, which he called "epistemo-juridical." The technology of power is the key principle that encompasses both the penal system and the knowledge of man—the human sciences. Punishment creates the juridical subject and finally the man. There are two points here. The first is obvious, that the state creates the spectacle in order to compel and intimidate by example. The second point is far more subtle. By marking the body of the victim the state fashions the conduit for its power and thereby invents the subject out of an empirical individual. In the case of the spectacle, this is done by means of the criminal's body.[6] The body counts above all else, because it is the focus of the power-information exerted on behalf of the law.[7] "But the body is also directly involved in a political field; power relations have an immediate hold on it; they invest it, mark it, train it, torture it, force it to carry out tasks, to perform ceremonies, to emit signs. This political investment of the body is bound up, in accordance with complex reciprocal relations, with its economic use."[8]

Foucault's effort to recover the process of the creation of the subject out of power relations is admirable. His sociopsychological monism is subtle, and for many cultural theorists, persuasive. But there is a very strange gap, perhaps a paradox, in his method. It may be the monistic ontology, or the Marxist sociology to which Foucault is committed here, that makes him forget that the body is not an object—a map, or even a corpse. The body does not register pain; the person does. Foucault's lengthy description of Damiens's execution is loaded with resentment against state power, but it is oddly lacking in empathy for the victim. Though his brutal execution was ripe with symbolism, Damiens's body was not a billboard; it was, first and foremost the center of Damiens's consciousness and pain. Due to a strange aloofness, Foucault fails to notice, or emphasize, a very striking aspect of the spectacle. The quote from Bouton relates the following:

> Manseiur Le [sic] Breton, the clerk of the court, went up to the patient several times and asked him if he had anything to say. He said he had not; at each torment, he cried out, "Pardon, my God! Pardon, Lord." . . . Monseiur le Breton went up to him again and asked him if he had anything to say; he said no. Several confessors went up to him and spoke to him at length; he willingly kissed the crucifix that was held out to him; he opened his lips and repeated: "Pardon, Lord."

Foucault failed to take notice that the state, in the form of its court officials and executioners, was not just applying brute force to the body of its victim. It was, rather, executing a formal procedure, a ritual, imbued with meaningful religious elements, in which the accused was expected to play an active and willing part. The execution, in other words, was a pseudoconfessional rite, or perhaps a conversion or reconciliation. And Damiens, indeed, acted as a willing participator in the rite (if not the execution itself), not as a passive object that registered the signs of a technology of power, but as a subject of some consolation and potential redemption.

Due to this omission, at the very least, Foucault cannot serve as a reliable guide for pursuing one of the main agendas of his own work. If we want to understand the role of religious and legal procedure in the making of the modern subject, we need a more subtle analysis of the ritual aspects of penal tortures, and, more specifically, the theological-penitential models on which they are constructed. Such an analysis is precisely what this chapter offers.

Of course, "the modern subject" is a hopelessly vague concept. Instead, this chapter will look at the emergence to prominence of the modern conscience, or more precisely, the sense of guilt—the very apparatus that Freud regarded as a universal and transhistorical aspect of the human psyche. I will demonstrate the important role of religious inquisitions and tortures in the formation of this aspect of modern consciousness.[9] In the process I will share Foucault's rejection of a metaphysical "self." But while his work rests on a Marxist ontology, the present work is phenomenological and grants special privilege to experience and consciousness. I will show how the experience of pain in key juridical contexts led to some modern metaphors of the guilty conscience.

Pain, Guilt, and the Juridical Model of the Conscience

> Told to tell in detail what she had done she replied "I have already told you the truth." Then she screamed and said "Tell me what you want for I don't know what to say." She was told to say what she had done, for she was tortured because she had not done so, and another turn of the cord was ordered. She cried "Loosen me, Senores and tell me what I have to say: I do not know what I have done, O Lord, have mercy on me, a sinner!"[10]

Despite the lack of clarity in the meaning and function of guilt and conscience in psychological literature, many writers regard both as historically contingent phenomena. Paul Ricoeur famously connects guilt in human history with stain and contagion: "The idea of guilt represents the extreme form of interiorization which we have seen sketched in the passage from stain to sin."[11] John Carroll similarly argues that guilt has a historical dimension, and adds that the psychology of guilt suggests that "societies may differ widely in the degree in which their members are under the thrall of the gray eminence."[12] In historic and geographic places where guilt does in fact emerge, it is defined as aggression turned back against the self. Freudian theory posits that this aggression is stimulated by anxiety, which is the fear of conscience, or forces associated with superego. For Freud these forces are intrinsic and universal to the human race, explained in terms of the conflict between drives (instincts) and the constraints of civilization.[13] Any variation in the experiential face of guilt arises from the content of the superego, from the cultural ideas and taboos that shape conscience. But, of course, Freud was better at constructing universal mechanisms than at identifying local features.

The case of the Inquisition calls for a more flexible and anthropological approach to the psychology of the guilty subject. The medieval or archaic person must be understood in relational terms. She was an empirical person who experienced herself in relationship to family, community, or local church. She possessed little sense of interiority, or an identity located within her "center," but identified with external relational loci. This psychology could easily be compared with that of traditional societies anywhere, even totemic communities.[14] The local parish or church actively participates in this relational web, which is characterized by the use of charms and amulets; the worship of saints and their relics; the performance of magical rituals—often involving parish priests—for healing, exorcism, agricultural benefits, and even black magic.[15] Guilt in such an archaic world—superficial and nondispositional—is often experienced as debt, or as pollution, and the realms of natural events and moral judgment are not clearly differentiated. This was surely the case in medieval Europe where misfortunes were blamed on divine anger or human failings, as the plague (Black Death) of 1348 was considered the work of Jews, or lepers.[16] Scapegoat communities were identified for sacrificial destruction, for the removal of communal pollution and guilt and the control of the powers that governed nature.[17] In such a world, one does not turn inward to introspect on one's guilt or one's faults. Instead these are broadcast in a humiliating fashion as *mala fama* (infamy) and are publicized for the community at large. The concept of infamy became a technical one, with legal consequences at the hands of the Inquisition. But far more significant from the psychological point of view was the experience of culpability as shame, as the loss of reputation in the community that defined the person.[18] In the archaic and magical world of premodern Europe, guilt could be ascertained by magical means—by ordeals, for example, not because the ordeal uncovered the hearts of humans but because guilt hovered outside in the world, as did the ubiquitous spirits and demons.

The Inquisition did not singlehandedly change these ways of experiencing guilt; they still survive today. However, the inquisitional ritual played a profound role in those aspects relating to moral introspection and the sense of guilt, along with the need for corporal punishment as a mitigator of fault. From the moral and psychological point of view then, the Inquisition straddled the boundary between the archaic and the modern. It capitalized on the relational ontology of individuals by shaming them, then isolating and disorienting them. It insisted on introspection as an act of discovering (or creating) guilt "inside" oneself, and it uncovered this guilt with efficiency by means of torture. Finally, the Inquisition replaced the magical concept of the scapegoat as the locus of fault, and pointed its finger at everyman and everywoman. In fact, the (Spanish) Inquisition left the totally marginal (the gypsy, the expelled Jew) alone, and hounded the *conversos* and heretics only inasmuch as they were potentially ordinary, future members of the community. The painful rituals of the Inquisition, in short, provided the model for the modern sense of guilt. But the painful work of the Inquisition cannot be understood only in terms of the juridical conception of pain as the remover of fault. Inquisitional pain was also the medical and alchemical agent of change that transformed a confused soul into a saved one in a manner that defies easy condemnation.[19]

It may seem facile to say that inquisitional tortures were not so horrible after all, that there are cases on record of children defeating their torturers by keeping silent.[20] It may also ring false to claim that Europeans of the thirteenth to seventeenth centuries were tougher and more immune to pain than we are. But there is also some truth here. Pain with no analgesics pervaded life in Europe and held a coherent meaning. Aside from the ubiquity of minor irritants and the recurring submission of women to labor, there were more symbolically significant pains as well. Barber-surgeons, dentists, and bonesetters were familiar and horrifying professionals also, much like executioners. Their work generated extreme pain. For amputation, the fourteenth-century French surgeon Manderville could only offer: "The limb which is to be cut off should be ligated by two cords . . . so that the patient will feel the operation less acutely because of the constriction."[21] Medical illustrations of the period identify the surgeon with an executioner and the patient with a Christlike figure being tormented in a variety of manners, from flagellation to a crucifixion on a frightening rack. The bonesetter, or the surgeon who repaired dislocations, pulled the bone into place by elongating the limb of the patient who was suspended on a rack. The pain can only be imagined and the artists made no effort to communicate it.

But there is more. The technology of pain—if not pain itself—involved bodily fluids, especially blood. It was a technology of pollution and danger—not the work of proper physicians but of socially marginal practitioners who, like alchemists, were awesome. But here also lay their power to transform their patients: "The surgeon saw the body over which he laboured as being something like the athanor of the alchemists: the seat of incessant boiling, combustion and calcinations, on which the lungs blow like a blacksmith's bellows. And indeed the surgeon was not unlike a smith or jeweller as he wielded his white-hot pincers—his cauterizing tools—frequently used to evacuate or keep away evil humors."[22] The point then is not that life was painful and so the Inquisition did not seem so horrible. The point, rather, was that pain was prevalent and familiar, and so it was meaningful, easily coopted by a positive ideology.

Conditions for the Rise of the Inquisitions

Historians are reasonably clear on the circumstances that surrounded the rise of the medieval Inquisition and later the Spanish Inquisition. A distinct convergence of political and legal factors combined with ideological and psychological facts in both cases. From the perspective of the inquisitorial ritual and the internalization of guilt, a brief account of the blending of the political with the ideological and psychological should be adequate. Four major developments stand out in this regard: centralization, juridicalization, rationality, and the primacy of experience.

Centralization

The medieval institution of the Inquisition emerged early in the years of Pope Gregory IX, between 1227 and 1233.[23] It was one among several turning points in an ongoing struggle by the Church to shore up a weakening political, economic, and doctrinal hegemony. The events that led to the founding of the Holy Office were extremely diverse and included the fall of Jersusalem to Islam in 1187, the running battle with the twin heresies of the Cathars and the Waldensians, the excommunication of Emperor Frederick II of Swabia (1229), the rise of the Mendicant Orders of the Dominicans and Franciscans, the Albigensian Crusade (ended 1209), and others. The transitional and chaotic twelfth and thirteenth centuries marked the ebb and flow of the Church's authority in the face of centrifugal forces. Its response was to fortify the center with a bureaucracy of power.

The same holds true in a general sense for the establishment of the Spanish Inquisition in 1478. There too it was a battle to consolidate political and economic power by a Church that was united with royalty in the person of Ferdinand.[24] Though in the Spanish case the Holy Office was nominally a weapon against Judaism and Judaisers—those among the *conversos* who secretly practiced Judaism—the true reason for its foundation was a desire to eliminate the contesting power of urban middle classes. This culminated with the expulsion of all the Jews from Spain in March 1492, but the work of the Inquisition was only beginning at that point as far as identifying secret heresies was concerned. The Inquisition was thus a primary tool, both royal and ecclesiastic, for the "reconquest" of Spain for Christianity, for the aristocracy, and for the racially pure.[25] Half a century later the Spanish Inquisition shifted its attention from the *conversos,* who were now thoroughly integrated into the elite of Old Christians. It now focused on other forces threatening the center, namely the "centrifugal action of the fueros," the Moslems, the Lutheran immigrants from France or newer converts to Lutheranism, the Mariscos.[26] By the mid-sixteenth century the New Christians (*conversos*) were no longer targets, but paradoxically, neither were the gypsies, despite their penchant for blasphemy and immorality. As noted, the first group was now a part of the center; the second group was too marginal to threaten the center.

Juridicalization

The consolidation of central authority and power by the Church resonated with more subtle and meaningful developments in jurisprudence, religious ideology, and medieval psychology. The most notable among these was, perhaps, the reemergence of Roman law in twelfth-century Italy. Medieval laws up till the mid-twelfth century—for instance, Germanic law—recognized a variety of secular and religious crimes and punished them severely. The German Church prescribed branding with hot iron and practiced public shaming, mutilations, and so forth.[27] But when Roman legal studies recommenced in Bologna under Gratian in the eleventh and twelfth centuries, an old instrument was rediscovered for the systematic suppression of dissent and the strengthening of the Church's authority. What Roman law brought into play was not so much the use of corporal punishment, but a renowned ideology of authority, the concept of heresy as treason against the central authority, and the notion of infamy (*mala fama*). These concepts supplemented juridical developments that might have come about anyway due to political factors, and, to some extent, they promoted the rise of humanism and rationalism in the sphere of jurisprudence. Chief among these latter developments was the replacement of Germanic accusatory law with proper criminal law based on an examination of crimes by state officials, an inquisitorial approach. This was modeled on the ancient Roman precedent, instituted gradually starting in the second century BCE and formalized by the emperor Hadrian in 125 BCE.[28] Previously the Roman state had taken no active role in initiating legal action—not even "criminal." Adjudication involved the settling of disputes between litigants, one of whom brought action (*accusatio*) against another to redress damages—even where loss of limb or life was concerned. The rule of Augustus brought an enormous amount of centralized power into the hands of the state, which assumed a greater interest in controlling legal affairs by establishing a bureaucracy that initiated action against citizens, based on information gathered by official examiners conducting investigations (*inquisitio*). The interest of a central authority in crimes and misdemeanors implied that mutual acts among individuals produced more than debt, pollution, or some form of magical substance ("bad blood"). The accountability to such central authority implied blame, a moral-legal category that was not detectable magically through divination because it was integral to the agent's bond with the state—his legal motives.[29]

Rationality

By 1230, similar centralizing legal dynamics were taking place in Europe under the rule of kings, lords, and popes. The Roman canonical procedural law was displacing local practices that were based on the accusatory procedure of redressing damages.[30] But just as important, and perhaps linked to this development, was the replacement of medieval evidentiary rituals with rational procedures. In practical terms this means that the rituals of the judicial duel, the ordeal, and the compurgation (common oath) were replaced with meticulous questioning and torture.[31] The older methods, dominant in medieval Europe, were based on the assumption that God may intervene in ascertaining truth. This was replaced by the thirteenth century with a rational and human-centered method of investigation leading to the uncovering of truth. It is important to note that, like torture, the ordeals often also involved pain, but the evidence emerged not only from the courage to withstand the hurt but from the marks that the ordeal left on the body of the subject. Torture (*inquisitio*) was assumed to be an effective and logical procedure for uncovering hidden truths, especially when the claimants were no longer two citizens but the state and one of its subjects. By 1215 the Lateran Council prohibited ordeals, and in the Verona decree of Lucius III, recognized forms of canonical "purgation" were prescribed for the examination of suspected heretics.[32] The Lateran Council was deeply responsible for the juridicalization of individual psychology by means of sacramental rituals. As Foucault noted, obligatory penances and confession institutionalized the introspection and moral self-scrutiny of the individual and made it (in a germinal form) an instrument of social control.[33] In 1252 Innocent IV published a bull (*Ad extripanda*) that adopted this decree and legitimized the use of torture for heresy.

The institution of procedural tortures and their application to suspected heretics implies a dominant religious center and human-based rationalism acting in its service. Both of these assumptions rest on Roman precedents. But the same also holds true for the conception of heresy as a grievous crime against that center, as treason. Both Greek and Roman law had refrained from applying torture to citizens of the state. Torture was acceptable only in the case of slaves, who lacked legal personality, or in the case of treason, where the authority of the state itself was challenged.[34] Maximus was the first Roman ruler in 385 to execute heretics (Gnostics and Manichaeans) for their beliefs. The Church itself, at that time, still refrained from torturing or executing heretics despite the pressure that was building up on ideological and political grounds. St. Augustine asked the Prefect of Africa not to execute Donatists but to apply charity to them instead. However, by 447, Leo I legitimized the most violent response to heresy conforming to Jerome's earlier advice that temporal punishment was merciful to heretics, sparing them from the eternal torments of hell.[35] A constitution of 453 by the emperors Balentian III and Marcian wedded church doctrine with imperial interest when it stated that paganism was treasonous—the holding of imperial laws in contempt.[36] These, and similar decrees (e.g., Codex Theodosianus of 534) institutionalized corporal punishments for heresy and provided the foundation for twelfth century canonical law on heresy and treason.

The severity of the legal view of treason was mitigated, at least theoretically, by the ecclesiastical notion that the law was therapeutic and not vindictive.[37] The precedent for such a pious view goes as far back as Plato. In the medieval context this meant that the prosecution and torture of the heretic served not only as a protection of the center (church, state) but as the restoration of the heretic's spiritual standing, conceived initially not in psychological but social terms. Augustine had used the phrase "compel them to come in" in connection with heretics, or insisted that the laws against heretics were meant to return them to "the feast of God."[38] This was consistent, of course, with his relative mildness in legal matters.

The Primacy of Experience

The dramatic rise of heresy in the eleventh through thirteenth centuries was in fact an ecclesiastical characterization of intellectual and political ferment—a threat to the institutional and scriptural authority insisted on by the Church of Rome. In fact, the rise of the Mendicant Orders, especially the Dominicans and Franciscans, and later the powerful mystical orders of Spain, was part of the same phenomenon.[39] Although the Church abided by and sanctioned the new mystical orders, their quick rise to prominence was symptomatic of the dynamic energy of the period, and particularly the new authority invested in religious experience. The direct pursuit of divine knowledge and its capacity for undermining traditional hierarchy thus pervaded both sides of the Church boundaries. But the passion with which the Dominicans and Franciscans sought religious truth experientially was turned by the Church into an instrument for battling the other religious sects of the period, primarily Cathars and Waldensians, who were labeled heretics. What this meant, in practical terms, was that the fasts, vigils, scourging, and every other form of voluntary self-torture that the mystics inflicted on their own persons were turned against the heretics as an instrument of law.[40] The Church, as noted previously, imagined the Holy Office as an arm of penance, spiritual reconciliation, and the restoration of the wayward back to the community of the faithful. Its tortures were modeled after ascetic practices, and even the burning of the heretic at the stake was based on readings of scripture, and on the penitential model of purifying fires as a purgatorial blessing.[41]

The insistence on the direct experience of truth had its flip side in the demand by the Church for uncovering the hidden truths in the souls of its members, above and beyond their actions. External and practical conformity was no longer the gauge for spiritual authenticity. The Inquisition, run mainly by members of the Dominican order, thus marks a major transitional point in medieval religious psychology. This was a transition from the archaic medieval person to the premodern individual; a transition from a relational and community-based ontology with a concomitant magical orientation to the world, to a world of increasingly discrete and separate persons (moral agents). Such persons' inner life may, as always, be transparent to the all-knowing God, but remains hidden from their social and spiritual betters.

Procedure and the Ritualization of Guilt

In many ways the inquisitional process was not altogether different from that of secular courts. The public summons and the notification of arrest were humiliating and terrifying in both cases. The isolation and discomforts, not to say torments, of prison were similar: a dark cell, meager rations, straw bed, disease, lack of information and representation, prolonged delays. The interrogation, often accompanied by threats or blows, was something every thief and robber came to expect. Public executions for notorious criminals were extremely common throughout Europe until the nineteenth century. If anything, the Inquisition's procedures were milder than those of the secular courts: Inquisitional prisons tended to be somewhat more humane, and the interrogators were constrained by more rigid rules of procedure.[42]

The detailed procedure was determined to a very large extent by the guiding ideology of the Inquisition. The Inquisition was never conceptualized as an institution of civil and criminal prosecution. Instead, it was a paternalistic instrument of the Church, a Holy Office, designed to identify the secret sins of heresy or other forms of religious guilt, and save the souls of those who had erred. The inquisitor was the spiritual father of the accused, and the target of his inquest was the inner thought and belief of the accused, not merely overt actions. The guilt (culpability, not subjective feeling) of those investigated was assumed in advance because the officials of the Inquisition were fully aware just how difficult it was to be a blameless believer.

Above all, the Inquisition looked for confessions from its accused. That was the primary goal of the entire procedure—to elicit a voluntary admission of the facts and a confession of culpability.[43] Tied with the confession was a public profession of conversion and repentance, for guilt implied a loss of membership in the community of good Christians. Reconversion and repentance, accompanied by penance, returned the wayward to the flock. And indeed, the Inquisition, strictly speaking, was not authorized to punish the guilty. It could torture the accused to elicit confessions, and it could impose penances in order to facilitate the healing process of the stray soul, but it could not impose punishment in the secular sense of the term. Prisoners who refused to confess at all costs were "relaxed" to the secular authorities, who would burn them at the stake.

Genuine conversion and repentance were indicated by verbal assertion. But the Inquisition also expected of the accused, as the Church expected of all the faithful at the time of confession, that all known "accomplices" also be named. Turning in one's friends and relatives—something that seems like betrayal to us—was an indication that the accused genuinely felt that he was helping those other souls, hence, that he was properly converted himself. Therefore, underlying the aspect of the Inquisition that seems most insidious was a certainty of its own benevolence, or virtue. This determined much of what happened in the procedure of the Inquisition.

The investigation usually began before its subject was even aware of anything untoward. It could begin with a denunciation by an acquaintance or could be initiated by officers of the Inquisition based on other evidence. The investigation could take years and include a collection of minute and wide-ranging bits of information on every detail of the subject's life. When enough material was assembled, the subject of the investigation was notified and summoned. The summons would often be posted in a public place such as a church or community gathering place. The charges were virtually never stated, but the damage in reputation to the accused was deep and shameful.

The accused would make his appearance and take an oath. He (or she) still did not know the charges, but was required to confess. If there was strong evidence against the accused at this early point, but he refused to confess, he was charged with obstinacy along with the original indictment. This rendered him equivalent to a heretic and a parricide, even if the original charges were nothing of the kind. Except in unusual circumstances, where the accused was an exceptionally distinguished individual, arrest followed the oath. The accused was placed in one of the inquisitional dungeons, which were somewhat better than the secular holding cells. The drawbacks, however, were significant. Chief among these was the absence of information given to the accused of the suspicions or charges against him, the secrecy surrounding the entire case, and the capacity of the Inquisition to hold the accused in the cell for years before any formal procedure was initiated.

Interrogations were extremely protracted and thorough. They were conducted by well-trained personnel, usually Dominican monks, before any torture was even mentioned, but they were exhausting and lasted for long periods. The goal of the interrogation was not only to elicit admission of acts performed but also a confession of religious guilt, of being a sinner. The following is an example of such an interrogation:[44]

> When a heretic is first brought up for examination, he assumes a confident air, as though secure in his innocence. I ask him why he has been brought before me. He replies, smiling and courteous, "Sir, I would be glad to hear the cause from you."
>
> I. "You are accused as a heretic, and that you believe and teach otherwise than Holy Church believes."
>
> A. (Raising his eyes to heaven, with an air of the greatest faith) "Lord, thou knowest that I am innocent of this, and that I never held any faith other than that of true Christianity."
>
> I. "You call your faith Christian, for you consider ours as false and heretical. But I ask whether you have ever believed as true another faith than that which the Roman Church holds to be true?"
>
> A. "I believe the true faith which the Roman Church believes, and which you openly preach to us."
>
> I. "Perhaps you have some of your sect at Rome whom you call the Roman Church. I, when I preach, say many things, some of which are common to us both, as that God liveth, and you believe some of what I preach. Nevertheless you may be a heretic in not believing other matters which are to be believed."
>
> A. "I believe all the things that a Christian should believe."
>
> I. "I know your tricks. What the members of your sect believe you hold to be that which a Christian should believe. But we waste time in this fencing. Say simply, Do you believe in one God the Father, and the Son, and the Holy Ghost?"
>
> A. "I believe."
>
> I. "Do you believe in Christ born of the Virgin, suffered, risen, and ascended to heaven?"
>
> A. (Briskly) "I believe."
>
> I. "Do you believe the bread and wine in the mass performed by the priests to be changed into the body and blood of Christ by divine virtue?"
>
> A. "Ought I not to believe this?"
>
> I. "I don't ask if you ought to believe, but if you do believe."
>
> A. "I believe whatever you and other good doctors order me to believe."
>
> The inquisitor was able to smell this hedging about and sparring continued for some time. The prisoner managed to avoid saying what the inquisitor is clearly trying to get him to say. Then the subject of an oath came up:
>
> I. "Will you then swear that you have never learned anything contrary to the faith which we hold to be true?"
>
> A. (Growing pale) "If I ought to swear, I will willingly swear."
>
> I. "I don't ask whether you ought, but whether you will swear."

A. "If you order me to swear, I will swear."
I. "I don't force you to swear, because as you believe oaths to be unlawful, you will transfer the sin to me who forced you; but if you will swear, I will hear it."

> The prisoner will refuse to swear, but he will say, "Sir, if I have done amiss I aught, I will willingly bear the penance, only help me to avoid the infamy of which I am accused through malice and without fault of mine." The inquisitor is told not to fall into this trap and to insist on a full and voluntary confession.

It is important to note that the willingness to confess was useless if one could not at that time convince the inquisitors that the confession derived from a genuine and complete search of one's soul. At issue was not obedience or conformity, but spiritual truth, as the Inquisition saw it.

If the isolation and meager rations of the cell, along with the protracted interrogations, did not persuade the prisoner to confess, additional measures were put into place. The case could simply be allowed to drag, while the accused languished in jail supported only by a financially strapped family on the verge of ruin. At times, spies were placed in the cells to gain information that could be used more persuasively than the anonymous evidence brought up at the interrogation.[45] Families might be contacted and told to plead with the prisoner, or else the entire property might be confiscated, or members of the family harassed. In cases where all these measures failed, torture was put into play. Such torture did not involve rampant or random use of force, but a carefully ordered sequence of actions in conformity to guides or manuals. The best known among these were written by Nicolas Eymerich and Bernard Gui. Both called for "moderation," which is defined, perhaps, by the care not to cause permanent damage to the prisoner, let alone death. Both manuals also insisted that a bishop and inquisitor be present at the torture, though the actual work was to be done by a secular functionary.

The prisoner was first shown the implements of torture and told to speak. If he refused he was sent back to his cell for a day or two, to contemplate his options. The following time, the prisoner—man or woman—was stripped down to undershirt and bound to a torture implement. He was then told to speak, and if he still refused he was sent back to the cell. Following refusal to speak (confess) the third time, the prisoner was then tortured. The torture was performed slowly and methodically. If at any point the prisoner wished to speak the torture was suspended. It was never officially stopped because according to the manuals torture could only be inflicted "once." If the prisoner decided to confess he was unbound and taken off the torture machines. As confession could only be accepted if "free and spontaneous" the prisoner might be sent to his cell and his confession taken later.

It was an extremely rare case in which the accused was simply exonerated. Usually the outcome of the case was either confession or condemnation. In the case of confession, the Inquisition assigned a variety of penances, depending on the severity of the charges. The models for penance were monastic penitential practices, such as those of St. Dominic. They included poverty (confiscation of property), dietary injunctions (living on bread and water), pilgrimages, scourging, public humiliation, and others. If a prisoner refused to confess but could not refute the charges against him, he was condemned as an obstinate heretic. He was then relaxed to the secular authorities for burning at the stake. Execution at the stake was not a uniquely religious form of punishment. Thomas Aquinas distinguished the religious from the secular execution by means of the opportunities given to the convict to recant. And indeed, before the fuel was lit, heretics were twice given the chance to recant and join the community of the faithful. In cases of a confession or reconversion at the stake the heretic was either strangled before being burned, or taken down and imprisoned for life. If still obstinate, the convict would be burned alive while tied to a post, with faggots laid around his feet. Eymerich's instruction to the priests attending the execution was to see that none of this happened too fast, that the convict did not expire quickly, that he or she was conscious of the proceedings at all times. In a case where the convict had died during the long inquisitorial process, which could last for years, his corpse or bones would be dug up and burned; if the prisoner had escaped, or was otherwise unavailable, the burning would still take place in effigy.

Interrogation and Torture

The Inquisition possessed as large an arsenal of torture implements as the secular courts, but used mainly three: the *garrucha, toca,* and *potro.*[46] The *garrucha* was a pulley mechanism in which the prisoner, hands bound behind his back, was attached to a cord at his wrists, and hauled off the ground. He would then be dropped, either a short distance or the full length of the cord, and jerked to a stop. Stubborn prisoners had weights attached to their ankles to add persuasion. The *toca* apparatus was an inclined rack to which the prisoner was bound with ropes. A cloth (*toca*) would be placed across his face and over his mouth, which was forced open. Varying quantities of water would be slowly poured over the cloth in tandem with the questioning. As the cloth became soaked and heavy it would slide into the throat of the prisoner, producing an agonizingly slow drowning sensation. Meanwhile, the ropes around the prisoner's limbs could be tightened, burning the skin, tearing into the muscles and joints. The *potro* was a rack, to which the prisoner was bound by ropes that were attached to pulleys. With the turn of the wheel the ropes would stretch the prisoner, pulling his full skeletal structure—muscles, tendons, and nerves—and slowly tearing him apart. The three implements, along with other less frequently used ones, were repeatedly illustrated by a variety of artists throughout the centuries. These included Bernard Picart, Modesto Rastrelli, G. del Valle, Fracisco Goya, Jacques Callot, Pieter Bruegel the Elder, and others. The effect on the modern bystander is chilling; the impact on the accused who was first brought in for a view could only have been horrifying.

The Torture of Juan de Salas

On February 14, 1527, a physician called Juan de Salas was arrested by the Inquisition in the diocese of Palencia. He was arrested based on the evidence of another Inquisition prisoner who claimed that Salas had said that the evangelists were liars. Salas claimed that the facts were not correctly stated in the charge. Despite the strong arguments Salas put forth in his own defense, the inquisitor Moriz, without the concurrence of his colleague Alvarado, decreed that Salas should be tortured, as guilty of concealment. In this act the following deposition is found: "We ordain that the said torture be employed in the manner and during the time that we shall think proper, after having protested as we still protest, that, in case of injury, death, or fractured limbs, the fault can only be imputed to the said licentiate Salas."

The lengthy interrogatory procedure, in which charges, denials, and countercharges aired at length, ended with the beginning of the torture phase of the case. At this point verbal sparring and argumentation were absent and the procedure had an entirely different tenor. The interrogator merely warned the victim to speak the truth, and the victim said very little at all:

> At Valladolid, on the 21st of June 1527, the licentiate Moriz, inquisitor, caused the licentiate Juan de Salas to appear before him, and the sentence was read and notified to him. After the reading, the said licentiate Salas declared, that he had not said that of which he was accused; and the said licentiate Moriz immediately caused him to be conducted to the chamber of torture, where, being stripped to his shirt, Salas was put by the shoulders into the Chevrolet [*toca*], where the executioner, Pedro Porras, fastened him by the arms and legs with cords of hemp, of which he made eleven turns round each limb; Salas, during the time that the said Porras was tying him thus, was warned to speak the truth several times, to which he always replied, that he had never said what he was accused of.

> He recited the creed, "Quicumque vult," and several times gave thanks to God and our Lady; and the said Salas being still tied as before mentioned, a fine wet cloth was put over his face, and about a pint of water was poured into his mouth and nostril, from an earthen vessel with a hole at the bottom, and containing about two quarts: nevertheless, Salas still persisted in denying the accusation. Then Pedro de Porras tightened the cords on the right leg, and poured a second measure of water on the face; the cords were tightened a second time on that same leg, but Juan de Salas still persisted in denying that he had ever said any thing of the kind; and although pressed to tell the truth several times, he still denied the accusation. Then the said licentiate Moriz, having declared that the torture was BEGUN BUT NOT FINISHED, commanded that it should cease.[47]

The criminal processed by the secular courts knew what he had done, or at least why he had been arrested; victims of the Inquisition usually remained in the dark. The most fundamental fact of the inquisitional ritual was the ignorance of the prisoner and the omniscience of the inquisitor. A cursory look at the cases cited above, and countless others, shows the interrogation beginning with the accused professing ignorance of his or her fault and asking the inquisitors what to confess: "Senores, why will you not tell me what I have to say?" An accused may even be willing to confess heresy, if told to do so by the inquisitors. But that would violate the rules. The inquisitors knew what the specific sin was, at least in their own minds. The accused may have known she was charged with heresy, or even with a specific act (refusing to eat pork), but she had absolutely no idea what the inquisitors knew, how much they knew, and how much they wanted her to acknowledge. The explicit rules demanded that she confess, not everything (too trite), but exactly the right things. The accused, whether guilty or not, was simply not able to give a blanket confession, but she was unwilling to state more than she thought the inquisitors should hear. So the accused began by trying to determine what the inquisitors knew, and the shrewd Dominicans who had seen it all were on to her. Despite all the pain, the record of the torture is thus clearly a give-and-take, as seen even in the case of poor Elvira del Campo.

> She was tied to the *potro* with the cords, she was admonished to tell the truth and the garrotes were ordered to be tightened. She said "Senor, do you not see how these people are killing me? Senor, I did it—for God's sake let me go." She was told to tell it. She said "Senor, remind me of what I did not know—Senores have mercy on me—let me go for God's sake—they have no pity on me—I did it—take me from here and I will remember what I cannot here."[48]

The interrogation was thus a chess game for truth, as well as a jockeying for the appearance of sincerity. Of course, if the accused was completely innocent, that is, not a heretic, the load on his shoulders was even heavier. The inquisitors may have stated the broad charge (heresy), but no more. Nor did they name the accusers (informers) or reveal any of the information given by such people, who may have been neighbors, colleagues, or even family. Consequently, the innocent prisoner, though completely ignorant of his fault, would develop a profound sense of unease and fear, experienced as free-floating anxiety guilt. He was commanded—at pains to his body—to look into his soul for the sins he had committed, growing to believe perhaps that he had indeed done something. But the position of the "true" heretic (say, a Judaiser) was not much better because she did not know how much of what she had in fact done was known to the inquisitors. Moreover, the inquisitors did not just want a confession of acts committed; those were often not in dispute. They wanted an assertion of motive, a psychological confession of the prisoner's identity, who she truly was (Jew, Protestant, etc.) under the mask.

Viewed in this light, the process looked like a spiral beginning with broad statements and working inward to the specific. It began with a general statement by the inquisitors, a response—say, an acceptance by the accused—followed by a clarification by the inquisitor and a movement to a more specific proposition that was logically subsidiary to the first. This went on until something rang false to the inquisitors, who knew what they were looking for anyway. Ready assent by the prisoner, quick confessions, statement of fault were not easily accepted by the examiners. Words counted profoundly for the accused in an age of magical psychology. An invitation to take an oath could send terror in the soul of the accused who feared swearing falsely. The inquisitors too insisted that the oath be voluntary, horrified by the prospect of a forced false oath, which would cast its misfortune on them. The inquisitors were after right motives, sincerity, purity of heart. They expected the reconciled prisoner to reveal his accomplices in heresy, the supreme test of true conversion. Only prisoners who were persuaded of the Inquisition's virtue would "voluntarily" turn in their friends and family for an opportunity to be saved by the Holy Office.

Indeed, the heart of the inquisitional ritual was the pious fiction of "voluntary" confession. This fiction was maintained despite the use of torture. A careful reading of the case of Elvira del Campo's tortures, side by side with that of George van Hoflaquen, reveals that the torturers were working very precisely. While police and political torturers simply brutalized the victim into behavioristically conditioned assent, the inquisitors used pain like the pricking of an artificial conscience.[49] Like Plutarch, who compared conscience to "an ulcer in the flesh," Philo once said that "it stabs as with a goad, and inflicts wounds that know no healing."[50] Both men meant this in a metaphorical sense, using pain as a simile. But not so the Inquisition. Here pain was applied precisely as a goad might lead a beast on the true path. It is very important to emphasize that although there were abuses and sadistic torturers—that goes without saying—the inquisitional theory and the guidelines of Eymerich and Gui insisted on a carefully modulated application of pain.[51] Pain was timed precisely to coincide with insincerity, as the meticulous records indicate when you listen to Elvira's groans: "I did it, I did it . . . loosen me, loosen me and I will tell it." She was told to tell it and said, "I don't know what I have to tell—Senor, I did it—I have nothing to tell—O my arms!" Or, in another case described with a bit more distance: "He was admonished to tell the truth. He said he knew no more and if he did he would say so; when he made this reply, they ordered another three turns of the cord."[52]

Clearly, any prisoner who was ignorant of the precise nature of his heresy (if any) would suffer enormously. The procedure would lead to intense, even desperate "introspection." That means that the prisoner would have to try and recall every minute incident in the last several years, which might have been construed as heretical, go over every remark stated to family or even strangers. The discovery of sin became an act of recollection, and introspection was set up as the uncovering of what was hidden from one's immediate consciousness but was somehow known to the Holy Office. Pain helped to uncover the truth; it was the literal instrument of this ritualized conscience, while confession ended the suffering. But the psychological mechanism was subtle, because the torture did not seem to have triggered stream-of-consciousness narratives but stubborn and pathetic duels with the inquisitor.

Torture and Rough Psychoanalysis

The Inquisition and its procedures look, above all, like a system of social control. Nothing seems more coercive than raw power, exerted by means of pain. Pain influences people effectively; it rams the collective will down the throat of its victims. Sociologists of the Inquisition view the matter like the common observer. They merely add that social coercion has to be legitimated by an effective ideology. In this case, the power of the Inquisition is expressed in terms of the inevitability that links guilt to penance, and the dependence of penance on punishment or medicine. The Holy Office looks like the KGB, whose secret prisons are psychiatric hospitals and gulags.[53]

The coercive weight of the Inquisition on its victims was too obvious to deny. But the assumption that good citizens were defined by their identity as passive subjects of terror—like leftists in Argentina—is historically inaccurate from a psychological and ideological perspective. The inquisitional ritual was a procedure for transforming the ideology of penance from its juridical form of representation to a sacrificial and passage model. The social control applied by inquisitors was "internalized" effectively—and the ideological transformation was effective—when the ritual changed the perception of pain into a pseudo-voluntary, sacrificial form. This happened both as a ritual event and through the psychological exchange that took place between inquisitor and "patient." Psychologically speaking, the session was no mere behavior-modification or brainwashing through pain. It is necessary to think about the torture session as more than forced confession leading to painful penance for the purpose of cleansing sins and fortifying orthodoxy. Instead, it was a ritual for defining and institutionalizing a specific version of dispositional guilt (self-directed aggression). "The psychological line separating modern societies from primitive ones . . . is that guilt has become dispositional and as a result the remissions of a superficial guilt culture no longer work."[54] When the Inquisition had completed the brunt of its work in Europe, ritualized penances and purification, pilgrimages and vows, were no longer sufficient for purifying one's conscience (eliminating superficial guilt). The anxiety that accompanies guilt in the Christian world—starting with Catholic societies under the reign of the Inquisition—had to become a type of aggression against the self. It had to create what John Carroll calls dispositional guilt. But merely torturing a subject of investigation does not turn her anxiety into self-directed aggression. Far more has to happen.[55]

The relationship between interrogator and the patient of the Inquisition was surprisingly intimate. Although the inquisitor's manuals (Gui, Eyemerich) scripted the scene in such a way that the patient usually could not see his interrogator standing behind, the voice was there, as well as the expectant silence in between questions and commands. It would not be a stretch to characterize this relationship as "analysis," a rude psychological fixing, construed in a broad sense and understood, perhaps, with the aid of Lacan.[56] With visual feedback eliminated, voice became critical—the speech of the analyst-inquisitor and the entire Church on one side, and the critically important speech of the patient on the other. Under carefully regulated torture—pain applied when the inquisitor nodded to the torturer in response to a note of falseness or obstinacy—the patient spoke. Only words that did not produce pain were legitimated, and as the speech of the subject they "determine[d] the status of the subject as subject."[57] The patient, of course, wanted to please the interrogator. They may have spent months together and he controlled her bodily feelings. Her speech had to sound just right in his ears. His response—voice, silence, or pain—became the "Other," Lacan's "le grand Autre," who existed at the place where speech and truth combined. A transference might have taken place, but not the commonly understood transference of psychotherapy, which is the giving of assent to the power of the analyst.[58] Instead, this was a resistant transference, one in which communication from the patient's unconscious was interrupted ("Tell me what I have to remember Senor"). The discourse of the past—true recollection—was closed off due to terror or resentment, and was replaced with the words coming from the mouth of the analyst, or with the goading of pain, from the mouth of the patient on behalf of the analyst. As long as the patient exclaimed "tell me what to say," she met with pain. Eventually, as a result of transference, his voice will have become her own, and her speech would no longer produce pain. This was a gradual process, not of behavior modification, but of remaking the self, through a hypnoticlike dissociation triggered by pain. Very few individuals could resist it successfully without being crushed.

The subject was not emotionally detached. Torture produced aggression in the patient, but the inquisitor, in absenting himself from the scene (except as voice) avoided offering himself as the object of her rage and aggression. In psychoanalytical terms he avoided "offering to the patient an idea of the analyst's person that can be co-opted into the defensive maneuvers of the patient's ego."[59] Instead, the object of aggression was the ego itself, the organizing ground of subjectivity, the *agent provocateur* who summoned pain through disingenuousness. Lacan has argued, and enlisted Melanie Klein here, that the ego is the unification of an "original organic disarray" in which the infant exists. This unification, which is essentially narcissistic, is profoundly satisfying and generates enormous energy in the ego ("narcissistic passion"). According to Muller and Richardson's close reading of Lacan, the threatening of this unity produces aggressivity.[60] Pain does this—it disrupts the flow of information (control) between the ego as organizing principle and subsidiary aspects of the individual's self. The disruption is experienced as the loss of unity. But inquisitional pain was timed to match false assertions, and it was instigated by an abstract voice, which gradually (in transference) became the patient's own. And so, the aggression was turned inward and initiated the work of dispositional guilt, which we have defined as self-directed aggression. The sessions could radically transform an individual who thought and felt in terms of hiding from an external authority, into one whose center of authority was internalized and inescapable but not before anger censored and muted the voice of the customary self. In other words, the victim of the Inquisition emerged with an intrinsic sense of guilt.

Punishment

But there was more pain. The investigative tortures were only the first step in the Holy Office's redemptive agenda. The prisoner who refused to confess and was condemned as a flagrant heretic was turned over to the secular authorities who executed him by burning at the stake. In contrast, the accused who confessed persuasively, and became reconciled to the church, was sentenced to penance, which included public displays of contrition, penitential procedures such as pilgrimages, or scourging. Both the burning at the stake and the penance were fairly elaborate rituals. What bears emphasizing at this point is that the use of pain in these ritual contexts was based on penitential and eschatological models, conforming to known salvific forms. This was as true for the execution of the Inquisition's prisoners as it was for secular criminals.[61] Such a pain served a supplementary function to go with the condemnation of conscience, both in late medieval Europe and today.

Just as the public execution of heretics was never merely about intimidating the population, so the investigative tortures were not just about eliciting facts. The prisoner did not merely disclose information; the inquisitors, after all, had already judged him guilty. What he did instead was to make an ontological confession and acknowledge being a sinner of a specific kind. Torture, as we have seen, was thus an instrument of spiritual introspection. Consequently, the penitential and executional tortures at the end of the inquisitorial process, following the *auto de fe*, were continuous with investigative tortures. The penance and the burning at the stake were transformative tools, sequential with the earlier pains in the theological psychology of the Inquisition.

> All the reconciled went in procession, to the number of 750 persons, including both men and women. They went in procession from the church of St. Peter Martyr in the following way. The men were all together in a group, bareheaded and unshod, and since it was extremely cold they were told to wear soles under their feet which were otherwise bare; in their hands were unlit candles. The women were together in a group, their heads uncovered and their faces bare, unshod like the men

> with candles. . . . They went along howling loudly and weeping and tearing out their hair, no doubt more for the dishonour they were suffering than for any offence they had committed against God. . . . At the door of the church were two chaplains who made the sign of the cross on each one's forehead, saying, "Receive the sign of the cross, which you denied and lost through being deceived." . . . When this was over they were publicly allotted penance and ordered to go in procession for six Fridays, disciplining their body with scourges of hempcord, barebacked, unshod, and bareheaded; and they were to fast for those six Fridays. . . . And they were ordered that if they relapsed, that if they fell into the same error again, and resorted to any of the aforementioned things, they would be condemned to the fire.[62]

In secular Western punishments, even today to some extent, the repeated opportunity given to the criminal to confess during the ritual of the execution incorporates both elements (confessional-ontological and transformative) in one context. Legal tortures and painful executions were, of course, common throughout Europe. Even England, the cradle of constitutional law, inflicted horrific tortures on traitors, heretics, and the common criminal. At the time when the Spanish Inquisition was active, the English drew and quartered their criminals, disemboweled them alive, hung the accused spread eagle from four stakes and placed heavy rocks on their midsection.[63] But even well into the eighteenth century several English authors—Henry Fielding, Charles Jones—and the popular press debated the relative mildness of hanging for hardened criminals. Many thought that breaking the criminal on the wheel, castrating him, or having him bitten by rabid dogs would be a more suitable deterrent than simple death by hanging.[64] Foucault missed this aspect of the punishment in the ritual execution of Damiens with which *Discipline and Punish* began. When officials and priests repeatedly approached the tormented convict and bent over him for his words, they were playing out their part of a redemptive ritual. They listened to his words for a simple reason: The transformative potency of punitive pain came to life only when the pain became voluntary. The victim had to give assent to his own suffering and to assume an active role in his part of the ritual. This fact was recognized, at least implicitly, in many of the execution ceremonies in Europe over the centuries.[65]

Several centuries later the magical quality of ritual assent (confession) reached a modern level of organizational consciousness. The efficacy of assent evolved into spiritual introspection, the convict enjoined to look into his soul for the source of his corruption and for hope of redemption. In 1842 in England, a prisoner, whether about to be executed or not, was likely to hear a similar sermon:

> Prisoners, were it in my power, I would touch your feelings and consciences to the quick—I would lay your hearts open to your own eyes—so that, by contemplating the desperate wickedness which lies there, you might be struck with horror at its appearance; so that before the gates of mercy are closed upon you forever, you might turn to the Lord your God, and humbling yourselves before Him, in deep and sincere sorrow for your past lives, devoutly and unceasingly pray for the assistance of his blessed spirit in guiding you through the narrow way which leads to eternal life.[66]

The sermon called for remorse, for sorrow in the absence of a shame that comes only from a social consciousness. This sermon was thus a product of a modernized sensibility. During the height of the Inquisition's reign, the pricks of remorse would have been felt most sharply as shame. It was the Inquisition itself, paradoxically, that accounted for the mixing of shame with guilt. The Inquisition capitalized on the social bonds that lead to shame, but it also worked to instill a genuine inner sense of fault. The gradual loss of shame was related inversely to the use of elaborate shaming devices such as wearing the absurd dunce cap or facing the public through the pillory.[67] The medieval Inquisition, and the Spanish Holy Office as well, imagined their mission as the returning of wayward souls into their community. The elaborate rituals of penance and execution can be studied separately as miniature dramas enacting the primordial Fall—confession, penance, and redemption—with a powerful role assigned to the crowds.[68] These shamed and humiliated the prisoners during the stages of the ritual leading up to and including part of the penance. With the application of penitential pains—self-flagellation or scourging, for example—the mirth turned to empathy and rejection was replaced with the embracing of the penitents. This applied even in the cases of execution, as the following case demonstrates:

> On August 24, 1719 an auto was held at Logrono in which a Judaizer would be burned at the stake. As the burning torch was passed before his face he was warned to repent. With perfect serenity he said, "I will convert myself to the faith of Jesus Christ," words which he had not been heard to utter until then. This overjoyed all the religious who began to embrace him with tenderness and gave infinite thanks to God for having opened to them a door for his conversion. . . . At this moment the criminal saw the executioner, who had put his head out from behind the stake, and asked him, "Why did you call me a dog before?" The executioner replied, "Because you denied the faith of Jesus Christ; but now that you have confessed, we are brothers, and if I have offended you by what I said, I beg your pardon on my knees." The criminal forgave him gladly, and the two embraced. . . . I went round casually behind the stake to where the executioner was, and gave him the order

> to strangle him immediately because it was very important not to delay. This he did with great expedition. The pyre was then torched and the dead man reduced to ashes.[69]

One cannot help but notice how important the shaming was to the man about to be executed, and how sincerely the executioner apologized to a man he was about to kill. The victim, in turn, took the removal of his shame as profound consolation, the existential equal of his impending death.

These examples illustrate an important fact. Pain inflicted as punishment or as penance not only prevented the torments of hell. That is a theoretical point. Subjectively the pain removed a greater source of mental suffering—shame and humiliation. The penitent who flailed his skin harshly and to the point of intense pain (under order of the Inquisition) knew with every blow that his shame was removed, that the door to social reacceptance was opening more widely. The pain of penance thus became a solution to the problem of sin (conceived in archaic psychological terms)—that is, shame and isolation. From a model of juridical punishment, pain came to be experienced as an instrument of readmission—initiation or passage. The process involving the penitents, as Henry Lea showed, was a gradual transition back into the life of community.[70]

EIGHT

Anesthetics and the End of "Good Pain"

Sacred Pain is an unusual work in assuming that pain has served humanity in a variety of constructive religious and social ways.[1] This is a hard argument to make in light of the Inquisition's work and a difficult notion for the modern reader to accept. Pain, common sense insists, is a medical problem with a clinical or pharmaceutical solution. Martyrs and saints are odd, hells and inquisitions perverse. This clarity is a modern phenomenon, a product of distinct cultural and medical developments that took place in the nineteenth century. The present chapter will look at these developments, particularly the invention of surgical and obstetric anesthetics, and will discover some reasons for the collective cultural amnesia that we share in reference to religious pain. It will also look at some of the ideological side effects of these medical breakthroughs: With the invention of anesthetics pain became strictly a medical problem and a matter that pertains to the body rather than the entire person. The individual in pain evolved into a patient, which is a juridical and ethical category—a possessor of rights over one's body and a temporary resident of a medical institution (the hospital). This replaced the premodern person in pain, who was first and foremost a member of a true community, and whose pain meant something far more significant than tissue damage.

The invention and then application of chemicals—ether and chloroform—to anesthetize patients undergoing surgery and women in labor ranks as one of the great achievements of nineteenth-century medicine. It brought to an abrupt end the most gruesome and frightful aspects of premodern healing, and almost immediately blinded humanity to any value pain might have previously possessed. The benefit of painless medical procedures was so overwhelming that commonplace scenes of pain in the great clinics of Europe have been largely forgotten.

It is no exaggeration to say, in fact, that Charles Darwin's great career in biology owes as much to the pain of medical procedure as to any other single event in his life. If chloroform or ether had been in use during his days as a medical student at the University of Edinburgh, Darwin might have completed his studies and become a physician rather than the evolutionary biologist he eventually became. As it was, Darwin attended two operations at the university—one on a child—but rushed away in horror before either was completed. He later claimed in his autobiography that the two cases "haunted" him for many long years.[2]

The American physician Jonathan Mason Warren, like many others, went to Paris—the medical center of the world at that time—and observed the greatest clinicians of the first half of the century: men like Dupuytren, Roux, Lisfranc, Velpeau, and others. They performed a variety of surgeries in their clinics including amputations, reduction of dislocations, rhinoplasty (reconstruction of the nose), staphylorraphy (closing a cleft), suture of a ruptured perineum, enterostomy (making an artificial anus), lithotomy (incising the bladder and extracting stones), removing cataracts, tonsillectomy, draining fistulas and abscesses, removing fragments of cartilage from the knee, removing tumors and cancers—all without surgical anesthetics.[3] The instruments were not esoteric but were variations or modifications on some very ancient instruments such as knives; saws; the lancet (a short single-edged blade used in opening vessels for blood letting—a pre-anesthetics procedure for dulling pain); scissors; the *gorget tranchant*, which was a spoonlike instrument with sharp edges; and the *bistouri* or scalpel, a single-edged blade fixed in a handle.[4] Other instruments were used for probing and dilating an opening. There were also tubes for injecting fluids, pincers, hooks, needles, speculums, vices, cauterizing instruments, and many others.

Due to the painful nature of the operation, speed was greatly prized—both in the prestigious Parisian clinics and elsewhere. Lord Nelson of the British Navy described his surgeon as a man who could amputate an arm at the shoulder in 30 seconds or less. In December 1832, Jonathan Warren wrote a letter to his father, in which he described Dupuytren's great skill. The physician was removing tonsils from a patient who was neither named nor described in the letter. Using hooked forceps the surgeon seized the tonsils and cut them off with a probe-tipped knife that had half its blade covered with cloth. The next day Warren saw the amputation of an elbow joint due to cancer: "The operation was performed by first making an incision of about 6 inches across the elbow. A second incision was then made opposite to the first on the anterior part of the arm. Their centers were then joined by a transverse cut and the two flaps dissected up. The humerous was now sawed through an inch above the joint and the joint carefully dissected out. The operation was terminated by sawing through the two bones of the forearm. During the operation the patient did not seem to suffer greatly." One can only speculate what suffering "greatly" could have meant for the observing physician who does not even tell us who the patient was.[5]

A more reliable gauge for the sensations associated with pre-anaesthetic surgery comes from the patient under the knife. Such a description was given by the American woman Franny Burney, who underwent a mastectomy in 1810 in a Parisian hospital at the hands of the great surgeon Dominique-Jean Larrey:

> M. Dubois placed me upon the Mattress, & spread a cambric handkerchief upon my face. It was transparent, however & I saw through it that the Bed stead was instantly surrounded by the 7 men and my nurse, I refused to be held; but when, right through the cambric, I saw the glitter of polished steel—I closed my eyes. . . .
>
> Yet—when the dreadful steel was plunged into the breast—cutting through veins—arteries—flesh—nerves—I needed no injunctions not to restrain my cries. I began a scream that lasted unintermittingly during the whole time of the incision—& I almost marveled that it rings not in my Ears still! So excruciating was the agony. When the wound was made, & the instrument was withdrawn, the pain seemed undiminished, for the air that suddenly rushed into those delicate parts felt like a mass of minute but sharp & forked poniards, that were tearing the edges of the wound,—but when again I felt the instrument—describing a curve—cutting against the grain, if I may so say, while the flesh resisted in a manner so forcible as to oppose & tire the hand of the operator, who was forced to change from the right to the left—then, indeed, I thought I must have expired, I attempted no more to open my eyes.[6]

One shudders to think that the mere three minutes described here will stretch on for the full duration of the surgery, and that Fanny Burney will experience all of it. In fact, her description extends to several pages of extreme suffering. All operations were not so traumatic, of course, and as noted, speed had a lot to do with suffering. The same Larrey who operated on Burney describes an amputation he performed during the military seige of St. Jean d'Arce. General Caffarelli had had his elbow joint shattered by a bullet. The surgeon noted: "Such a disorder necessitated the amputation of the arm; the general himself demanded this; he also put up with it with extreme courage, and perhaps with too much concentration, because he did not utter a single word. Being very attached to this brave general, I operated on him with all speed possible in order to shorten his pains."[7]

The advent of surgical and obstetric anesthetics was a great boon to patients and physicians alike, but it was not an overnight miracle. A variety of soporific, narcotic, and analgesic agents (and procedures) such as opiates and several plants were known for a very long time. In 1772 Joseph Priestly discovered nitrous oxide, later known as "laughing gas." Humphry Davy noted that this substance was effective at reducing pain, but his observations were ignored.[8] In 1824 Henry Hill Hickman operated painlessly on animals anesthetized by carbon dioxide—but he too was ignored. The dominant manner of desensitizing patients to pain at the beginning of the century was not chemical at all, but was a form of hypnotism known at the time as mesmerism or "animal magnetism" (the term "hypnotism" would only be coined in 1843 by James Braid).[9] Interestingly, the strongest impetus for applying anesthetics came from professional dentistry. The three chemical agents of nineteenth-century anesthetics were already known in America and Europe by the early 1830s. These were ether, nitrous oxide, and chloroform. In 1844 a Connecticut dentist, Horace Wells, tried nitrous oxide on himself while volunteering to have one of his own teeth extracted. After this, a colleague, Dr. William T. G. Morton, convinced the great Harvard physician John C. Warren to use nitrous oxide while performing surgery before his class. Early in 1847 James Simpson, a professor of obstetrics at Edinburgh, began using ether for his more difficult deliveries, and later that year he switched to chloroform, which he found more agreeable than ether.[10] The first specialist in anesthetics was John Snow who administered chloroform to Queen Victoria on two births.

The Debates over Anesthetics

Once ether and chloroform took their place in the operation and delivery rooms of hospitals and in dental offices in Great Britain, France, and America, there was no turning back. Patients loved the new procedures, which guaranteed painless operations, and they were willing to ignore the unpleasant side effects, especially of ether, including irritation of the throat and lungs, bronchitis, convulsions, and pneumonia. Soon physicians were able to record hundreds of cases of successful applications of anesthetics. In fact, medical statistics began with the counting of procedures undertaken with anesthetics in the late 1840s. Still, the acceptance of anesthetics for surgery and obstetrics was neither smooth nor universal. For a number of years both the medical literature and the popular press aired numerous and heated debates on the pros and cons of pain and painlessness. And though one might expect that the most passionate arguments would come from organized religion, on grounds of either biblical literalism or moral puritanism, this was not the case. The religious opposition was, in fact, far broader in tone and scope. And although some medical conservatives voiced religious arguments, such arguments were overstated by those who cited them when defending the use of anesthetics.[11] The major responsibility for this lay with James Y. Simpson, the Edinburgh professor of obstetrics who introduced chloroform into the delivery room and who took the lead in defending anesthetics from its detractors.

The arguments against painless surgery and delivery on religious grounds took a number of forms. Most basic, though rarely heard, was the fundamentalist claim that women ought to give birth in pain due to the Genesis curse. A New York dentist wrote in 1848 that mothers ought to fulfill "the edict of bringing forth children 'in sorrow.'"[12] The city of Zurich banned all use of anesthetics due to the curse of the primal sin.[13] René Fulop-Miller reports that "Calvinist Scotland" responded to Simpson's advocacy of painless delivery—in the press and pulpits presumably—by declaring Simpson a blasphemer and heretic, who utters words that Satan has put into his mouth. "Did not the Almighty pronounce his primal curse? Pain during childbirth was God's will."[14] Threats were sounded that children delivered in painless birth would be refused the sacrament of baptism. Simpson's own publications made it clear that he had heard, at least informally, the claims on behalf of biblical literalism. He argued in response, that the language of the curse in Genesis was not "sorrow," but "labor" or "toil." His proof was that the very next verse describes Adam's curse as eating out of the ground with "sorrow"—meaning, not physical pain, but toil. Just as we do not dream that pulling out thistles from the ground is a torture, neither is painless delivery lacking toil.[15]

In fact, though the argument based on Genesis may have been sounded informally, in church sermons and publications, the more common arguments based on religious doctrine were entirely different. They included the following:

1. Pain, especially obstetric, may not be divine punishment, but it is spiritually uplifting, and in the case of women it produces sublime emotions. A New York gynecologist, who may have been reared on Ralph W. Emerson's view of pain as a producer of spiritual rewards ("compensation"), wrote: "I feel that these compensations are not limited to the mere physical strengthening of other . . . facilities . . . this baptism of pain and privation has regenerated the individual's whole nature . . . by the chastening made but a little lower than the angels."[16]
2. This spiritual benefit of pain is a reflection not of God's wrath but

his love, evidence of his paternal affection for humanity. To eliminate pain is to do the work of the devil. William Henry Atkinson, the first president of the American Dental Association, made the following statement:

> I think anesthesia is of the devil, and I cannot give my sanction to any Satanic influence which deprives a man of the capacity to recognize the law! I wish there were no such thing as anesthesia! I do not think men should be prevented from passing through what God intended them to endure.[17]

This sentiment was repeated by an English physician, Robert Brown, who felt that nature and God "walked hand in hand" and that the meddling that produced unnatural painlessness in delivery was an invention of the Devil.[18]

3. Other religious arguments did not apply directly to the elimination of pain as much as to the production of side effects that were offensive to religion. For instance, the American temperance movement regarded etherization as a form of intoxication that posed a threat to the virtue and respectability of female patients.[19] Even supporters of anesthetics, such as G. T. Gream in Great Britain, felt that women would rather be put through the tortures of hell than suffer the humiliation of finding out what they had done under chloroform. Gream cited the example of a patient (woman in labor) who "drew an attendant to her to kiss as she was in the second stage of narcotism."[20] Even Charles Meigs, a distinguished Philadelphia physician, felt that chloroform was more of an intoxicant than a soporific, and therefore should be avoided on moral grounds.[21]

The replies on behalf of anesthetics rarely took religion head-on. The physicians administering ether or chloroform were as likely to be religious as their opponents. They preferred to extend the debate to medical and ethical grounds and take the matter away from the pulpit. Some cited religion precisely to sanction anesthetics, but such a position was rare. Dr. Eliza L. S. Thomas regarded anesthesia as a "second dispensation," a gift from God to show his forgiveness for our sin, and another physician, pointing to a God of love and mercy, argued on similar religious grounds for anesthetics.[22]

If the debates over ending surgical and obstetric pain reflected a profound shift in nineteenth-century worldviews, organized religion is not the place to track such a revolution. Far more profound and interesting arguments were made both against and on behalf of anesthetics strictly within the medical community. These go to the heart of the newly emerging medical ethics, the view of the patient as an autonomous person in a free economy, and the physiological-psychological understanding of the human subject. While the majority of practitioners favored the use of ether or chloroform, a large number of physicians and physiologists are on record voicing either concern or opposition. These include Tyler Smith, G. T. Gream, Francois Magendie, Charles Meigs, B. Cooper, R. Barnes, and virtually every naturopath in America and Europe—including homeopaths (Hahnemann), hydropaths, herbalists, vegetarians, and followers of Rush's "heroic" medicine. The arguments aired by these opponents can be sorted into four major types, excluding simple conservatism, which insists that any innovation be held at bay due to potential risks.

The Danger of Anesthetics

Direct evidence still showed that anesthetics posed significant chemical and physiological risks, and that was the primary line of conservative medical opposition. The rapidly increasing use of ether and chloroform yielded evidence of extremely harmful side effects. In 1852, army surgeon John B. Porter stated in an article published in the *American Journal of the Medical Sciences* that the inhalation of ether in sufficient quantities to produce insensitivity to pain poisons the blood, destroys or diminishes nervous influence and muscle contractility, and puts the wounds in "an unfavorable state for recovery."[23] The AMA's Committee on Surgery noted "convulsions more or less severe and protracted, prolonged stupor, high cerebral excitement, alarming and long continued depression of vital powers, and asphyxia. As secondary effects, bronchitis, pneumonia, and inflammation of the brain."[24] Several critics expressed the horrific fear that anesthetics did not really remove pain at all but caused partial paralysis followed by amnesia. So the patient was tortured horribly with no capacity to respond, then emerged with no recollection of that hell.[25] In the case of obstetric use of chloroform, critics argued that the chemical agent could affect the health of the infant by entering its bloodstream. However, medical opposition, especially on the obstetric front, focused more directly on the physiological function of pain in the process of birth.

The Function of Pain

The arguments for the necessity of labor pain sound antiquated today, but they were voiced by some of the leading obstetric experts of the mid-nineteenth century and were based on medical observations, if not experiments. The chief concerns were those of Charles Meigs, professor of obstetrics in Philadelphia, and Tyler Smith. Smith argued in an article in *Lancet* (March 1847) that labor pain induced the mother to cry. Her cry "by opening the glottis, takes away all expiratory pressure, and leaves the uterus acting alone," which was beneficial to parturition.[26] The pain sometimes acted as a stimulant to the birthing process, an essential feature of the contractions.[27] Meigs felt that there was a functional connection between the contraction of the womb, the dilation of the uterine opening, and pain, all of which guaranteed the successful delivery of the baby. By anesthetizing the mother to the pain of the contractions, the contractions themselves ceased and the birthing process slowed down to the detriment of both child and mother. Finally, Charles Meigs, Tyler Smith, Francis Ramsbotham, and others felt that labor was a natural process that relied on something they called "life force" and that etherization weakened this force.[28] This allusion to life force played its largest role in the debates over obstetric anesthesia—a debate that still continues incidentally. Surgical anesthesia was not as vulnerable to a critique based on the "naturalness" of procedural pain. Still, even here, "life force" was used in argument.

A large and significant element in nineteenth-century medicine recognized a force called "sympathy" or "vitality" that functioned in traditional forms of medicine such as counterirritation. Benjamin Rush, who was the leading figure of "heroic" medicine, argued for curing the disease with its equivalent, much like homeopathy:

> All evils cured by evil [sic]. Diseases cure each other, as gout and mania, dropsy, consumption, &c. Even remedies are nothing but the means of exciting new diseases. Whipping a dog prevents the effect of Nux Vomica. . . . What would be the effect of hot iron after swallowing poison?[29]

The *New York Journal of Medicine* declared that pain is essential to surgical procedure, and that its removal was harmful to the patient.[30] Even Francois Magendie, the great French physiologist and neurologist, felt that pain was essential to life and was connected with the vital essence of the living organism and that anesthetics rendered the "patient a corpse."[31] The vital spirit of the patient would be critical to his healing both during and after the operation. Some surgeons claimed that the lusty bawling of their operative patients assured them that the patient would recover. These surgeons perceived a connection between the passive silence of the unconscious patient and a failure to recover and live.

Natural Medicine

The practitioners of the various natural disciplines listed earlier, especially in America, substituted "Nature" for the "God" of the more theologically inclined opponents of anesthetics. To naturopaths, any procedure that circumvented nature's own way of healing, including the pain that attends both illness and healing, was morally evil and medically unsound. Pain was a signal for violating some natural physical law—a punishment, in a sense. It had to be felt if one were to heal. The various schools of natural medicine relied on different principles—water, vegetarian diet, sleep regimen—but all of them recognized in the body's natural sensitivity to pain a profound natural fact and not a mere symptom of illness. Consequently anesthetics do not just mask a symptom, which is bad enough, but subvert the natural process as a whole. This point applied even to physiologists—like Magendie—who posited the "life force" (or "vital force") at the basis of life and health.

Medical Ethics

Some of the best arguments raised against the use of anesthetics were based on ethical considerations: doctor-patient relations, demographics, and the autonomy of the patient. The rise of anesthetics was closely associated with the bureaucratizing of medicine in Europe and in America, with the reduction of the person to the status of patient and statistical sample. Deciding whether to anesthetize or not required a measurement of benefit and harm, and the keeping of medical statistics—both positive developments. But in fact, the use of anesthetics quickly came to reflect the demographics of sex, race, ethnicity, class, and nationality of patients. The application of the new boon was highly selective and seemed to reflect either indifference to the suffering of underprivileged classes, or worse, the assumption that the poor or members of minorities (African Americans, Native Americans, immigrants) suffered pain differently. Of course, neither ether nor chloroform was responsible for prejudice, but they were associated with other mid-century developments reflecting the changes in the relationship between the individual and the community.

The complementary side of the reduction of the person to medical statistic was the elevation of the physician to the status of both commercial entrepreneur and a godlike ruler over the destiny of an insentient patient. As one French physician put it early in the nineteenth century: "It is important for the happiness of all that man be placed under the sacred power of the physician."[32] Meanwhile physicians like Morton, who wanted to patent and monopolize ether, were acting in an increasingly capitalist and consumerist medical environment. The decline in the "gentleman ideal" of medicine led to fears that anesthetics put patients at risk of sexual abuse, or worse, that anesthetics allowed the incompetent physician to cover his bungling. The unconscious patient, who had taken an active role in the surgical and obstetric procedures of old, was now rendered a passive object who could neither guide the doctor nor voice any point of view. In short, ether completely eliminated the patient's autonomy. Emily Dickinson wrote in 1861: "Give Balm—to Giants/—And they'll wilt, like Men."[33]

The *Philadelphia Presbyterian* also stated in 1847, "Let every one who values free agency beware of the slavery of etherization." Magendie, again, added in a more abstract fashion that depriving a patient of consciousness is dehumanizing and reduces medicine to the cutting of meat.[34] An Iowa physician argued that he wanted the patient to know what is going on.[35]

It is difficult today to imagine that arguments against the elimination of pain would carry much weight. It has become so self-evident that patients are entitled to a painless surgical or other medical treatment that one too easily shrugs off as quaint any claims on behalf of pain. However, what we take for granted today is a development traceable precisely to the decade or two under discussion, a time at which prestigious authorities split on the issue. The brevity of the responses cited below should not be construed as meaning that the merit of anesthetics was obvious at the time. I focus primarily on the criticism of anesthetics in order to recover the meaning of an earlier worldview, which has now expired and given way to the modern and self-evident perspective on pain.

The arguments in favor of anesthetics also covered the full spectrum of issues, from the theology of divine forgiveness, to the safety of painless procedures, to the rights of patients who insist on waiving the opportunity to know in favor of painlessness. Protheroe Smith and William Channing defended obstetric anesthetics by proving—empirically—that there was no causal relation between pain and contractions. Simpson argued repeatedly, and based on numerous instances, that the absence of pain in fact relaxed the pelvic muscles and allowed for a quicker and healthier delivery of the infant. Numerous physicians discussed their feelings of empathy for the squirming and crying patient who suffered excruciating pain under the knife and proclaimed it a higher ethical stance to eliminate pain than to allow the patient to have his (screaming) voice. On a deeper physiological level, medical practice increasingly differentiated between the symptoms of various illness (including pain) and its physiological causes, and demonstrated that the elimination of pain has no bearing on the battle with the disease.

At their most rarefied level the debates over anesthetics resolved themselves over the matter of consciousness and its role both in healing and in defining the dignity of the patient. These were not theoretical concerns but went to the very heart of what it meant to be human, and healthy as well. At mid-century, consciousness was associated with the soul, a distinctly human—and perhaps divinely given—instrument of essential vitality. To render the patient unconscious was to deprive him of both humanity and the power to heal. It would thus take the transition from soul to mind to mute such arguments.

The Science of Pain and the Metaphysics of Consciousness

Twenty to twenty-five years went by before physiologists could explain precisely why ether and chloroform anesthetized patients. In fact, the developments in chemistry that made the production and use of anesthetics possible preceded their use and the debates that ensued by several decades. Men like Joseph Priestly, Humphry Davy, and Michael Faraday had known for decades—based on empirical observation—that some chemicals can render humans insentient to pain. In 1818 Faraday observed in *The Quarterly Journal of Science and the Arts*:

> When the vapour of ether mixed with common air is inhaled it produces effects very similar to those occasioned by nitrous oxide . . . a stimulating effect is at first perceived at the epiglottis, but soon becomes very much diminished. . . . By the imprudent inspiration of ether, a gentleman was thrown into a very lethargic state, which continued with occasional periods of intermission for more than 30 hours.[36]

The effects of gases on the consciousness of "gentlemen" was known, because scientists—physiologists, chemists, physicians—tried these substances on themselves and on their colleagues. Experimental science required such firsthand observation, as in fact it does today. The result was a severe splitting between experimental and empirical precision on the one hand, and theoretical understanding of the phenomena observed. This, again, is still a feature of empirical science. And it is this gap that opens up science to the hermeneutical effects of worldviews, political and economic assumptions—in a word, ideology.

Many of the discoveries in physiology and neurology that preceded the elimination of surgical pain were precisely of this empirical nature. Some predated the use of anesthetics by nearly a century. Robert Whytt (1711–66) discovered the spinal reflexes in vertebrates and coined the term *stimulus*. Charles Bell (in 1811) and somewhat later Francois Magendie discovered that the dorsal side of the spine carried sensory neural input while the ventral carried motor neural output. In 1850 Helmholtz was able to measure the speed of the neural impulse (at ninety feet per second for the frog he studied and fifty to one hundred feet per second for man). He thus discovered a gap between the mind's command and the body's response, or vice versa in the case of input. This allowed theorists like Thomas Laycock and Wilhelm Griesinger to argue that thought or feeling are interrupted reflexes, which provided the foundation of neurophysiology and scientific psychiatry in the 1840s. Pierre Fourens, working on pigeons, was able to map out the functional anatomy of the brain and specify that "the function of the cerebral lobes is willing, judging, remembering, seeing, hearing, in a word, perceiving."[37] In 1833 J. J. Lister discovered, using the newly improved microscope, that the gray matter in the brain is cellular, and in 1839 Nasse found that a severed nerve continues to function from the point of enervation, but that from the cut to the periphery it degenerates. This degeneration allowed Waller to map the course of the peripheral nerves with great precision.[38]

The experimental work in physiological psychology produced a massive amount of information bearing on pain and its control. The studies I have briefly mentioned—and many others—applied to the transmission and processing of information by the peripheral and central nervous systems. This information would not only impact patients of surgery or women in the delivery room. It would also bear on the age-old philosophical debates between empiricists and associationists on the one hand and various forms of a priori theorists and the doctrine of faculties on the other.[39] Modern psychology would emerge from these debates, and the course of nineteenth-century arts and theology would be deeply affected by experimental work on the nerves and the brain.

But the study of pain and its elimination during the mid-nineteenth century, much like today, was deeply influenced by another matter: the paradigm of specificity. Like all paradigms, specificity was not just a conscious theory but an a priori assumption operating below the level of conscious awareness in a large variety of scientific fields.[40] Specificity required that every organ and every anatomical region perform one function that is specific to it, and no other.[41] A recent definition of specificity with regard to pain regards it as "a one-to-one relationship between receptor type, fiber size, and the kind of painful stimulus (cutting, burning, and so forth) in a fixed stimulus-response relationship."[42]

In the field of pain research, the specificity paradigm seemed obvious when the reports of patients were taken into account. For centuries, clinicians who listened to their patients recognized that different conditions produce different types of pain. This observation was helpful in diagnosis, as it still is with the use of the McGill Pain Questionnaire. At the beginning of the nineteenth century F. X. Bichat described, in *Anatomie Generale,* a patient who asked his physician why—during amputation of his leg—the pain he felt when his skin was cut was so different from the pain he felt when the flesh was sectioned, and that from the sectioning of the marrow.[43] In a less dramatic but more pervasive way the question was raised in philosophical discussions. Given the enormous richness of the world that our senses present, how does the nervous system function to convey such variety? Are there separate nerves for colors and for tastes (for example), and do these break down into specific nerves for red and for green? In physiology the specificity paradigm implied that distinct nerves convey distinct forms of pain, or at another level, distinct parts of the brain receive different signals.

Like all paradigms, specificity was not a consistent and universally applicable position. The evidence that seemed obvious based on specificity (distinct pain sensations) raised other issues not so easily resolved. The most profound issue was one of integration of raw information. If the nervous system transmitted specific and separate information (the redness of the rose and its smell), how did such sensations become integrated into a cohesive perceptual world? The more scientific the studies of nerve function and nervous energy, the more dramatic became the need to reconcile phenomenal experience with "electricity" and similar forces in terms of the specificity paradigm. This led to the formulation of competing theories or models on the nature of neural transmission and integration, which were very much at odds during the debates over anesthetics at mid-century.

The two primary competing models relating to the transmission of impulse were the mechanisitic model and the vitalistic model. The mechanistic model argued that the nervous system operated like a machine—something along the lines of the industrial revolution's great mechanical inventions. It was a self-regulating machine, perhaps like the steam engine, but it transmitted signals of an electrical nature. The mechanical model required a center, both as regulator of input and output (the Bell-Magendie experiments provided that), but more important, as the decoder of incoming signals and their translator into phenomena. This was the central processing model, which owes a good deal to Kant and Thomas Reid but was formulated to a large extent through their misreading by Victor Cousin. This model focused on regions or sites of the brain (Longet's work in France) that specialized in perceptions and even contained faculties such as intelligence and free will.[44]

The vitalist model insisted that the nervous system transmitted some type of nonmechanical energy such as vital spirit. This was susceptible to reading by the mind, or did not require translation from one category of being (matter) into another (consciousness). Robert Whytt's famous experiments on frogs illustrate the possibilities: He removed the brain from a frog and pricked its peripheral organs finding that the animal still jumped in response to the stimulation. The only condition for the continuation of this response is that the limbs, such as the legs, were still connected to the spinal column.[45] Whytt's experiment, of course, was widely cited in support of the vitalistic model. As late as the 1840s vitalism was in favor with the political authorities who funded research projects and universities. Several men, including

Friedrich Eduard Beneke as well as Ludwig Buchner and his followers, lost their university positions because they were proponents of materialistic science, which ran afoul of conservative (religious) academic bodies.[46] Even in 1850, the United States Senate invited John Bovee Dods to present lectures on the psychology of the day, titled "electrical psychology." Dods, who was a Universalist minister, said to his listeners:

> The brain is invested with a living spirit, which, like an enthroned deity presides over and governs . . . all the voluntary motions of this organized corporeal universe; while its living presence, and its involuntary self-moving powers cause all the involuntary functions of life.[47]

Clearly, the perceived effects of anesthetics on consciousness—the threat of stupor on vital energy—and the consequent resistance in wide medical circles were largely grounded in vitalistic assumptions, which were both scientific and profoundly metaphysical. At mid-century the scientific scene in relation to the nervous system and particularly its transmission of pain was a complex combination of rich experimental observation and several irreconcilable theoretical positions. A monumental survey of mid-nineteenth-century neurology and physiology, with a significant synthesis, is found in Johannes Muller's *Elements of Physiology*, which was by far the most influential work in physiology in that century. Muller's work indicates that the specificity paradigm was far from exhausted, even though he was aware of its severe limitations. If a specific fiber is required to transmit unique sensations (the redness of a flower in one, the whiteness of another going through another fiber), an infinite number of nerve fibers would be required. At the same time he also knew that an identical stimulation (say, electrical impulse) applied to different nerves produces different sensations. At the optical nerve it produced a flash; at the taste nerves it produced a strange taste. One could never smell with one's optical nerves nor see with the oracular. Facing such contradictions, Muller could not explain the diversity of visual, olfactory, and other sensations based on the specificity paradigm, but he strongly upheld the specific and unique energy of the five types of sensory nerves (vision, taste, and the rest). He regarded this energy as ultimately "metaphysical."[48] In the absence of precise information on the central cerebral localization and processing of nerve stimuli, Muller had to resort to that same "vital energy" (the equivalent of "life force") that courses through the nerves and allows them to function in a homogeneous fashion with the stimuli for which they were designed.

Muller's great work contained additional metaphysical assumptions—for instance, in reference to higher cerebral functions. They are found in the ninth and tenth "laws" of Muller's synthetic formulation of neural physiology and function:

> Our imagination and our experience (and not the nerves themselves) inform us that modifications in the state of the nerves reflect modifications in the external world. It is thus "the soul" which forms images and ideas, and which gives them precision and clarity.[49]

The vital energy previously mentioned guaranteed that what reached the brain were not only modifications in the states of the biochemical processes, but also indirect information on the qualities and changes in the external world appropriate to each nerve according to its qualities or sensory energies (Muller's eighth law). In other words, the type of mental perceptions that we have of the world require both a central perceiving soul and a nervous system that transmits biochemical information in a manner that is readable in a mental way. Muller discussed the phenomenon of phantom-limb pain at some length (as did Descartes). He combined a modified peripheralism (the pain originated in the severed nerves at the stump) with a central-perceiver that is mandated by the extreme clarity and vividness of the phantom sensations.

As noted, Muller's *Elements of Physiology* was by far the most widely distributed work on physiology in the nineteenth century.[50] His treatment of perception and of pain indicates that at mid-century the issue of pain could not be separated from metaphysical concerns relating to vital energy, spiritism, and soul. The theoretical debates over anesthetics, grounded in neurophysiology as they were, need to be understood in the context of the inescapable metaphysics and even theology of consciousness. A surrender to unconscious therapy meant relinquishing the aspect of the human patient that both defined him as deserving of dignity and allowed him to recover more effectively.

Medical Sociology

The medical and philosophical debates over anesthetics shrink compared to the speed with which surgical anesthetics spread. This is simple to explain in terms of patients' desire to avoid pain, regardless of ideology or religious dogma. But other developments reinforced patients' interests and rights. Fifty years earlier medical practice, both in England and America, was dominated by the liberal gentleman-practitioner ideal.[51] Physicians were trained in the liberal arts and practiced in a local community, much like the local vicar. These physicians did not acquire specialized medical training, and their primary professional relationship was not with other physicians, but with members of their "parish."

Medical practice was thus highly individualized and based on community relations, on a lifelong familiarity with one's patients. The medicine was noninterventionist and consisted to a large extent of ethico-medical principles, such as proper diet, moderation and discipline in lifestyle, and so forth. Medicine was often naturopathic or homeopathic, and self-healing coupled with forbearance under duress were expected. All were indicated by the local practitioner's familiarity with the patient's personal habits, character, and physical disposition.

The end of the Napoleonic wars, the rise of urban centers in the wake of the industrial revolution, and the mass migration of rural populations into the cities had profound effects on medical practice.[52] Large urban medical centers, in the major cities such as London and New York but just as importantly in new centers such as Edinburgh and Philadelphia, were directly connected with the demise of the gentlemanly ideal and its replacement with a professional class of physicians. England, Europe, and most of the states in America began to impose standards of medical proficiency and licensing. The economics of the industrial and commercial state began to permeate the medical field. Licensing, for instance, was geared to minimize competition by regulating the number of new physicians in the field, though the large medical schools campaigned against limits because their faculties were supported by tuition. In the 1840s most of the hospitals were still funded by private sources, including charity and religious endowments. The hiring of faculty and the endowment of teaching chairs, for instance, were subject to scrutiny by these sources of money and power.[53] Although the nursing staff and ideals were closely linked to religious institutions, increasingly after 1834 in England (with the New Poor Law), hospitals were funded by the state and run by employees of the state.[54]

The sudden and extremely well-publicized use of anesthetics in the hospitals, for surgery and certainly for obstetrics, needs to be evaluated in the context of these broad changes. On top of everything else, the wholesale administration of a powerful narcotic to strangers in a large medical institution flew in the face of the personal practice that the conservatives had valued so deeply. Everyone knew that anesthetics could not be administered haphazardly or in the same quantity to different patients. Too much could kill a patient, too little brought torture. Opponents of anesthetics mocked the idea of a universally administered medication of any kind. Traditional medicines, and the extremely pervasive natural remedies, could only be given on the basis of close familiarity with the patient. Supporters of anesthetics could produce, in defense of the new practice, altogether new techniques of evaluating patients who were strangers. These included such statistical criteria as age, gender, weight, race, nationality, and so forth. Dosage depended on bureaucratic and statistical calculations that reduced patients from persons (members of a community) to consumers and objects of technology. Naturally, the emergence of medical ethics as a separate domain of concern (tied to licensing) owes to the professionalization of medicine and commercialization of health. Again, many of the conservative opponents of anesthetics were concerned for patients who, under anesthetics, were entirely at the mercy of an impersonal and perhaps uncaring physician. The bureaucratic response was to institutionalize the rights of patients over their health and over their bodies. The debates reflect such a concern in the new language of rights, which is a juridical and civil concept now applied to the relationship between physician and patient, but more important, between the patient and his or her own body. The patient has a right not to hurt, or a right to remain conscious, or a right to keep a gangrenous leg, and these rights may be enforced in civil courts. This should not be taken to mean that previously the patient was at the total mercy of his physician, while now the doctor needed permission for everything. It meant, on a deeper level, that previously both patient and physician shared the assumption that the medical man knew what was best for the patient based on familiarity and wisdom. The new, modern medicine took this shared assumption away. The physician was now in command of technical information. What remains for the patient is not ontological (his being in the world) but juridical—the right to feel better, or not hurt.

The new physiology of pain and technologies for its control, coupled with the social and economic changes taking place early in the nineteenth century produced a revolutionary, and paradoxical, reevaluation of pain. On the one hand, pain became naturalized and medicalized. The neurological mechanisms for the transmission and perception of pain became increasingly understood. Pain was gradually turning into an optional aspect of medical phenomena, not a spiritual and religious currency in one's dealing with God. And certainly, the nineteenth century proves that given the choice between hurting or being medicated, the vast majority would opt for painlessness. On the other hand, since pain was both a medical matter and an option, anyone choosing to hurt had to be, in some sense, abnormal. This latter point of view took a couple of decades to catch on, but when it did, it was applied anachronistically as well. By the 1860s a general amnesia set in as to the reasons anyone would opt for pain, given a choice. Historical as well as contemporary cases of extreme austerities and self-hurting, phenomena that had previously found their place in religious literature, were now judged also by medical criteria. Certainly, neurophysiology and neurology—Jean-Martin Charcot comes to mind first—following the victory of medical anesthetics could only look at such phenomena through a medical lens.

Pain and Hysteria

The rapid acceptance of anesthetics in the 1840s after two failed arrivals decades earlier indicates that social and ideological conditions were ripe for its acceptance. According to Caton, mid-century medicine had achieved a deep separation between illness and religion—pain had lost its religious connotations. Although the debates show that this is an overstatement, undoubtedly medicine was rapidly becoming biologized and pain medicalized. But this created a monumental paradox that resulted in the Victorian period's flood of hysteria cases. The hysteric represents a competition between the following dynamics: On the one hand, people are encouraged to think of themselves as patients, to treat their own bodies as medical objects through a new type of somatic introspection. On the other hand, this very same gaze produces a plethora of symptoms which, when scrutinized by a more objective gaze, display no material "causes." This paradox resulted in the frequent diagnosis of hysteria, which was a conversion illness—symptoms with no cause that mimic true disease. Until J.-M. Charcot systematized the plethora of symptoms and classified hysteria as a neurological-mental disease in its own right, hysteria became medically conflated with "malingering" or faking. Hysteria, then, reflected a culture of medical disbelief: The clinician's work included—very prominently—the need to identify true disease and separate it from false. Pain complaints, which were often characteristic of hysteric patients, required techniques of verification. While pain behavior had evolved in a social manner for proper healing and was based on the transparency of pain signals, now displays of pain became suspect and pain itself became increasingly isolating. And finally, those whose lives were steeped in pain, or those who seemed to pursue it voluntarily in religious fervor, became conflated with hysterics or other neurological and mental patients.

The phenomena that come under the overwide umbrella designation of hysteria were familiar for millennia before the nineteenth century. However, the neurological approach to diagnosing hysterical phenomena began with William Cullen's *First Lines of the Practice of Physic* (1796). The first modern study of hysteria as a "conversion" illness—a disease that imitates others and takes on their symptoms—was by Thomas Sydenham, who wrote about one hundred years earlier.[55] Sydenham's work was still being republished in the nineteenth century, and the 1848 edition of his work on hysteria claimed that hysterical disorders made up a full two-thirds of all chronic diseases and were, indeed, most typically female.

> The frequency of hysteria is no less remarkable than the multiformity of the shapes which it puts on. Few of the maladies of miserable mortality are not imitated by it. Whatever part of the body it attacks, it will create the proper symptom of that part. Hence, without skill and sagacity the physician will be deceived.[56]

Weir Mitchell (1829–1914) was the most distinguished expert in America on hysteria, along with other "women's diseases," and Paul Briquet was the immediate predecessor to Jean-Martin Charcot, with whose name hysteria is usually linked. His study *Traite clinique et therapeutique de l'hysterie* (1859) was the first systematic and empirical study of the disease based on clinical observation of a substantial sample of patients.

As noted, the phenomena that came to be designated hysterical were extremely diverse and included, prominently, fainting, convulsions, paleness and weakness, tics, tremors, speech disorders, sudden sensory failure, and others. However, because hysteria "imitated" other diseases, as Sydenham claimed, it could actually take any shape whatsoever, and thus, by the mid-nineteenth century included a monumental plethora of "symptoms." In fact, hysteria came to designate the game of communication that goes on between the patient and the doctor. If the physician believed the patient (and the patient's body), he would certify a proper illness behind the symptoms. Failure to persuade the physician of the authenticity of the disease could result in a diagnosis of "malingering" or hysteria—that physiomoral aberration that mimics illness. It was Jean-Martin Charcot (1825–1893) who sorted out the diverse phenomena of hysteria and diagnosed it as a legitimate psychoneurotic disease. He identified major stages in the hysterical attack: the epileptoid stage (with its many symptoms such as falling and fainting, preceded by warning signs such as tremors, coughs, yawning); the next stage was commonly called the stage of clownism (strange bending and posturing of the body); the next stage was called *attitude passionelles* in which

> the patient begins to give himself to expressive mimicry, indicating the sentiments . . . which move him; pleasure, pain, fear, even fright, love hatred, etc. . . . Mimicry mostly takes the first place, but some patients also scream in connection with their sentiments, and some make long speeches.[57]

Other symptoms included somnambulism, anesthesia, hyperesthesia, fits of laughter and crying, and of course, a large variety of symptoms that mimic other illnesses. In his clinic at the Salpêtrière, Charcot handled his numerous patients with relative dignity as legitimate patients and developed systematic treatments for hysteria. These included "frictions, massage and passive movements applied to the paralysed limbs, including those movements which are produced by the application of a faradic current to the muscles."[58] In addition to restoring mobility to the limbs of the prostrate patient, Charcot applied more general somatic therapies such as hydrotherapy (cold water), balneotherapy, gymnastics, tonics and restorants, along with the faradic (static) electricity. At the same time the Salpêtrière insisted on "moral" therapies as well: isolation from parents or relatives whose laxness or misconduct may have brought on the attacks, the promotion of discipline, and "intellectual hygiene."[59]

Both Pierre Janet and Sigmund Freud studied Charcot's work with hysterics. Janet elaborated on the dissociative aspects of hysteria and explored its implications vis-à-vis hypnotism.[60] His work proved influential on Hilgard and neodissociation, as we have seen in Chapter 5, which dealt with possession and exorcism. Freud had visited the Salpêtrière in 1885–86 and wrote an obituary for Charchot in 1893. Like Charcot, whose lectures he attended, Freud believed early on that hysteria involved a distinct mental state behind the somatic manifestations. The unique situation of the hysteric patient is that she is not conscious of the connection between her mental state and outer symptoms:

> This asserted that hysterical symptoms arose when the affect of a mental process cathected with a strong affect was forcibly prevented from being worked over consciously in the normal way and was thus diverted into a wrong path. In cases of hysteria, according to this theory, the affect passed over into an unusual somatic innervation ("conversion"), but could be given another direction and got rid of ("abreacted"), if the experience was revived under hypnosis.[61]

Freud was thus not content with a neurological explanation of hysteria and insisted that the process of conversion itself was mental, which required a subconscious mechanism or series of mechanisms such as repression. It would be some time before Freud would fully develop his theory of the unconscious, of drives and the oedipal conflict, of masochism as an erotic impulse. His insights on hysteria came earlier, and in fact, many of the patients who provided him with the data for the prominent psychoanalytical theories were hysterics. There is thus a link between hysteria and masochism, but it developed only gradually as Freud's thought evolved to include the drives, repression, conversion, cathexis, and other mechanisms that link a relationship trauma to clinical pathology.[62]

Hysteria, Neurosis, and Religion

The proliferation of hysteria as a characteristically Victorian illness and the prevailing mood of optimism in identifying and treating its many symptoms created a fertile ground for extending neuropsychology to cultural and religious phenomena. In fact, hysteria, while it lasted as a dominant psychological diagnosis, always remained a profoundly social and moral form of illness—even after it was medicalized. It was a small stretch for Charcot and his colleagues to extend their psychology to some of the major religious phenomena of the day, beginning with the miracle healing craze of Lourdes. In 1864 the Church officially recognized the miraculous powers of the pool discovered in 1858 by Marie-Bernarde Soubirous. It became a sanctioned and immensely popular pilgrimage site in which numerous miracles of spontaneous healing took place.[63] At the Salpêtrière, meanwhile, Charcot had a high degree of success in also getting paralyzed patients to get up and walk, either by the application of electrical stimulation to the muscles or by "injunctive therapy": ordering the patient to get up and walk.[64] It was easy to argue then that the healing of Lourdes worked with hysterical symptoms, and the concept of miracle was thus easily naturalized.

Other deeply enshrined religious institutions similarly fell under the broad umbrella of neurological and mental disorders. People with stigmata, who were previously thought to have received manifestation of a miraculous favor, were now tested in the laboratory, like any other biological subjects. Louise Lateau (1850–83) was studied, with the approval of the Church, by Lefebvre, a professor at Louvain University. She had exhibited many of the classical stigmata phenomena, including bleeding, blisters, extreme headaches and burning sensations—all at the appropriate places matching the wounds of Christ. But she was now examined under a magnifying glass; indeed, the blood was viewed through a microscope showing "an abundance of white corpuscules, larger than the normal state, and a notably higher proportion of serum, which was related . . . to the patient's chloro-anaemia."[65] There were others exhibiting stigmata during those decades, most notably Teresa Neumann, whose case descriptions were published in the same journals (*Progress Medical*) in which Charcot published his studies. These individuals were diagnosed, among other things, as suffering from a neurological "compatience" or extreme sympathy, which manifested itself in somatic identification with the suffering of others. It may be only a coincidence, but the word used by European clinicians for the manifestations of hysteria—but not other conditions—was not symptom but stigmata.

Possession, whether spontaneous or consciously induced in ritual context, and exorcism were also reduced to the concept of hysteria—as I have shown in Chapter 5 of this book. There were cases of grand or mass hysteria both in secular contexts (prison riots, mass demonstrations) and religious contexts such as celebrations, pilgrimages, and retrospectively, to the witch hunts and mass executions.[66] The constant fasting, even refusal to eat, formerly associated with extreme religious zeal became nervous anorexia according to William Gull in England and Lasegue in France—one of Charcot's predecessors at the Salpêtrière.[67]

Even saints who had already attained the highest levels of reverence in the Catholic world were not spared the reduction to clinical pathology, including hysteria. St. Teresa of Avila, St. Catherine of Genoa, St. Marguerite, St. Maria Maddalena de' Pazzi, Mme. Guyon, St. Therese of Lisieux, and male mystics and saints all came under psychological scrutiny. St. Teresa, the patron saint of headaches, was facetiously dubbed the patron saint of hysteria. Her acute and medically inexplicable pains were attributed to hysterical causes: "pains about the heart so acute that it seemed at times as if it was being torn to pieces by sharp teeth."[68] The ambiguity of the pains she felt in her abdomen, the delightful quality of the "ineffable wound" presented an open invitation to sexual interpretation, suggestive of the erotic dimension of theatrical hysteria as masochism. St. Teresa manifested many of the classic hysteric symptoms according to Rouby, including anorexia, contractions (and convulsions), occasional paralysis, exaggerated emotions, and anesthesia or hyperesthesia.[69]

The late nineteenth-century French nun Therese of Lisieux was critically analyzed, even before beatification, for psychological proclivities. Although she was not much of a self-hurter, she reported a great deal of suffering in her own life and highly glorified the life of pain. Even her sympathizers felt that much of her writing on suffering was instigated by abnormal sensitivity to criticism and a neurotic temperament manifested in extreme emotional displays.[70] She occasionally failed to live up to her own standards of brave suffering. Once, when she was refused pain medication she exclaimed in a very modern tone of bitterness, "What is the good of writing beautiful things about suffering? . . . It means nothing, nothing! When you are going through it, then you know the worthlessness of all this eloquence."[71] Therese's conduct thus pales in contrast with the famous self-hurters—mystics and saints. In other words, she seemed unable to exhibit any pleasure or satisfaction in the sensation of pain, a paradox that Nietzsche, then Freud and his colleagues placed at the center of the erotic component of masochistic behavior—including moral masochism. The masochistic pleasure takes on its full effect in the interplay between the victim and the "executioner." In such a topology the masochistic position has often been defined as that of a consenting and demanding victim: "*victima*, a person immolated in order to appease the gods."[72] From a clinical perspective the executioner or hurter need not be literally there because the superego takes on the role of that powerful figure. Many of the symptoms exhibited by hysterics involve a display of sexual suggestiveness or "immoderation." The connection of religious masochism with erotic impulses thus predates the systematic reduction of psychology to the two drives and their traumatization in the oedipal conflict.[73] Therese may be one of the first postmasochism saints of the Church, a product of the neurological and psychoanalytical age that judged the conduct of mystics by psychological standards. Her excellence had more to do with a tolerance for her own failings and the circumstances around her than with the voluntary pain she inflicted on herself. On this standard some modern victims—even martyrs—who failed to bear their misfortune silently and may have cried out loud in pain, failed the test of beatification.

The reduction of religious phenomena to psychological causes still persists today, though moderated by a greater sensitivity to the distinction between social-symbolic behavior and individual pathology. While not all contemporary psychologists, and few historians, would explain mystical self-hurting in terms of clinical masochism, neurosis, or hysteria, one legacy has persisted since the 1880s. We have lost our capacity to understand why and how pain would be valuable for mystics, members of religious communities, and perhaps humanity as a whole. The role of pain, before it was displaced, was rich and nuanced, and ultimately situated persons within broader social and religious contexts. Our failure to remember—to recognize—this fact is a direct legacy of the nineteenth century's medicalization of pain and elevation of nervous disorders (followed by psychoanalytical pathology) to the understanding of human religious behavior.

Teleological Psychology

It is doubtful that our attitude toward pain could have developed in any other way. Given the option of meaningful pain or not hurting, most humans choose painlessness. However, the failure to remember the value pain had in the past, which entails a fundamental shift in social and religious values, is linked directly to scientific positivism, along with social and political developments that characterized the mid-nineteenth century. Many of these views were excoriated by Pius IX in the Syllabus of 1864 as anathema to religion. They included naturalism (with scientific positivism and materialism at its core), absolute rationalism, liberalism, nationalism, socialism, and communism. While the scientific revolution continued to extend its reach over broader and more humanistic domains, including even religious practices, the Church went about the business of beatifying and canonizing individuals who were very intimate with pain. Even today, as Padre Pio is on the verge of canonization, his stigmata and his painful struggles with demons remain at the forefront. It is important to remember that the Church did not significantly oppose surgical and obstetric anesthesia in the 1840s, and none of the items in the syllabus reflects a rejection of medical progress. Catholic medical ethics insist that consciousness—the issue at the heart of the debates on anesthesia—is valuable only when the patient is able to participate in religious rites such as confession. Relief of pain is a flexible matter that takes into account the passage of the dying patient, or his spiritual needs if he is recovering, but painlessness does not represent a moral evil for the patient.

While many of the prominent psychologists in the nineteenth century were Catholic—chief among these were Johannes Muller and Franz Brentano—the break between organized religion and experimental psychology was sharp. The search in physiological psychology for the neurological foundations of mental functions implied that the individual was not governed by the soul, and that ultimately material substance and processes constitute the entire person. In the face of materialism, major Catholic psychologists were not altogether able to renounce Thomistic dualism in favor of materialistic monism in the development of experimental psychology. Thus, Muller was in fact a vitalist and Brentano became an apostate.

We know today that despite the body-mind break declared by Descartes and the two centuries of supremacy by materialistic monism beginning with La Mettrie (1709–51), the issue is far from resolved. It is interesting to speculate how psychology might have developed without the astounding progress of experimental physiology and neurology and the effect of these on psychoanalysis, behaviorism, and other dominant modern approaches. Henryk Misiak and Virginia Staudt suggested, in 1954, that had the scholastic and Greek theory of hylomorphism (the absolute codependence of body and form) been familiar to the founding scientific psychologists, modern psychology might have taken a different direction.[74] This is probably true about any number of ideas and events in the history of science, but it is important to note that all traces of a soul psychology, or a psychology based on consciousness and intentionality, have not been wiped out by positivism. Brentano, for instance, developed a systematic psychology based on acts of intentionality—forms of consciousness with mental objects as their content. Emotions and cognitions are intentional states that enfold psychic objects—the emotion, the thought, and so forth. This psychology, which does not represent a radical break from medieval scholasticism (or for that matter Spinoza), influenced Christian von Ehrenfels, who was a precursor to Gestalt psychology. Among Brentano's students was also Edmund Husserl, the founder of modern phenomenology. Both of these men refused to reduce psychology to materialism or material causality. More recently, the psychology of intentional states has led to ethical or humanistic approaches and even semiotic psychoanalysis.

Thomas S. Szasz has been the most vocal critic of positivistic medicine and psychology. In several works, including *The Myth of Mental Illness* (1961) and *The Manufacture of Madness* (1970) he has argued that Charcot and hysteria mark the beginning of modern medicine in a very negative manner. Szasz is referring to the medicalization of what he regards as a symbolic form of (somatic) communication that is not pathological but meaningful. His is a strong case: The proliferation of hysteria cases in Victorian Europe (on which both Charcot and Freud built their practice) came to an abrupt end for cultural reasons, indicating that hysteria always had an irreducible cultural dimension.[75]

Chance might have led psychology to develop in a teleological and ecological way, to emphasize the context in which the person moves and the relationships with that context above individual psychology and mental illness. Such a psychology might have been Christian, for instance, or it might have been Marxist.[76] While "Marxist psychology" was indeed developed in the 1920s by V. N. Voloshinov, Lev Vygotsky, and A. R. Luria and explored by a non-Marxist thinker like M. Bakhtin, Christian psychology remains largely hypothetical. Like Marxist psychology, it would undoubtedly have been a teleological construction, according to the impression one gets by reading a theologian like the Greek Orthodox John D. Zizioulas. Teleological means, as Thomas Aquinas has it, that all things are related to a goal—an end—and are both ordered by and dependent on such a goal: "The end is the measure of things ordered to the end."[77] This end cannot be the person or the individual, according to Zizioulas, but Christ taken as an absolute relational entity. The modern person—the autonomous individual (or patient)—is a fragmentation of what had been a monistic conception for the Greeks. If the archaic person was a mask or accretion to that unity ("Being"), the modern person, identified with the biological entity, is essentially separate from the unity of Being. It comes to exist in birth and disappears at death, its existence thus marked by an essential tragedy. Zizioulas quotes Dostoevsky's Krilove (in *The*

Possessed) who declares that any man who desires total freedom must be courageous enough to end his own life.[78] Christian psychology would not abandon the modern concern for health or the body but would situate these within an ever-widening ecology of community and Christ. In this psychology pain would not necessarily represent damage or rupture but would be taken as a meaningful sign of something. If Thomas Szasz can claim that a therapist may (and Freud should have!) read and interpret the pains of a hysteric as a hidden language, then a Christian psychology might provide one key. Pain, on this reading, may not be mere biological damage or disfunction, but psychic alienation from the end (telos) of the person's being.

As noted, the Marxist psychologists—especially in the pre-Stalin USSR—worked out a "relational" or telic psychology in some detail. Voloshinov was the first to call on Marxism to construct "a genuinely objective psychology, which means a psychology based on sociological, not physiological or biological principles."[79] The fulcrum of such a psychology would be consciousness and the task of the researcher to show to what extent this consciousness—or the self—is shaped by others. Both Vygotsky and Luria accepted consciousness as an essential aspect of individual psychology but were aware that consciousness had to be linked to a more fundamental principle. For them, consciousness was determined by social relationships: "The mechanism of social behavior and the mechanism of consciousness are the same. . . . We are aware of ourselves, for we are aware of others, and in the same way as we know others."[80] Higher mental functions are products of mediated activity—social tools—that are formed through communication. Both Vygotsky and Luria were interested in neurology and the sensory-motor functions associated with psychological tools, and neither reduced mental function to material causes. On the contrary, they recognized a dialectical relationship between brain and mind. At the same time, Voloshinov, Vygotsky, and following them Bakhtin regarded consciousness as an inner language, or a dialogue with others inwardly projected. Consciousness thus mediates social phenomena and neurological function, a fact that Luria demonstated experimentally and Bakhtin showed in the works of authors such as Dostoevsky.[81]

Marxist psychology shares a fundamental feature with the hypothetical Christian psychology I have mentioned earlier. Both situate the individual within a broader ontological context, not just in a moral sense but in a more fundamental psychological manner. The person is constituted by relationships to the broader social environment, which itself is geared toward a goal or a telos. This is the type of psychology that Durkheim would identify at the core of archaic societies—Bakhtin was an admirer of the French sociologist. Such a relational or teleological psychology does not justify or sanction self-inflicted pain but it holds the tools for understanding such pain without reducing it to mental illness. It would not only illuminate the conduct of mystics and ritual participants, but more important, it would also explain certain aspects of contemporary chronic pain behavior.

Conclusion

No modern reader who opens the pages of *Sacred Pain* thinks that pain is a good thing. Jacob Goren, who has suffered chronic phantom-limb pain since 1960, thinks of pain as a destroyer, an unrelenting enemy. And it is Goren's puzzlement over Good Friday practices in the Philippines and Shi'ite practices at Karbala that inspired the writing of *Sacred Pain*. Why hurt if you don't have to, Goren asked, and what does physical pain have to do with religion? The questions resonate in many forms: What does the poet mean when he writes, "Mysterious alchemy, that has transmuted/Such torment into passion"?[1] What is Teresa of Avila experiencing in her pain, which is so deep that it feels like "the sweetness of this greatest pain?" Or why does a Sufi poet—Rumi—exclaim insistently, "Seek pain, Seek pain, pain, pain!"[2]

We feel a greater kinship with Job, who curses the day he was born when his pain becomes unbearable, and like Job we describe our pain with vicious metaphors, industrial, military, bestial, or even fantastic: "there, there's a, ah, ama, a demon, a monster, something very horro, horrible lurking around banging the insides of my body, ripping it apart."[3] Those who fail to rebel against their pain puzzle us: One pain clinician calls them "little martyrs"—men and women who think they deserve to hurt. The derision reaches beyond the few who feel that they deserve to be punished and extends to any individual who shows some ambivalence toward pain. Such an attitude is dysfunctional and perhaps pathological. So the modern pain patient, perhaps a reader of this book, is situated on one side, while Rumi and St. Ignatius, along with hysterics, masochists, and teenage self-mutilators, are assigned to the other side of the pain divide. One publisher, in turning down a proposal for a book on religious pain, called the religious perspective "superstitious" and "insane." He could be right, of course, but he will have missed something important and interesting in, for instance, Simone Weil's assertion that "nothing is worse than exteme affliction which destroys the 'I' from outside, because after that we can no longer destroy it ourselves."[4] That publisher will also have overlooked the concept of "redemptive suffering" as the detailed unfolding of an "alchemy" that transforms "pain to passion." *Sacred Pain* offers no elixir, of course, only a psychology and neurology carefully applied to the monk and the nun, the novice and initiate, pilgrim and mourner, and those practitioners who voluntarily hurt themselves or others as a matter of religious practice and in the service of spiritual goals. They all share one basic fact: No matter what theology or cosmology informs their imaginations, it is a desire for the personal experience of religious ideals that leads them to hurt the body. Experience, more than any doctrine, shows them that pain can make self-transcending realities accessible and vivid.

That pain works in practice we know from reading hundreds of religious narratives. How it works in theory is another matter, and *Sacred Pain* offers a hypothesis that is based on the systemic nature of the central and peripheral nervous systems and on the neuropsychological grounds of agency and self. To sum up three chapters in three sentences, the more irritation one applies to the body in the form of pain, the less output the central nervous system generates from the areas that regulate the signals on which a sense of self relies. Modulated pain weakens the individual's feeling of being a discrete agent; it makes the "body-self" transparent and facilitates the emergence of a new identity. Metaphorically, pain creates an embodied "absence" and makes way for a new and greater "presence." Weil, again, describes this as emptying ourselves of the "false divinity with which we were born." This helps put the following words into perspective: "Where there is pain, the cure will come; where the land is low, water will run."[5] The new identity, for the mystics, is almost always what they expected or set out to achieve: Christ, Truth, Murugan. As the empirical agency gives way to a more highly esteemed reality, the center of being shifts outward, situating the sense of self in a greater center of "Being." This applies not only to the mystic but to any religious individual—a pilgrim, for example. In the words of one, "At one moment everything is pain. But at the next moment everything is love (anpu). Everything is love for the Lord."[6]

But this hardly mitigates the problem for the reader who is not merely curious about mystics and initiates, but is suffering from pain and its consequences. Even if psychology can explain religious pain without reducing the practitioners to lunatics, what does that have to do with modern patients? As modern persons, they are simply too different from the religious person in pain. Their shared humanity cannot span the gap between what it means to be a modern person and a mystic or archaic person. John D. Zizioulas has discussed this distinction in some detail, as we saw in the last chapter.[7] For the mystic, or for the member of some traditional societies—Greece, for example—being a person is not an essential aspect of being. The person, instead, is an accretion of layers, of masks that merely cover what is real—true Being. Personhood thus implies distance and alienation. The truly religious recognize that the empirical reality (of persons) consists of suffering (*duhkha* or *dard*) because it represents a separation from what is True. For the Christian mystic—Julian of Norwich, for instance—that separation is called sin. The person is a lie, an accumulation that alienates from God. The modern view stands in diametrical opposition to this. The person is not a mask that distances from Being but the presence of one self in conversation (or confrontation) with another (person or God). The fabric of personhood does not call for unmaking—that is a tragedy—but for strengthening as a discrete self. That is the goal worth striving for in a meaningful, even religious life. Suffering, for the person who is a patient, is not distance from Truth or the Beloved; it is the rupture caused to the person by the thwarting of his or her goals—happiness, prosperity, health.

The medicine of the former, more archaic suffering is religious pain: "When pain transcends all boundaries, it becomes medicine." This is because pain-as-medicine shifts the focus from individual agency to a greater center, from distance and lack to intimacy and presence. In contrast, the medicine for "modern" suffering (including Job's) is the curing of physical pain. The great mystery of sacred pain is how one type of pain can become the other, and how pain can be redefined in relation to suffering. I have shown how modern Europeans largely lost the capacity to do this during the years of great medical discoveries in the nineteenth century, especially the invention of anesthetics. Tolstoy's Ivan Ilyich, who occupied this moment in history, was very much the modern patient in his pained misery. But Tolstoy had not forgotten the other manner of experiencing pain and suffering, and he finally saved his protagonist—from suffering, not pain. "The doctor said his physical agony was dreadful, and that was true; but even more dreadful was his moral agony, and it was this that tormented him most."[8] It was this recognition of moral agony (meaninglessness) that induced Ilyich, in the presence of the simple villager Gerasim, to wonder: "What if my entire life, my entire conscious life, simply was not *the real thing*?" Wondering finally what "the real thing" was, sensing that it was not too late even on his deathbed to find "the real thing," Ilyich for the first time truly *saw* his family standing around his bed, and felt deeply sorry for them. He discovered a selfless empathy for his surviving wife and children whom he had previously despised. At that instant his pain stopped hurting. Ilyich felt it but pain failed to torment him. Tolstoy shared a worldview with us as modern patients, but he was still able to look backward and see pain as medicine (a sign of social rupture).

I dare not ask anyone to do this, least of all Jacob Goren. As I write these words my own back hurts from subluxation of the fourth and fifth vertebrae and that gets in the way of typing. Goren himself mixes a dangerous cocktail of painkillers in order to get through every night and day. A medical discovery that would finally explain phantom-limb pain and lead to effective treatment would make his life infinitely better. This is a fact I could never dispute. But what can *Sacred Pain* add to this frustrated certainty?

As Goren himself knows, pain clinics today no longer treat the isolated symptoms, or complaints, of the pain patient. The clinic represents a holistic approach to pain relief, and treats the entire lived world of the patient—his body in its multiple contexts of the emotional life, family relations, work, culture, and even worldview and religion. Implicit here are two complementary assumptions. The first is that pain affects not just the physical functioning of the patient, but every other area of existence in a widening span of disruption. As a result, the treatment also focuses on how the patient acts in these multiple contexts and levels of suffering. A patient with a backache who cannot work is more likely to feel anxiety and depression, and his family relations will suffer. The complementary assumption is even more significant. It holds that the suffering of the chronic pain patient consists, to a large extent, of emotional, social, professional, and ideological elements. Here pain does not radiate "outward" to color an otherwise neutral life, but an opposite movement prevails. The patient's back hurts worse because his family relations are disrupted and because he no longer feels productive. Pain experience is caused and magnified by depression, isolation, lack of productivity, and philosophical upheaval. Much of what is called "the pain of the patient" is, in fact, such multilayered suffering, what Melzack and his followers have characterized as "top-down" or "center-periphery" factors.

Pain researchers and many patients know that it is possible to feel pain, to know that it is there, but not really care. Athletes sometimes give strong evidence for this phenomenon. George ("Sparky") Anderson, the former manager of the Detroit Tigers, once quipped about an injured player, "pain don't hurt."[9] Morphine has this effect on strong pain, but so does hypnosis, and to a lesser extent even mild dissociation caused by inattention. William James described this phenomenon in 1890:

> In a perfectly healthy young man who can write with a planchette [a device like a pointer on a Ouija board], I lately found the hand to be entirely anesthetic during the writing act. I could prick it severely without the subject knowing the fact.[10]

It seems, then, that the *anguish* that modern chronic pain victims feel is tied up with being situated in a transitional and ambiguous moment in medical history. On the one hand, medical technology promises relief from pain for the benefit of the individual patient—the person who occupies a body and has economic and legal rights to insist on the body's health. On the other hand, it also turns out that pain experience is not just localized in the body but represents a disruption of wider contexts (family, community, culture, God), and that the patient is never an isolated figure. As long as hospitals treated chronic pain as an isolated biomedical symptom of a discrete body, suffering tended to persist. This is what the newer pain clinics seek to overcome and in the process they seem to have drawn on the premodern approach to the patient as part of a lived world.

The role of religion in this picture is complex and ambiguous. Some patients do feel that they deserve to be punished, but this is likely a psychological problem rather than a religious or philosophical question of theodicy. But even when pain is perceived as punishment it may help relieve feelings of guilt and may thus allow the patient to endure the pain with relative tranquility.[11] Other patients use prayer or religious ritual to help tolerate the pain. Meaning can indeed modify sensation. One leading chronic pain specialist, Steven F. Brena, has drawn on diverse religious texts, such as the *Bhagavadgita,* the book of Job, the *New Testament* and the *Qur'an* to formulate appropriate responses to pain, including even "unselfish work and devotional love."[12] In fact, *Sacred Pain* clearly shows that in religious contexts pain is seldom just an aversive force. Pain may be medicine, a test, a rite of passage, or an alchemical agent of inner transformation. Consequently religion can act as consolation, as a challenge, or as a basis for social solidarity and not only as a sword hanging over the heads of sinners.

Although *Sacred Pain* focuses on religion, other ideologies can transform "pain into passion" when they situate the patient in a self-transcending meaningful context. Goren's example can illustrate this. Nearly 80 years old now, Goren was injured in Italy in March, 1945. Long decades of pain have failed to shatter the value of his life, despite the damage to his family life and career. In his case the redeeming factor was not a belief in God but a passionate adherence to a highly valued secular ideology—social Zionism. Goren, like many of his contemporaries, has subsumed his individual life to the ideological demands and rewards of Israeli socialism and Zionism. His life and consciousness have been quite literally the collective life of these movements. So while the phantom-limb pain has persisted and the search for medicine never stopped, Goren is no Ivan Ilyich whose isolation and moral confusion were the true sources of torture.

Sacred Pain does not aim to give relief or consolation, but it may help explain how a life can be painful and meaningful at the same time. Perhaps, in a minor way, understanding can then filter downward and help separate pain from suffering.

Notes

INTRODUCTION

1. William C. Chittick, *The Sufi Path of Love: The Spiritual Teachings of Rumi* (Albany: SUNY, 1983), 208.
2. Quoted in Patrick D. Wall and Mervyn Jones, *Defeating Pain: The War Against a Silent Epidemic* (New York: Plenum Press, 1991), 150–151. Italics are the Pope's. Paul Brand, former president of the International Christian Medical and Dental Society, has been equally eloquent on behalf of pain, if less overtly theological. See, for example, Paul Brand and Philip Yancey, "And God Created Pain," *Christianity Today*, Jan. 10, 1994, 18–23.
3. Simone Weil, "The Love of God and Affliction." See Miklos Veto, *The Religious Metaphysics of Simone Weil*, trans. Joan Dargan (Albany: SUNY, 1994), 77–78.
4. Elaine Scarry, *The Body in Pain: The Making and Unmaking of Worlds* (New York: Oxford University Press, 1985). The most notable exception to my generalization is David B. Morris, *The Culture of Pain* (Berkeley: University of California Press, 1991). However, although he focuses on pain and culture, religion receives limited attention.
5. Though wrong, this is not an outrageous assumption. See, for instance, Armando R. Favazza, *Bodies under Seige: Self-mutilation and Body Modification in Culture and Psychology* (Baltimore: Johns Hopkins University Press, 1996).
6. Steven F. Brena, *Pain and Religion: A Psychophysiological Study* (Springfield, IL: Charles C. Thomas, 1972), 134. According to Brena, who worked at the University of Washington at Seattle, the religious element among chronic pain patients came almost always in the form of guilt. F. D. Hart calls them "little martyrs." See F. D. Hart, "Pain as an Old Friend," *British Medical Journal*, 1 (1979), 1405–07. See also Howard M. Spiro, *Doctors, Patients and Placebos* (New Haven, CT: Yale University Press, 1986), 98.
7. Richard A. Shweder, *Thinking Through Cultures: Expeditions in Cultural Psychology* (Cambridge, MA: Harvard University Press, 1991).
8. Patricia Smith Churchland, *Neurophilosophy: Toward a Unified Science of the Mind/Brain* (Cambridge: MIT, 1998), chapter 7.

ONE

1. For the clinical definition see Harold Merskey, "Pain Terms," *Pain*, 6 (1979), 249–52.
2. Quoted in Roselyne Rey, *The History of Pain*, Louise Elliott Wallace et al., trans. (Cambridge, MA: Harvard University Press, 1993), 3.
3. See Chapters 2 and 3 of this volume.
4. Julie Scott Mesami, trans., *The Sea of Precious Virtues (Bahr al-Fava' id): A Medieval Islamic Mirror for Princes* (Salt Lake City: University of Utah Press, 1991), 20.
5. Ivan G. Marcus, *Piety and Society: The Jewish Pietists of Medieval Germany* (Leiden: Brill, 1981).
6. Rey, *The History of Pain*, 5.
7. R. Akiva said: "The King (God) has four sons, one, when struck (*lakah*) suffers in silence, the second kicks, the third prays, and the fourth says to his father 'strike me.'" Semahoth, VIII.
8. Friedrich Nietzsche, *The Genealogy of Morals*, Walter Kaufmann, trans. (New York: Vintage, 1967), 117. The Buddha was wary of such a performer of austerities because "he torments and tortures himself, despite his yearnings for pleasure and despite his repungnance to pain." *Kandaraka Sutta*, quoted in Lord Chalmers, trans., *Further Dialogues of the Buddha* (London: Humphrey Milford, 1926), 248. E. M. Cioran marked another paradox at the heart of asceticism. He pronounced saintliness "imperialistic"and voluptuous, and claimed that it interests him for "the delirium of self-aggrandizement hidden beneath its meekness, its will to power masked by goodness." *Tears and Saints*, Ilinca Zarifopol-Johnston, trans. (Chicago: University of Chicago Press, 1995), viii. Nietzsche would undoubtedly have approved.
9. *Prometheus Bound*, 402–03, David Grene, trans. (Chicago: University of Chicago Press, 1957); see also Cicero's version in Carl Kerenyi, *Prometheus: Archetypal Image of Human Existence*, Ralph Manheim, trans. (Princeton, NJ: Princeton University Press, Bollingen Series 65, I, 1963), 113–14. The theme of unjust suffering, inflicted whimsically or even by an evil agent, is extremely pervasive in Greek tragedy (*Electra, Hipppolytus, Oedipus Rex*). Its psychological underpinnings are explored in Eli Sagan, *The Lust to Annihilate: A Psychoanalytic Study of Violence in Ancient Greek Culture* (New York: Psychohistory Press, 1979), 115–43.
10. Genesis 3:16–17. According to the commentary of R. Samson Raphael Hirsch, the pain of childbirth is a sacrificial one—based on the idea that happiness comes by way of sacrifice. However, delivery under anesthetics is not against Jewish (or Christian) medical ethics. See Rabbi Reuven P. Bulka, *The Jewish Pleasure Principle* (New York: Human Sciences, 1987), 138, note 29.
11. Marshall Sahlins, "The Sadness of Sweetness: The Native Anthropology of Western Cosmology," *Current Anthropology*, 37 (1996), 396.
12. Virgil claims that even the gods who control Tartarus are backed up by justice: "Being warned, Learn justice; reverence the gods." *Aeneid* VI. 650; The psalmist is not always sure: for a vindictively punishing God, see Psalm 38:2. The connection between suffering and the removal of sin deserves a book of its own. The operative mechanism is extremely subtle in both psychological and cultural ways. For a cocksure view on this link see Dorothee Soelle, *Suffering*, trans. E. Verett R. Kalin (Philadelphia: Fortress Press, 1975), 20–21. She stands in contrast to a monumental corpus of anguished theodicies. For one example, see Michael J. Taylor, ed., *The Mystery of Suffering and Death* (New York: Alba House, 1973).
13. Harold Gardiner, ed., *The Imitation of Christ* (New York: Image Books, 1989), 66–67. The pain may act as indication of God's anger, and consequent future hurt. See al-Qushayri, *Principles of Sufism*, B. R. von Schlegel, trans. (Berkeley: Mitzan, 1990), 82.

14. J. T. McNeill and H. M. Gamer, eds., *Medieval Handbooks of Penance* (New York: Columbia University Press, 1938), 354.
15. H. J. Thurston, *Butler's Lives of the Saints*, vol. 1 (Westminster, MD: Christian Classics, 1990), 27.
16. Palladius (524), Lausiac History 2.24; 83–84 (Meyer's translation); in Oswei Temkin, *Hippocrates in a World of Pagans and Christians* (Baltimore: Johns Hopkins University Press, 1991), 155.
17. *Talmud*, Tractate Arkhin; see also *Genesis* 22:13, *Book of Ruth* 4:7. "The chicken is my substitute, and my ransom shall be killed," says Agnon's rabbi in Samuel Agnon, *The Days of Awe* (New York: Shocken, 1948), 19.
18. Quoted in Patrick D. Wall, *Defeating Pain: The War against a Silent Epidemic* (New York: Plenum, 1991), 151.
19. *Protagoras* 357e, *Republic* 444b, *Timaeus* 86b, *Phaedo* 113d–14c.
20. See the case of Abdin in Gananth Obeyesekere, *Medusa's Hair: An Essay on Personal Symbols and Religious Experience* (Chicago: University of Chicago Press, 1981). Obeyesekere is careful to show that much more than mere barter is at work from a psychological point of view. See also G. Obeyesekere, *The Work of Culture: Symbolic Transformation in Psychoanalysis and Anthropology* (Chicago: University of Chicago Press, 1990), 3–7. A more conventional psychoanalytical interpretation of the same data can be found in Dan W. Forsyth, "Ajatasattu and the Future of Psychoanalytical Anthropology. Part II: The Imperative of the Wish," *International Journal of Hindu Studies*, 1 (1997), 314–36. See also Elizabeth Fuller Collins, *Pierced by Murugan's Lance: Ritual, Power, and Moral Redemption among Malaysian Hindus* (Dekalb: Northern Illinois University Press, 1997), 82.
21. Thomas Hobbes, *Leviathan*. See also William Ian Miller, *Humiliation: And Other Essays on Honor, Social Discomfort, and Violence* (Ithaca, NY: Cornell University Press, 1993).
22. P. V. Kane, *History of Dharmasastra* (Pune: Bandharkar Oriental Research Institute, 1974), 4.370–71. The ordeal by fire or heat is still used in India, but not in judicial contexts. For a magical context see, Ariel Glucklich, *The End of Magic* (New York: Oxford University Press, 1997), 93. For more on ordeals in ancient India, see Richard W. Larivierre, trans., *The Divyatattva of Raghunandana Bhattacarya* (New Delhi: Manohar, 1981).
23. Robert Bartlett, *Trial by Fire and Water: The Medieval Judicial Ordeal* (Oxford: Clarendon, 1986).
24. Patricia Terry, trans., "The Third Lay of Gudrun," in *Poems of the Vikings. The Elder Edda* (Indianapolis and New York: University of Indiana Press, 1969), 204. The connection between heat and sexual infidelity or the testing of faithfulness is a powerful theme. See, for comparison, the *Ramayana*'s test of Sita, the Spanish *Fuero de Cuenca*, and also Adolph Franz, ed., *Das Rituale von St. Florian aus dem zwolften Jahrhundert* (Frieburg im Breisgau, 1904). The connection between ordeals and women's sex crimes (adultery) in European history is matched in the *Mishnah*, which limits the use of ordeal to women accused of adultery, and there too the ordeal relies on fire (Sotah 2.2).
25. Michel Foucault, "Le combat de las chastete," quoted in T. Asad, "Notes on Body Pain and Truth in Medieval Christian Ritual," *Economy and Society*, 12 (1983), 310–11.
26. Kamala Tiyavanich, *Forest Recollections: Wandering Monks in Twentieth Century Thailand* (Honolulu: University of Hawaii Press, 1997), 111. "Pleasure is the seed of pain," states a Japanese Buddhist proverb, and "pain is the seed of pleasure." *The Buddhist Writings of Lafacadio Hearn* (Santa Barbara, CA: Ross-Erikson, 1977), 181. This equanimity is associated with a middle-of-the-road opposition to

extreme austerities, which is characteristic of Buddhism. See, for instance, Arthur Braverman, trans., *Warrior Zen: The Diamond-hard Wisdom Mind of Suzuki Shosan* (New York: Kodansha, 1994), 42: "You should not engage in unreasonable practices or excessive zazen." See also *Sunyasampadane*, M. S. Sunkapur and Armando Menezes, trans. (Dharwar: Karnataka University Press, 1972), 399. In Hinduism see also Kaushitaki Upanishad 2.15; 1.7, Bhagavadgita 2.14–18: "The sense contacts, O Son of Kunti, are those that cause heat and cold, pleasure and pain. Impermanent, they come and go; endure them with patience, O Son of Bharata." See also Patanjali's *Yoga Sutras* 1.14–15. Similar sentiments are to be found in Western mysticism as well. Hazrat Inayat Khan puts the matter thus: "If it were not for pain, one would not enjoy the experience of joy . . . for everything is distinguished by its opposite." *The Complete Sayings of Hazrat Inayat Khan* (New Lebanon, NJ: Sufi Order, 1978), 182. A dramatically conflicting evaluation of pain, one that rings almost Jewish in its rejection of the value of pain, is found in a tale from the *Masnavi* (of Rumi) called "The Striker and the Stricken, the Dilemma of Mystical Bewilderment." See A. J. Arberry, *Tales from the Masnavi* (London: George Allen & Unwin, 1961), 212.

27. The second clause of the Shema prayer commands Jews to love God with all their heart, possessions, and soul. Baraitha Berakhot 61b reports that R. Akiva told his students, who were witnessing the torture, that he had always known that he loved God with all his heart and possessions. Here, finally, was his chance to see if he loved God with all his soul as well. See also David R. Blumenthal, *Facing the Abusing God: A Theology of Protest* (Louisville, KY: Westminster, 1993), 151–52. Compare Hazrat Inayat Khan who claimed: "Devotion is proved by sacrifice." *The Complete Sayings*, 26.
28. Hebrews 2:18; see also Matthew 4:1, Luke 4:2, Hebrews 2:14–17. For Maimonides the forbearance of pain should come about precisely from the opposite stance, that is, our very inability to fathom its meaning. Mishneh Torah, Laws of Opinions, 4: 4. See also Talmud Gittin, 70a.
29. Saint Athanasius, *Life of Saint Antony*, Robert T. Meyers, trans. (Westminster, MD: Newman, 1950), 9, 28.
30. And Proverbs 22:15 states, "Foolishness is bound up in the heart of a child; The rod of discipline will remove it far from him."
31. 2 Samuel 7:14–15. See also Proverbs 3:11–12; Hebrews 5:11–14.
32. Clement, *Stromateis*, 7.11, quoted in Darrel W. Amundsen, *Medicine, Society, and Faith in the Ancient and Medieval Worlds* (Baltimore: Johns Hopkins University Press, 1996), 91.
33. Prudentius, *Peristephanon*, 10. Michael John Roberts, *Poetry and the Cult of Martyrs: The Liber Peristephanon of Prudentius* (Ann Arbor: University of Michigan Press, 1993).
34. Macarius, *Homilien*, 48.4. The Jewish approach at the time was more pragmatic and sympathetic to medicine. "The Lord created medicines out of the earth; and a prudent man will have no disgust at them." Sirach 38, 4; see also Midrash Samuel IV, 27b; see D. Blumenthal, *Facing the Abusing God*, 154.
35. O. Temkin, *Hippocrates in a World of Pagans and Christians* (Baltimore: Johns Hopkins University Press, 1991), 9. On pain as counterirritant (a medical concept), see Saint Basil, *The Long Rules*, Q. 51–52. In Monica Wagner, trans., *Saint Basil: Ascetical Works* (New York: Father of the Church, 1950), 328–29.
36. Temkin, *Hippocrates*, 16.
37. *Wagner, Saint Basil: Ascetical Works*, 329; Basil quoted scripture for support: "For behold this selfsame thing, that you were made sorrowful according to God, how great carefulness it works in you"(2 Corinthians 7:11).

38. Mesami, *The Sea of Precious Virtues*, 27.
39. Annemarie Schimmel, *Pain and Grace: A Study of Two Mystical Writers of Eighteenth-Century Muslim India* (Leiden: Brill, 1976), 59.
40. Ibid. See also Rumi: "Oh Love! Each person names you differently; Last night I gave you another name, pain without cure." Quoted in Javed Nurbakhsh, *Sufi Symbolism* (London: Khaniqahi-Nirmutullahi, 1991), vol. V, 154. The connection between love and pain is divine: pain indicates "an experience which arrives suddenly from the Beloved, such that the lover cannot tolerate it" (Ibid., 153).
41. Job 6:4.
42. Atharvaveda, 6.90.
43. Jeremiah 30:12–14.
44. The historic origins of the dualistic antagonism between soul and body in Zoroastrianism, Gnosticism, and ancient Greece are familiar enough to bypass here. Specifically, the ascetic impulse in early Christianity owes a great debt to the Pythagoreans and to Plato's dualistic conception of the divine soul as the prisoner of the worldly body.
45. Randall C. Gleason, *John Calvin and John Owen on Mortification: A Comparative Study in Reformed Spirituality* (New York: Peter Lang, 1995), 60–61. A prolonged Calvinistic (Scottish) discourse on the spiritual war can be read in Andrew Gray, *The Spiritual Warfare: Or Some Sermons Concerning the Nature of Mortification* (Boston: S. Kneeland, 1720). See Paul in 2 Corinthians 12:10: "for when I am weak, then I am strong."
46. St. Augustine, *The Confessions*, J. G. Pilkington, trans. (New York: Liveright, 1943), 8.5, 170–71.
47. Temkin, *Hippocrates*, 153. John Climacus yelled out: "Let us kill this flesh, let us kill it just as it has killed us with the mortal blow of sin." Piero Camporesi, *The Incorruptible Flesh: Bodily Mutation and Mortification in Religion and Folklore* (Cambridge: Cambridge University Press, 1988), 45. St. Margaret of Cortona (1297) told her confessor who was trying to stop her self-mutilations, "Between me and my body there must needs be a struggle till death." Thurston, *Butler's Lives*, 397. See also Heraclidis Pradeisos 1, quoted in E. R. Dodds, *Pagan and Christian in an Age of Anxiety* (Cambridge: Cambridge University Press, 1968), 30 and note 1.
48. Thurston, *Butler's Lives*, vol. 1, 20.
49. *The Letters of Catherine of Siena, Letter 1*, Suzanne Noffke, trans. (Binghamton, NY: Medieval and Renaissance Texts, 1988), 38.
50. Mesami, *The Sea of Precious Virtues*, 13.
51. *Ibid.*, 13–14.
52. Henry Suso also began to think of himself as a knight fighting in the the service of God, not against heathens but his own body. Frank Tobin, ed and trans., *Henry Suso: The Exemplar with two German Sermons* (New York: Paulist Press, 1989), 99–100.
53. V. A. Oldfeather, trans., *Epictetus* (London: W. Heinemann, 1928), II, 151.
54. See also 1 Peter 4:12 and Hebrews 12:1, 4. As noted earlier, the prevailing Jewish approach to pain at that time was nonascetic. But there were striking exceptions. Akiva accepted his torture with love (see test model above). Avot D'Rabbe Nathan (41: 4) stated that Jewish life was to "eat bread with salt, to drink water in measure, to sleep on the ground, and live a life of pain." The text may have been descriptive rather than prescriptive.
55. Colin Eisler, "The Athlete of Virtue: The Iconography of Asceticism," in Millard Meiss, ed., *Essays in Honor of Erwin Panofsky* (New York: New York University Press, 1961), I. 83.
56. Alexander Roberts and James Donaldson, eds., *The Ante-Nicene Fathers* (New York: 1903), III. 638–39; Prudentius, *The Crowns of Martyrdom* and *The Psychomachia*.

57. Virginia Woods Callahan, trans., *Saint Gregory of Nyssa: Ascetical Works* (Washington DC: Catholic University, 1966), 241.
58. Schimmel, *Pain and Grace*, 134. Leonard W. Levy (*Blasphemy*, 80) indicates that those who recanted their blasphemy were still made to carry firewood for the burning of other blasphemers in order to symbolize their own immolation.
59. *Satapatha Brahmana*, 5.4.4.7.
60. Jan Heesterman, *The Ancient India Royal Consecration* (The Hague: Mouton, 1957), 156–57. The explicit rationalization for the beating contradicts the implicit, possibly archaic motive. The pun can hardly be expected to have been the motive for the ritual act. For a more general discussion, see E. E. Evans Pritchard, "The Divine Kingship of the Shilluk of the Nilotic Sudan," the Frazer Lecture of 1948, in *Social Anthropology and Other Essays* (New York: Free Press, 1962) and Godfrey Lienhardt, *Divinity and Experience: The Religion of the Dinka* (Oxford: Clarendon, 1961). For pain and fertility in Islamic North Africa, see Nadia Abu-Zahra, *The Pure and Powerful: Studies in Contemporary Muslim Society* (Berkshire: Ithaca, 1997), 29–31.
61. E. Heinrich Kisch, *The Sexual Life of Woman in Its Physiological and Hygienic Aspect* (New York: Medical Art Agency, 1916), chapter 17.
62. See Mircea Eliade, *Patterns in Comparative Religion* (New York: New American Library, 1958), chapters 8–9.
63. Emile Durkheim, *The Elementary Forms of the Religious Life* (New York: Free Press, 1965), 353–54; for a brief overview of this widely discussed topic, see M. Eliade's "Initiation: An Overview," in *The Encyclopedia of Religion* (New York: Macmillan, 1987), vol. 7.
64. See George Riley Scott, *The History of Corporal Punishment* (London: T. Werner Laurie, 1938), 25.
65. Walter O. Kaelber, *Tapta Marga: Asceticism and Initiation in Vedic India* (Albany: SUNY, 1989).
66. The translation varies according to the root *tap*, with Bloomfield taking it as "hurting" and Blair more literally as "burning." See *Tapta Marga*, 49.
67. *Satapatha Brahmana*, 3,4,3.2; quoted by Kaelber, *Tapta Marga*, 55.
68. Stephen Eskildsen, *Asceticism in Early Taoist Religion* (New York: SUNY, 1998), 92.
69. Dodds, *Pagan*, 7–36; R. Numbers, *Caring and Curing*, 53.
70. Quoted in Caroline Walker Bynum, *The Resurrection of the Body in Western Christianity, 200–1336* (New York: Columbia University Press, 1995), 61 and fn. 7. Helinand of Froimont, a late medieval Cistercian monk, wrote the "Verses on Death":

    A well-fed body and delicate complexion
    Are but a tunic of worms and fire.
    The body is vile, stinking, and withered.
    The pleasure of the flesh is by nature poisoned and corrupt.

    Quoted in Jacques Le Goff, *The Medieval Imagination*, trans. Arthur Goldhammer (Chicago: University of Chicago Press, 1988), 84.
71. St. Bernard Abbot of Clairvaux, *Meditationes piisimae ad humanae conditionis* (1679). Quoted in P. Camporesi, *The Incorruptible Flesh*, 108.
72. Camporesi, *The Incorruptible Flesh*, 110.
73. See James Frazer, *The Golden Bough* (London: Macmillan, 1911–15), 11:171. The most comprehensive collection of such rituals is Wayland D. Hand, *Magical Medicine: The Folkloric Component of Medicine in the Folk Belief, Custom, and Ritual of the Peoples of Europe and America* (Berkeley: University of California Press, 1980), 133–85. A different view of purification can be seen in the Yom Kippur

concept of *memarkin* or scouring, which is a punishment that purifies (Leviticus 16: 30). See Pinchas Peli, *Soloveitchik on Repentance* (New York: Paulist, 1984), 267.

74. *Pali Tipikas* (2 vols.) (Delhi: Kalinga, 1999), I. 230–31; Ariel Glucklich, *The Sense of Adharma* (New York: Oxford University Press, 1994); I. Marcus, *Piety*, 84.
75. Baha'u'llah, "The Seven Valleys," in *The Seven Valleys and the Four Valleys*, Ali-kuli Khan, trans., assisted by Marzieh Gail (Wilmette, IL: Bahai Publishing Trust, 1931, rev. ed. 1974), 8.
76. Shelly Girard, "Why Have Natural Childbirth," quoted by Margaret Talbot, "Pay on Delivery," *New York Times Magazine*, Oct. 31 1999, 19. See also Pamela A. Klassen, "The Birthing Body in Pain," paper read at the American Academy of Religion meeting, November 1999.
77. Marjorie Williams, "Normalizing Suicide," *Washington Post*, Nov. 14, 1999, B7.
78. A striking example is Father Donissan in Georges Bernanos, *Under the Sun of Satan*, Harry L. Binsse, trans. (New York: Pantheon, 1949). See also Peter J. Braunlein, "Performing Jesus' Death: Philippine Crucifixion Rituals as Performative Events," paper presented at American Academy of Religion meeting, November 1998. It is central to Judaism as well: "Whoever rejoices in the afflictions which are brought upon the self brings salvation to the world," Talmud Avot 3: 14. The circumcision ritual blessing omits "sheheheyanu" out of empathy for the boy's pain. Moshe Perlman, *Midrash HaRefuah* (Tel Aviv: Dvir, 1926) 1:47, note 76.
79. *Oedipus Rex*, David Grene, trans. (Chicago: University of Chicago Press, 1957), 93–94. On Miasma see Jean-Pierre Vernant and Pierre Vidal-Naquet, *Myth and Tragedy in Ancient Greece*, Janet Lloyd, trans. (New York: Zone Books, 1988), 131.
80. Pamela Eisenbaum, "Suffering, Discipline, and Perfection in Hebrews," in Leif E. Vaage and Vincent L. Wimbush eds., *Asceticism in the New Testament* (New York: Routledge, 1999), 337.
81. Noffke, *The Letters*, letter 18, 76.
82. Edmund Colledge and James Walsh, trans., *Julian of Norwich: Showings, Classics of Western Spirituality* (New York: Paulist Press, 1978), Long Text 178.
83. Zohar Ahare Mot 56b, 57b. Philip Goodman, *The Yom Kippur Anthology* (Philadelphia: Jewish Publication Society, 1971), 41–42.
84. *Mingzhen ke*, 24b; quoted in Eskildsen, *Asceticism*, 119.
85. See for instance, William C. Bushell, "Psychophysiological and Comparative Analysis of Ascetico-Meditational Discipline: Toward a New Theory of Asceticism," in Vincent L. Wimbush and Richard Valantis, eds., *Asceticism* (New York: Oxford University Press, 1995), 553–75. Note that neurophysiological principles cannot act as a conceptual model for pain in a prescientific age. Even today the language of neuropeptides fails to account for the phenomenology of experience.
86. Fakir, "Editorial: Changes-of-Bodystate," in *Body Play: And Modern Primitives*, vol. 1, no. 3, pp. 4–5. On the ecstasies of shamanic ordeals, see M. Eliade, *Shamanism: Archaic Techiques of Ecstasy* (Princeton: Princeton University Press, 1974), especially 36. See also Gananath Obeyesekere, *Medusa's Hair: An Essay on Personal Symbols and Religious Experience* (Chicago: University of Chicago Press, 1981), 145–46.
87. The normative "theories" are particularly rich, and especially in Christianity where moral and retributivist theologies are actively promoted, along with psychologies and philosophies of atonement. See, for example, C. Gunton, *The Actuality of the Atonement* (Edinburgh: T& T Clark, 1988); R. Swinburne, *Responsibility and Atonement* (Oxford: Oxford University Press, 1988); Timothy Gorringe, *God's Just Vengeance* (Cambridge: Cambridge University Press, 1996).
88. It is not necessary for a good theory to explain every instance of pain in religious history. Certainly my own theory will not do this. What is essential, however, is

that the reductive theory be situated within the field in its full complexity, and that it account for its own limitations by clarifying the nature of its explanatory range.

89. I am using "type" in contrast to "model" as a strictly theoretical construct, rather than a normative or descriptive form of discourse that is accessible to informants.
90. The Roman poet Martial was awed by the condemned warrior-victim "Mucius Scaevola" who put his sword hand in the altar fire and watched it burn: "What we observe as a sport in the arena of Caesar was in the time of Brutus the summit of glory. See how the hand grasps the flame and enjoys the punishment." Quoted in Carlin A. Barton, *The Sorrows of the Ancient Romans: The Gladiator and the Monster* (Princeton, NJ: Princeton University Press, 1993), 60. Barton argues that the gladiatorial ordeal became a matter of voluntary suffering, structured like my notion of sacred pain.
91. I am indebted to Peter J. Braunlein from the University of Bremen for the information on these performances.
92. Paul C. Rosenblatt et al., *Grief and Mourning in Cross-Cultural Perspective* (New York: HRAF Press, 1976), 23–24.
93. Emile Durkheim, *The Elementary Forms of the Religious Life* (New York: Free Press, 1965), 436.
94. Maurice Bloch and Jonathan Parry, eds., *Death and the Regeneration of Life* (Cambridge: Cambridge University Press, 1982).
95. Renato Rosaldo, *Culture and Truth: The Remaking of Social Analysis* (Boston: Beacon, 1989).
96. Peter Metcalf and Richard Huntington, *Celebrations of Death: The Anthropology of Mortuary Ritual* (Cambridge: Cambridge University Press, 1991).
97. On mourning and ambivalence see Susan Letzler Cole, *The Absent One: Mourning Ritual, Tragedy, and the Performance of Ambivalence* (University Park: Pennsylvania State University Press, 1991).
98. There is also a methodological issue at stake: Spontaneous eruptions of emotion are an appropriate subject for psychological reduction while choreographed ritualized action is not. The problematic separation between psychological and social explanation has generated a great deal of debate. For a summary of the positions see I. M. Lewis, *Ecstatic Religion: A Study of Shamanism and Spirit Possession*, 2nd ed., (London: Routledge, 1989), especially chapter 7.
99. V. W. Turner and E. Turner, *Image and Pilgrimage in Christian Culture: Anthropological Perspectives* (Oxford: Basil Blackwell, 1978); John Eade and Michael J. Sallnow, *Contesting the Sacred: The Anthropology of Christian Pilgrimage* (London: Routledge, 1991).
100. E. Valentine Daniel, *Fluid Signs: Being a Person the Tamil Way* (Berkeley: University of California, 1987), 246–78.
101. Ibid., 255.
102. Ibid., 267.
103. Ibid., 268.
104. Ibid., 269. For a strikingly similar transformation of suffering into love in another pilgrimage, see Ruth Harris, *Lourdes: Body and Spirit in the Secular Age* (New York: Viking, 1999), 311.

TWO

1. Nirmal Dass, trans., *Songs of Kabir from the Adi Grant* (New York: SUNY Press, 1991), 148–49.

2. Mircea Eliade, *Rites and Symbols of Initiation: The Mysteries of Birth and Rebirth* (New York: Harper Torchbooks, 1958); see also Lawrence E. Sullivan, *Icanchu's Drum: An Orientation to Meaning in South American Religions* (New York: Macmillan, 1988), and Bruce Lincoln, *Emerging from the Chrysalis: Studies in Rituals of Women's Initiation* (Cambridge, MA: Harvard University Press, 1981).
3. Montague Summers, trans., *Malleus Maleficarum* (New York: Benjamin Blom, 1970), vol. 3, 195 Anne Llewellyn Barstow, *Witchcraze: A New History of the European Witch Hunts* (New York: Pandora, 1994), 143–45.
4. Of course, for Freud there is no such thing as the holy. Masochism is always a clinical condition, always connected with sexuality, and often, with sadism. See *Civilization and Its Discontents*, James Strachey, trans. (New York: Norton, 1962), and *Beyond the Pleasure Principle*, James Strachey, trans. (New York: Norton, 1989). See also Marie Bonaparte, "Some Biopsychical Aspects of Sado-Masochism," in Margaret Ann Fitzpatrick Hanly, ed., *Essential Papers on Masochism* (New York: New York University Press, 1995), 432–52.
5. For a critique of psychoanalysis in comparative cultural studies, see Victor Turner, *The Forest of Symbols: Aspects of Ndembu Ritual* (Ithaca, NY: Cornell University Press, 1967), 35–38.
6. For neuropsychology consider the influential article by Arnold Mandell, "Toward a Psychobiology of Transcendence: God in the Brain," in Julian M. Davidson and Hohn Richards, eds., *The Psychobiology of Consciousness* (New York: Plenum Books, 1980), 117–35. More recent research is included in Armando Favazza, *Bodies under Seige: Self-Mutilation and Body Modification in Culture and Psychiatry* (Baltimore: Johns Hopkins University Press, 1992), 261–64. Prominent ethological theories are contained in the following works: Konrad Lorenz, *The Foundations of Ethology* (New York: Springer-Verlag, 1981); Desmond Morris, *The Human Animal: A Personal View of the Human Species* (New York: Crown, 1994); Edward O. Wilson, *On Human Nature* (Cambridge, MA: Harvard University Press, 1978).
7. Elaine Scarry, *The Body in Pain: The Making and Unmaking of the World* (New York: Oxford University Press, 1985). A brief list of articles in religious journals influenced by her work can include Maureen Flynn, "The Spiritual Uses of Pain in Spanish Mysticism," *Journal of the American Academy of Religion*, 64:2 (1996), 257–78; Maureen A. Tilley, "The Ascetic Body and the (Un)Making of the World of the Martyr," *Journal of the American Academy of Religion*, 59:3 (1990), 467–79; Paula M. Cooey, "Experience, Body, and Authority," *Harvard Theological Review*, 82:3 (1989), 325–42; Kristin Boudreau, "Pain and the Unmaking of Self in Toni Morrison's *Beloved*," *Contemporary Literature*, 36:3 (1995), 447–65; Pamela A. Smith, "Chronic Pain and Creative Possibility: A Psychological Phenomenon Confronts Theologies of Suffering," in Maureen A. Tilly and Susan A. Ross, eds., *Broken and Whole: Essays on Religion and the Body*, Annual Publication of the College Theology Society, vol. 39 (New York: University Press of America, 1993).
8. Scarry, *Body in Pain*, 162.
9. Flynn, "Spiritual Uses of Pain," 274.
10. Eric Lomax, *The Railway Man: A True Story of War, Remembrance, and Forgiveness* (New York: Ballantine Books, 1995), 141–43.
11. Virginia Woolf, "On Being Ill," in Virginia Woolf, *The Moment and Other Essays* (New York: Harcourt, Brace, 1948), 11.
12. The notion that pain is indeed subject to communication is not novel to *Sacred Pain*. See Jean Jackson, "Chronic Pain and the Tension between the Body, as Subject and Object," in T. J. Csordas, ed., *Embodiment and Experience*, 202–28; Talal Asad, "Agency and Pain: An Exploration," in *Culture and Religion*, 1:1 (2000), 29–60.

13. Ronald Melzack, "The McGill Questionnaire: Major Properties and Scoring Methods," *Pain*, 1 (1975), 277–99; Dennis C. Turk and Ronald Melzack, *Handbook of Pain Assessment* (New York: Guiford Press, 1992).
14. Scarry, *Body in Pain*, 15; For Scarry, the result of such metaphorical extensions of experience is the conflation of pain with power, a political observation.
15. Kumarasambhava, 1.20.
16. This list represents an extremely brief selection, based mostly on dictionary sources. I have gone over the *Sushruta Samhita* and *Caraka Samhita*, ancient medical texts, and found dozens of additional terms, which space precludes from listing in the text. *Sushruta Samhita*, 1.22.11, alone has these types of pain: *todana* (pricking), *bhedana* (breaking), *tāḍana* (beating), *chedana* (cutting), *ayamana* (knotting), *manthana* (churning), *vikṣepaṇa* (shaking).
17. For pain terms in classical Greek, see Roslyne Rey, *The History of Pain* (Cambridge, MA: Harvard University Press, 1995), 12–14. For a grammatical analysis for English and Romance languages, see Horacio Fabrega, Jr., and Stephen Tyma, "Language and Cultural Influences in the Description of Pain," *British Journal of Medical Psychology*, 49 (1976), 349–71. For Thai and Japanese, see Horacio Fabrega, Jr., and Stephen Tyma, "Culture, Language and the Shaping of Illness: An Illustration Based on Pain," in *Journal of Psychosomatic Research*, 20 (1976), 323–37.
18. Adrian Akmajian et al., *Linguistics: An Introduction to Language and Communication* (Cambridge, MA: MIT, 1990), 41; Andrew Ortony, ed., *Metaphor and Thought* (Cambridge: Cambridge University Press, 1993).
19. Akmajian, *Linguistics*, 41. The foundational role of metaphorical semantics has been championed by George Lakoff and Mark Johnson, *Metaphors We Live By* (Chicago: University of Chicago Press, 1980), and George Lakoff, *Women, Fire, and Dangerous Things* (Chicago: University of Chicago Press, 1987).
20. This entire topic is discussed in philosophical circles as the question of other minds. Philosophers try to determine how one can know that others have similar mental states, or any at all. See, for instance, John Wisdom, *Other Minds* (Oxford: Clarendon, 1956). I will stay away from this agenda in this work.
21. See for instance, K. Koffka, *Principles of Gestalt Psychology* (New York: Harcourt, Brace, and World, 1935), 55–67.
22. Wolfgang Kohler, *Gestalt Psychology: An Introduction to New Concepts in Modern Psychology* (New York: Liveright, 1947), 225. According to several theorists, the appropriate term is *the unity of the senses*. For the precise epistemology, see George W. Harmann, *Gestalt Psychology: A Survey of Facts and Principles* (New York: Ronald Press Company, 1935), 141–51. A vivid description of synesthesia and its role in learning and memory is contained in A. R. Luria, *The Mind of a Mnemonist* (Cambridge, MA: Harvard University Press, 1987).
23. Douglas R. Hofstadter, *Metamagical Themas: Questing for the Essence of Mind and Pattern* (New York: Basic Books, 1985), 179.
24. Quoted in ibid., 180.
25. Ibid., 181.
26. Kohler, *Gestalt Psychology*, 248–49.
27. Susanne K. Langer, *Philosophy in a New Key: A Study in the Symbolism of Reason, Rite, and Art* (New York: New American Library, 1961), 193. The synesthetic effect in art is discussed by E. H. Gombrich, who owes his account to Roman Jakobson. See *Art and Illusion: A Study in the Psychology of Pictorial Representation*, Bollingen Series 35.5 (New York: Pantheon, 1960), 370.
28. Oliver Sacks, *Migraine* (New York: Vintage, 1992), 294–95.
29. Fyodor Dostoevsky, *Notes from the Underground* (New York: A Signet Classic, 1980), 84.

30. Freud, quoted in Stanley J. Coen, "The Excitement of Sadomasochism," in Hanly, ed., *Essential Papers on Masochism*, 383–84.
31. Dostoevsky, *Notes*, 86.
32. The reader who wishes to experiment with these ideas or observe his or her reaction to the appalling "torture of the rat" may look up Octave Mirbeau, *Torture Garden* (New York: Citadel Press, 1948), 192–94.
33. Harold Merskey, "Pain Terms," *Pain*, 6 (1979), 249–52.
34. See the comments by R. Havard, M.D., in the Appendix to C. S. Lewis, *The Problem of Pain* (London: Geoffrey Bles, 1950).
35. See the discussion of Maria Maddalena de' Pazzi in Chapter 4 of this book.
36. Patrick D. Wall and Mervyn Jones, *Defeating Pain: The War against the Silent Epidemic* (New York: Plenum, 1991), 137.
37. For a convenient summary, see Ronald Melzack, "Phantom-Limb and the Brain," in Burkhart Bromm and John E. Desmedt, eds., *Pain and the Brain: From Nociception to Cognition*. Advances in Pain Research and Therapy, vol. 22 (New York: Raven Press, 1995).
38. René Descartes, *The Principles of Philosophy*, 4. 196, in John Veitch, trans., *The Meditations and Selections from the Principles* (La Salle, IL: Open Court, 1968), 200–01.
39. Ibid.
40. The studies that document these figures are listed in Ronald Melzack, "Phantom-Limb Pain and the Brain," 79. See also Joel Katz, "The Role of the Sympathetic Nervous System in Phantom Limb Pain," *Physical Medicine and Rehabilitation*, 10: 1 (1996), 153–75.
41. E.S.M. Saadah and R. Melzack, "Phantom Limb Experience in Congenital Limb-Deficient Adults," *Cortex*, 30 (1994), 479–85. George Grouios, "Phantom Limb Perceptuomotor 'Memories' in a congenital Limb Child," *Medical Science Research*, 24 (1996), 503–04. For a peripheralist theory of phantom-limb pain (blood clots, gangrene, stump problems), see Samuel A. Weiss and Brad Lindell, "Phantom Limb Pain and Etiology of Amputation in Unilateral Lower Extremities Amputees," *Journal of Pain and Symptom Management*, 11 (1996), 3–17.
42. Melzack's theory has appeared in several publications and studies. Among the clearest statements are "Phantom-Limb Pain and the Brain"; "Pain: Past, Present and Future," *Canadian Journal of Experimental Psychology*, 47 (1993), 615–29; and in the most accessible context: Melzack, "Phantom Limbs," *Scientific American*, 261 (April 1992), 120–26.
43. Melzack, "Phantom-Limb Pain," 75–76.
44. Wolfgang Kohler, *The Task of Gestalt Psychology* (Princeton, NJ: Princeton University Press, 1969), 66.
45. Melzack, "Phantom-Limb Pain," 79–80.
46. V. S. Ramachandran et al., "Touching the Phantom Limb," *Nature*, 377:6549 (1995), 489–90. See also Maomora Muraoka et al., "Psychosomatic Treatment of Phantom Limb Pain with Post-Traumatic Stress Disorder: A Case Report," *Pain*, 66 (1996), 385–88.
47. Ramachandran, "Touching the Phantom Limb," 490.
48. Geoffery Schultz and Ronald Melzack, "Visual Hallucinations and Mental State: A Study of 14 Charles Bonnet Syndrome Hallucinators," *Journal of Nervous and Mental Disease*, 181 (1993), 639–43. Hallucinations are also known to be auditory, tactile, olfactory, and gustatory.
49. Hallucinations are complex psychological and physiological events. Sensory deprivation is only one cause, even among the deliberate methods of inducing such mental states. See Peter D. Slade and Richard P. Bentall, *Sensory Deception: A Scientific Analysis of Hallucinations* (Baltimore: Johns Hopkins University Press, 1988), 15–16.

50. The variables affecting the contents of hallucinations range from psychological factors such as stress and pathology to intelligence and language skills, suggestibility and responsiveness to instructions, environmental stimulation, cultural values, and others (Slade and Bentall, *Sensory Deprivation*, 82–109).
51. The term *hallucination* is ontologically neutral and refers in this context merely to mental phenomena produced by the overfiring of neuronal output.
52. Oscar D. Ratnoff, "The Psychogenic Purpuras: A Review of Autoerythrocyte Sensitization, Autosensitization to DNA, 'Hysterical' and Factitial Bleeding, and the Religious Stigmata," *Seminars in Hematology* 17 (July 1983), 192–213; on Hunt and Chapman, see Ted Harrison, *Stigmata: A Medieval Mystery in a Modern Age* (New York: Penguin, 1994).
53. J. Vernon and T. E. McGill, "Sensory Deprivation and Pain Thresholds," *Science*, 133 (1961), 330–31.
54. On information theory and perceptual psychology, see Ralph Norman Haber, "Information Processing," in Edward C. Carterrette and Morton P. Friedman, eds., *Handbook of Perception*, 11 vols. (New York: Academic Press, 1974), vol. 1, 313–31. On the more specific feedback features of the system, see John P. Zubek, "Sensory and Perceptual-Motor Effects," in John P. Zubek, ed., *Sensory Deprivation: Fifteen Years of Research* (New York: Appleton-Century-Crofts, 1969), 444–46. A similar and perhaps related phenomenon is called "hyperstimulation analgesia." This may be due, however, to the release of natural opiates caused by sharp pain, rather than the disruption of the body-self template by constant dull pain. See William C. Bushell, "Psychophysiological and Comparative Analysis of Asceticism," in Vincent L. Wimbush and Richard Valantis, eds., *Asceticism* (New York: Oxford University Press, 1995), 553–75.
55. I have argued elsewhere that this phenomenal simplicity defines the very nature of purity in Hinduism and conforms to the religious purpose of bathing in India. See Ariel Glucklich, *The Sense of Adharma* (New York: Oxford University Press, 1994), 66–88.
56. D. I. McCloskey, "Signals of Proprioception in Man," in D. Garlick, ed., *Proprioception, Posture and Emotion* (Kensington, Australia: CPME, 1988), 14–22.
57. There are several ways of defining neurological and cognitive schemas. They share a recognition that coordinated and complex action requires that the organism operate on abstracted "models" or "frames" rather than direct physical reality. Schemata apply both to physical action (James J. Gibson, Ulric Neisser) and to cognitive operations and information processing (Jean Piaget, Marvin L. Minsky). For a brief summary see Michael A. Arbib, "Schemas," in R. L. Gregory ed., *The Oxford Companion to the Mind* (Oxford: Oxford University Press, 1987), 695–97; see also George Lakoff, *Women, Fire, and Dangerous Things: What Categories Reveal about the Mind* (Chicago: University of Chicago Press, 1984); James J. Gibson, "The Theory of Affordances," in Robert E. Snow and John Bransford, eds., *Perceiving, Acting and Knowing: Toward an Ecological Psychology* (Hillsdale, NJ: Lawrence Erlbaum, 1977), 33–48; Ulric Neisser, *Cognition and Reality: Principles and Implications of Cognitive Psychology* (San Francisco: Freeman, 1976); Jean Piaget, *Biology and Knowledge: An Essay on the Relations between Organic Regulations and Cognitive Processes* (Edinburgh: Edinburgh University Press, 1971); Marvin L. Minsky, "A Framework for Representing Knowledge," in Patrick H. Winston, ed., *The Psychology of Computer Vision* (New York: McGraw-Hill, 1975), 211–77.
58. It is important to note that systematic chronic pain does not erase learning; it does not "erase the world," in Scarry's words. What it unmakes is the sense of self—the phenomenal aspect of the body-self template (or schema). This results in the *reinforcing* of certain learned ideas such as religious ideas that minimize the value of

the self in relation to God. For instance, inscribing the presence of Jesus—an "other" self—on the body of the self-tormenting mystic whose own sense of self weakens is a way of making a world. F. Tobin, *Henry Suso*, 70.

59. This state will be discussed in detail in Chapter 4.
60. John T. McNeill and Helena M. Gamer, eds., *Medieval Handbooks of Penance* (New York: Columbia University Press, 1938), 223.
61. *The Sea of Precious Virtues (Bahr al-Fava'id): A Medieval Islamic Mirror for Princes,* (Julie Scott Mesami, trans. (Salt Lake City: University of Utah Press, 1991), 13. It would be too easy to multiply the number of examples of pain; readers should refer to the models of Chapter 1.
62. Annemarie Schimmel, *Pain and Grace: A Study of Two Mystical Writers of Eighteenth-Century Muslim India* (Leiden: Brill, 1979), 197.
63. David Bakan, *Disease, Pain and Sacrifice: Toward a Psychology of Suffering* (Chicago: University of Chicago Press, 1968).
64. Ibid., 59.

THREE

1. There are other solutions to the problem raised by Elain Scarry's influential argument that pain "resists" language. For instance, Thomas J. Csordas has offered the suggestion that since language need not be representational it can serve to communicate the unique experience of pain. "Introduction: The Body as Representation and Being-in-the-World" in T. J. Csordas, ed., *Embodiment and Experience: The Existential Ground of Culture and Self* (New York: Cambridge University Press, 1994), 11.
2. Robert Vischer, *Uber das optische Fromgefuhl: Ein Beitrag zur Aesthetik* (Leipzig, 1873).
3. Ibid., 30. See Moshe Barasch, *Modern Theories of Art*, vol. 2 (New York: New York University Press, 1998), 104. Empathy has strong cultural implications ranging from family relations to magic and mysticism. This is explored in David Freedberg, *The Power of Images: Studies in the History and Theory of Response* (Chicago: University of Chicago Press, 1989), chapter 8. For a critique, see James Elkins, *Pictures of the Body: Pain and Metamorphosis* (Stanford, CA: Stanford University Press, 1999), 24. Elkins accentuates the political relations between the subject and object in his concept of metamorphosis, which stands over against pain.
4. But see the Rorschach test in Barasch, *Modern Theories*, 110.
5. Theodor Lipps, *Grundlegung der Aesthetic* (Hamburg and Lepzig: Voss, 1903) and Theodor Lipps, "Aesthetische Einfuhlung," *Zeitschrift Psychologie*, 22 (1900), 415–50.
6. Karl Groos, quoted in Edmunde Burke Feldman, *Varieties of Visual Experience: Art as Image and Idea* (New York: Harry Abrams, nd), 353. M. Barasch, *Modern Theories*, 111.
7. Lipps, *Aesthetische Einfuhlung*, 415, quoted in Rudolf Arnheim, "The Gestalt Theory of Expression," in Mary Hanle, ed., *Documents of Gestalt Psychology* (Berkeley: University of California Press, 1961), 307. See also Rudolph Arnheim, *Art and Visual Perception: A Psychology of the Creative Eye* (Berkeley: University of California Press, 1971) 433–34.
8. Langer, *Philosophy in a New Key*, 193; see also Susanne K. Langer, *Mind: An Essay on Human Feeling*, vol. 1 (Baltimore: Johns Hopkins University Press, 1967), chapter 4. She was preceded, of course, by William James: "I cannot help remarking that the disparity between motions and feelings, on which these authors lay so much stress, is somewhat less absolute than at first sight it seems. Not only temporal succession, but such attributes as intensity, volume, simplicity or complication, smooth or impeded change, rest or agitation, are habitually predicated of both

physical facts and mental facts." Quoted in Arnheim, *Art and Visual Expression*, 428. William James was bested by Aristotle in *Politics*: "By their true nature rhythms and tunes are copies of anger and mildness, courage and temperance." Quoted in E. H. Gombrich, *Art and Illusion*, 359.

9. Arnheim, *The Gestalt Theory of Expression*, 309.
10. C. Richard Chapman, "Pain, Perception, and Illusion," in Richard A. Sternbach, ed., *The Psychology of Pain* (New York: Raven Press, 1986), 153–79.
11. Arnheim, *The Gestalt Theory*, 311.
12. Ibid., 310, n. 4.
13. Wassily Kandinsky, *Concerning the Spiritual in Art*, M.T.H. Sadler, trans. (New York: Dover, 1977), 32.
14. Wassily Kandinsky, *Point and Line to Plane* (New York: Dover, 1979), 68; see also Paul Klee, *Pedagogical Sketchbook*, Sibyl Mohloy-Nagy, trans., (London: Faber and Faber, 1968), 28–29. Arnheim, *Art and Visual Perception*, 414–16.
15. Rudolf Arnheim, *The Split and the Structure: Twenty-Eight Essays* (Berkeley: University of California Press, 1996).
16. Arnheim, *The Gestalt Theory*, 313.
17. Carolyn A. Ristau, "Aspects of the Cognitive Ethology of an Injury-feigning Bird, the Piping Plover," in Carolyn A. Ristau, ed., *Cognitive Ethology: Essays in Honor of Donald R. Griffin* (Hillsdale, NJ: Lawrence Erlbaum, 1991), 91–106.
18. Marc D. Hauser, *The Evolution of Communication* (Cambridge, MA: MIT, 1999), 588.
19. Vicki Bruce and Andy Young, *In the Eye of the Beholder: The Science of Face Perception* (Oxford: Oxford University Press, 1998). See also Robert A. Sobieszek, *Ghost in the Shell: Photographs and the Human Soul 1850–2000* (Cambridge, MA: MIT and L.A. County Museum of Art, 1999).
20. J. A. Russell, "Is There Universal Recognition of Emotion from Facial Expression? A Review of Cross-cultural Studies," *Psychological Bulletin*, 115 (1994), 102–41; for a contrasting analysis, see P. Ekman, "Facial Expressions of Emotion: An Old Controversy and New Findings," *Philosophical Transactions of the Royal Society of London*, 335 (1992), 63–70.
21. T. Dabelstein and S. B. Pederson, "Song and Information about Aggressive Response of Blackbirds, Turdus merula: Evidence from Interactive Playback Experiments with Territory Owners," *Animal Behavior*, 40 (1990), 1158–68.
22. Hauser, *The Evolution*, 490, Table 7.2.
23. Charles Darwin; *The Expression of the Emotions in Man and Animals* (Chicago: University of Chicago Press, 1965), 72.
24. Stephen G. Dennis and Ronald Melzack, "Perspectives on Phylogenetic Evolution of Pain Expression," in Ralph L. Kitchell et al., eds., *Animal Pain: Perception and Alleviation* (Bethesda, MD: American Physiological Association, 1983), 151–60; W. D. Willis, "The Pain System: The Neural Basis of Nociceptive Transmission in the Mammalian Nervous System," in P. L. Gildenberg, ed., *Pain and Headache*, vol. 58 (New York: Krager, 1985), 77–92.
25. C. Richard Chapman, "Pain, Perception, and Illusion," in R. A. Sternbach ed., *The Psychology of Pain*, 2nd ed. (New York: Raven, 1986), 153–79; Gary B. Rollman, "Pain Responsiveness," in Morton Heller and William Schiff, eds., *The Psychology of Touch* (New York: Lawrence Erlbaum, 1991), 91–114.
26. Chapman, "Pain, Perception," 158.
27. Dennis and Melzack, "Perspectives," 153.
28. Walter B. Cannon, *Bodily Changes in Pain, Hunger, Fear and Rage* (New York: D. A. Appleton, 1929).
29. Ibid., 193.

30. Chapman, "Pain, Perception," 163.
31. W. R. Garner, "Good Patterns Have Few Alternatives," *American Scientist*, 58 (1970), 34–42; R. A. Sternbach, *Pain Patients—Traits and Treatment* (New York: Academic Press, 1974); Chapman, "Pain, Perception," 169.
32. Howard L. Fields, *Pain* (New York: McGraw Hill, 1987); Ronald Phillip Pawl, *Chronic Pain Primer* (Chicago: Year Book Medical Publications, 1979).
33. Noreen T. Meinhart and Margo McCaffery, *Pain: A Nursing Approach to Assessment and Analysis* (Norwalk, CT: Appleton-Century-Crofts, 1983), 324.
34. Paul Karoly and Mark P. Jensen, *Multimethod Assessment of Chronic Pain* (Oxford: Pergamon, 1987), 1–25; Dennis C. Turk, Donald Meichenbaum, and Myles Genest, *Pain and Behavioral Medicine: A Cognitive-Behavioral Perspective* (New York: Guilford, 1983).
35. R. Melzack, "The McGill Pain Questionnaire: Major Properties and Scoring Methods," *Pain*, 1 (1975), 281.
36. Marion V. Smith, "Talking about Pain," in Bernadette Carter, ed., *Perspectives on Pain: Mapping the Territory* (London: Arnold, 1998), 26–45.
37. The guiding principle here is phenomenology, which avoids the Cartesian and objectivist separation between subject and world. See Mary-Jo DelVecchio Good et al., eds., *Pain as Human Experience: An Anthropological Perspective* (Berkeley: University of California Press, 1992).
38. M. C. Rawlinson, "The Sense of Suffering," *Journal of Medicine and Philosophy*, 11 (1986), 39–62.
39. DelVecchio Good, ed., *Pain as Human Experience*.
40. G. Bendelow and S. Williams, "Transcending the Dualisms: Toward a Sociology of Pain," *Sociology of Health and Illness*, 17 (1995), 146.
41. Judith Thwaite, "Pain Lashes Out: A Personal Story of Pain," in B. Carter, ed., *Perspectives on Pain*, 4.
42. Ibid., 2.

FOUR

1. Andre Vauchez, *Sainthood in the Later Middle Ages*, Jean Birrell, trans. (Cambridge: Cambridge University Press, 1977), 197, 374, 365.
2. Caroline Walker Bynum, *Holy Feast and Holy Fast* (Berkeley: University of California Press, 1987), 391, n. 77.
3. Frank Tobin, ed. and trans., *Henry Suso: The Exemplar, with Two German Sermons* (New York: Paulist Press, 1989).
4. Jennifer Egan, "The Thin Red Line," *New York Times Magazine*, July 27, 1997, 21–25.
5. Armando R. Favazza, *Bodies under Siege: Self-mutilation and Body Modification in Culture and Psychology* (Baltimore: Johns Hopkins University Press, 1996).
6. Ibid., xvii–xix.
7. M. J. Russ, "Self-Injurious Behavior in Patients with Borderline Personality Disorder: Biological Perspectives," *Journal of Personality Disorders*, 6 (1992), 64–81.
8. There are dozens of theories for thousands of clinical cases in this one category alone, which breaks down into numerous types. See, for instance, Anna Freud, *The Ego and the Mechanisms of Defense* (New York: International Universities Press, 1946), 56; Bruno Bettelheim, *Symbolic Wounds* (London: Thames and Hudson), 19; and A. Favazza, *Bodies*, 272–80.
9. J. Egan, "The Thin Red Line," 24. On the feelings of empowerment and mastery generated by self-abuse (for instance, anorexia), see Rudolph M. Bell, *Holy Anorexia* (Chicago: University of Chicago Press, 1985), 17–20; Bell argues that the phenomenological and historical voice of the subject ought to be taken into account.

10. Anonymous, "Self-help for Self-injury." Internet document ("Self-Mutilation"); available at www.gurlpages.com., 1998.
11. See Favazza, *Bodies*, 45.
12. Vicenzo Puccini, *The Life of Suor Maria Maddalena de Patsi, 1619*. D. M. Rogers, ed., *English Recusant Literature 1558–1640*. (Menston, England: The Scholar, 1970), 108–09.
13. The controversy over her clinical status was generated by Eric Dingwall's *Very Peculiar People: Portrait Studies in the Queer, the Abnormal and the Uncanny* (New Hyde Park, NY: Clarion, 1962), 119–44. Dingwall regarded Maria Maddalena as a "masochistic exhibitionist," spurring numerous vocal rebuttals. See Bell, *Holy Anorexia*, 172.
14. Puccini, *Life*, 9.
15. Ibid., 50.
16. Ibid., 38, 140–41, 108–09.
17. Ibid., 78.
18. Ibid., 144.
19. Ibid., 101.
20. Ibid., 20.
21. Cristina Mazzoni, *Saint Hysteria: Neurosis, Mysticism, and Gender in European Culture* (Ithaca, NY: Cornell University Press, 1996). This topic will be taken up again in Chapter 9.
22. Ibid., 14; quoting Legrand du Saulle, doctor at the Salpêtrière and expert on hysteria.
23. C. G. Jung, *Psychology and Religion: West and East* (Bollingen Series; Princeton, NJ: Princeton University Press, 1969), 252–80.
24. Michael Washburn, *The Ego and the Dynamic Ground: A Transpersonal Theory of Human Development* (Albany: SUNY, 1995), ix.
25. Of course, for Freud there is no such thing as the holy. Masochism is always a clinical condition, always connected with sexuality, and often, with sadism. See *Civilization and Its Discontents*, trans. James Strachey (New York: Norton, 1962), 66–67; Paul Ricoeur, *Freud and Philosophy* (New Haven: Yale University Press, 1972), 300–02. See also, Marie Bonaparte, "Some Biopsychical Aspects of Sado-Masochism," in Margaret Ann Fitzpatrick Hanly, ed., *Essential Papers on Masochism* (New York: New York University Press, 1995), 432–52.
26. Fyodor Dostoevsky, *The Brothers Karamazov* (Constance Garnett trans. (New York: Norton, 1976), 554; in some translations "vile" is "wretch" or "wicked."
27. On analgesic pain as a therapeutic device, see Roselyne Rey, *The History of Pain* (Cambridge, MA: Harvard University Press, 1995), 140.
28. Freud recognized three forms of masochism and reduced them all to erotogenic masochism. Moral masochism may have been consciously desexualized, but it originates in the oedipus complex. In fact, Freud even asserted that "Kant's Categorical Imperative is the direct heir of the oedipus complex." Quoted in Hanly, ed., *Essential Papers on Masochism*, 281.
29. Melanie Klein, *Love, Guilt and Repression* (London: Hogarth, 1975); Leon Wurmser, *The Mask of Shame* (Baltimore: Johns Hopkins University Press, 1981).
30. Roy F. Baumeister, *Masochism and the Self* (Hillsdale, NJ: Lawrence Erlbaum, 1989), 3.
31. Rudolph M. Loewenstein, "A Contribution to the Psychoanalytical Theory of Masochism," in Hanly, ed., *Essential Papers on Masochism*, 37.
32. See for instance, Victor Turner, *The Forest of Symbols: Aspects of Ndumbu Ritual* (Ithaca, NY: Cornell University Press, 1967), 33–38. Psychoanalytical theory has been decisive in the way ritual (devotional) self-mutilation in India has been ex-

plained. It has mostly been interpreted as symbolic self-castration due to a culturally unresolved oedipal complex. See a discussion of such ethnocentric theorizing in Stanley N. Kurtz, *All the Mothers Are One: Hindu India and the Cultural Reshaping of Psychoanalysis* (New York: Columbia University Press, 1992).

33. Heinz Kohut, *The Restoration of the Self* (Madison, WI: International Universities Press, 1996), 117. The interactional and the self psychology theories of psychoanalysis are more consistent than drive theory with a systemic biological view of the human mind and with its neurological foundations.

34. V. S. Ramachandran and Sandra Blakeslee, *Phantoms in the Brain: Probing the Mysteries of the Human Mind* (New York: William Morrow, 1998), 54. Augustine knew this: "Pain of body is simply suffering of soul arising from the body; it is, as it were, the soul's disapproval of what is happening to the body." Saint Augustine, *The City of God*, abridged ed., Gerald G. Walsh et al., trans. (Garden City, NY: Image Books, 1958), 314.

35. There is a vast literature on the effect of psychological and even cultural factors on the perception of pain. A pioneer in this area is Mark Zborauski, *People in Pain* (San Francisco: Jossey-Bass, Inc., 1969); for comprehensive surveys and analyses see Paul Karoly and Mark P. Jensen, *Multimethod Assessment of Chronic Pain* (New York: Pergamon Press, 1987); Ronald Melzack and Patrick D. Wall, *The Challenge of Pain* (New York: Basic Books, 1983); Richard A. Sternbach, ed., *The Psychology of Pain*, 2nd ed. (New York: Raven, 1986); Bernadette Carter, ed., *Perspectives on Pain: Mapping the Territory* (London: Arnold, 1998).

36. The reader who doubts this should try a classic pain experiment: Put your hand in ice cold water after it has been in cool water, then try it after the hand has been in very warm water. Context can be decisive. See John Broome, "More Pain or Less?" *Analysis*, 56 (1996), 116–18.

37. Asenath Petrie, *Individuality in Pain and Suffering* (Chicago: University of Chicago Press, 1967), 16–38.

38. See Robert J. Gatchel and Dennis C. Turk, eds., *Psychosocial Factors in Pain: Critical Perspectives* (New York: Guilford Press, 1999).

39. For a convenient summary of the "gate-control theory," see Ronald Melzack, "Pain: Past, Present and Future," *Canadian Journal of Experimental Psychology*, 47 (1993), 615–29.

40. Melzack's neuromatrix should not be confused with Penfield's map of the homunculus, although from a functional and epistemological point of view they are parallel. See W. Penfield and T. Rasmussen, *The Cerebral Cortex of Man: A Clinical Study of Localization of Function* (New York: MacMillan, 1950), 25–27. The homunculus is the neurological representation of elements in the sensory and motor sequence. Regions with greater sensory sensitivity such as genitalia, lips, or toes are represented in Penfield's map as proportionally larger within a cartoonlike figure of the body-image.

41. A. R. Luria, *The Working Brain* (London: Penguin, 1973); the major pioneer in this field was Henry Head, *Aphasia and Kindred Disorders of Speech*, vol. 1 (Cambridge: Cambridge University Press, 1926); C. D. Van der Velde, "Body Images of One's Self and of Others: Development and Clinical Significance," *American Journal of Psychiatry*, 142 (1985), 527–37.

42. The body-image is "the picture that the person has of the physical appearance of his body." A. C. Traub and J. Orbach, "Psychological Studies of Body Image," *Archives of General Psychiatry*, 11 (1964), 57. The body schema is "knowledge [implicit] of the body's current position and possible future positions, which the individual utilizes during movement, without even thinking." Donald Moss, "Brain, Body, and World:

Body Image and Psychology of the Body," in Ronald S. Valle and Steen Holling, eds., *Existential-phenomenological Perspectives in Psychology* (New York: Plenum, 1989), 64.

43. M. Merleau-Ponty, *Phenomenology of Perception* (London: Routledge & Kegan Paul, 1962), and M. Mereau-Ponty, *The Structure of Behavior* (Boston: Beacon Press, 1963).
44. William James, *Essays in Radical Empiricism* (Cambridge, MA: Harvard University Press, 1976), 289, n. 170.
45. Jaques Lacan, "The Mirror Stage as Formative of the Function of the I as Revealed in Psychoanalytic Experience," in Jacques Lacan, *Ecrits* (New York: W. W. Norton, 1977), 1–7.
46. Van der Velde, "Body Images," 531; See also, Bruce Fink, *The Lacanian Subject: Between Language and Jouissance* (Princeton: Princeton University Press, 1995), 37.
47. These include the embodied, passionate, executive, mnemonic, unified, vigilant, conceptual, and social selves. The names are not always felicitous but the phenomenology and neurological anatomy are beyond the capacity of a historian of religion to dispute. See Ramachandran and Blakeslee, *Phantoms*, 247–55. See also, Arnold H. Modell, *The Private Self* (Cambridge, MA: Harvard University Press, 1997), especially chapter 4.
48. Jerome Bruner, *Acts of Meaning* (Cambridge, MA: Harvard University Press, 1990), and Jerome Bruner, *Actual Minds, Possible Worlds* (Cambridge, MA: Harvard University Press, 1986).
49. A. R. Luria, *The Working Brain*, 31; cultural-cognitive creations "are recognized as essential elements in the establishment of functional connections between individual parts of the brain." This thesis has been taken up in a variety of ways by more recent neuropsychological approaches such as connectionism. See, for instance, Stephen Jose Hanson, *Brain Function: The Developing Interface* (Cambridge, MA: MIT, 1990).
50. Elkhonon Goldberg, ed., *Contemporary Neuropsychology and the Legacy of Luria* (Hillsdale, NJ: Lawrence Erlbaum, 1990).
51. Luria, *The Working Brain*, 93–94.
52. Lev Vygotsky, *Mind in Society: The Development of Higher Psychological Processes* (Cambridge, MA: Harvard University Press, 1978), 27.
53. David Bakan, *Disease, Pain and Sacrifice: Toward a Psychology of Suffering* (Chicago: University of Chicago Press, 1968), 35.
54. Wolfgang Kohler, *Gestalt Psychology: An Introduction to New Concepts in Modern Psychology* (New York: Liveright, 1992), 50–252.
55. Merleau-Ponty, *The Structure of Behavior*, 47.
56. J. A. Scott Kelso, *Dynamic Patterns: The Self-Organization of Brain and Behavior* (Cambridge, MA: MIT Press, 1995).
57. Ibid., 37–43.
58. J. Lacan, *The Seminar of Jacques Lacan*, book 2, S. Tomaselli, trans. (Cambridge: Cambridge University Press, 1988); R. D. Laing, *The Divided Self* (London: Tavistock, 1960); Robert Kennedy, *The Elusive Human Subject: A Psychoanalytical Theory of Subject Relations* (New York: Free Association Books, 1998).
59. James J. Gibson, *The Ecological Approach to Visual Perception* (Boston: Houghton Mifflin, 1979); David Lee and P. E. Reddish, "Plummeting Gannets: A Paradigm of Ecological Optics," *Nature*, 292 (1981), 293–94.
60. Bakan, *Disease, Pain and Sacrifice*, 31–38.
61. Sigmund Freud, *The Ego and the Id*, Joan Riviere, trans. (London: Hogarth, 1950), 31.

62. Quoted in Gertrude and Rubin Blanck, *Ego Psychology II: Psychoanalytic Developmental Psychology* (New York: Columbia University Press, 1979), 16.
63. Heinz Hartmann, *Essays on Ego Psychology* (New York: International Universities Press, 1964).
64. Blanck, *Ego Psychology*, 18.
65. Kelso, *Dynamic Patterns*, 67; William Condon, "Cultural Microrhythms," in Martha Davis, ed., *Interaction Rhythms: Periodicity in Communicative Behavior* (New York: Human Sciences, 1982), 66.
66. According to Melzack's "paradox of pain," medical definitions of pain that directly link it with tissue damage are wrong.
67. Bakan, *Disease, Pain and Sacrifice*, 59.
68. Richard Alexander, *Darwinism and Human Affairs* (Seattle: University of Washington Press, 1979), and Richard Alexander, *The Biology of Moral Systems* (New York: Aldine De Gruyter, 1987).
69. See Blanck, *Ego Psychology*, 21–22. See also Donald Winnicott, *Playing and Reality* (New York: Basic Books, 1971).
70. However, some soldiers do inflict injuries on themselves in an intentional manner, usually to remove an extreme threat, or for similarly traumatic reasons. This is true for prisoners, slaves, even animals in captivity. The "intention" to commit self-mutilation has a neurological foundation in extreme distress.
71. This is the answer that prevails in the literature on sacred pain. See bibliography in Chapter 2, n. 6.
72. Wurmser, *The Mask of Shame* 9–12.
73. Ibid., 9.
74. Kohut, *The Restoration of the Self*, 127.
75. J. Reid Meloy, "Concept and Percept Formation in Object Relation Theory," *Psychoanalytic Psychology*, 2 (1985), 35–45.
76. D. Winnicott, *Playing and Reality*, 11; see also W. W. Meissner, *Psychoanalysis and Religious Experience* (New Haven, CT: Yale, 1984).
77. Margaret Mahler, *Selected Papers of Margaret Mahler* (New York: Jason Aronson, 1979). See also J. Reid Meloy, *Violent Attachments* (Northvale, NJ: Jason Aronson, 1998); L. Gomez, *An Introduction to Object Relations* (New York: New York University Press, 1997).
78. Kennedy, *Elusive Human Subject*, 68.
79. Ramachandran and Blakeslee, *Phantoms*, 61.

FIVE

1. Puccini, *Life*, 144.
2. *Diagnostic and Statistical Manual of Mental Disorders* (*DSM III-R*) (Washington, DC: American Psychiatric Press, 1987). See Colin A. Ross, *Dissociative Identity Disorder: Diagnosis, Clinical Features, and Treatment of Multiple Personality* (New York: John Wiley, 1997); Stanley Kripner, "Cross-Cultural Treatment Perspectives on Dissociative Disorders," in Steven J. Lynn and Judith W. Rhue, eds., *Dissociation: Clinical and Theoretical Perspectives* (New York: Guilford Press, 1994), 336–61.
3. Suddhir Kakar, *Shamans, Mystics and Doctors: A Psychological Inquiry into India and Its Healing Traditions* (Bombay: Oxford University Press, 1990), 70–71.
4. Suryani and Jensen, *Trance and Possession in Bali: A Window on Western Multiple Personality, Possession Disorder, and Suicide* (Kuala Lumpur: Oxford University Press, 1993); Michel Leiris, *La Possession et ses Aspects Theatreaux chez Les Ethiopiens de Gandar* (Paris: Plon, 1958); J. Boddy, "Spirits and Selves in Northern Sudan:

The Cultural Therapies of Possession and Trance," *American Ethnologist*, 15 (1988), 4–27.

5. Luke 8:26–39.
6. Sheila C. Walker, *Ceremonial Spirit Possession in Africa and Afro-America: Forms, Meanings, and Functional Significance for Individuals and Social Groups* (Leiden: E. J. Brill, 1972), 26.
7. T. K. Oesterreich, *Possession: Demoniacal and Other among Primitive Races, in Antiquity, the Middle Ages, and Modern Times* (Secaucus, NJ: University Books, 1966), 38.
8. Because I am interested in the effects of pain on personality and identity, my material is intentionally tilted toward painful cases. At the same time I am not shooting for an ethnographic survey and some of the most notorious cases, such as Brazilian Candomble, the African Orisha cult, Iraqi Dervishes and Sufis, are hardly touched. Several bibliographies are available on the more dramatic cases. See for instance, Gilbert Rouget, *Music and Trance: A Theory of the Relation between Music and Possession*, Brunhilde Biebuyk, trans. (Chicago: University of Chicago Press, 1985), and Vincent Crapanzano and Vivian Garrison, *Case Studies in Spirit Possession* (New York: John Wiley, 1977).
9. Pierre Janet, "Un cas des possession et d'exorcisme moderne," *Nevroses et idees fixes*, 1, 1898; quoted in T. K. Oesterreich, *Possession*, 111–12.
10. Vincent Crapanzano, *The Hamadsa: A Study in Moroccan Ethnopsychiatry* (Berkeley: University of California Press, 1973), 144.
11. Crapanzano, *The Hamadsa*, 152.
12. Ariel Glucklich, *The End of Magic* (New York: Oxford University Press, 1997), 141–42, 177–79.
13. Lawrence A. Babb, *The Divine Hierarchy: Popular Hinduism in Central India* (New York: Columbia University Press, 1975), 135–38.
14. J. Koss-Chioino, *Women as Healers, Women as Patients: Mental Health Care and Traditional Healing in Puerto-Rico* (Boulder, CO: Westview Press, 1992), 38–39; N. P. Spanos, "Hypnosis, Demonic Possession, and Multiple Personality: Strategic Enactments and Disavowels of Responsibility for Actions," in C. Ward, ed., *Altered States of Consciousness and Mental Health: A Cross-cultural Perspective* (Newbury Park, CA: Sage, 1989), 96–124; see also Krippner, 341–50.
15. Oesterreich, *Possession*, 51–52; see also Jean-Joseph Surin, *Triomphe de l'Amour Divin sur les Puissance de l'Enfer* (Grenoble: Jerome Millon, 1990). The Loudun affair has received enormous coverage due to the number and distinction of the personalities involved. A splendid retelling (in English) of the entire travesty is Aldous Huxley's *The Devils of Loudun* (New York: Carroll & Graf, 1996). Jean-Joseph Surin appears again in Michel de Certeau, *The Mystic Fable*, vol. I (Chicago: University of Chicago Press, 1992), 208, where he reports being told the following by a young man who is an "angel/guide": "He told me that, to the extent that a soul was more in a hurry to attain perfection, it was necessary to do violence to oneself . . . the greatest misfortune was that people did not bear up well under bodily suffering and infirmities, in which God had great designs, and He unites with the soul through pain."
16. Rouget, *Music and Trance*, 5, 144, 265, etc.
17. See Chapter 2.
18. Felicitas D. Goodman, *How about Demons? Possession and Exorcism in the Modern World* (Bloomington: Indiana University Press, 1988), 3.
19. Marilee Strong, *A Bright Red Scream: Self-Mutilation and the Language of Pain* (New York: Viking, 1998), 36–38.
20. Pierre Janet, *L'automatisme psychologique* (Paris: Alcan, 1889).

21. Etzel Cardena, "The Domain of Dissociation," in Steven Jay Lynn and Judith W. Rhue eds., *Dissociation: Clinical and Theoretical Perspectives* (New York: Guilford Press), 15. Many of the anthropological works dealing with possession discuss the altered states of consciousness as "trance" or sometimes "ecstasy." Both of these conditions are culturally circumscribed states, unlike "dissociation," in the sense with which I use it: the neurodynamic process underlying the former two, along with others. See P. H. van der Walde, "Trance States and Ego Psychology," in Raymond Prince, ed., *Trance and Possession States* (Montreal: Proceedings of the Second Annual Conference of the R. M. Bucke Memorial Society, 1968), 57–68.
22. See Michael G. Kenny, *The Passion of Ansel Bourne: Multiple Personality in American Culture* (Washington, DC: Smithsonian Institute, 1986), 68; see also the case of Anna Eckland told in Adam Crabtree, *Multiple Man: Explorations in Possession and Multiple Personality* (New York: Praeger, 1985), 95–101.
23. Winston Davis, *Dojo: Magic and Exorcism in Modern Japan* (Stanford: Stanford University Press, 1980), 135.
24. *DSM-III-R*, 271–72.
25. Ibid., 269.
26. Ibid., 269–277.
27. Frank W. Putnam, *Diagnosis and Treatment of Multiple Personality Disorder* (New York: Guilford, 1989). Full bibliography in Suzette Boon and Nel Draijer, *Multiple Personality Disorder in the Netherlands* (Amsterdam: Swets & Zeitlinger, 1993), 30.
28. John F. Kihlstrom, "One Hundred Years of Hysteria," in Lynn and Rhue, *Dissociation*, 365–94.
29. E. Cardena, "The Domain of Dissociation," 28.
30. Steven Jay Lynn and Judith W. Rhue, "Introduction: Dissociation and Dissociative Disorders in Perspective," in Lynn and Rhue, *Dissociation*, 3.
31. Ernest R. Hilgard, *Divided Consciousness: Multiple Controls in Human Thought and Action* (New York: John Wiley, 1977).
32. There is evidence that the uniqueness and proprietary nature of such consciousness is a product of historic developments unique to the West. The rigid identity of the solitary individual with his or her one-pointed consciousness is the product of such a development—which I shall explore in a later chapter. See John R. Wikse, *About Possession: The Self as Private Property* (University Park: Pennsylvania State University Press, 1977); Richard A. Shweder, *Thinking through Cultures: Expeditions in Cultural Psychology* (Cambridge, MA: Harvard University Press, 1991), 122–23. Recognition of this fact has been decisive since Wilhelm Wundt and William James. The number of studies that back up the complex-systemic view of the self is now staggering. See, for example, Jaine Strauss and George R. Goethals, eds., *The Self: Interdisciplinary Approaches* (New York: Springer-Verlag, 1991), especially the following chapter: Charles S. Carver and Michael F. Scheier, "Self-Regulation and the Self" (168–204).
33. "Neodissociation Theory," p. 47; for a critical evaluation of our overreliance on these automatic functions, see Ellen J. Langer, *Mindfulness* (Reading, MA: Perseus Books, 1989).
34. Ernest R. Hilgard, "Neodissociation Theory," in Lynn and Rhue, 38.
35. Ibid.
36. Hilgard, *Neodissociation*, 39.
37. Ernest R. Hilgard and Josephine R. Hilgard, *Hypnosis in the Relief of Pain* (Los Altos, CA: William Kaufman, 1975), 35–37; Ernest R. Hilgard, "Neodissociation Theory," 38–39; see also Ernest R. Hilgard, "Hypnosis and Pain," in Richard A. Sternbach, ed., *The Psychology of Pain*, 2nd ed. (New York: Raven, 1986), 197–221; Paul Sacerdote, "Technique of Hypnotic Intervention with Pain Patients," in Joseph Bar-

ber and Cheri Adrian, eds., *Psychological Approaches to Pain Management* (New York: Brunner/Mazel, 1982), 60–83.

38. Ramachandran, *Phantoms in the Brain.*
39. Hilgard, "Neodissociation Theory," 48.
40. See Rouget, *Music and Trance,* 47.
41. Robert M. Pirsig, *Zen and the Art of Motorcycle Maintenance* (New York: Bantam, 1975), 84–85.
42. Huxley, *The Devils,* 86.
43. Thomas J. Csordas, *The Sacred Self: A Cultural Phenomenology of Charismatic Healing* (Berkeley: University of California Press, 1994), 165.
44. Ibid., 169
45. Anna Freud, *The Ego and the Mechanisms of Defence,* Cecil Baines, trans. (New York: International Universities Press, 1950), 47; 73.
46. Ibid., 48ff.
47. Peter Buckley, ed., *Essential Papers on Object Relations* (New York: New York University, 1986); Sheldon Cashdan, *Object Relations Theory: Using the Relationship* (New York: W. W. Norton, 1988).
48. Richard P. Kluft, "The Diagnosis and Treatment of Dissociative Identity Disorder," in *The Hatherleigh Guide to Psychiatric Disorders* (New York: Hatherleigh Press, 1996), 56–57.
49. Heinz Hartmann, *Ego Psychology and the Problem of Adaptation,* David Rapaport, trans. (Madison: International Universities Press, 1992).
50. P. Bromberg, "Shadow and Substance," in *Psychoanalytical Psychology,* 10:2 (1993), 147–68; S. Mitchell, *Hope and Dread in Psychoanalysis* (New York: Basic Books, 1993); Mitchell and Black, *Freud and Beyond.*
51. J. R. Greenberg and Stephen A. Mitchell, *Object Relations in Psychoanalytical Theory* (Cambridge, MA: Harvard University Press, 1983); Melanie Klein, *Contributions to Psychoanalysis, 1921–45* (New York: McGraw-Hill, 1964); Csordas, *The Sacred Self.*
52. E. Kathleen Gough, "Cults of the Dead among the Nayars," in Milton Singer, ed., *Traditional India: Structure and Change* (Philadelphia: American Folklore Society, 1959). Stanley Kurtz, however, focuses on voluntary possessions and acts of self-mutilation as a representation of "the ongoing consolidation of an ego of the whole." *All the Mothers Are One,* 167. In other words, such acts represent the identity change associated with the uniquely Indian way of resolving oedipal conflict, where pain—in the form of self-sacrifice—induces positive changes of identity through the possession of the Goddess.
53. Bruce Kapferer, "Mind, Self, and Other in Demonic Illness: The Negation and Reconstruction of Self," *American Ethnologist,* 6:1 (1979), 110–33; *A Celebration of Demons: Exorcism and the Aesthetics of Healing in Sri Lanka* (Bloomington: Indiana University Press, 1983). See also Elizabeth Fuller Collins, *Pierced by Murugan's Lance: Ritual, Power, and Moral Redemption among Malaysian Hindus* (De Kalb: Northern Illinois University Press, 1997).
54. Richard Lannoy, *The Speaking Tree: A Study of Indian Culture and Society* (London: Oxford University Press, 1971), 199.
55. L. Wittgenstein, *Notebooks, 1914–1916,* G. von Wright and G. E. M. Anscombe, eds. (Oxford: Basil Blackwell, 1961), August 5, 1916.
56. Csordas, *The Sacred Self,* 5.
57. This discussion is based on William James, *The Varieties of Religious Experience* (New York: Collier Books, 1961), 140–67, 218–49; The clearest and most dramatic statements William James made on the nonmetaphysical self are in *The Principles of Psychology* in the famous chapter, "Consciousness of Self."

58. James, *The Varieties*, 160.
59. Ibid., 164; see also William James, *Psychology: Briefer Course* (New York: Holt, 1892).
60. In the case of Ansel Bourne, James felt it was a "post epileptic partial loss of memory." Kenny, *The Passion*, 69. It was this disintegration that allows for the intrusion of what James called "supernormal forces."

SIX

1. Considering the works written by psychoanalysts like Freud, Jung, Bettelheim, and Reik, one quickly gives up on a multidisciplinary list of works on passage. In addition to the anthropological works that will be cited in the course of the chapter, the following have been especially useful: T. O. Beidelman, "Circumcision," in *The Encyclopedia of Religion* (New York: Macmillan, 1987), 3:511–14; James L. Brain, "Boys' Initiation Rites among the Luguru of Eastern Tanzania," *Anthropos*, 75 (1980), 369–82; Page Dubois, *Sowing the Body* (Chicago: University of Chicago Press, 1988); D. Riches, ed., *The Anthropology of Violence* (Oxford: Basil Blackwell, 1986); Simon Ottenberg, *Boyhood Rituals in an African Society* (Seattle: University of Washington Press, 1989); Nancy C. Lutkenhous and Paul B. Roscoe, eds., *Gender Rituals: Female Initiation in Melanesia* (New York: Routledge, 1995).
2. Gilbert Lewis, *Day of Shining Red: An Essay on Understanding Ritual* (Cambridge: Cambridge University Press, 1980), 111.
3. Alice Schlegel and Hubert Barry, III, "Adolescent Initiation Ceremonies: A Cross-cultural Code," *Ethology*, 18 (1979), 199–210.
4. Favazza, *Bodies*, 186–87; Beidelman, "Circumcision," 511.
5. More so perhaps than any other ritual, everyone has an opinion on passage pain. At a recent Georgetown colloquium I found out that the commonsensical view is that youngsters should be tested before they could meet the rigors of adult life, and that perhaps we should mourn the loss of this rite in our own culture.
6. Mircea Eliade, "Mystery and Spiritual Regeneration in Extra-European Religions," *Papers from Eranos-Yearbooks*, Joseph Campbell, ed., Bolingen Series, vol. 30 (New York: Pantheon, 1964), 3–36.
7. Mircea Eliade, *Rites and Symbols of Initiation: The Mysteries of Birth and Rebirth* (New York: Harper Torchbooks, 1958), xii.
8. Ibid.; Eliade was a prolific and imaginative thinker. One could find in his work three or four distinct and specific explanations for ritual pain, such as the achievement of symbolic androgyny, passage through narrow spaces, death and rebirth. All share the assumption that traditional people, like Christians, become spiritually reborn by these rituals. Additional detailed discussions can be found in *Shamanism: Archaic Techniques of Ecstasy* (Princeton: Princeton University Press, 1974), 33–144.
9. Konrad Lorenz, *On Aggression* (New York: Bantam Books, 1963), 54–59.
10. Victor Turner, *The Forest of Symbols: Aspects of Ndembu Ritual* (Ithaca, NY: Cornell University Press, 1967); Max Gluckman, *Essays on the Ritual of Social Relations* (Manchester: Manchester University Press, 1962); Arnold Van Gennep, *The Rites of Passage* (Chicago: University of Chicago Press, 1960); Vincent Crapanzano, "Rite of Return: Circumcision in Morocco," in Werner Muensterberger and L. Bryce Boyer, eds., *The Psychoanalytic Study of Society*, 9 (1981), 15–36; Sam D. Gill, "Hopi Kachina Cult Initiation: The Shocking Beginning to the Hopi's Religious Life," *Journal of the American Academy of Religion*, 45: 2, supplement (June 1977), 447–64. These rituals are discussed in detail by Catherine Bell, *Ritual Perspectives and Dimension* (New York: Oxford University Press, 1997), 52–59.
11. V. Turner quoted in Bell, *Ritual Perspectives*, 53. See also Karen Ericson Paige and

Jefferey M. Paige, *The Politics of Reproductive Ritual* (Berkeley: University of California Press, 1981).

12. Leora N. Rose, "Adolescent Initiation: Whiting's Hypothesis Revisited," in L. B. Boyer and E. A. Brolnick, eds., *Psychoanalytic Study of Society*, vol. 12 (Hillsdale, NJ: Analytic Press, 1989), 131–55. See also John Whiting, Richard Kluckhohn, and Albert Anthony, "The Function of Male Initiation Ceremonies at Puberty," in E. E. Maccoby, T. M. Newcomb, and E. L. Harlley, eds., *Readings in Social Psychology* (New York: Holt, Reinhart & Winston, 1958), 359–70. See also S. Kurtz, *All the Mothers Are One*.
13. G. Lewis, *Day of Shining*, 110–112.
14. I. Hogbin, *The Island of Menstruating Men* (Scranton, PA: Chandler, 1970), 88.
15. Charles S. Peirce, *Collected Papers*, 8 vols. (Cambridge, MA: Harvard University Press, 1931–58), 2: 228.
16. Corinne A. Kratz, *Affecting Performance* (Washington, DC: Smithsonian Institution Press, 1994), 40.
17. Roy A. Rappaport, *Ritual and Religion in the Making of Humanity* (Cambridge: Cambridge University Press, 1999), 112.
18. Ibid.
19. Ibid., 148; see also Michael Jackson, "Thinking through the Body: An Essay on Understanding Metaphor," *Social Analysis*, 14 (1983), 127–49.
20. Judith Butler, *Bodies That Matter: On the Discursive Limits of "Sex"* (New York: Routledge, 1993).
21. Pierre Bourdieu, *Outline of a Theory of Practice* (Cambridge: Cambridge University Press, 1977); Carol Laderman and Marina Roseman, eds., *The Performance of Healing* (New York: Routledge, 1996). On sociolinguistics, performative-utterance, and rhetorical-persuasive approaches, see the following seminal works: Roman Jakobson, "Closing Statement: Linguistics and Poetics," in Thomas A. Sebeok, ed., *Style in Language* (Cambridge, MA: MIT, 1960), 350–77; Gregory Bateson, *Naven* (Cambridge: Cambridge University Press, 1936); Richard Bauman, *Verbal Art as Performance* (Prospect Heights, IL: Waveland Press, 1984); Stanley Tambiah, *The Cosmological and Performative Significance of a Thai Cult of Healing through Meditation*. Reprinted in *Culture, Thought, and Social Action: An Anthropological Perspective* (Cambridge, MA: Harvard University Press, 1985).
22. Scarry, *The Body in Pain*.
23. See T. O. Beidelman, *The Cool Knife: Imagery of Gender, Sexuality, and Moral Education in Kaguru Initiation Ritual* (Washington, DC: Smithsonian Institution Press, 1997), 251.
24. Beidelman, *The Cool Knife*, 179; Alan Morinis, "The Ritual Experience of Pain and the Transformation of Consciousness," *Ethos*, 13 (1985), 150–74.
25. See Robert Solomon, *The Passions* (New York: Anchor, 1977), 185–86. See also Robert Solomon, "Getting Angry: The Jamesian Theory of Emotion in Anthropology," in R. A. Shweder and R. A. Leickine, eds., *Cultural Theory: Essays on Mind, Self, and Emotion* (Cambridge: Cambridge University Press, 1984).
26. The social and cultural construction of emotion currently dominate ethnographic and anthropological writings. See, for instance, Catherine A. Lutz and Lila Abu-Lughod, *Language and the Politics of Emotion* (New York: Cambridge University Press, 1990); Owen M. Lynch, ed., *Divine Passions: The Social Construction of Emotion in India* (Berkeley: University of California Press, 1990); G. White and J. Kirkpatrick, eds., *Person, Self, and Experience: Exploring Pacific Ethnopsychologies* (Berkeley: University of California Press, 1985); Helen Morton, *Becoming Tongan: An Ethnography of Childhood* (Honolulu: University of Hawai'i Press, 1996).

27. Paul Griffiths lists six headings under which the "propositional attitude theory" can be rejected: objectless emotions, reflex emotions, unemotional evaluations, judgements undermine emotions, emotional response to imagination, physiological responses. *What Emotions Really Are* (Chicago: University of Chicago Press, 1997), 28–30. My own approach is a hybrid in which the "object" of the emotion is the phenomenal body.
28. Robert Plutchik, *Emotion: A Psychoevolutionary Synthesis* (New York: Harper & Row, 1980); Michael Lewis and Jeannette M. Haviland, *Handbook of Emotions* (New York: Guilford Press, 1993); Richard S. Lazarus, *Emotion and Adaptation* (New York: Oxford University Press, 1991).
29. Richard S. Lazarus, *Emotion and Adaptation* (New York: Oxford University Press, 1991), 6; see also K. Strongman, *The Psychology of Emotions* (New York: Wiley, 1973), 1–2.
30. See the following, for example: Bessel A. van der Kilk, "The Body Keeps the Score: Memory and the Evolving Psychobiology of Posttraumatic Stress," *Harvard Review of Psychiatry*, 1 (1994), 253–65; Nathan Schwartz-Salant and Murray Stein, eds., *The Body in Analysis* (Wilmette, IL: Chiron Publications, 1986); Andrew Olsen, *Body Stories: A Guide to Experiential Anatomy* (Barrytown, NY: Station Hill Press, 1991); James Kepner, *Body Process: A Gestalt Approach to Working with the Body in Psychotherapy* (New York: Gestalt Institute of Cleveland Press, 1987).
31. Myron Sharaf, *Fury on Earth* (New York: St. Martin's Press, 1983); quoted in Robert Marrone, *Body of Knowledge: An Introduction to Body/Mind Psychology* (Albany: SUNY, 1990), 26.
32. Charles Darwin, *The Expression of the Emotions in Man and Animals* (Chicago: University of Chicago Press, 1965), 7–8.
33. Wilhelm Reich, *Character Analysis*, 3rd ed. (New York: Noonday Press, 1997).
34. Steen Halling and Judy Dearborn Nill, "Demystifying Psychopathology: Understanding Disturbed Persons," in Ronald S. Valle and Steen Halling, eds., *Existential-Phenomenological Perspectives in Psychology* (New York: Plenum Press, 1989), 179–92.
35. Marrone, *Body Knowledge*, 99.
36. Alexander Lowen, *Bioenergetics* (New York: Coward, McCann & Geoghegan, 1975), 83.
37. See George Lakoff and Mark Johnson, *Metaphors We Live By* (Chicago: University of Chicago Press, 1980).
38. Lowen, *Bioenergetics*, 85–89; Marrone, *Body Knowledge*, 103–04.
39. See the articles and bibliographies in Garlick, ed., *Proprioception, Posture and Emotion*.
40. Lazarus, *Emotion and Adaptation*, 26; Social-constructive reasons and explanations for the part of the body that is hurt are invariably symbolic and unrelated to the biology of the body or its sensations. See Beidelman, *The Cool Knife*, 251.
41. See Lazarus, *Emotion and Adaptation*, chapter 2.
42. T. J. Scheff, *Catharsis in Healing, Ritual, and Drama* (Berkeley: University of California Press, 1979), 3–15.
43. Victor Turner, *The Forest of Symbols: Aspects of Ndembu Ritual* (Ithaca, NY: Cornell University Press, 1967), 216–18.
44. Splitting, according to Anna Freud, is a gradually developed defensive response, but can happen instantaneuously, as with repression, under conditions of trauma and dissociation. See A. Freud, *The Ego and the Mechanisms of Defence*.
45. D. W. Winnicot, *Psychoanalytic Explorations* (Cambridge, MA: Harvard University Press, 1989).

46. Turner, *The Forest of Symbols*, 217; "Three Symbols of Passage in Ndembu Circumcision Ritual," in M. Gluckman, ed., *Essays in the Ritual of Social Relations* (Manchester, England: Manchester University Press, 1962), 156–58.
47. On "primitive" defense mechanisms, see Otto F. Kernberg, *Internal World and External Reality* (New York: Aronson, 1980), 219–20. See also John M. Ingham, *Psychological Anthropology Reconsidered* (Cambridge: Cambridge University Press, 1996), 180.
48. The following are only works I have consulted, out of the wealth of available material: Joseph G. Jorgensen, *The Sun Dance Religion: Power for the Powerless* (Chicago: University of Chicago Press, 1972); Thomas H. Lewis, *The Medicine Men: Oglala Sioux Ceremony and Healing* (Lincoln: University of Nebraska Press, 1990); Fred W. Voget, *The Shoshoni-Crow Sun Dance* (Norman: University of Oklahoma Press, 1984); Robert H. Lowie, "The Sun Dance of the Shoshone, Ute and Hidatsa," *American Museum of Natural History Anthropological Papers*, 26 (1919), 393–410; Joseph Epes Brown, "Sundance," in Mircea Eliade, ed., *The Encyclopedia of Religions* (New York: Macmillan, 1987); Thomas Yellowtail, *Yellowtail: Crow Medicine Man and Sun Dance Chief* (Norman: University of Oklahoma Press, 1991); Manny Twofeathers, *The Road to the Sundance: My Journey into Native Spirituality* (New York: Hyperion, 1996); Thomas E. Mails, *Sundancing: The Great Sioux Piercing Ritual* (Tulsa: Council Oak Books, 1998).
49. Jorgensen, *Sun Dance Religion*, 7.
50. Brown, "Sundance," 143; Voget, *Shoshoni-Crow*, 78.
51. Lewis, *Medicine Men*, 53.
52. Voget, *Shoshoni-Crow*, 86.
53. Many of the available descriptions are extremely detailed. Particularly convenient, however, is Jorgensen's summary and variables in the appendix, *Sundance Religion*, 305–40.
54. Ibid., 206.
55. Felicitas Goodman literally induced such an event accidentally by the pain from the heat of a difficult trek: *Where the Spirits Ride the Wind: Trance Journeys and Other Ecstatic Experiences* (Bloomington: University of Indiana Press, 1990), 32–38.
56. This is Ten Bears's account in Voget, p. 264.
57. Mails, *Sundancing*, 142.
58. Ibid., 133.
59. Twofeathers, *Road to Sundance*, 89–94.
60. Catherine Bell, *Ritual Theory, Ritual Practice* (New York: Oxford University Press, 1992).
61. A. H. Modell, *Object Love and Reality* (New York: International Universities Press, 1968), 82.
62. Semiotic-cognitive analysis highlights the educational value of initiation as acquisition of deeper levels of cultural meanings. Unfortunately, pain becomes merely a reinforcer, a motivator or behavior modifier, which may be true but too simple. See Beidelman, *The Cool Knife*, 7–9.
63. R. A. Spitz, *The First Year of Life* (New York: International Universities Press, 1965), 147.
64. S. J. Blatt and C. M. Wild, *Schizophrenia: A Developmental Analysis* (New York: Academic Press, 1976); quoted in Edward M. Hundert, *Philosophy, Psychiatry, and Neuroscience: Three Approaches to the Mind* (Oxford: Clarendon, 1990), 144.
65. Modell, *Object Love*, 83.
66. The implications of stages of separation are widely recognized in developmental psychological literature. See, for instance, Margaret Mahler, *Selected Papers of Margaret S. Mahler* (New York: Jason Aronson, 1979); J. Bowlby, "Some Pathological

Processes Set in Train by Early Mother-Child Separation," *Journal of Mental Science*, 99 (1953), 265–72; J. Bowlby, *Attachment and Loss*, vol. 2, *Separation, Anxiety and Anger* (New York: Basic Books, 1973). The consequences of loss of attachment as far as pathological violence is concerned is discussed in J. Reid Meloy, *Violent Attachments* (New York: Jason Aronson, 1997).

67. Favazza, *Bodies under Seige*, 231.
68. See, for instance, Laurel Kendall, "Initiating Performance: The Story of Chini, a Korean Shaman," in Carol Laderman and Marina Roseman, eds. *The Performance of Healing* (New York: Routledge, 1996), 50.
69. Bell, *Ritual Theory*, 221.
70. "Ndembu maintain the fiction that the novices take the initiative in calling for the rites, though in practice it is their parents who inaugurate them." Turner, "Three Symbols," 151.

SEVEN

1. Henry Charles Lea, *A History of the Spanish Inquisition*, 4 vols. (New York: American Scholar Publications, 1966), vol. 3, 24–26. For additional signs of Judaizers see Salo Witt Mayer Baron, *A Social and Religious History of the Jews*, 2nd ed. (New York: Columbia University Press, 1969), vol. 13, 36; Yitzhak Baer, *Toledot ha Yehudim biSefarad haNotzrit*, 2 vols. (Tel Aviv: Dvir, 1945).
2. Michel Foucault, *Discipline and Punish: The Birth of the Prison* (New York: Vintage Books, 1995), 3.
3. Ibid., 11.
4. Critiques of Foucault run on several levels from his linguistic constructionism to his ahistorical reductions. For present purposes it may be worthwhile to note that he gets his facts wrong on the development of the penitentiary and its displacement of the torture spectacle. See Michael Ignatieff, *A Just Measure of Pain: The Penitentiary in the Industrial Revolution 1750–1850* (London: Penguin, 1978); Peter Linebough and E. P. Thompson, eds., *Albion's Fatal Tree: Crime and Society in Eighteenth-Century England* (London: Allen Lane, 1975). Foucault also oversimplified the transition from physical punishment to incarceration and surveillance—in other words, the emergence of contemporary technology of power—into one moment. That was the moment when it became "more profitable in terms of the economy of power to place people under surveillance than to subject them to some exemplary penalty." *Power/Knowledge: Selected Interviews and Other Writings 1972–1977* (New York: Pantheon Books, 1980), 38–39. The implication is that a single idea dominated a complex and drawn-out transition (ignoring economics, politics, and government), and if Foucault got the century wrong—which he did—the whole thing falls flat on its own terms. See Keith Windschuttle, *The Killing of History* (New York: Free Press, 1996), 121–57. An incisive critique of Foucault's handling of the body/mind issue along the lines of my agenda is found in Terence Turner, "Bodies and Anti-bodies: Flesh and Fetish in Contemporary Social Theory," in Thomas J. Csordas, ed., *Embodiment and Experience: The Existential Ground of Culture and Self* (Cambridge: Cambridge University Press, 1997), 27–47.
5. Foucault, *Power/Knowledge*, 27. Other types of critique can be found in Pieter Spierenberg, *The Spectacle of Suffering and the Evolution of Repression* (Cambridge: Cambridge University Press, 1984); David Garland, *Punishment and Modern Society* (Oxford: Clarendon, 1990); Talal Asad, "Notes on Body Pain and Truth in Medieval Christian Ritual," *Economy and Society*, 12 (1983), 287–327.
6. Foucault, *Discipline*, 25–26. It only operates as a sign for others in being a surrogate victim, a sacrifice on behalf of all potential subjects. See Girard, *Violence and the Sacred*.

7. Foucault's work has produced an immense cottage industry of books on culture and embodiment. The strange common denominator many of these works share is the privileging of words and signs in relation to power ("society inscribes its truths on the body"). The case of pain should balance some of this top-heavy bias.
8. Foucault, *Discipline*, 25–26.
9. Though less explicitly detailed in his analysis of torture, Norbert Elias is more subtle in his estimation of the raw power of the state over the individual. His analysis of shame and embarrassment, violence, and rationality have been influential in the way I read the inquisitional torture. See Norbert Elias, *The Civilizing Process* (Oxford: Basil Blackwell, 1994), 480. See also "The Genesis of Sport in Antiquity," in N. Elias, ed., *On Civilization, Power, and Knowledge* (Chicago: University of Chicago Press, 1998), 167.
10. In Lea, *Spanish Inquistion*, 24.
11. "Guilt, Ethics, and Religion," in C. E. Ellis Nelson, ed., *Conscience: Theological and Psychological Perspectives* (New York: Newman, 1973), 15.
12. John Carroll, *Guilt: The Grey Eminence behind Character, History, and Culture* (London: Routledge and Kegan Paul, 1985), 97. Leon Wurmser indicates that it was Democritus who first substituted the older concept of shame with a new concept of shame one can feel alone. See *The Mask of Shame*, 17.
13. "It has long been our contention that the 'dread of society' is the essence of what is called conscience." Conscience is the superego in its moralizing social agenda, but in guilt, it acts as a condemning judge, a punitive aggressor. Quoted and discussed in Paul Lehman, "The Decline and Fall of Conscience," 38.
14. The sociological and psychological literature on the relational subject is vast, as previously noted. It ranges from Indian ethnography to ancient Greek history and contemporary Marxist neuropsychology. Jane Harison described the situation nicely in reference to classical Greek society: "We are still apt to put the cart before the horse, to think of the group as made up of an aggregate of individuals rather than of individuals as a gradual segregation of the group." *Themis* (New Hyde Park, NY: University Books, 1962), 470. See also Erich Neuman, *The Origins and History of Consciousness* (Princeton: Princeton University Press, 1970), 121.
15. Richard Kieckhefer, *Magic in the Middle Ages* (Cambridge: Cambridge University Press, 1997), chapter 4. Alan C. Kors and Edward Peters, *Witchcraft in Europe 1100–1700* (Philadelphia: University of Pennsylvania Press, 1999). Keith Thomas, *Religion and the Decline of Magic* (New York: Charles Scribner's Sons, 1971), chapter 2; Simon Kemp, *Medieval Psychology* (New York: Greenwood Press, 1990), chapter 8. See also Simon Kemp, "Demonic Possession and Mental Disorder in Medieval and Early Modern Europe," *Psychological Medicine*, 17 (1987), 21–29.
16. David Nirenberg, *Communities of Violence: Persecution of Minorities in the Middle Ages* (Princeton: Princeton University Press, 1996), 142, 234.
17. David Nirenberg convincingly criticizes René Girard's thesis (which is based on Freud and Durkheim) on the value of eliminating the scapegoat for the purification of the community. The critique is empirical, though, showing that the Jewish minority, though scapegoated, was not eliminated cataclysmically. The violence against it was periodical and controlled. *Communities*, 241–43. See also R. I. Moore, *The Formation of Persecuting Society* (Oxford: Oxford University Press, 1987), chapter 3. See also Malcolm Barber, "The Plot to Overthrow Christendom in 1321," *History*, 66 (1981), 1–17.
18. Shame was magnified by stripping the prisoner (male or female) during torture, though not always revealing the full body. This applied most notoriously to suspected witches, but few were spared embarrassment in milder forms. A pathetic example is

given in Lingard's *History of England,* quoted in Abbott, *Tortures,* 15–16. See also Elias, *On Civilization, Power,* 19.

19. Thomas Aquinas advises: "The mouth should accuse only what the conscience possesses." *Summa Theologia.* John Mahoney, who quotes Aquinas, states that the theologian's justification for confessing all one's sins is medical, not juridical. "A doctor does not treat just one ailment, but the whole state of the patient and its complications." The medicine is penance, of course. John Mahoney, *The Making of Moral Theology: A Study of the Roman Catholic Tradition* (Oxford: Clarendon, 1987), 20, note 84. See also Giovanni da San Gimignano's explicit and detailed identification of penance and medicine, cited in Joseph Ziegler, *Medicine and Religion c. 1300* (Oxford: Clarendon, 1998), 65.
20. In 1607 in Valencia, a girl of thirteen was subjected to torture, but overcame it without confessing. Henry Kamen, *The Spanish Inquisition* (New York: New American Library, 1965), 174.
21. Marie-Christine Pouchelle, *The Body and Surgery in the Middle Ages,* Rosemary Morris, trans., (New York: Polity Press, 1990), 76.
22. Ibid., 71.
23. Edward Burman, *The Inquisition: The Hammer of Heresy* (Northamptonshire: Aquarian Press, 1984), 31.
24. Kamen, *Spanish Inquisition,* 40.
25. Kamen's clearly realist account discards the explicit ideology of the Church in favor of what he calls the interests of the "lay and ecclesiastical aristocracy." Kamen, *Spanish Inquisition,* 8.
26. William Monter, *Frontiers of Heresy: The Spanish Inquisition from the Basque Lands to Sicily* (Cambridge: Cambridge University Press, 1990), 321; Jean-Pierre Dedieu, *L'Administration de La Foi: L'Inquisition de Toledo XVIe–XVIIIe Siecle* (Madrid: Casa de Velazquez, 1987). There were also visitors from Protestant countries who simply had the bad luck of arriving at the wrong time. Mary Brearely, *Hugo Gurgeny: Prisoner of the Lisbon Inquisition* (New Haven: Yale University Press, 1948); Yosef Hayim Yerushalmi, "The Inquisition and the Jews of France in the Time of Bernard Gui," *Harvard Theological Review,* 63 (1970), 317–76; Cecil Roth, *The Spanish Inquisition* (New York: Norton, 1964), 99–105.
27. Edward Peters, *Inquisition* (New York: Free Press, 1988) 44. W. W. Buckland, *A Textbook of Roman Law from Augustus to Justinian,* 3rd ed. (Cambridge: Cambridge University Press, 1975).
28. Ibid., 21–13.
29. Thomas, *Decline of Magic,* 27–28.
30. Ibid., 15–16.
31. Charles Henry Lea, *Torture* (First published 1866; Philadelphia: University of Pennsylvania, 1973), viii; Edward Peters, *Torture* (New York: Basil Blackwell, 1985), 40–44; Talal Asad, "Notes on Body Pain," 289. See also Heinrich Kramer and James Spenger, *The Malleus Maleficarum,* trans. Montague Summers (New York: Dover, 1971), 233.
32. Charles Henry Lea, *A History of the Inquisition of the Middle Ages* (New York: Russell & Russell, 1958), 1: 421; Peters, *Torture,* 44–54.
33. Foucault, *History of Sexuality* (New York: Pantheon, 1978), 58.
34. Lea, *Torture,* x–xi; Page duBois, *Torture and Truth* (New York: Routledge, 1991), 47–62.
35. Lea, *A History of the Inquisition of the Middle Ages,* 213–15.
36. Peters, *Inquisition,* 29.
37. Ibid., 30.

38. Roland H. Bainton, *Concerning Heretics* (New York: Columbia University Press, 1935), 27; Peters, *Torture,* 30.
39. Edward Peters, *Heresy and Authority in Medieval Europe* (Philadelphia: University of Pennsylvania, 1980). On the fine line between heresy and orthodoxy, see Steven Ozment, *The Age of Reform 1250–1550* (New Haven, CT: Yale University Press, 1980), 94; Edward Muir, *Ritual in Early Modern Europe* (Cambridge: Cambridge University Press, 1997), 65–66.
40. Lea, *A History of the Inquisition of the Middle Ages,* 238, 462; Edward Muir, *Ritual in Early Modern Europe* (Cambridge: Cambridge University Press, 1997), 64–65.
41. Maureen Flynn, "Mimesis of the Last Judgement: The Spanish *Auto de fe,*" *Sixteenth Century Journal,* 22 (1991), 292; see also St. John of the Cross, *Dark Night of the Soul,* chapters 5–8, 10; St. Ignatius, *The Spiritual Exercises,* first week, fifth exercise.
42. Some criminals committed heresy in order to be transferred to inquisitional prisons. See Kamen, *Spanish Inquisition,* 169–70. The manuals indicated a preference for allowing the accused to languish in prison until he confessed. See Bernard Gui, *Manuel de L'Inquisiteur,* French translation by G. Mollat (Paris: Librarie Ancienne, 1926), 1.55. Walter L. Wakefield, *Heresy, Crusade, and Inquisition in Southern France 1100–1250* (Berkeley: University of California Press, 1974); for the moderate stance of Tomas de Torquemada, see Baron, *A Social and Religious History,* vol. 13, 324 note 42.
43. Peters, *Torture,* 50; "Torture was not a means of proof, but a means of obtaining a confession." But for a counterexample, the Inquisition as a tool of sheer terror, see Nicholas Eymerich quoted in Bartolome Bennassar, "Patterns of the Inquisitorial Mind as a Basis for a Pedagogy of Fear," in Angel Alcala, ed., *The Spanish Inquisition and the Inquisitorial Mind* (Boulder, CO: Social Science Monographs, 1987), 178. On the monastic modeling of inquisitional procedure, see Salo Witt Mayer Baron, *A Social and Religious History of the Jews,* 2nd ed. (New York: Columbia University Press, 1969), vol. 13, 35.
44. Lea, *A History of the Inquisition of the Middle Ages,* 411–14.
45. Claude-Henri Freches, *Antonio Jose da Silva et L'Inquisition* (Paris: Fundacao Calouste Gulbenkian, 1982), 86–87.
46. Kamen, *Spanish Inquisition,* 174. Roth, *Spanish Inquisition,* 95–96. For a subjective description ("They stretched my limbs with all their might . . ."), see John Coustos, *An Account of the Unparalleled Sufferings of John Coustos* (Norwich, CT: J. Trumbull, 1798).
47. Juan Antonio Llorente, *A Critical History of the Inquisition of Spain* (English ed.) (published in 1823; Williamstown, MA: John Lilburne, 1967), 119–22.
48. In Lea, *Spanish Inquisition,* 25.
49. The meaning of the merely totalitarian pain dissolves into its function of identifying the victim with filth or crime, but the pain he suffers neither purifies nor absolves. See William T. Cavanaugh, *Torture and Eucharist* (Oxford: Blackwell, 1998), 28–30.
50. Ellis C. Nelson, ed., *Conscience: Theological and Psychological Perspectives* (New York: Newman, 1973), 30.
51. At times the inquisitor lost his professional detachment and, according to the witnesses, went insane with rage: "Although he was a learned man and of noble family, [he] was so demented by fury that he began to inflict torture with his own hands," clearly in violation of the major guides of Gui and Eyemerich. Quoted by David Burr at http://www.Fordham.edu/halsall/source/clareno—inq.htm. 9/9/98. The manuals insisted on professionalism and a balance between security and compassion. In Gui's guide (*Manuel*), see chapter iv. See also Lea, *Medieval Inquisition,* 1, 367–68.
52. Kamen, *Spanish Inquisition,* 176. Some prisoners were capable only of moaning and

begging for help while tortured (Vincenzo Ianello, March 20, 1552). Then at other times they were able to make long-winded speeches even while suspended in midair! See Pierroberto Scaramella, *Con La Croce Al Core: Inquisizione ed eresia in Terra di Lavoro* (Roma: La Citta de Sale, 1995), 117–20. The prisoner's pathetic cries for mercy (120) make Elvira sound stoic.

53. Bartolome Escandell, "The Persistence of the Inquisitorial Model of Social Control," in Angel Alcala, ed., *The Spanish Inquisition*, 669, 673, 675; David Burr uses American equivalents—FBI, CIA.
54. Carroll, *Guilt*, 131.
55. Anxiety can trigger both aggression and flight (shame). The inability to escape the source of anxiety increases aggressive reaction. See Wurmser, *The Mask of Shame*, 54.
56. See Thomas S. Szasz, *The Manufacture of Madness* (New York: Delta, 1970).
57. Jacques Lacan, *The Four Fundamental Concepts of Psychoanalysis*, Jacques-Alain Miller, ed., (New York: Norton, 1978), 126 ("The Presence of the Analyst").
58. See Thomas S. Szasz, "The Concept of Transferrence," *International Journal of Psychoanalysis*, 44, (1963) 432–43.
59. John P. Muller and William J. Richardson, *Lacan and Language: A Reader's Guide to Ecrits* (New York: International Universities Press, 1982), 45.
60. Ibid., 49.
61. The theological-eschatological aspect of criminal executions is clearly discussed in numerous works, including the following: Lionello Puppi, *Torment in Art: Pain, Violence, Martyrdom* (New York: New York University Press, 1991); Mitchell B. Merback, *The Thief, the Cross, and the Wheel: Pain and the Spectacle of Punishment in Medieval and Renaissance Europe* (Chicago: University of Chicago Press, 1998); Pieter Spierenburg, *The Spectacle of Suffering: Executions and the Evolution of Repression: From a Pre-industrial Metropolis to the European Experience* (Cambridge: Cambridge University Press, 1984); Esther Cohen, "To Die a Criminal for the Public Good: The Execution Ritual in Later Medieval Paris," in Bernard S. Bacharach and David Nicholas, eds., *Law, Custom, and the Social Fabric in Medieval Europe: Essays in Honor of Bruce Lyon* (Studies in Medieval Culture, xxviii) (Kalamazoo: Western Michigan University, 1990), 285–304.
62. Quoted in Kamen, *Spanish Inquisition*, 188–89.
63. And the Tower in London had its tiny cells called "Little Ease," cords (cf. *Strappado*) for suspending the prisoner, the thumbscrew, the boots and wedge, the rack ("Exeter's Daughter"), the "Scavenger's Daughter." These and others easily equalled and surpassed the three typical inquisitional tortures in ferocity and pain. Frederick Howard Wines, *Punishment and Reformation* (New York: AMS Press, 1975), 91–94. See also G. Abbott, *Tortures of the Tower of London* (London: David & Charles, 1986).
64. J. M. Beattie, *Crime and the Courts in England 1660–1800* (Princeton: Princeton University Press, 1986), 525–58. Beattie notes that paradoxically, it was the threat of using the executed body for dissection in medical colleges that acted as the greatest source of terror.
65. A dramatic case is reported in a seventeenth-century Spanish picaresque novel in which the convict ascends the hangman's ladder, turns to the judge, and points out that one of the rungs is broken and should be fixed. Cited in Spierenberg, *The Spectacle of Suffering*, 94.
66. Ignatieff, *A Just Measure*, 5.
67. Ibid., 21.
68. Flynn, "Mimesis of the Last Judgement"; on the reaction of the crowd see Muir, *Ritual*, 65.
69. Quoted in Kamen, *Spanish Inquisition*, 193–94.

70. Henry Charles Lea, *A History of Auracular Confession and Indulgences in the Latin Church* (Philadelphia: 1896), vol. 1, 24.

EIGHT

1. But it is not unique. See Daniel de Moulin, "A Historical-phenomenological Study of Bodily Pain in Western Man," *Bulletin of the History of Medicine*, 48 (1974), 540–70; Esther Cohen, "Toward a History of European Sensibility: Pain in the Later Middle Ages," *Science in Context*, 8 (1995), 47–74.
2. Nora Barlow, ed., *The Autobiography of Charles Darwin* (London: Collins, 1958), 48.
3. Jonathan Mason Warren, *The Parisian Education of an American Surgeon* (Philadelphia: American Philosophical Society, 1978), 35. On the French medical influence in America and its medical students, see John Hurley Warner, *Against the Spirit of System: The French Impulse in Nineteenth-Century American Medicine* (Princeton, NJ: Princeton University Press, 1998), 255–757; Anne La Berge and Mordechai Feingold, eds., *French Medical Culture in the Nineteenth Century* (Amsterdam-Atlanta: Rodopi, 1994).
4. J. Warren, *The Parisian Education*, 34, 36; There were two types of bloodletting—general and local. In general bloodletting, the blood was collected in a large vase; the procedure was meant to reduce fever and the risk of hemorrhage and was both a pre- and postoperative procedure. In local bloodletting, leeches were commonly applied to the site of the disease, where inflammation and swelling marked the painful spot.
5. Ibid. 87–88; Warren describes (134–35) a ghastly procedure (removal of a testicle) that unintentionally reveals the author's astounding indifference to the patient.
6. Roy Porter, *The Greatest Benefit to Mankind: A Medical History of Humanity* (New York: W. W. Norton, 1995), 365.
7. Quoted in Roselyne Rey, *The History of Pain* (Cambridge, MA: Harvard University Press, 1995), 138.
8. Meyer Friedman and Gerald F. W. Friedland, *Medicine's 10 Greatest Discoveries* (New Haven, CT: Yale University Press, 1998), 96–98.
9. Thomas E. Keys, *The History of Surgical Anesthesia* (New York: Schuman's, 1945), 18; Guy Williams, *The Age of Miracles: Medicine and Surgery in the Nineteenth Century* (London: Constable, 1981), 49–50. The first anesthetized surgical patient in Britain was Frederick Churchill, who had both legs amputated at the thighs on December 21, 1846. "Animal magnetism" was not a simple-folk pseudo-medical concept but a central pillar in early nineteenth-century psychology. Its displacement was bound to generate tremendous ideological resistance. See Ann Taves, *Fits, Trances & Visions: Experiencing Religion and Explaining Religious Experience from Wesley to James* (Princeton, NJ: Princeton University Press, 1999), 121–27. See also Henry Ellensberger, *Discovery of the Unconscious* (New York: Basic Books, 1970).
10. J. Duns, *Memoir of Sir James Y. Simpson, Bart.* (Edinburgh: Edomonston and Douglas, 1873).
11. John Duffy, "Anglo-American Reaction to Obstetrical Anesthesia," in Philip K. Wilson, ed., *Methods and Folklore* (New York: Garland, 1996), 34; A. D. Farr, "Religious Opposition to Obstetric Anesthesia: A Myth?" in Wilson, *Methods*, 161; Rey, *The History of Pain*, 188–89.
12. Quoted in Martin S. Pernick, *A Calculus of Suffering: Pain, Professionalism, and Anesthesia in Nineteenth Century America* (New York: Columbia University Press, 1985), 50.
13. Pernick, *A Calculus*, 56; but see his discussion at 283, fn. 104, in which he evaluates

his sources (*Harper's* 1865 and *Western Lancet* 1847 along with other sources, which may not be entirely accurate).

14. René Fulop-Miller, *Triumph over Pain* (New York: Literary Guild, 1938), 335–36.
15. "Letter to Mr. Waldie 14 November," in Farr, "Religious Opposition," 161; a first-hand argument by Simpson is contained in J. Y. Simpson, "Notes on the Employment of the Inhalation of Sulphuric Ether in the Practice of Midwifery," in Wilson, *Methods* (no pp.). See also Duns, *Memoir*, 255–56.
16. Augustus K. Gardner, *Our Children* (Hartford: Belknap & Bliss, 1872), 25–51, quoted in Pernick, *A Calculus*, 47; Ralph W. Emerson, *Essays, First Series* (1888), 89–122.
17. Raper, *Man against Pain: The Epic of Anesthesia*, 105.
18. *Lancet* 2 (1849), 537, quoted in A. J. Youngson, *The Scientific Revolution in Victorian Medicine* (New York: Holmes & Meier, 1979), 111.
19. *Annalist*, 1 (Jan. 1847), 190.
20. G. T. Gream, *Remarks on the Employment of Anaesthetic Agents in Midwifery* (London: John Churchill, 1848), quoted in Youngson, *The Scientific Revolution*, 105.
21. Duns, *Memoir of Sir James Y. Simpson*, 253.
22. Eliza Thomas, "On the Property of Anaesthetic Agents in Surgical Operations" unpublished M.D. thesis. Female Medical College of Pennsylvania, February 1, 1855; quoted in Pernick, 79. See also the euphoric and pious comments of the Duchess of Argyll about the blessing of painlessness, echoed by Dr. George Wilson in Dunn, *Memoir*, 262.
23. John B. Porter, "Medical and Surgical Notes of Campaigns in the War with Mexico," *American Journal of Medical Science*, 23 (1852), 33.
24. *Transactions of the American Medical Association*, 1 (1848), 189–96.
25. See Robert Barnes in *American Journal of the Medical Sciences*, 21 (1857), 254.
26. W. Tyler Smith, "A Lecture on the Utility and Safety of the Inhalation of Ether in Obstetric Practice," *Lancet*, 1 (1847), 321–23; Duffy, "Anglo-American Reaction," 34; Samuel Gregory of Boston was quoted in the *Edinburgh Medical Journal* as saying that the cry of the mother was a safety valve allowing air to escape if the contraction was too forceful, creating too much pressure. The release of pressure would thus reduce the physical harm both to the mother and the infant. See Robert Barnes in *American Journal of Medical Sciences*, 21 (1851), 252–53, cited in James Y. Simpson, *Anaesthesia, or the Employment of Chloroform and Ether in Surgery, Midwifery, etc.* (Philadelphia: Lindsay & Blakiston, 1849), 232. See also Samuel Gregory, *Man-Midwifery Exposed and Corrected* (Boston: G. Gregory, 1848), 43.
27. Charles Meigs, letter to Walter Channing, "A Treatise on Etherization in Childbirth," in Wilson, ed. *Methods and Folklore*, 14.
28. Duffy, "Anglo-American Reaction," 35.
29. Benjamin Rush, "Commonplace Book," in *The Autobiography of Benjamin Rush*, George W. Corner, ed., 1948 entry of August 5, 1793, 231; see also Rey, *The History of Pain*, 140.
30. *New York Journal of Medicine*, 9 (1847), 122–25; see John Duffy, *History of Public Health in New York City 1625–1866* (New York: Russell Sage Foundation, 1968–74), 463.
31. Quoted in Fulop-Miller, *Triumph over Pain*, 211.
32. Erwin H. Ackernecht, *Paris Hospital*, 154.
33. *The Poems of Emily Dickinson*, edited by Thomas H. Johnson (London: Faber, 1963), vol. 1, 181; see also Aldous Huxley, *Brave New World* (New York: Harper, 1960), 163.
34. Cited in Pernick, *A Calculus*, 59.
35. Duffy, "Anglo-American Reaction," 43.

36. Keys, *The History of Surgical Anesthesia,* 18.
37. J. C. Flugel, *A Hundred Years of Psychology* (New York: International Universities Press, 1970), 43.
38. Ibid., 73.
39. Andrew Peacock, "The Relationship between the Soul and the Brain," in F. Clifford Rose and W. F. Bynum, eds., *Historical Aspects of the Neurosciences* (New York: Raven, 1982), 83–98.
40. Thomas S. Kuhn, *The Structure of Scientific Revolutions* (Chicago: University of Chicago Press, 1996). See Flourens's words: "The great fact of specificity of action by various parts of the nervous system [is] a fact to the demonstration of which physiologists have devoted their noblest efforts." Clearly "fact" here means axiomatic worldview, not hypotheisis. Francis Schiller, "Neurology: The Electric Root," in Clifford and Bynum, eds., *Historical Aspects,* 2.
41. Rey, *The History of Pain,* 135.
42. Howard M. Spiro, *Doctors, Patients, and Placebos* (New Haven: Yale University Press, 86), 100–01.
43. Rey, *The History of Pain,* 98.
44. Rey, *The History of Pain,* 161; Reed, *From Soul to Mind,* 32.
45. Joravsky, *Russian Psychology* 7–8; these experiments have fascinated scientists to this very day and even Sir John Eccles, the eminent contemporary dualist philosopher, has performed them.
46. Flugel, *A Hundred Years,* 28; Reed, *From Soul to Mind,* 9.
47. Reed, *From Soul to Mind,* 2.
48. Rey, *The History of Pain,* 194.
49. Ibid., 195.
50. Johannes Muller, *Elements of Physiology* (London: Murray, 1838).
51. John V. Pickstone, "Establishment and Dissent in Nineteenth-Century Medicine: An Exploration of Some Correspondence and Connections between Religious and Medical Belief-Systems in Early Industrial England," in W. J. Sheils, ed., *The Church and Healing* (Oxford: Basil Blackwell, 1982), 165–89; Pernick, *A Calculus,* 23–29, 125–35; Andrew Wear et al., eds., *Doctors and Ethics: The Earlier Historical Setting of Professional Ethics* (Amsterdam-Atlanta: Rodopi, 1985). The need for professional ethics owes to the erosion of traditional healing communities, as doctors were told how to treat strangers with the courtesy one shows to a member of one's community—no more and no less. In France, professionalization of medicine with all its attendant symptoms took place earlier. George Weisz, "The Development of Medical Specialization in Nineteenth Century Paris," in A. La Berge and M. Feingold, eds., *French Medical Culture,* 149–87.
52. Albert S. Lyons and R. Joseph Pertrucelli, *Medicine: An Illustrated History* (New York: Harry Abrams, 1987), 497.
53. Michael Barfoot, ed., *"To Ask the Suffrages of the Patrons": Thomas Laycock and the Edinburgh Chair of Medicine, 1855* (London: Wellcome Institute for the History of Medicine, 1995). In the United States, see Paul Starr, *The Social Transformation of Medicine* (New York: Basic Books, 1982).
54. On the Medical Act of 1858, which ratified the professionalization of medicine in Britain, see W. F. Bynum, *Science and the Practice of Medicine in the Nineteenth Century* (Cambridge: Cambridge University Press, 1994), 149. See also Anne Digby, *The Evolution of British General Practice 1850–1948* (Oxford: Oxford University Press, 1999), 8–9. The dehumanizing effects of the medicalization of illness is discussed by Sander L. Gilman, "The Image of the Hysteric," in S. L. Gilman, H. King, R. Porter, G. S. Rousseau, and E. Showalter, eds., *Hysteria beyond Freud* (Berkeley: University of California Press, 1993), 345–52. Richard Harrison Shryock, *Medical*

Licensing in America 1650–1965 (Baltimore, MD: Johns Hopkins University Press, 1967), 3–30. Matthew Ramsey, "The Politics of Professional Monopoly in Nineteenth Century Medicine: The French Model and Its Rivals" in G. L. Geison, ed., *Professions and the French State 1700–1900* (Philadelphia: University of Pennsylvania Press, 1984), 225–305.

55. Mardi J. Horowitz, ed., *Hysterical Personality* (New York: Jason Aronson, 1977), 25.
56. M. Horowitz, *Hysterical Personality*, 26. On male hysteria, see Jan Goldstein, "The Uses of Male Hysteria: Medical and Literary Discoveries in Nineteenth-Century France," in A. La Berge and M. Feingold, *French Medical Culture*, 210–47.
57. A. R. G. Owen, *Hysteria, Hypnosis and Healing: The Work of J.-M. Charcot* (New York: Garrett, 1971), 64.
58. Georges Guillain, *J.-M. Charcot 1825–1893: His Life—His Work* (London: Pitman, 1959), 141.
59. Guillain, *J.-M. Charcot*, 142.
60. Like Charcot, Janet linked neurological illness with the behavior of saints, especially anorexic saints. See Pierre Janet, *The Major Symptoms of Hysteria*, 2nd ed. (New York: 1920), 227–44.
61. Ilse Grubrich-Simitis, *Early Freud and Late Freud: Reading Anew Studies on Hysteria and Moses and Monotheism* (New York: Routledge, 1997), 17.
62. Josef Breuer and Sigmund Freud, *Studies on Hysteria* (New York: Basic Books, 1957), 9.
63. Owen, *Hysteria*, 140. A recent treatment of hysteria in its literary contexts is Christina Mazzoni, *Saint Hysteria: Neurosis, Mysticism, and Gender in European Culture* (Ithaca, NY: Cornell University Press, 1996). See also Ruth Harris, *Lourdes: Body and Spirit in the Secular Age* (New York: Viking, 1999), chapter 10. See especially Jan Goldstein, "The Hysteria Diagnosis and the Politics of Anti-Clericalism in Late Nineteenth-century France," *Journal of Modern History*, 54 (1982), 209–39.
64. Owen, *Hysteria*, 124–26.
65. Rene Biot, *The Enigma of the Stigmata*, P. J. Hefpurne-Scott, trans. (New York: Hawthorn Books, 1962), 34. See also Desire-Magloire Bourneville, *Science et miracle: Louise Lateau, ou la stigmatisee belge* (Paris: Delahaye, 1878).
66. Both the witch's possession and ritualized frenzy of her execution may exhibit hysteria (or neuropathology)—see especially the test for her anesthesia to pain. Thomas S. Szasz, *The Manufacture of Madness* (New York: Delta, 1970), 72.
67. Owen, *Hysteria*, 137.
68. James Leuba, *The Psychology of Religious Mysticism* (London: Routledge, 1972), 150.
69. Rouby, *L'Hysterie de Sainte Therese* (Paris: Bureaux Du Progres Medical, 1902), 11–13.
70. Etienne Roba, *Two Portraits of St. Therese of Lisieux* (Chicago: Henry Regnery, 1955), 127–29.
71. Monica Furlong, *Therese of Lisieux* (sl: Virago Pantheon Pioneers, 1987), 119.
72. Victor N. Smirnoff, "The Masochistic Contract," in Margaret Hanly, ed., *Essential Papers on Masochism* (New York: New York University Press, 1995), 66. See also Wilhelm Reich, *The Mass Psychology of Fascism*, Vincent Carfagno, trans. (New York: Farrar, Straus and Giroux, 1970), quoted in C. Mazzoni, *Saint Hysteria*, 41, fn. 70.
73. Breuer and Freud, "Preliminary Communication (1893)," in *Studies on Hysteria*.
74. Henryk Misiak and Virginia M. Staudt, *Catholics in Psychology: A Historical Survey* (New York: McGraw-Hill, 1954), 10.
75. Thomas S. Szasz, *The Manufacture of Madness*, and *The Myth of Mental Illness* (New York: Delta, 1961). See also Morris, *The Culture of Pain*, chapter 5.

76. Contemporary cultural psychology has undergone recent developments in the direction of sociocentric or culturally constituted notions of the person. It has provided some of the most visible critiques of positivistic psychologies in recent times. See, for instance, Richard A. Shweder, *Thinking through Cultures* (Cambridge, MA: Harvard University Press, 1991), and Michael Cole, *Cultural Psychology: A Once and Future Discipline* (Cambridge, MA: Harvard University Press, 1996).
77. Joel James Shulman, *The Body of Compassion: Ethics, Medicine, and the Church* (New York: Westview, 1999), 83.
78. John D. Zizioulas, *Being as Communion: Studies in Personhood and the Church* (Crestwood, NY: St. Vladimir's Seminary Press, 1997), 42–43. See Fyodor Dostoevsky, *Demons* (formerly *The Possessed*) (New York: Vintage, 1994), 115–16.
79. V. N. Voloshinov, *Marxism and the Philosophy of Language* (New York: Seminar, 1973), 25.
80. Lev Vygotsky, *Thought and Language* (Cambridge, MA: MIT Press, 1997), xxiv.
81. Luria aimed to synthesize consciousness with physiology in what he called a "romanitic science." This ultimately leads to particular and embedded narratives as objects of analysis. See A. R. Luria, *The Making of Mind* (Cambridge, MA: Harvard University Press, 1979), 174. See also Mikhail Bakhtin's words: "Unity not as an innate one-and-only, but as a dialogic *concordance* of unmerged twos or multiples." In "Toward a Reworking of the Dostoevsky Book," in *Problems of Dostoevsky's Poetics*, C. Emerson ed./trans. (Minneapolis: University of Minnesota Press, 1984), 289. See also Gary Saul Morson and Caryl Emerson, *Mikhail Bakhtin: Creation of a Prosaics* (Stanford: Stanford University Press, 1990), chapter 5.

CONCLUSION

1. Thomas Cashet, *A Breviary of Torment* (San Francisco: GLB Publishers, 1991), 39.
2. William C. Chittick, *The Sufi Path of Love: The Spiritual Teachings of Rumi* (Albany: SUNY, 1983), 208.
3. Mary-Jo DelVecchio Good, ed., *Pain as Human Experience*, 36.
4. Simone Weil, *Gravity and Grace*, Arthur Wills, trans. (New York: Octagon Books, 1983), 71.
5. These are Rumi's words again in Chittick, *The Sufi Path*, 208.
6. E. V. Daniel, *Fluid Signs: Being a Person the Tamil Way* (Berkeley: University of California Press, 1987), 269.
7. John D. Zizioulas, *Being as Communion: Studies in Personhead and the church* (Crestwood, NY: St. Vladimir Seminary Press, 1997), 42–43.
8. Leo Tolstoy, *The Death of Ivan Ilyich*, Lynn Solotaroff, trans. (New York: Bantam, 1981), 126.
9. Quoted by David Mayo, "Tigers' Sparky Sly and Successful," *Kalamazoo Gazette*, 2 April 1989: G2.
10. William James, *Principles of Psychology* (New York: Henry Holt, 1890) 208.
11. Meinhart and McCoffery, *Pain*, 100.
12. Steven F. Brenna, *Chronic Pain: America's Hidden Epidemic* (New York: Atheneum\SMI, 1971), 219.

Selected Bibliography

Abbott, G. *Tortures of the Tower of London.* London: David & Charles, 1986.
Abu-Zahra, Nadia. *The Pure and Powerful: Studies in Contemporary Muslim Society.* Berkshire: Ithaca, 1997.
Agnon, Samuel. *The Days of Awe.* New York: Shocken, 1948.
Akmajian, Adrian et al. *Linguistics: An Introduction to Language and Communication.* Cambridge, MA: MIT, 1990.
Alcala, Angel, ed. *The Spanish Inquisition and the Inquisitorial Mind.* Boulder, CO: Social Science Monographs, 1987.
Alexander, Richard. *The Biology of Moral Systems.* New York: Aldine De Gruyter, 1987.
———. *Darwinism and Human Affairs.* Seattle: University of Washington Press, 1979.
al-Qushayri. ʿAbd Al-Karim *Principles of Sufism.* B. R. von Schlegel, trans. Berkeley: Mitzan, 1990.
American Psychiatric Association. *Diagnostic and Statistical Manual of Mental Disorders (DSM III-R).* Washington, DC: American Psychiatric Press, 1987.
Amundsen, Darrel W. *Medicine, Society, and Faith in the Ancient and Medieval Worlds.* Baltimore, MD: Johns Hopkins University Press, 1996.
Arberry, A. J. *Tales from the Masnavi.* London: George Allen & Unwin, 1961.
Arbib, Michael A. "Schemas." In *The Oxford Companion to the Mind.* R. L. Gregory, ed. Oxford: Oxford University Press, 1987, 695–97.
Arnheim, Rudolf. *Art and Visual Perception: A Psychology of the Creative Eye.* Berkeley: University of California Press, 1971.
———. "The Gestalt Theory of Expression." In *Documents of Gestalt Psychology.* Mary Hanle, ed. Berkeley: University of California Press, 1961, 301–12.
———. *The Split and the Structure: Twenty-Eight Essays.* Berkeley: University of California Press, 1996.
Asad, Talal. "Agency and Pain: An Exploration." *Culture and Religion,* 1:1 (2000), 29–60.
———. "Notes on Body Pain and Truth in Medieval Christian Ritual." *Economy and Society,* 12 (1983), 287–327.
Babb, Lawrence A. *The Divine Hierarchy: Popular Hinduism in Central India.* New York: Columbia University Press, 1975.
Baer, Yitzhak. *Toledot ha Yehudim biSefarad haNotzrit.* 2 vols. Tel Aviv: Dvir, 1945.

Baha'u'llah. "The Seven Valleys." In *The Seven Valleys and the Four Valleys.* Ali-kuli Khan, trans., assisted by Marzieh Gail. Wilmette, IL: Bahai Publishing Trust, 1931. rev. 1974.

Bainton, Roland H. *Concerning Heretics.* New York: Columbia University Press, 1935.

Bakan, David. *Disease, Pain and Sacrifice: Toward a Psychology of Suffering.* Chicago: University of Chicago Press, 1968.

Bakhtin, Mikhail. "Toward a Reworking of the Dostoevsky Book." In *Problems of Dostoevsky's Poetics.* C. Emerson, ed. and trans. Minneapolis: University of Minnesota Press, 1984.

Barasch, Moshe. *Modern Theories of Art,* vol. 2. New York: New York University Press, 1998.

Barber, Malcolm. "The Plot to Overthrow Christendom in 1321." *History,* 66 (1981), 1–17.

Barfoot, Michael, ed. *"To Ask the Suffrages of the Patrons": Thomas Laycock and the Edinburgh Chair of Medicine, 1855.* London: Wellcome Institute for the History of Medicine, 1995.

Barlow, Nora, ed. *The Autobiography of Charles Darwin.* London: Collins, 1958.

Baron, Salo Witt Mayer. *A Social and Religious History of the Jews.* 2nd ed. New York: Columbia University Press, 1969.

Barstow, Anne Llewellyn. *Witchcraze: A New History of the European Witch Hunts.* New York: Pandora, 1994.

Bartlett, Robert. *Trial by Fire and Water: The Medieval Judicial Ordeal.* Oxford: Clarendon, 1986.

Barton, Carlin A. *The Sorrows of the Ancient Romans: The Gladiator and the Monster.* Princeton: Princeton University Press, 1993.

Bateson, Gregory. *Naven.* Cambridge: Cambridge University Press, 1936.

Bauman, Richard. *Verbal Art as Performance.* Prospect Heights, IL: Waveland Press, 1984.

Baumeister, Roy F. *Masochism and the Self.* Hillsdale, NJ: Lawrence Erlbaum, 1989.

Beattie, J. M. *Crime and the Courts in England 1660–1800.* Princeton, NJ: Princeton University Press, 1986.

Beidelman, T. O. "Circumcision." *The Encyclopedia of Religion,* vol. 3, 511–14. New York: Macmillan, 1987.

———. *The Cool Knife: Imagery of Gender, Sexuality, and Moral Education in Kaguru Initiation Ritual.* Washington, DC: Smithsonian Institution Press, 1997.

Bell, Catherine, *Ritual Perspectives and Dimension.* New York: Oxford University Press, 1997.

———. *Ritual Theory, Ritual Practice.* New York: Oxford University Press, 1992.

Bell, Rudolph M. *Holy Anorexia.* Chicago: University of Chicago Press, 1985.

Bendelow, G., and S. Williams. "Transcending the Dualisms: Toward a Sociology of Pain." *Sociology of Health and Illness,* 17 (1995), 141–55.

Bernanos, Georges. *Under the Sun of Satan.* Harry L. Binsse, trans. New York: Pantheon, 1949.

Biot, Rene. *The Enigma of the Stigmata.* P. J. Hefpurne-Scott, trans. New York: Hawthorn Books, 1962.

Blanck, Gertrude, and Rubin Blanck. *Ego Psychology II: Psychoanalytic Developmental Psychology.* New York: Columbia University Press, 1979.

Blatt, S. J., and C. M. Wild. *Schizophrenia: A Developmental Analysis.* New York: Academic Press, 1976.

Bloch, Maurice, and Jonathan Parry, eds. *Death and the Regeneration of Life.* Cambridge: Cambridge University Press, 1982.

Blumenthal, David R. *Facing the Abusing God: A Theology of Protest.* Louisville, KY: Westminster, 1993.

Boddy, J. "Spirits and Selves in Northern Sudan: The Cultural Therapies of Possession and Trance." *American Ethnologist,* 15 (1988), 4–27.

Bonaparte, Marie. "Some Biopsychical Aspects of Sado-Masochism." In *Essential Papers on Masochism.* Margaret Ann Hanly Fitzpatrick, ed. New York: New York University Press, 1995, 432–52.

Boon, Suzette, and Nel Draijer. *Multiple Personality Disorder in the Netherlands.* Amsterdam: Swets & Zeitlinger, 1993.

Boudreau, Kristin, "Pain and the Unmaking of Self in Toni Morrison's *Beloved.*" *Contemporary Literature,* 36:3 (1995), 447–65.

Bourdieu, Pierre. *Outline of a Theory of Practice.* Cambridge: Cambridge University Press, 1977.

Bourneville, Desire-Magloire. *Science et miracle: Louise Lateau, ou la stigmatisee belge.* Paris: Delahaye, 1878.

Bowlby, J. *Attachment and Loss.* Vol. 2, *Separation, Anxiety and Anger.* New York: Basic Books, 1973.

———. "Some Pathological Processes Set in Train by Early Mother-Child Separation." *Journal of Mental Science,* 99 (1953), 265–72.

Brain, James L. "Boys' Initiation Rites among the Luguru of Eastern Tanzania." *Anthropos,* 75 (1980), 369–82.

Brand, Paul, and Philip Yancey. "And God Created Pain." *Christianity Today,* Jan. 10, 1994, 18–23.

Braverman, Arthur, trans. *Warrior Zen: The Diamond-hard Wisdom Mind of Suzuki Shosan.* New York: Kodansha, 1994.

Brearely, Mary. *Hugo Gurgeny: Prisoner of the Lisbon Inquisition.* New Haven: Yale University Press, 1948.

Brena, Steven. *Chronic Pain: America's Hidden Epidemic.* New York: Atheneum\SMI, 1971.

———. *Pain and Religion: A Psychophysiological Study.* Springfield, IL: Charles C. Thomas, 1972.

Breuer, Josef, and Sigmund Freud. *Studies on Hysteria.* New York: Basic Books, 1957.

Bromberg, P. "Shadow and Substance." *Psychoanalytical Psychology,* 10:2, (1993), 147–68.

Broome, John. "More Pain or Less?" *Analysis,* 56 (1996), 116–18.

Brown, Joseph Epes, "Sundance." *The Encyclopedia of Religions,* Mircea Eliade, ed. New York: Macmillan, 1987.

Bruce, Vicki, and Andy Young. *In the Eye of the Beholder: The Science of Face Perception.* Oxford: Oxford University Press, 1998.

Bruner, Jerome. *Acts of Meaning.* Cambridge, MA: Harvard University Press, 1990.

———. *Actual Minds, Possible Worlds.* Cambridge, MA: Harvard University Press, 1986.

Buckland, W. W. *A Textbook of Roman Law from Augustus to Justinian.* 3rd ed. Cambridge: Cambridge University Press, 1975.

Buckley, Peter, ed. *Essential Papers on Object Relations.* New York: New York University, 1986.

Bulka, Reuven P. *The Jewish Pleasure Principle.* New York: Human Sciences, 1987.

Burman, Edward. *The Inquisition: The Hammer of Heresy.* Northamptonshire: Aquarian Press, 1984.

Bushell, William C. "Psychophysiological and Comparative Analysis of Asceticism." In *Asceticism,* Vincent L. Wimbush, and Richard Valantis, eds. New York: Oxford University Press, 1995, 553–75.

Butler, Judith. *Bodies That Matter: On the Discursive Limits of "Sex."* New York: Routledge, 1993.

Bynum, Caroline Walker. *Holy Feast and Holy Fast.* Berkeley: University of California Press, 1987.

———. *The Resurrection of the Body in Western Christianity, 200–1336.* New York: Columbia University Press, 1995.

Bynum, W. F. *Science and the Practice of Medicine in the Nineteenth Century.* Cambridge: Cambridge University Press, 1994.

Callahan, Virginia Woods, trans. *Saint Gregory of Nyssa: Ascetical Works.* Washington DC: Catholic University, 1966.

Camporesi, Piero. *The Incorruptible Flesh: Bodily Mutation and Mortification in Religion and Folklore.* Cambridge: Cambridge University Press, 1988.

Cannon, Walter B. *Bodily Changes in Pain, Hunger, Fear and Rage.* New York: D. A. Appleton, 1929.

Carroll, John. *Guilt: The Grey Eminence behind Character, History, and Culture.* London: Routledge and Kegan Paul, 1985.

Carter, Bernadette, ed. *Perspectives on Pain: Mapping the Territory.* London: Arnold, 1998.

Cashdan, Sheldon, *Object Relations Theory: Using the Relationship.* New York: W. W. Norton, 1988.

Cavanaugh, William T. *Torture and Eucharist.* Oxford: Blackwell, 1998.

Certeau, Michel de. *The Mystic Fable* vol. I. Chicago: University of Chicago Press, 1992.

Chalmers, Lord, trans. *Further Dialogues of the Buddha.* London: Humphrey Milford, 1926.

Chapman, C. Richard. "Pain, Perception, and Illusion." In *The Psychology of Pain.* 2nd ed. R. A. Sternbach, ed. New York: Raven, 1986, 153–79.

Chittick, William C. *The Sufi Path of Love: The Spiritual Teachings of Rumi.* Albany: State University of New York Press, 1983.

Churchland, Patricia Smith. *Neurophilosophy: Toward a Unified Science of the Mind/Brain.* Cambridge: MIT, 1998.

Cioran, E. M. *Tears and Saints.* Ilinca Zarifopol-Johnston, trans. Chicago: University of Chicago Press, 1995.

Cohen, Esther. "To Die a Criminal for the Public Good: The Execution Ritual in Later Medieval Paris." In *Law, Custom, and the Social Fabric in Medieval Europe: Essays in Honor of Bruce Lyon.* Bernard S. Bacharach and David Nicholas, eds. Studies in Medieval Culture, 28. Kalamazoo: Western Michigan University, 1990, 285–304.

———. "Toward a History of European Sensibility: Pain in the Later Middle Ages." *Science in Context,* 8 (1995), 47–74.

Cole, Michael. *Cultural Psychology: A Once and Future Discipline.* Cambridge, MA: Harvard University Press, 1996.

Cole, Susan Letzler. *The Absent One: Mourning Ritual, Tragedy, and the Performance of Ambivalence.* University Park: The Pennsylvania State University Press, 1991.

Colledge, Edmund, and James Walsh, trans. *Julian of Norwich: Showings, Classics of Western Spirituality.* New York: Paulist Press, 1978.

Collins, Elizabeth Fuller. *Pierced by Murugan's Lance: Ritual, Power, and Moral Redemption among Malaysian Hindus.* Dekalb: Northern Illinois University Press, 1997.

Condon, William. "Cultural Microrhythms." In *Interaction Rhythms: Periodicity in Communicative Behavior.* Martha Davis, ed. New York: Human Sciences, 1982, 61–76.

Cooey, Paula M. "Experience, Body, and Authority." *Harvard Theological Review*, 82:3 (1989), 325–42.

Coustos, John. *An Account of the Unparalleled Sufferings of John Coustos*. Norwich, CT: J. Trumbull, 1798.

Crabtree, Adam. *Multiple Man: Explorations in Possession and Multiple Personality*. New York: Praeger, 1985.

Crapanzano, Vincent. *The Hamadsa: A Study in Moroccan Ethnopsychiatry*. Berkeley: University of California Press, 1973.

———. "Rite of Return: Circumcision in Morocco." Werner R. Muensterberger and L. Bryce Boyer, eds. *Psychoanalytic Study of Society*, 9 (1981), 15–36.

Crapanzano, Vincent, and Vivian Garrison. *Case Studies in Spirit Possession*. New York: John Wiley, 1977.

Csordas, Thomas J. *The Sacred Self: A Cultural Phenomenology of Charismatic Healing*. Berkeley: University of California Press, 1994.

Dabelstein, T., and S. B. Pederson. "Song and Information about Aggressive Response of Blackbirds, *Turdus merula*: Evidence from Interactive Playback Experiments with Territory Owners." *Animal Behavior*, 40 (1990), 1158–68.

Daniel, E. Valentine. *Fluid Signs: Being a Person the Tamil Way*. Berkeley: University of California, 1987.

Darwin, Charles. *The Expression of the Emotions in Man and Animals*. Chicago: University of Chicago Press, 1965.

Dass, Nirmal, trans. *Songs of Kabir from the Adi Grant*. New York: State University of New York Press, 1991.

Davis, Winston. *Dojo: Magic and Exorcism in Modern Japan*. Stanford, CA: Stanford University Press, 1980.

Dedieu, Jean-Pierre. *L'Administration de La Foi: L'Inquisition de Toledo XVIe–XVIIIe Siecle*. Madrid: Casa de Velazquez, 1987.

Dennis, Stephen G., and Ronald Melzack. "Perspectives on Phylogenetic Evolution of Pain Expression." In *Animal Pain: Perception and Alleviation*. Ralph L. Kitchell et al., eds. Bethesda, MD: American Physiological Association, 1983, 151–60.

Descartes, René. *The Principles of Philosophy*, vol. 4, 196. In *The Meditations and Selections from the Principles*. John Veitch, trans., La Salle, IL: Open Court, 1968.

Dickinson, Emily. *The Poems of Emily Dickinson*. Thomas H. Johnson, ed. London: Faber, 1963.

Digby, Anne. *The Evolution of British General Practice 1850–1948*. Oxford: Oxford University Press, 1999.

Dingwall, Eric. *Very Peculiar People: Portrait Studies in the Queer, the Abnormal and the Uncanny*. New Hyde Park, NY: Clarion, 1962.

Dodds, E. R. *Pagan and Christian in an Age of Anxiety*. Cambridge: Cambridge University Press, 1968.

Dostoevsky, Fyodor. *The Brothers Karamazov*. Constance Garnett, trans. New York: Norton, 1976.

———. *Demons*, formerly *The Possessed*. New York: Vintage, 1994.

———. *Notes from the Underground*. New York: A Signet Classic, 1980.

Douglas R. Hofstadter. *Metamagical Themas: Questing for the Essence of Mind and Pattern*. New York: Basic Books, 1985.

Dubois, Page. *Sowing the Body*. Chicago: University of Chicago Press, 1988.

———. *Torture and Truth*. New York: Routledge, 1991.

Duffy, John. "Anglo-American Reaction to Obstetrical Anesthesia." In *Methods and Folklore*. Philip K. Wilson, ed. New York: Garland, 1996.

———. *History of Public Health in New York City 1625–1866*. New York: Russell Sage Foundation, 1968–74.

Duns, J. *Memoir of Sir James Y. Simpson, Bart.* Edinburgh: Edomonston and Douglas, 1873.

Durkheim, Emile. *The Elementary Forms of the Religious Life.* New York: Free Press, 1965.

Egan, Jennifer. "The Thin Red Line." *New York Times Magazine.* (July 27, 1997), 21–25.

Eisenbaum, Pamela. "Suffering, Discipline, and Perfection in Hebrews." In *Asceticism in the New Testament.* Leif E. Vaage and Vincent L. Wimbush, eds. New York: Routledge, 1999, 332–44.

Eisler, Colin. "The Athlete of Virtue: The Iconography of Asceticism." In *Essays in Honor of Erwin Panofsky.* Millard Meiss, ed. New York: New York University Press, 1961, I., 73–82.

Ekman, P. "Facial Expressions of Emotion: An Old Controversy and New Findings." *Philosophical Transactions of the Royal Society of London,* 335 (1992), 63–70.

Eliade, Mircea. "Initiation: An Overview." *Encyclopedia of Religion,* vol. 7. New York: Macmillan, 1987.

———. "Mystery and Spiritual Regeneration in Extra-European Religions."

———. *Papers from Eranos-Yearbooks.* Joseph Campbell, ed. Bolingen Series xxx. New York: Pantheon, 1964, 3–36.

———. *Patterns in Comparative Religion.* New York: New American Library, 1958.

———. *Rites and Symbols of Initiation: The Mysteries of Birth and Rebirth.* New York: Harper Torchbooks, 1958.

———. *Shamanism: Archaic Techniques of Ecstasy.* Princeton, NJ: Princeton University Press, 1974.

Elias, Norbert. *The Civilizing Process.* Oxford: Basil Blackwell, 1994.

———. "The Genesis of Sport in Antiquity." In *On Civilization, Power, and Knowledge.* Chicago: University of Chicago Press, 1998, 154–72.

Elkins, James. *Pictures of the Body: Pain and Metamorphosis.* Stanford, CA: Stanford University Press, 1999.

Ellensberger, Henry. *Discovery of the Unconscious.* New York: Basic Books, 1970.

Escandell, Bartolome. "The Persistence of the Inquisitorial Model of Social Control." In *The Spanish Inquisition and the Inquisitorial Mind.* Alcala, Angel, ed. Boulder, CO: Social Science Monographs, 1987, 667–79.

Eskildsen, Stephen. *Asceticism in Early Taoist Religion.* New York: State University of New York Press, 1998.

Evans-Pritchard, E. E. "The Divine Kingship of the Shilluk of the Nilotic Sudan." The Frazer Lecture of 1948. In *Social Anthropology and Other Essays.* New York: Free Press, 1962.

Fabrega, Horacio, Jr., and Stephen Tyma. "Culture, Language and the Shaping of Illness: An Illustration Based on Pain." *Journal of Psychosomatic Research,* 20 (1976), 323–37.

———. "Language and Cultural Influences in the Description of Pain." *British Journal of Medical Psychology,* 49 (1976), 349–71.

Favazza, Armando R. *Bodies under Seige: Self-mutilation and Body Modification in Culture and Psychology.* Baltimore: Johns Hopkins University Press, 1996.

Feldman, Edmunde Burke. *Varieties of Visual Experience: Art as Image and Idea.* New York: Harry Abrams, nd.

Fields, Howard L. *Pain.* New York: McGraw-Hill, 1987.

Fink, Bruce. *The Lacanian Subject: Between Language and Jouissance.* Princeton, NJ: Princeton University Press, 1995.

Flugel, J. C. *A Hundred Years of Psychology.* New York: International Universities Press, 1970.

Flynn, Maureen. "Mimesis of the Last Judgement: The Spanish *Auto de fe.*" *Sixteenth Century Journal,* 22 (1991), 292.

———. "The Spiritual Uses of Pain in Spanish Mysticism." *Journal of the American Academy of Religion,* 64:2 (1999), 257–78.

Forsyth, Dan W. "Ajatasattu and the Future of Psychoanalytical Anthropology. Part II: The Imperative of the Wish." *International Journal of Hindu Studies,* 1 (1997), 314–36.

Foucault, Michel. *Discipline and Punish: The Birth of the Prison.* New York: Vintage Books, 1995.

———. *History of Sexuality.* New York: Pantheon, 1978.

———. *Power/Knowledge: Selected Interviews and Other Writings 1972–1977.* New York: Pantheon Books, 1980.

Franz, Adolph, ed. *Das Rituale von St. Florian aus dem zwolften Jahrhundert.* Frieburg im Breisgau, 1904.

Frazer, James. *The Golden Bough.* London: Macmillan, 1911–15.

Freches, Claude-Henri. *Antonio Jose da Silva et L'Inquisition.* Paris: Fundacao Calouste Gulbenkian, 1982.

Freedberg, David. *The Power of Images: Studies in the History and Theory of Response.* Chicago: University of Chicago Press, 1989.

Freud, Anna. *The Ego and the Mechanisms of Defense.* New York: International Universities Press, 1946.

Freud, Sigmund. *Beyond the Pleasure Principle.* James Strachey, trans. New York: Norton, 1989.

———. *Civilization and Its Discontents.* James Strachey, trans. New York: Norton, 1962.

———. *The Ego and the Id.* Joan Riviere, trans. London: Hogarth, 1950.

Friedman, Meyer, and Gerald F. W. Friedland. *Medicine's 10 Greatest Discoveries.* New Haven, CT: Yale University Press, 1998.

Fulop-Miller, René. *Triumph over Pain.* New York: Literary Guild, 1938.

Furlong, Monica. *Therese of Lisieux.* sl: Virago Pantheon Pioneers, 1987.

Gardner, Augustus K. *Our Children.* Hartford: Belknap & Bliss, 1872.

Garland, David. *Punishment and Modern Society.* Oxford: Clarendon, 1990.

Garner, W. R. "Good Patterns Have Few Alternatives." *American Scientist,* 58 (1970), 34–42.

Gatchel, Robert J., and Dennis C. Turk, eds. *Psychosocial Factors in Pain: Critical Perspectives.* New York: Guilford Press, 1999.

Gibson, James J. *The Ecological Approach to Visual Perception.* Boston: Houghton Mifflin, 1979.

———. "The Theory of Affordances." In *Perceiving, Acting and Knowing: Toward an Ecological Psychology.* Robert E. Snow and John Bransford eds. Hillsdale, NJ: Lawrence Erlbaum, 1977, 33–48.

Gill, Sam D. "Hopi Kachina Cult Initiation: The Shocking Beginning to the Hopi's Religious Life." *Journal of the American Academy of Religion,* 45:2, supplement (June 1977), 447–64.

Gilman, Sander L. "The Image of the Hysteric." In *Hysteria beyond Freud.* S. L. Gilman, H. King, R. Porter, G. S. Showalter, and E., Rousseau eds. Berkeley: University of California Press, 1993 345–52.

Gleason, Randall C. *John Calvin and John Owen on Mortification: A Comparative Study in Reformed Spirituality.* New York: Peter Lang, 1995.

Glucklich, Ariel. *The End of Magic.* New York: Oxford University Press, 1997.

———. *The Sense of Adharma.* New York: Oxford University Press, 1994.

Gluckman, Max. *Essays on the Ritual of Social Relations.* Manchester, England: Manchester University Press, 1962.

Goldberg, Elkhonon, ed. *Contemporary Neuropsychology and the Legacy of Luria.* Hillsdale, NJ: Lawrence Erlbaum, 1990.

Goldstein, Jan. "The Hysteria Diagnosis and the Politics of Anti-Clericalism in Late Nineteenth-century France." *Journal of Modern History,* 54 (1982), 209–39.

———. "The Uses of Male Hysteria: Medical and Literary Discoveries in Nineteenth-Century France." In *French Medical Culture.* A. La Berge and M. Feingold, eds. Atlanta, GA: Rodopi, 1994, 210–47.

Gombrich, Richard. *Art and Illusion: A Study in the Psychology of Pictorial Representation.* Bollingen Series xxxv, 5. New York: Pantheon, 1960.

Gomez, L. *An Introduction to Object Relations.* New York: New York University Press, 1997.

Good, Mary-Jo DelVecchio et al., eds. *Pain as Human Experience: An Anthropological Perspective.* Berkeley: University of California Press, 1992.

Goodman, Felicitas D. *How about Demons? Possession and Exorcism in the Modern World.* Bloomington: Indiana University Press, 1988.

———. *Where the Spirits Ride the Wind: Trance Journeys and Other Ecstatic Experiences.* Bloomington: University of Indiana Press, 1990.

Goodman, Philip. *The Yom Kippur Anthology.* Philadelphia: Jewish Publication Society, 1971.

Gorringe, Timothy. *God's Just Vengeance.* Cambridge: Cambridge University Press, 1996.

Gough, E. Kathleen. "Cults of the Dead among the Nayars." In *Traditional India: Structure and Change.* Milton Singer, ed. Philadelphia: The American Folklore Society, 1959.

Gray, Andrew. *The Spiritual Warfare: Or Some Sermons Concerning the Nature of Mortification.* Boston: S. Kneeland, 1720.

Gream, G. T. *Remarks on the Employment of Anaesthetic Agents in Midwifery.* London: J. Churchill 1848.

Greenberg, J. R., and Stephen A. Mitchell. *Object Relations in Psychoanalytical Theory.* Cambridge, MA: Harvard University Press, 1983.

Gregory, Samuel. *Man-Midwifery Exposed and Corrected.* Boston: G. Gregory, 1848.

Grene, David, trans. *Prometheus Bound.* Chicago: University of Chicago Press, 1957.

Griffiths, Paul. *What Emotions Really Are.* Chicago: University of Chicago Press, 1997.

Grouios, George. "Phantom Limb Perceptuomotor 'Memories' in a Congenital Limb Child." *Medical Science Research,* 24 (1996), 503–04.

Grubrich-Simitis, Ilse. *Early Freud and Late Freud: Reading Anew Studies on Hysteria and Moses and Monotheism.* New York: Routledge, 1997.

Gui, Bernard. *Manuel de L'Inquisiteur.* French translation by G. Mollat. Paris: Librarie Ancienne, 1926.

Guillain, Georges. *J.-M. Charcot 1825–1893: His Life—His Work.* London: Pitman, 1959.

Gunton, C. *The Actuality of the Atonement.* Edinburgh: T& T Clark, 1988.

Haber, Ralph Norman. "Information Processing." In *Handbook of Perception.* Edward C. Carterrette and Morton P. Friedman, eds. 11 vols. New York: Academic Press, 1974 vol. 1, 313–31.

Halling, Steen, and Judy Dearborn Nill. "Demystifying Psychopathology: Understanding Disturbed Persons." In *Existential-Phenomenological Perspectives in Psychology.* Ronald S. Valle and Steen Halling, eds. New York: Plenum Press, 1989, 179–92.

Hand, Wayland D. *Magical Medicine: The Folkloric Component of Medicine in the Folk Belief, Custom, and Ritual of the Peoples of Europe and America.* Berkeley: University of California, 1980.

Hanson, Stephen Jose. *Brain Function: The Developing Interface.* Cambridge, MA: MIT, 1990.

Harison, Jane. *Themis.* New Hyde Park, NY: University Books, 1962.

Harmann, George W. *Gestalt Psychology: A Survey of Facts and Principles*. New York: Ronald Press Company, 1935.
Harris, Ruth. *Lourdes: Body and Spirit in the Secular Age*. New York: Viking, 1999.
Harrison, Ted. *Stigmata: A Medieval Mystery in a Modern Age*. New York: Penguin, 1994.
Hart, F. D. "Pain as an Old Friend." In *British Medical Journal*, 1 (1979), 1405–07.
Hartmann, Heinz. *Ego Psychology and the Problem of Adaptation*. David Rapaport, trans. Madison, WI: International Universities Press, 1992.
———. *Essays on Ego Psychology*. New York: International Universities Press, 1964.
Hauser, Marc D. *The Evolution of Communication*. Cambridge, MA: MIT, 1999.
Head, Henry. *Aphasia and Kindred Disorders of Speech*, vol. 1. Cambridge: Cambridge University Press, 1926.
Heesterman, Jan. *The Ancient India Royal Consecration*. The Hague: Mouton, 1957.
Hilgard, Ernest R. *Divided Consciousness: Multiple Controls in Human Thought and Action*. New York: John Wiley, 1977.
———. "Hypnosis and Pain." In *The Psychology of Pain*, 2nd ed. Richard A. Sternbach, ed. New York: Raven, 1986, 197–221.
Hilgard, Ernest R., and Josephine R. Hilgard. *Hypnosis in the Relief of Pain*. Los Altos, CA: William Kaufman, 1975.
Hogbin, F. *The Island of Menstruating Men*. Scranton, PA: Chandler, 1970.
Horowitz, Mardi J., ed. *Hysterical Personality*. New York: Jason Aronson, 1977.
Hundert, Edward M. *Philosophy, Psychiatry, and Neuroscience: Three Approaches to the Mind*. Oxford: Clarendon, 1990.
Huxley, Aldous. *Brave New World*. New York: Harper, 1960.
———. *The Devils of Loudun*. New York: Carroll & Graf, 1996.
Ignatieff, Michael. *A Just Measure of Pain: The Penitentiary in the Industrial Revolution 1750–1850*. London: Penguin, 1978.
Ingham, John M. *Psychological Anthropology Reconsidered*. Cambridge: Cambridge University Press, 1996.
Jackson, Jean. "Chronic Pain and the Tension between the Body, as Subject and Object." In *Embodiment and Experience: The Existential Ground of Culture and Self*. T. J. Csordas, ed. New York: Cambridge University Press, 1994, 201–28.
Jackson, Michael. "Thinking through the Body: An Essay on Understanding Metaphor." *Social Analysis*, 14 (1983), 127–49.
Jakobson, Roman. "Closing Statement: Linguistics and Poetics." In *Style in Language*. Thomas A. Sebeok, ed. Cambridge, MA: MIT, 1960, 350–77.
James, William. *Essays in Radical Empiricism*. Cambridge, MA: Harvard University Press, 1976.
———. *Principles of Psychology*. New York: Henry Holt, 1890.
———. *Psychology: Briefer Course*. New York: Holt, 1892.
———. *The Varieties of Religious Experience*. New York: Collier Books, 1961.
Janet, Pierre. *L'automatisme psychologique*. Paris: Alcan, 1889.
———. *The Major Symptoms of Hysteria*. 2nd ed. New York: Macmillan 1920.
Jorgensen, Joseph G. *The Sun Dance Religion: Power for the Powerless*. Chicago: University of Chicago Press, 1972.
Jung, C. G. *Psychology and Religion: West and East*. Bollingen Series; Princeton, NJ: Princeton University Press, 1969.
Kaelber, Walter O. *Tapta Marga: Asceticism and Initiation in Vedic India*. Albany, NY: State University of New York Press, 1989.
Kakar, Suddhir. *Shamans, Mystics and Doctors: A Psychological Inquiry into India and Its Healing Traditions*. Bombay: Oxford University Press, 1990.
Kamen, Henry. *The Spanish Inquisition*. New York: New American Library, 1965.

Kandinsky, Wassily. *Concerning the Spiritual in Art.* M.T.H. Sadler, trans. New York: Dover, 1977.

———. *Point and Line to Plane.* New York: Dover, 1979.

Kane, P. V. *History of Dharmasastra.* Pune: Bandharkar Oriental Research Institute, 1974.

Kapferer, Bruce. *A Celebration of Demons: Exorcism and the Aesthetics of Healing in Sri Lanka.* Bloomington: Indiana University Press, 1983.

———. "Mind, Self, and Other in Demonic Illness: The Negation and Reconstruction of Self." *American Ethnologist,* 6:1 (1979), 110–33.

Karoly, Paul, and Mark P. Jensen. *Multimethod Assessment of Chronic Pain.* Oxford: Pergamon, 1987.

Katz, Joel. "The Role of the Sympathetic Nervous System in Phantom Limb Pain." *Physical Medicine and Rehabilitation,* 10:1 (1996), 153–75.

Kelso, J. A. Scott. *Dynamic Patterns: The Self-Organization of Brain and Behavior.* Cambridge, MA: MIT Press, 1995.

Kemp, Simon. "Demonic Possession and Mental Disorder in Medieval and Early Modern Europe." *Psychological Medicine,* 17 (1987), 21–29.

———. *Medieval Psychology.* New York: Greenwood Press, 1990.

Kempis, Thomas à. *The Imitation of Christ.* Harold Gardiner, ed. New York: Image Books, 1989.

Kendall, Laurel. "Initiating Performance: The Story of Chini, a Korean Shaman." In *The Performance of Healing.* Carol Laderman and Marina Roseman, eds. New York: Routledge, 1996.

Kennedy, Robert. *The Elusive Human Subject: A Psychoanalytical Theory of Subject Relations.* New York: Free Association Books, 1998.

Kenny, Michael G. *The Passion of Ansel Bourne: Multiple Personality in American Culture.* Washington, DC: Smithsonian Institute, 1986.

Kepner, James. *Body Process: A Gestalt Approach to Working with the Body in Psychotherapy.* New York: Gestalt Institute of Cleveland Press, 1987.

Kerenyi, Carl. *Prometheus: Archetypal Image of Human Existence.* Ralph Manheim, trans. Princeton, NJ: Princeton University Press, Bollingen Series, 65, I, 1963.

Kernberg, Otto F. *Internal World and External Reality.* New York: Aronson, 1980.

Keys, Thomas E. *The History of Surgical Anesthesia.* New York: Schuman's, 1945.

Khan, Hazrat Inayat. *The Complete Sayings of Hazrat Inayat Khan.* New Lebanon, NJ: Sufi Order, 1978.

Kieckhefer, Richard. *Magic in the Middle Ages.* Cambridge: Cambridge University Press, 1997.

Kisch, E. Heinrich. *The Sexual Life of Woman in Its Physiological and Hygienic Aspect.* New York: Medical Art Agency, 1916.

Klee, Paul. *Pedagogical Sketchbook.* Sibyl Mohloy-Nagy, trans. London: Faber and Faber, 1968.

Klein, Melanie. *Contributions to Psychoanalysis, 1921–45.* New York: McGraw-Hill, 1964.

———. *Love, Guilt, and Repression.* London: Hogarth, 1975.

Kluft, Richard P. "The Diagnosis and Treatment of Dissociative Identity Disorder." In *The Hatherleigh Guide to Psychiatric Disorders.* New York: Hatherleigh Press, 1996, 56–57.

Koffka, K. *Principles of Gestalt Psychology.* New York: Harcourt, Brace & World, 1935.

Kohler, Wolfgang. *Gestalt Psychology: An Introduction to New Concepts in Modern Psychology.* New York: Liveright, 1947.

———. *The Task of Gestalt Psychology.* Princeton, NJ: Princeton University Press, 1969.

Kohut, Heinz. *The Restoration of the Self.* Madison, WI: International Universities Press, 1996.

Kors, Alan C., & Edward Peters. *Witchcraft in Europe 1100–1700.* Philadelphia: University of Pennsylvania Press, 1999.

Koss-Chioino, J. *Women as Healers, Women as Patients: Mental Health Care and Traditional Healing in Puerto-Rico.* Boulder, CO: Westview Press, 1992.

Kramer, Heinrich, and James Spenger. *The Malleus Maleficarum.* Montague Summers, trans. New York: Dover, 1971.

Kratz, Corinne A. *Affecting Performance.* Washington, DC: Smithsonian Institution Press, 1994.

Kripner, Stanley. "Cross-cultural Treatment Perspectives on Dissociative Disorders." In *Dissociation: Clinical and Theoretical Perspectives.* Steven J. Lynn and Judith W. Rhue eds. New York: Guilford Press, 1994, 336–61.

Kuhn, Thomas S. *The Structure of Scientific Revolutions.* Chicago: University of Chicago Press, 1996.

Kurtz, Stanley N. *All the Mothers Are One: Hindu India and the Cultural Reshaping of Psychoanalysis.* New York: Columbia University Press, 1992.

La Berge, Anne, and Mordechai Feingold, eds. *French Medical Culture in the Nineteenth Century.* Amsterdam-Atlanta: Rodopi, 1994.

Lacan, Jacques. *The Four Fundamental Concepts of Psychoanalysis.* Jacques-Alain Miller, ed. New York: Norton, 1978.

———. "The Mirror Stage as Formative of the Function of the I as Revealed in Psychoanalytic Experience." In Jacques Lacan. *Ecrits.* New York: W. W. Norton, 1977, 1–7.

———. *The Seminar of Jacques Lacan,* book 2: S. Tomaselli, trans. Cambridge: Cambridge University Press, 1988.

Laderman, Carol, and Marina Roseman eds. *The Performance of Healing.* New York: Routledge, 1996.

Laing, R. D. *The Divided Self.* London: Tavistock, 1960.

Lakoff, George. *Women, Fire, and Dangerous Things.* Chicago: University of Chicago Press, 1987.

Lakoff, George, and Mark Johnson, *Metaphors We Live By.* Chicago: University of Chicago Press, 1980.

Langer, Ellen J. *Mindfulness.* Reading, MA: Perseus Books, 1989.

Langer, Susanne K. *Mind: An Essay on Human Feeling,* vol. 1. Baltimore: Johns Hopkins University Press, 1967.

———. *Philosophy in a New Key: A Study in the Symbolism of Reason, Rite, and Art.* New York: New American Library, 1961.

Lannoy, Richard. *The Speaking Tree: A Study of Indian Culture and Society.* London: Oxford University Press, 1971.

Larivierre, Richard W., trans. *The Divyatattva of Raghunandana Bhattacarya.* New Delhi: Manohar, 1981.

Lazarus, Richard S. *Emotion and Adaptation.* New York: Oxford University Press, 1991.

Le Goff, Jacques. *The Medieval Imagination.* Arthur Goldhammer, trans. Chicago: University of Chicago Press, 1988.

Lea, Charles Henry. *A History of Auracular Confession and Indulgences in the Latin Church.* New York: Greenwood Press, 1968.

———. *A History of the Inquisition of the Middle Ages.* New York: Russell & Russell, 1958.

———. *A History of the Spanish Inquisition.* 4 vols. New York: American Scholar Publications, 1966.

———. *Torture.* Philadelphia; University of Pennsylvania, 1973. (Originally pub. 1866.)

Leiris, Michel. *La Possession et ses Aspects Theatreaux chez Les Ethiopiens de Gandar.* Paris: Plon, 1958.

Leuba, James. *The Psychology of Religious Mysticism.* London: Routledge, 1972.

Lewis, C. S. *The Problem of Pain.* London: Geoffrey Bles, 1950.

Lewis, Gilbert. *Day of Shining Red: An Essay on Understanding Ritual.* Cambridge: Cambridge University Press, 1980.

Lewis, I. M. *Ecstatic Religion: A Study of Shamanism and Spirit Possession.* 2nd ed. London: Routledge, 1989.

Lewis, Michael, and Jeannette M. Haviland. *Handbook of Emotions.* New York: Guilford Press, 1993.

Lewis, Thomas H. *The Medicine Men: Oglala Sioux Ceremony and Healing.* Lincoln: University of Nebraska Press, 1990.

Lienhardt, Godfrey. *Divinity and Experience: The Religion of the Dinka.* Oxford: Clarendon, 1961.

Lincoln, Bruce. *Emerging from the Chrysalis: Studies in Rituals of Women's Initiation.* Cambridge, MA: Harvard University Press, 1981.

Linebough, Peter, and E. P. Thompson, eds. *Albion's Fatal Tree: Crime and Society in Eighteenth Century England.* London: Allen Lane, 1975.

Lipps, Theodor. "Aesthetische Einfuhlung." *Zeitschrift Psychologie,* 22 (1900), 415–50.

———. *Grundlegung der Aesthetic,* I. Hampburg and Lepzig: Voss, 1903.

Llorente, Juan Antonio. *A Critical History of the Inquisition of Spain.* English ed. Williamstown, MA: John Lilburne, 1967. (Originally pub. 1823.)

Lomax, Eric. *The Railway Man: A True Story of War, Remembrance, and Forgiveness.* New York: Ballantine Books, 1995.

Lorenz, Konrad. *The Foundations of Ethology.* New York: Springer-Verlag, 1981.

———. *On Aggression.* New York: Bantam Books, 1963.

Lowen, Alexander. *Bioenergetics.* New York: Coward, McCann & Geoghegan, 1975.

Lowie, Robert H. "The Sun Dance of the Shoshone, Ute and Hidatsa." *American Museum of Natural History Anthropological Papers,* 26 (1919), 393–410.

Luria, A. R. *The Making of Mind.* Cambridge, MA: Harvard University Press, 1979.

———. *The Mind of a Mnemonist.* Cambridge, MA: Harvard University Press, 1987.

———. *The Working Brain.* London: Penguin, 1973.

Lutkenhous, Nancy C., and Paul B. Roscoe, eds. *Gender Rituals: Female Initiation in Melanesia.* New York: Routledge, 1995.

Lutz, Catherine A., and Lila Abu-Lughod. *Language and the Politics of Emotion.* New York: Cambridge University Press, 1990.

Lynch, Owen M., ed. *Divine Passions: The Social Construction of Emotion in India.* Berkeley: University of California Press, 1990.

Lyons, Albert S., and R. Joseph Pertrucelli. *Medicine: An Illustrated History.* New York: Harry Abrams, 1987.

Mahler, Margaret. *Selected Papers of Margaret Mahler.* New York: Jason Aronson, 1979.

Mahoney, John. *The Making of Moral Theology: A Study of the Roman Catholic Tradition.* Oxford: Clarendon, 1987.

Mails, Thomas E. *Sundancing: The Great Sioux Piercing Ritual.* Tulsa: Council Oak Books, 1998.

Mandell, Arnold. "Toward a Psychobiology of Transcendence: God in the Brain." In *The Psychobiology of Consciousness.* Julian M. Davidson and Hohn Richards, eds. New York: Plenum Books, 1980, 151–67.

Marcus, Ivan G. *Piety and Society: The Jewish Pietists of Medieval Germany.* Leiden: Brill, 1981.

Marrone, Robert. *Body of Knowledge: An Introduction to Body/Mind Psychology.* Albany: SUNY, 1990.

Mazzoni, Cristina. *Saint Hysteria: Neurosis, Mysticism, and Gender in European Culture.* Ithaca, NY: Cornell University Press, 1996.
McCloskey, D. I. "Signals of Proprioception in Man." In *Proprioception, Posture and Emotion.* D. Garlick, ed. Kensington, Australia: CPME, 1988, 14–22.
McNeill, J. T., and H. M. Gamer, eds. *Medieval Handbooks of Penance.* New York: Columbia University Press, 1938.
Meinhart, Noreen T., and Margo McCaffery. *Pain: A Nursing Approach to Assessment and Analysis.* Norwalk, CT: Appleton-Century-Crofts, 1983.
Meissner, W. W. *Psychoanalysis and Religious Experience.* New Haven, CT: Yale, 1984.
Meloy, J. Reid. "Concept and Percept Formation in Object Relation Theory." *Psychoanalytic Psychology,* 2 (1985), 35–45.
———. *Violent Attachments.* New York: Jason Aronson, 1997.
Melzack, Ronald. "The McGill Questionnaire: Major Properties and Scoring Methods," *Pain,* 1 (1975) 277–99.
———. "Pain: Past, Present and Future." *Canadian Journal of Experimental Psychology,* 47 (1993), 615–29.
———. "Phantom-Limb and the Brain." In *Pain and the Brain: From Nociception to Cognition.* Burkhart Bromm and John E. Desmedt, eds., Advances in Pain Research and Therapy, vol. 22. New York: Raven Press, 1995.
———. "Phantom Limbs." *Scientific American,* 261 (April 1992), 120–26.
Melzack, Ronald, and Patrick D. Wall. *The Challenge of Pain.* New York: Basic Books, 1983.
Merback, Mitchell B. *The Thief, the Cross, and the Wheel: Pain and the Spectacle of Punishment in Medieval and Renaissance Europe.* Chicago: University of Chicago Press, 1998.
Merleau-Ponty, M. *Phenomenology of Perception.* London: Routledge & Kegan Paul, 1962.
———. *The Structure of Behavior.* Boston: Beacon Press, 1963.
Merskey, Harold. "Pain Terms." *Pain,* 6 (1979), 249–52.
Mesami, Julie Scott, trans. *The Sea of Precious Virtues (Bahr al-Fava' id): A Medieval Islamic Mirror for Princes.* Salt Lake City: University of Utah Press, 1991.
Metcalf, Peter, and Richard Huntington. *Celebrations of Death: The Anthropology of Mortuary Ritual.* Cambridge: Cambridge University Press, 1991.
Miller, William Ian. *Humiliation: And Other Essays on Honor, Social Discomfort, and Violence.* Ithaca, NY: Cornell University Press, 1993.
Minsky, Marvin L. "A Framework for Representing Knowledge." In *The Psychology of Computer Vision.* Patrick H. Winston, ed. New York: McGraw-Hill, 1975, 211–77.
Mirbeau, Octave. *Torture Garden.* New York: Citadel Press, 1948.
Misiak, Henryk, and Virginia M. Staudt. *Catholics in Psychology: A Historical Survey.* New York: McGraw-Hill, 1954.
Mitchell, S. *Hope and Dread in Psychoanalysis.* New York: Basic Books, 1993.
Modell, Arnold H. *Object Love and Reality.* New York: International Universities Press, 1968.
———. *The Private Self.* Cambridge, MA: Harvard University Press, 1997.
Monter, William. *Frontiers of Heresy: The Spanish Inquisition from the Basque Lands to Sicily.* Cambridge: Cambridge University Press, 1990.
Morinis, Alan. "The Ritual Experience of Pain and the Transformation of Consciousness." *Ethos,* 13, (1985), 150–74.
Morris, David B. *The Culture of Pain.* Berkeley: University of California Press, 1991.
Morris, Desmond. *The Human Animal: A Personal View of the Human Species.* New York: Crown, 1994.

Morson, Gary Saul, & Caryl Emerson. *Mikhail Bakhtin: Creation of a Prosaics.* Stanford, CA: Stanford University Press, 1990.

Morton, Helen, *Becoming Tongan: An Ethnography of Childhood.* Honolulu: University of Hawai'i Press, 1996.

Moss, Donald. "Brain, Body, and World: Body Image and Psychology of the Body." In *Existential-phenomenological Perspectives in Psychology.* Ronald S. Valle and Steen Holling, eds. New York: Plenum, 1989, 59–72.

Moulin, Daniel de. "A Historical-phenomenological Study of Bodily Pain in Western Man." *Bulletin of the History of Medicine,* 48 (1974), 540–70.

Muir, Edward. *Ritual in Early Modern Europe.* Cambridge: Cambridge University Press, 1997.

Muller, Johannes. *Elements of Physiology.* London: Murray, 1838.

Muller, John P., and William J. Richardson. *Lacan and Language: A Reader's Guide to Ecrits.* New York: International Universities Press, 1982.

Muraoka, Maomora, et al. "Psychosomatic Treatment of Phantom Limb Pain with Post-Traumatic Stress Disorder: A Case Report." *Pain,* 66 (1996), 385–88.

Neisser, Ulric. *Cognition and Reality: Principles and Implications of Cognitive Psychology.* San Francisco: Freeman, 1976.

Nelson, C. E. Ellis, ed. *Conscience: Theological and Psychological Perspectives.* New York: Newman, 1973.

Neuman, Erich. *The Origins and History of Consciousness.* Princeton, NJ: Princeton University Press, 1970.

Nietzsche, Friedrich. *The Genealogy of Morals.* Walter Kaufmann, trans. New York: Vintage, 1967.

Nirenberg, David. *Communities of Violence: Persecution of Minorities in the Middle Ages.* Princeton, NJ: Princeton University Press, 1996.

Noffke, Suzanne, trans. *The Letters of Catherine of Siena, Letter 1.* Binghamton, NY: Medieval and Renaissance Texts, 1988.

Nurbakhsh, Javed. *Sufi Symbolism.* London: Khaniqahi-Nirmutullahi, 1991.

Obeyesekere, Gananth. *Medusa's Hair: An Essay on Personal Symbols and Religious Experience.* Chicago: University of Chicago Press, 1981.

———. *The Work of Culture: Symbolic Transformation in Psychoanalysis and Anthropology.* Chicago: University of Chicago Press, 1990.

Oesterreich, T. K. *Possession: Demoniacal and Other, among Primitive Races, in Antiquity, the Middle Ages, and Modern Times.* Secaucus, NJ: University Books, 1966.

Olsen, Andrew. *Body Stories: A Guide to Experiential Anatomy.* Barrytown, NY: Station Hill Press, 1991.

Ortony, Andrew, ed. *Metaphor and Thought.* Cambridge: Cambridge University Press, 1993.

Ottenberg, Simon. *Boyhood Rituals in an African Society.* Seattle: University of Washington Press, 1989.

Owen, A.R.G. *Hysteria, Hypnosis and Healing: The Work of J.-M. Charcot.* New York: Garrett, 1971.

Ozment, Steven. *The Age of Reform 1250–1550.* New Haven, CT: Yale University Press, 1980.

Paige, Karen Ericson, and Jefferey M. Paige. *The Politics of Reproductive Ritual.* Berkeley: University of California Press, 1981.

Pawl, Ronald Phillip. *Chronic Pain Primer.* Chicago: Yearbook Medical Publications, 1979.

Peacock, Andrew. "The Relationship between the Soul and the Brain." In *Historical Aspects of the Neurosciences.* F. Clifford Bynum, and W. F. Rose, eds. New York: Raven, 1982, 83–98.

Peirce, Charles S. *Collected Papers.* 8 vols. Cambridge, MA: Harvard University Press, 1931–58.

Peli, Pinchas. *Soloveitchik on Repentance.* New York: Paulist, 1984.

Penfield, W., and T. Rasmussen. *The Cerebral Cortex of Man: A Clinical Study of Localization of Function.* New York: Macmillan, 1950.

Perlman, Moshe. *Midrash HaRefuah.* Tel Aviv: Dvir, 1926.

Pernick, Martin S. *A Calculus of Suffering: Pain, Professionalism, and Anesthesia in Nineteenth Century America.* New York: Columbia University Press, 1985.

Peters, Edward. *Heresy and Authority in Medieval Europe.* Philadelphia: University of Pennsylvania, 1980.

———. *Inquisition.* New York: Free Press, 1988.

———. *Torture.* New York: Basil Blackwell, 1985.

Petrie, Asenath. *Individuality in Pain and Suffering.* Chicago: University of Chicago Press, 1967.

Piaget, Jean. *Biology and Knowledge: An Essay on the Relations between Organic Regulations and Cognitive Processes.* Edinburgh: Edinburgh University Press, 1971.

Pickstone, John V. "Establishment and Dissent in Nineteenth-Century Medicine: An Exploration of Some Correspondence and Connections between Religious and Medical Belief-Systems in Early Industrial England." In *The Church and Healing.* W. J. Sheils, ed., Oxford: Basil Blackwell, 1982, 165–89.

Pirsig, Robert M. *Zen and the Art of Motorcycle Maintenance.* New York: Bantam, 1975.

Plutchik, Robert. *Emotion: A Psychoevolutionary Synthesis.* New York: Harper & Row, 1980.

Porter, John B. "Medical and Surgical Notes of Campaigns in the War with Mexico." *American Journal of Medical Science,* 23 (1852), 33–36.

Porter, Roy. *The Greatest Benefit to Mankind: A Medical History of Humanity.* New York: W. W. Norton, 1995.

Pouchelle, Marie-Christine. *The Body and Surgery in the Middle Ages.* Rosemary Morris, trans. New York: Polity Press, 1990.

Puccini, Vicenzo. *The Life of Suor Maria Maddalena de Patsi, 1619.* D. M. Rogers, ed. English Recusant Literature, 1558–1640. Menston, England: The Scholar, 1970.

Puppi, Lionello. *Torment in Art: Pain, Violence, Martyrdom.* New York: New York University Press, 1991.

Putnam, Frank W. *Diagnosis and Treatment of Multiple Personality Disorder.* New York: Guilford, 1989.

R. I. Moore, *The Formation of Persecuting Society.* Oxford: Oxford University Press, 1987.

Ramachandran, V. S. et al. "Touching the Phantom Limb." *Nature* 377:6549 (1995), 489–90.

Ramachandran, V. S., and Sandra Blakeslee. *Phantoms in the Brain: Probing the Mysteries of the Human Mind.* New York: William Morrow, 1998.

Ramsey, Matthew. "The Politics of Professional Monopoly in Nineteenth Century Medicine: The French Model and Its Rivals." In *Professions and the French State 1700–1900.* G. L. Geison, ed. Philadelphia: University of Pennsylvania Press, 1984, 225–305.

Rappaport, Roy A. *Ritual and Religion in the Making of Humanity.* Cambridge: Cambridge University Press, 1999.

Ratnoff, Oscar D. "The Psychogenic Purpuras: A Review of Autoerythrocyte Sensitization, Autosensitization to DNA, 'Hysterical' and Factitial Bleeding, and the Religious Stigmata." *Seminars in Hematology,* July 17, 1983, 192–213.

Rawlinson, M. C. "The Sense of Suffering." *Journal of Medicine and Philosophy,* 11 (1986), 39–62.

Reddish, David Lee, and P. E. Reddish "Plummeting Gannets: A Paradigm of Ecological Optics." *Nature*, 292 (1981), 293–94.

Reich, Wilhelm. *Character Analysis*. 3rd ed. New York: Noonday Press, 1997.

———. *The Mass Psychology of Fascism*, Vincent Carfagno, trans. New York: Farrar, Straus and Giroux, 1970.

Rey, Roselyne. *The History of Pain*. Louise Elliott Wallace et al., trans. Cambridge, MA: Harvard University Press, 1993.

Richesed, D. *The Anthropology of Violence*. Oxford: Basil Blackwell, 1986.

Ricoeur, Paul. *Freud and Philosophy*. New Haven, CT: Yale University Press, 1972.

Ristau, Carolyn A. "Aspects of the Cognitive Ethology of an Injury-feigning Bird, the Piping Plover." In *Cognitive Ethology: Essays in Honor of Donald R. Griffin*. Carolyn A. Ristau, ed. Hillsdale, NJ: Lawrence Erlbaum, 1991, 91–106.

Roba, Etienne, *Two Portraits of St. Therese of Lisieux*. Chicago: Henry Regnery, 1955.

Roberts, Michael John. *Poetry and the Cult of Martyrs: The Liber Peristephanon of Prudentius*. Ann Arbor: University of Michigan Press, 1993.

Rollman, Gary B. "Pain Responsiveness." In *The Psychology of Touch*. Morton Heller and William Schiff, eds. New York: Lawrence Erlbaum, 1991, 91–114.

Rosaldo, Renato. *Culture and Truth: The Remaking of Social Analysis*. Boston: Beacon, 1989.

Rose, Leora N. "Adolescent Initiation: Whiting's Hypothesis Revisited." In *Psychoanalytic Study of Society*, vol. 12. L. B. Boyer and E. A. Brolnick, eds. Hillsdale, NJ: Analytic Press, 1989, 131–55.

Rosenblatt, Paul C. et al. *Grief and Mourning in Cross-Cultural Perspective*. New York: HRAF Press, 1976.

Ross, Colin A. *Dissociative Identity Disorder: Diagnosis, Clinical Features, and Treatment of Multiple Personality*. New York: John Wiley, 1997.

Roth, Cecil. *The Spanish Inquisition*. New York: Norton, 1964.

Rouby, Dr. *L'Hysterie de Sainte Therese*. Paris: Bureaux Du Progres Medical, 1902.

Rouget, Gilbert. *Music and Trance: A Theory of the Relation between Music and Possession*. Brunhilde Biebuyk, trans. Chicago: University of Chicago Press, 1985.

Rush, Benjamin. *The Autobiography of Benjamin Rush*. George W. Corner, ed. Philadelphia: American Philosophical Society, 1948.

Russ, M. J. "Self-Injurious Behavior in Patients with Borderline Personality Disorder: Biological Perspectives." *Journal of Personality Disorders*, 6 (1992), 64–81.

Russell, J. A. "Is There Universal Recognition of Emotion fom Facial Expression? A Review of Cross-cultural Studies." *Psychological Bulletin*, 115 (1994), 102–141.

Saadah, E.S.M., and R. Melzack. "Phantom Limb Experience in Congenital Limb-Deficient Adults." *Cortex*, 30 (1994), 479–85.

Sacerdote, Paul. "Technique of Hypnotic Intervention with Pain Patients." In *Psychological Approaches to Pain Management*. Joseph Adrian, and Cheri, Barber eds. New York: Brunner/Mazel, 1982, 60–83.

Sacks, Oliver. *Migraine*. New York: Vintage, 1992.

Sagan, Eli. *The Lust to Annihilate: A Psychoanalytic Study of Violence in Ancient Greek Culture*. New York: Psychohistory Press, 1979.

Sahlins, Marshall. "The Sadness of Sweetness: The Native Anthropology of Western Cosmology." *Current Anthropology*, 37 (1996), 396.

Saint Athanasius. *Life of Saint Antony*. Robert T. Meyers, trans. Westminster, MD: Newman, 1950.

Saint Augustine. *The City of God*. Abridged ed. Gerald G. Walsh et al., trans. Garden City, NY: Image Books, 1958.

Saint Augustine. *The Confessions*. J. G. Pilkington, trans. New York: Liveright, 1943.

Scaramella, Pierroberto. *Con la Croce al Core: Inquisizione ed eresia in Terra di Lavoro.* Roma: La Citta de Sale, 1995.

Scarry, Elaine. *The Body in Pain: The Making and Unmaking of Worlds.* New York: Oxford University Press, 1985.

Scheff, T. J. *Catharsis in Healing, Ritual, and Drama.* Berkeley: University of California Press, 1979.

Schimmel, Annemarie. *Pain and Grace: A Study of Two Mystical Writers of Eighteenth-Century Muslim India.* Leiden: Brill, 1976.

Schlegel, Alice, and Hubert Barry, III. "Adolescent Initiation Ceremonies: A Cross-cultural Code." *Ethology,* 18 (1979), 199–210.

Schultz, Geoffery, and Ronald Melzack. "Visual Hallucinations and Mental State: A Study of 14 Charles Bonnet Syndrome Hallucinators." *Journal of Nervous and Mental Disease,* 181 (1993), 639–43.

Schwartz, Salant, and Murrary Stein, eds. *The Body in Analysis.* Wilmette, IL: Chiron Publications, 1986.

Scott, George Riley. *The History of Corporal Punishment.* London: T. Werner Laurie, 1938.

Sharaf, Myron. *Fury on Earth.* New York: St. Martin's Press, 1983.

Shryock, Richard Harrison. *Medical Licensing in America 1650–1965.* Baltimore, MD: Johns Hopkins University Press, 1967.

Shulman, Joel James. *The Body of Compassion: Ethics, Medicine, and the Church.* New York: Westview, 1999.

Shweder, Richard A. *Thinking through Cultures: Expeditions in Cultural Psychology.* Cambridge, MA: Harvard University Press, 1991.

Simpson, James Y. *Anaesthesia, or the Employment of Chloroform and Ether in Surgery, Midwifery, etc.* Philadelphia: Lindsay & Blakiston, 1849.

Slade, Peter D., and Richard P. Bentall. *Sensory Deception: A Scientific Analysis of Hallucinations.* Baltimore: Johns Hopkins University Press, 1988.

Smirnoff, Victor N. "The Masochistic Contract." In *Essential Papers on Masochism.* Margaret Hanly, ed. New York: New York University Press, 1995, 49–69.

Smith, Marion V. "Talking about Pain." In *Perspectives on Pain: Mapping the Territory.* Bernadette Carter, ed. London: Arnold, 1998, 26–45.

Smith, Pamela A. "Chronic Pain and Creative Possibility: A Psychological Phenomenon Confronts Theologies of Suffering." In *Broken and Whole: Essays on Religion and the Body.* Maureen A. Tilly and Susan A. Ross, eds. Annual Publication of the College Theology Society, vol. 39. New York: University Press of America, 1993, 113–27.

Smith, W. Tyler. "A Lecture on the Utility and Safety of the Inhalation of Ether in Obstetric Practice." *Lancet,* 1 (1847), 321–23.

Sobieszek, Robert A. *Ghost in the Shell: Photographs and the Human Soul 1850–2000.* Cambridge, MA: MIT and LA County Museum of Art, 1999.

Soelle, Dorothee. *Suffering.* E. Verett R. Kalin, trans. Philadelphia: Fortress Press, 1975.

Solomon, Robert. "Getting Angry: The Jamesian Theory of Emotion in Anthropology." In *Cultural Theory: Essays on Mind, Self, and Emotion.* R. A. Shweder and R. A. Leickine, eds. Cambridge: Cambridge University Press, 1984, 28–41.

———. *The Passions.* New York: Anchor, 1977.

Spanos, N. P. "Hypnosis, Demonic Possession, and Multiple Personality: Strategic Enactments and Disavowels of Responsibility for Actions." In *Altered States of Consciousness and Mental Health: A Cross-cultural Perspective.* C. Ward, ed. Newbury Park, CA: Sage, 1989, 96–124.

Spierenburg, Pieter. *The Spectacle of Suffering: Executions and the Evolution of Repression: From a Pre-industrial Metropolis to the European Experience.* Cambridge: Cambridge University Press, 1984.

Spiro, Howard M. *Doctors, Patients and Placebos.* New Haven, CT: Yale University Press, 1986.

Spitz, R. A. *The First Year of Life.* New York: International Universities Press, 1965.

Starr, Paul. *The Social Transformation of Medicine.* New York: Basic Books, 1982.

Sternbach, R. A. *Pain Patients—Traits and Treatment.* New York: Academic Press, 1974.

Sternbach, Richard A., ed. *The Psychology of Pain.* 2nd ed. New York: Raven, 1986.

Strauss, Jaine, and George R. Goethals, eds. *The Self: Interdisciplinary Approaches.* New York: Springer-Verlag, 1991.

Strong, Marilee. *A Bright Red Scream: Self-Mutilation and the Language of Pain.* New York: Viking, 1998.

Strongman, K. *The Psychology of Emotions.* New York: Wiley, 1973.

Sullivan, Lawrence E. *Icanchu's Drum: An Orientation to Meaning in South American Religions.* New York: Macmillan, 1988.

Surin, Jean-Joseph. *Triomphe de l'Amour Divin sur les Puissance de l'Enfer.* Grenoble: Jerome Millon, 1990.

Suryani, V., and K. Jensen, *Trance and Possession in Bali: A Window on Western Multiple Personality, Possession Disorder, and Suicide.* Kuala Lumpur: Oxford University Press, 1993.

Swinburne, R. *Responsibilty and Atonement.* Oxford: Oxford University Press, 1988.

Szasz, Thomas S. "The Concept of Transferrence." *International Journal of Psychoanalysis,* 44 (1963), 432–43.

———. *The Manufacture of Madness.* New York: Delta, 1970.

———. *The Myth of Mental Illness.* New York: Delta, 1961.

Tambiah, Stanley. *The Cosmological and Performative Significance of a Thai Cult of Healing through Meditation.* Reprinted in *Culture, Thought, and Social Action: An Anthropological Perspective.* Cambridge, MA: Harvard University Press, 1985.

Taves, Ann. *Fits, Trances and Visions: Experiencing Religion and Explaining Religious Experience from Wesley to James.* Princeton, NJ: Princeton University Press, 1999.

Taylor, Michael J., ed. *The Mystery of Suffering and Death.* New York: Alba House, 1973.

Temkin, Oswei. *Hippocrates in a World of Pagans and Christians.* Baltimore: Johns Hopkins University Press, 1991.

Terry, Patricia, trans. "The Third Lay of Gudrun." *Poems of the Vikings. The Elder Edda.* Indianapolis and New York: University of Indiana Press, 1969.

Thomas, Keith. *Religion and the Decline of Magic.* New York: Charles Scribner's Sons, 1971.

Thurston, H. J. *Butler's Lives of the Saints,* vol. 1. Westminster, MD: Christian Classics, 1990.

Tilley, Maureen A. "The Ascetic Body and the Unmaking of the World of the Martyr." *Journal of the American Academy of Religion,* 59:3 (1990), 467–79.

Tiyavanich, Kamala. *Forest Recollections: Wandering Monks in Twentieth Century Thailand.* Honolulu: University of Hawaii Press, 1997.

Tobin, Frank, ed. and trans. *Henry Suso: The Exemplar with Two German Sermons.* New York: Paulist Press, 1989.

Tolstoy, Leo. *The Death of Ivan Ilyich.* Lynn Solotaroff, trans. New York: Bantam, 1981.

Traub, A. C., and J. Orbach. "Psychological Studies of Body Image." *Archives of General Psychiatry,* 11 (1964), 55–62.

Turk, Dennis C., and Ronald Melzack. *Handbook of Pain Assessment.* New York: Guilford Press, 1992.

Turk, Dennis C., Donald Meichenbaum, and Myles Genest. *Pain and Behavioral Medicine: A Cognitive-behavioral Perspective.* New York: Guilford Press, 1983.

Turner, Terence. "Bodies and Anti-bodies: Flesh and Fetish in Contemporary Social Theory." In *Embodiment and Experience: The Existential Ground of Culture and Self.* Thomas J. Csordas, ed. Cambridge: Cambridge University Press, 1997, 27–47.

Turner, Victor. *The Forest of Symbols: Aspects of Ndumbu Ritual.* Ithaca, NY: Cornell University Press, 1967.

———. "Three Symbols of Passage in Ndembu Circumcision Ritual." In *Essays in the Ritual of Social Relations.* M. Gluckman, ed. Manchester, England: Manchester University Press, 1962, 146–179.

Turner, V. W., and E. Turner. *Image and Pilgrimage in Christian Culture: Anthropological Perspectives.* Oxford: Basil Blackwell, 1978.

Twofeathers, Manny. *The Road to the Sundance: My Journey into Native Spirituality.* New York: Hyperion, 1996.

Van der Kilk, Bessel A. "The Body Keeps the Score: Memory and the Evolving Psychobiology of Posttraumatic Stress." *Harvard Review of Psychiatry,* 1 (1994), 253–65.

Van der Velde, C. D. "Body Images of One's Self and of Others: Development and Clinical Significance." *American Journal of Psychiatry,* 142 (1985), 527–37.

Van der Walde, P. H. "Trance States and Ego Psychology." In *Trance and Possession States.* Raymond Prince, ed. Montreal: Proceedings of the Second Annual Conference of the R. M. Bucke Memorial Society, 1968, 57–68.

Van Gennep, Arnold. *The Rites of Passage.* Chicago: University of Chicago Press, 1960.

Vauchez, Andre. *Sainthood in the Later Middle Ages.* Jean Birrell, trans. Cambridge: Cambridge University Press, 1977.

Vernant, Jean-Pierre, and Pierre Vidal-Naquet. *Myth and Tragedy in Ancient Greece.* Janet Lloyd, trans. New York: Zone Books, 1988.

Vernon, J., and T. E. McGill. "Sensory Deprivation and Pain Thresholds." *Science,* 133 (1961), 330–31.

Veto, Miklos. *The Religious Metaphysics of Simone Weil.* Joan Dargan, trans. Albany: State University of New York Press, 1994.

Vischer, Robert. *Uber das optische Fromgefuhl: Ein Beitrag zur Aesthetik.* Leipzig: H. Credner 1873.

Voget, Fred W. *The Shoshoni-Crow Sun Dance.* Norman: University of Oklahoma Press, 1984.

Voloshinov, V. N. *Marxism and the Philosophy of Language.* New York: Seminar, 1973.

Vygotsky, Lev. *Mind in Society: The Development of Higher Psychological Processes.* Cambridge, MA: Harvard University Press, 1978.

———. *Thought and Language.* Cambridge, MA: MIT Press, 1997.

Wagner, Monica, trans. *Saint Basil: Ascetical Works.* New York: Father of the Church, 1950.

Wakefield, Walter L. *Heresy, Crusade, and Inquisition in Southern France 1100–1250.* Berkeley: University of California Press, 1974.

Walker, Sheila C. *Ceremonial Spirit Possession in Africa and Afro-America: Forms, Meanings, and Functional Significance for Individuals and Social Groups.* Leiden: E. J. Brill, 1972.

Wall, Patrick D., and Mervyn Jones. *Defeating Pain: The War against a Silent Epidemic.* New York: Plenum Press, 1991.

Warner, John Hurley. *Against the Spirit of System: The French Impulse in Nineteenth-Century American Medicine.* Princeton, NJ: Princeton University Press, 1998.

Warren, Jonathan Mason. *The Parisian Education of an American Surgeon.* Philadelphia: American Philosophical Society, 1978.

Washburn, Michael. *The Ego and the Dynamic Ground: A Transpersonal Theory of Human Development.* Albany: State University of New York Press 1995.

Wear, Andrew et al., eds. *Doctors and Ethics: The Earlier Historical Setting of Professional Ethics.* Amsterdam-Atlanta: Rodopi, 1985.

Weil, Simone. *Gravity and Grace.* Arthur Wills, trans. New York: Octagon Books, 1983.

Weiss, Samuel A., and Brad Lindell. "Phantom Limb Pain and Etiology of Amputation in Unilateral Lower Extremities Amputees." *Journal of Pain and Symptom Management,* 11 (1996), 3–17.

Weisz, George. "The Development of Medical Specialization in Nineteenth Century Paris." In *French Medical Culture in the Nineteenth Century.* A. La Berge and M. Feingold, eds. Amsterdam-Atlanta: Rodopi, 1994, 149–87.

White, G., and J. Kirkpatrick, eds. *Person, Self, and Experience: Exploring Pacific Ethnopsychologies.* Berkeley: University of California Press, 1985.

Whiting, John, Richard Kluckhohn, and Albert Anthony. "The Function of Male Initiation Ceremonies at Puberty." In *Readings in Social Psychology.* E. E. Maccoby, T. M. Newcomb, and E. L. Harlley, eds. New York: Holt, Reinhart & Winston, 1958, 359–70.

Wikse, John R. *About Possession: The Self as Private Property.* University Park: Pennsylvania State University Press, 1977.

Williams, Guy. *The Age of Miracles: Medicine and Surgery in the Nineteenth Century.* London: Constable, 1981.

Willis, W. D. "The Pain System: The Neural Basis of Nociceptive Transmission in the Mammalian Nervous System." In *Pain and Headache,* vol. 58. P. L. Gildenberg, ed. New York: Krager, 1985, 77–92.

Wilson, Edward O. *On Human Nature.* Cambridge, MA: Harvard University Press, 1978.

Windschuttle, Keith, *The Killing of History.* New York: Free Press, 1996.

Wines, Frederick Howard. *Punishment and Reformation.* New York: AMS Press, 1975.

Winnicot, D. W. *Playing and Reality.* New York: Basic Books, 1971.

———. *Psychoanalytic Explorations.* Cambridge, MA: Harvard University Press, 1989.

Wisdom, John. *Other Minds.* Oxford: Clarendon, 1956.

Wittgenstein, L. *Notebooks, 1914–1916.* G. von Wright and G.E.M. Anscombe, eds. Oxford: Basil Blackwell, 1961, 5 August 1916.

Woolf, Virginia. *The Moment and Other Essays.* New York: Harcourt, Brace, 1948.

Wurmser, Leon. *The Mask of Shame.* Baltimore: Johns Hopkins University Press, 1981.

Yellowtail, Thomas. *Yellowtail: Crow Medicine Man and Sun Dance Chief.* Norman: University of Oklahoma Press, 1991.

Yerushalmi, Yosef Hayim. "The Inquisition and the Jews of France in the Time of Bernard Gui." *Harvard Theological Review,* 63 (1970), 317–76.

Youngson, A. J. *The Scientific Revolution in Victorian Medicine.* New York: Holmes & Meier, 1979.

Zborauski, Mark. *People in Pain.* San Francisco: Jossey-Bass, 1969.

Ziegler, Joseph. *Medicine and Religion c. 1300.* Oxford: Clarendon, 1998.

Zizioulas, John D. *Being as Communion: Studies in Personhood and the Church.* Crestwood, NY: St. Vladimir's Seminary Press, 1997.

Zubek, John P. "Sensory and Perceptual-Motor Effects." In *Sensory Deprivation: Fifteen Years of Research.* John P. Zubek, ed. New York: Appleton-Century-Crofts, 1969, 441–48.

Index